VACHERON CONSTANTIN

Manufacture Horlogère. Genève, depuis 1755.

Quai de l'Ile

Quai de l'Ile: a history, a legend

The Quai de l'Ile, Vacheron Constantin's address since the 19th century, symbolises the watchmaking savoir-faire and high quality service that have shaped the brand's reputation according to the wish of François Constantin. A privileged meeting place of the brand's most celebrated customers, the Quai de l'Ile welcomed kings and queens, aristocrats and powerful leading families of the period, who came to order timepieces that met their most cherished wishes. Born out of this desire to create personalized watches, the Quai de l'Ile line pays tribute to the spirit of the Cabinotiers. The dream of conquering time, of inventing one's own time, has now become a reality and echoes the company's motto, "Do better if possible, and that is always possible".

Quai de l'Ile: personalized time

Made-to-measure audacity, technological ambition, aesthetic genius! At the crossroads of art and technical expertise, the Quai de l'Ile line is projecting Haute Horlogerie into a new era. Personalization, technology, design and security are at the core of this concept that pushes back the limits of excellence and exclusiveness. The unique construction of the cushion-shape case makes it possible to produce individual watches – almost 400 variations – using watchmaking expertise and high technology to capture time. And, reflecting the singularity of time, each model is as original and elegant as it is elusive and enigmatic.

A unique experience, the privilege of luxury

The noble materials and beautiful finishing of these timepieces are impeccably enhanced by their architecture. Drawing on transparency, the dials provide a glimpse of the wheels of time as they vanish into the complexity of the mechanism. Born from a combination of technical haute horlogerie and the science of security printing, the dials conceal a large number of details and sophisticated manufacturing processes. Beating at the heart of the Quai de l'Ile timepieces are two new mechanical movements, designed and manufactured by Vacheron Constantin and stamped with the famous Hallmark of Geneva.

QUAI DE L'ILE DAY-DATE AND
POWER-RESERVE PERSONALIZED

Self-winding mechanical movement
Caliber 2475 SC/1 ⚜ Hallmark of Geneva
Indication day and date with hands
Ø 41 mm
More than 400 combinations

QUAI DE L'ILE DATE SELF-WINDING
86050/000D-9343

Self-winding mechanical movement
Caliber 2460 QH ⚜ Hallmark of Geneva
Indication of the date by disc
Ø 41 mm
Palladium, Pink gold or Titanium

For information call 877-862-7555
www.vacheron-constantin.com/qdi.us

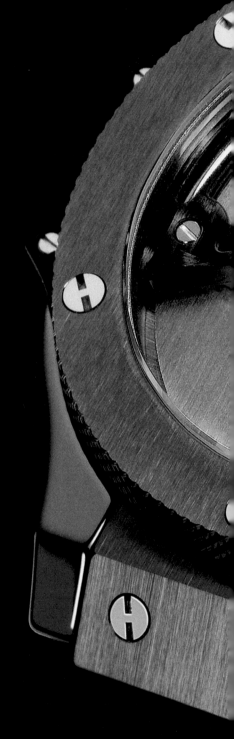

TOURBILLON
BAT BANG

THE ORIGINAL ANNUAL OF THE WORLD'S FINEST WRISTWATCHES

First published in the United States in 2009 by

TOURBILLON INTERNATIONAL
A MODERN LUXURY MEDIA, LLC COMPANY
11 West 25th Street, 8th Floor
New York, NY 10010
Tel: +1 (212) 627-7732   Fax +1 (312) 274-8418
www.modernluxury.com/watches

CHAIRMAN AND CEO
Michael Kong

VICE CHAIRMAN
Stephen Kong

COO
Michael Lipson

PUBLISHER
Caroline Childers

EDITOR IN CHIEF
Michel Jeannot

SENIOR VICE PRESIDENT OF FINANCE
John Pietrolungo

In association with **RIZZOLI** INTERNATIONAL PUBLICATIONS, INC.

300 Park Avenue South, New York, NY 10010

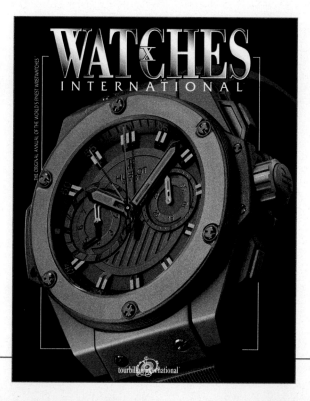

Rose gold case on alligator strap. Mechanical movement with manual winding, Cartier calibre 9452 MC (10 and 3/4 lines, 19 jewels, 21,600 vibrations per hour). Seconds indicated by the C-shaped tourbillon cage. Movement developed and assembled by the Cartier Manufacture in accordance with the Geneva Hallmark tradition: pieces with polished angles and file strokes, polished screw heads and jewels, bevelled geartrain wheels on both sides, polished pinion shanks and faces.

ballon bleu de *Cartier*
46 MM FLYING TOURBILLON 9452 MC CALIBRE

Cartier

one hundred years of passion and free spirit
1909 2009

CHANEL

CHANEL

J12

AUTOMATIC

J12

CALIBRE

3125

Note from the Chairmen

Michael Kong   Stephen Kong

Never Wince Twice

Purchase quality, the saying goes, and you wince only once. When it comes to watches, this is especially true, which is why we here at Modern Luxury Media consider *Watches International* to be such a valuable resource. Even in these challenging times, the market for luxury timepieces remains relatively robust. To help guide the way, we set out to provide discerning reviews of the finest, most exclusive and sought-after watches for those whose collections will not accommodate mediocrity.

As America's largest publisher of luxury city magazines, Modern Luxury consistently strives to offer readers the best information from the worlds of fashion, interior design, dining, travel, jewelry, and the arts. We're thrilled to report that Caroline Childers and her team here at *Watches International* and sister publication *Grand Complications* have applied the same level of expertise to their world since entering into the Modern Luxury fold two years ago.

The 2009 edition of *Watches International* is a perfect example: at a time when financial uncertainty is of great concern to the masses, the individuals who lead must consider this while maintaining a personal commitment to excellence. The pages that follow offer the best of the best, placing the emphasis on fine watchmaking. You, the readers and collectors, have come to expect this and, as you consider purchases for their aesthetic and technical qualities and for their potential to increase in value, *Watches International* is here to ensure that you can invest and collect with confidence—and to assure that you never wince twice.

Michael Kong

Stephen Kong

LEVIEV "Double Eagle" Platinum and Diamond Tourbillon

LEVIEV

EXTRAORDINARY DIAMONDS

LONDON · NEW YORK · MOSCOW · DUBAI
www.leviev.com

CELLINI JEWELERS
New York, NY

*Y*ves Saint-Laurent said it best: Fashions fade, but style is eternal. Cellini Jewelers personifies that ideal with an exquisite collection whose timeless beauty transcends fleeting trends.

BR 02 Instrument Blacktop Pro
(Bell & Ross)

The Adams family first opened Cellini's flagship location in the Hotel Waldorf-Astoria more than 30 years ago, later adding a second boutique among the posh shops that line Madison Avenue. Renowned for its personalized service, Cellini is a perennial favorite in reviews of the city's premier jewelers, drawing raves for having one of the most extensive selections of rare watches and jewelry in the world.

Sophisticated and discerning, the Cellini collection appeals to those who share a passion for life's finer things. For those who desire bejeweled scintillation, our showcases sparkle with the latest styles for everyday chic along with heirloom-quality pieces to be treasured for generations. For others who prefer haute horlogerie to haute couture, Cellini offers a rare opportunity to experience one of the largest collections of limited edition and one-of-a-kind timepieces found anywhere. Complicated mechanical watches from Europe's historic watch manufactures sit alongside daring creations from the growing number of independent watchmakers.

Whichever passions rule their hearts, they all come to Cellini to revel in the best of the best.

Colorful Carats: Natural fancy pink, yellow and white diamonds.

Cellini's flagship store was established in 1977 at the Hotel Waldorf-Astoria.

LEFT   Cellini's second boutique was established in 1987 at the epicenter of the world's
most elite shopping district, Madison Avenue
in New York City.

ABOVE   Filled with fine jewels and a striking collection of timepieces, Cellini's Madison
Avenue display windows never fail to stop
passers-by in their tracks.

Repetition Minute Zephyr
(Guy Ellia)

DISCERNING TASTE

More than just a gathering place for the handiwork of today's
best watchmakers, Cellini has become an important arbiter of style
thanks to its willingness through the years to introduce promising
watch brands.

Before going on to achieve much-deserved success, companies
like A. Lange & Söhne and Audemars Piguet found a home in America
at Cellini. "One of the things I'm most proud of is that we've never been
afraid to take a chance on something new or spend the time nurturing
a talented watchmaker," says the company's president, Leon Adams.
"Cultivating those long-standing relationships with the industry's ris-
ing stars is what's insured our access to hard-to-find watches today."

After introducing Guy Ellia and H. Moser & Cie. to its collection
in 2007, Cellini became the leading U.S. retailer for these hot new
brands. In 2008, each boutique added watches from Bell & Ross and
Giuliano Mazzuoli.

Cellini is also proud to be the first in the U.S. to offer Maîtres du
Temps, a brand that debuted this spring at the annual watch show
in Geneva. Founded by long-time watch veteran Steven Holtzman,
Maîtres du Temps represents a new concept in watchmaking, using
different teams of "masters" to develop unique watches. The first such
collaboration is called, fittingly, Chapter One. Developed with master
watchmaker Christophe Claret, this grand complication is the first to
combine a tourbillon movement with a mono-pusher column-wheel
chronograph, retrograde date, retrograde GMT, along with rolling bars
that indicate moonphase and day of the week.

Another rarity found at Cellini is the limited edition 1833 Collection from Jaeger-LeCoultre, a brand that celebrated 175 years in 2008. To mark the occasion, the watchmaker unveiled a series of exceptional Master Control watches.

LASTING BEAUTY

But watches tell only half the story. Cellini's superb selection of jewelry ranks among the city's best. To maintain its legendary reputation for excellence, Adams personally selects all of the gemstones featured in Cellini's one-of-a-kind pieces. "I take responsibility for maintaining our collection very seriously," he says. "Our clients expect an impeccably high standard of quality, which is why we use only diamonds that are rated VS1 or better in every piece we create."

From elegant understatement to over-the-top glitz, the only limit is your imagination. "We have an exceptional collection of flawless white and color diamonds, as well as rare and exotic gemstones," Adams says. "That range gives us the ability to hand-craft a personal masterpiece tailored to reflect your unique style."

Cellini offers a veritable rainbow of natural color diamonds, including pink, blue, green, orange and yellow. One of Cellini's standouts is a magnificent necklace that crackles with the high-watt intensity that only 42 carats can deliver. The necklace's 11 color diamonds, which weigh a total of four carats, are undoubtedly the stars of the show. Suspended tantalizingly from a trio of white marquises, the color diamonds—including blue pears, green and yellow radiants, pink asschers, and an orange heart—are each surrounded by white round brilliants.

Last year, Cellini unveiled matching earrings, as well as a bracelet that evokes the indulgent luxury of the necklace on the wrist. The platinum bracelet glitters with nearly 4 carats of color diamonds, which are complemented by more than 15 carats of white diamonds.

For those who appreciate the rarity of lasting beauty, the charm of Cellini's timeless style holds sway.

Symphony of Color: These one-of-a-kind pieces highlight Cellini's vast assortment of natural color diamonds with an extraordinary array of pink, blue, green, orange, and yellow stones.

WATCH BRANDS CARRIED

A. Lange & Söhne	Guy Ellia
Audemars Piguet	H. Moser & Cie.
Baume & Mercier	Hublot
Bell & Ross	IWC
Cartier	Jaeger-LeCoultre
Chopard	Jean Dunand
De Bethune	Maîtres du Temps
DeWitt	Parmigiani Fleurier
F.P. Journe	Panerai
Franck Muller	Piaget
Gérald Genta	Richard Mille
Girard-Perregaux	Ulysse Nardin
Giuliano Mazzuoli	Vacheron Constantin

STORE LOCATIONS

Hotel Waldorf-Astoria • 301 Park Avenue at 50th Street • New York, NY 10022 • 212-751-9824

509 Madison Avenue at 53rd Street • New York, NY 10022 • 212-888-0505

800-CELLINI • www.CelliniJewelers.com

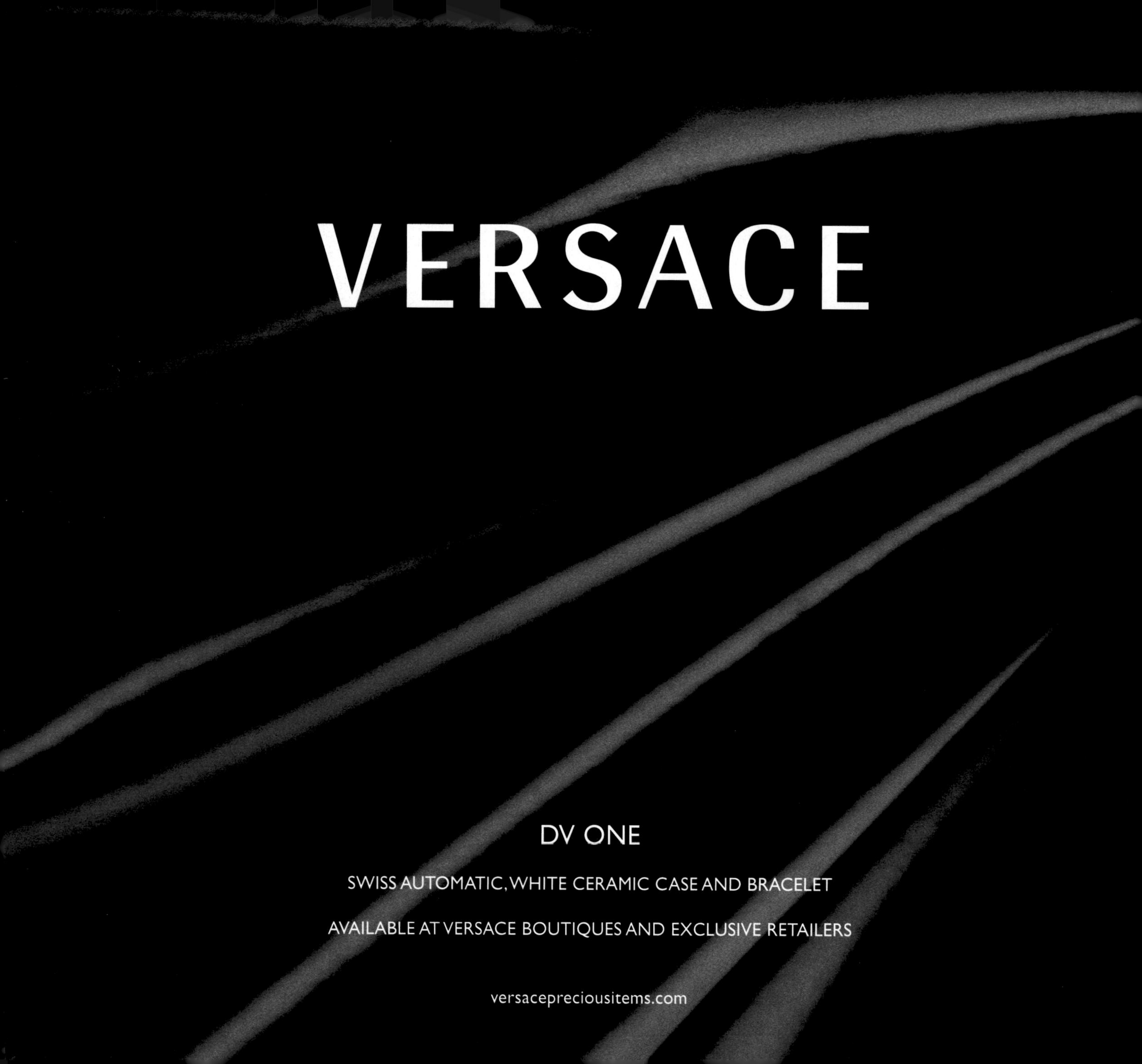

VERSACE

DV ONE

SWISS AUTOMATIC, WHITE CERAMIC CASE AND BRACELET

AVAILABLE AT VERSACE BOUTIQUES AND EXCLUSIVE RETAILERS

versacepreciousitems.com

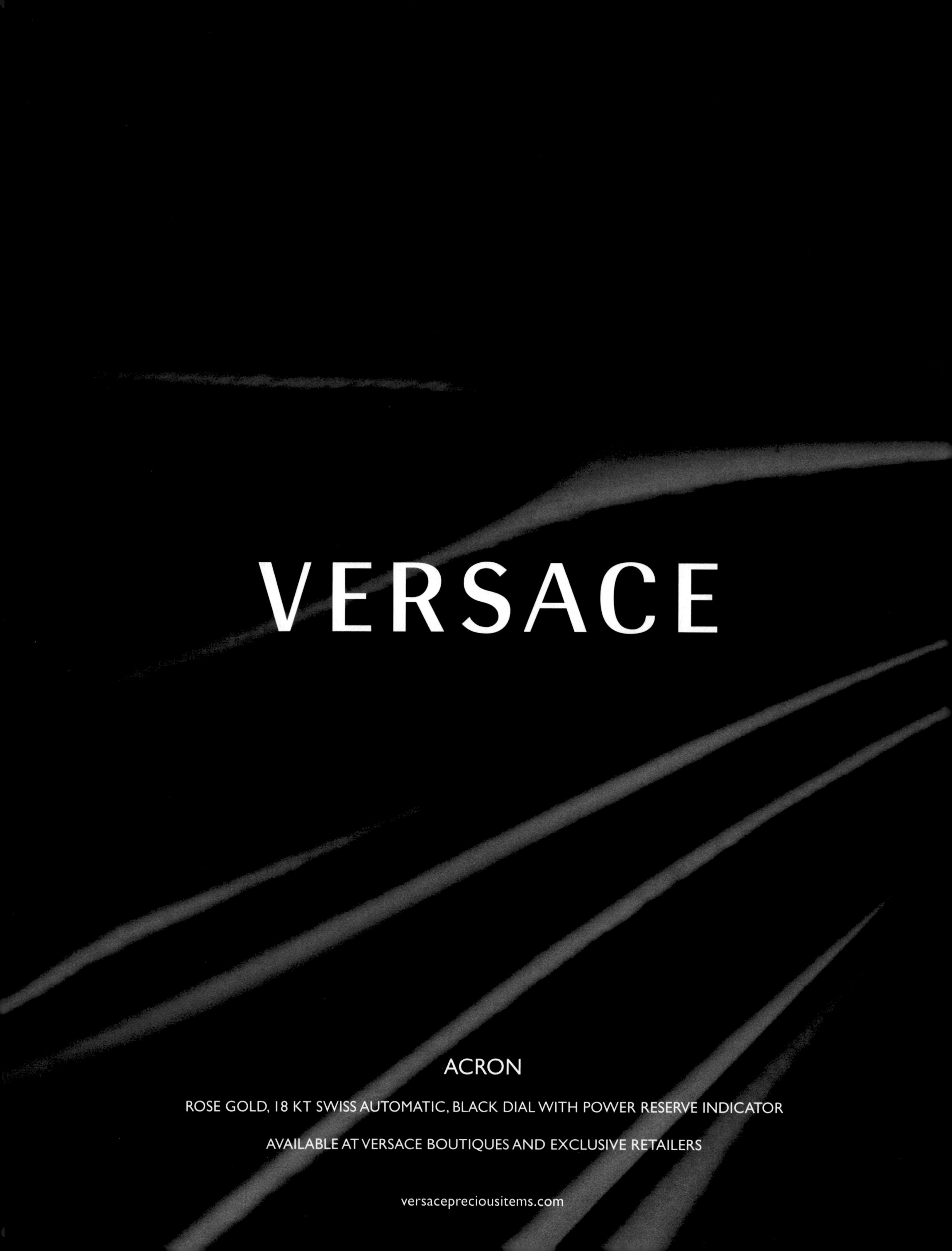

VERSACE

ACRON

ROSE GOLD, 18 KT SWISS AUTOMATIC, BLACK DIAL WITH POWER RESERVE INDICATOR

AVAILABLE AT VERSACE BOUTIQUES AND EXCLUSIVE RETAILERS

versacepreciousitems.com

Letter from the Publisher

Artists of the Mechanical

The figure of the watchmaker in the popular imagination is an old one: a man in a white shirt who passes his days behind a worktable, elbows around his ears and a loupe to his eye. This image is not completely divorced from reality, but it doesn't present the whole picture. What about the engineers, what about the constructors, what about the designers who have sought out unusual materials, invented ultra-complex movements and created the shapes of the future? And what about the marketing directors and the public relations departments, those hands-on teams who transport and sell these emotionally charged objects?

The roots of watchmaking lead us back to industrial imagery, but a look at today's haute horology reveals a whole new universe, one that rises to the level of artistic discipline. The evidence lies in the newest offerings from the world's watchmakers—the subject of this very book. They seem to reveal what we see in the paintings of the Old Masters: an indescribable emotion, an almost physical attraction for an object that has become suddenly, sometimes painfully, indispensable. Ask any professional working in horology today, any one will tell you that inside every watch hides a soul. And from emotion to passion, there is only one step, a step taken almost unconsciously.

Freed from the constraints of simply measuring time, a role that was born and grew along with the watch itself, today the timepiece explores virgin territory. It does this without restrictions and with determination, like the Fauvist painters from the beginning of the 20th century. They appropriated for themselves, among other things, the daring use of vivid colors, charting a path based on instinct. We see this all-consuming, fiery passion in the watches that push up against the limits of the field, that bring together the summits of technical excellence and aesthetic refinement, and wrap around our wrists. Creative magicians, these watchmakers have revolutionized the art of timekeeping by creating an horological osmosis, an exchange among a multitude of talents. Fine watchmaking has burst from its chrysalis, coming into its own as a beautiful butterfly.

Caroline Childers

♥ **A. LANGE & SÖHNE** Manon

Abplanalp Leon Adams Serge

Aebischer **ALAIN SILBERSTEIN** Ruediger

Amedro ♥♥♥ **ANONIMO** ♥♥♥ **ANTOINE**

Albers Marines Alvarez Melania Amati Gaëlle

Arabo Ginny Arakelyan **ARMAND NICOLET** ♥♥♥ **ARMIN**

PREZIUSO ♥♥♥ **AQUANAUTIC** Angela Arabo Jacob

Ashorn Sandrine Atamaniuk **AUDEMARS PIGUET** Flavio Audemars

STROM Herbert Arni **ARNOLD & SON** Yvan Arpa Rebecca

Bamert Mariam Bangall Jasmine Bapic Moshe Barokas Nisso Barokas Jack

Carole Augsburger **B.R.M** Jean-Christophe Babin Olivier Bacher Annette

BAUME & MERCIER Felix Baumgartner Matthieu Baumgartner **BÉDAT & CO.** Christian Bédat

Barouh Michele Barouh Eileen Barzola Céline Bassard Richard Baugh

Simone Bédat Cyril Bédat Jean-Christophe Bédos **BELL & ROSS**

Marianna Bellisario John-Henry Belmont Clelia Benhabiles François-Henry Bennahmias Annick Benoit-Godet Pascal Berclaz Jennifer Beretta Amélie Berger Giorgio Bernasconi

Marc Bernhardt Olivier Bernheim Patric Bernheim Vivian Bernstein Lise Berrod Camille Berthet Claire Berthet **BERTOLUCCI** Véronique Beuchat Françoise Bezzola Anne Biéler

Delphine Biver Jean-Claude Biver Murielle Blanchard Corinne Blanchard **BLANCPAIN** Ludovic Blanquer Léonie Bochot Marie Bodman Larry Boland Christophe Bolli Angelo Bonati

Philippe Bonay Jean-Marc Bories Adélina Bouché-Bellé **BOUCHERON** ♥♥ **BOVET** Carol Boyd Tristan Boyer de Bouillane Michael Brader-Araje Lauren Brand Pascal Brandt Martin Braun

BREGUET ♥♥♥ **BREITLING** Kathleen Bridoux Allen Brill Guillaume Brochard Shauna Brook Barbara Bucheli Linda Buckley Lance Burstyn Maximilian Büsser Stephen Butler **BVLGARI** Tom

Byrczek Mireille Cabezas Margherita Caccavale Alberto Caccia Angela Cahill Lisa Caiazzo Larry Califano Marc Calmonte Denise Campanelli François Candolfi Juan-Carlos Capelli Mitchell Caplan

CARL F. BUCHERER ♥♥♥ **CARTIER** Blandine Castaigne Alexandra Castro **CEDRIC JOHNER** Corinne Celeyron **CELLINI CENTURY** ♥♥♥ **CHANEL** ♥♥♥ **CHARLES OUDIN** Desiree Charles

CHARRIOL Philippe Charriol **CHAUMET PARIS** Thierry Chaunu Rudy Chavez **CHOPARD** Paola Chopard **CHRONOSWISS** Nicole Chuat Michael Cicero Christophe Claret **CLERC** Gerald Clerc

Nathalie Clerc Sophie Clottu Stefania Cocco Ellen Cohan Alberto Colangelo Barbara Colarieti Cristiana Colarieti Anne-Valérie Compain **CONCORD** Vanessa Conde Isabelle Corigny **CORUM** Antje

Costantino Laurence Courtois Lin Coyle Nathalie Crausaz Roberto Cristóbal Mimi Crume **CUERVO Y SOBRINOS** Lauren Curtin Geraldine Nagel D'Eternod Cristina Dagostino Pablo Dana **DANIEL**

MINK ♥♥♥ **DANIEL ROTH** Franck Dardenne **DAVID YURMAN** Roy Davidoff Caroline Dayen **De BEERS** ♥♥♥ **De BETHUNE** Maryline De Cesare Benoit de Clerck Marie de Foucaud **de GRISOGONO**

♥♥♥ **DE LA COUR** Alessandra De Martino Frederic de Narp Stanislas de Quercize Beatrice de Quervain Renaud de Retz Christine de Saint Andrieu Arnaud de Schytter Jérôme de Witt Olya Debrin

Olivier Degan Florence Degardin Nathalie Degrange Alain Delamuraz Lisa Delane **DELANEAU** Elisabeth Delannoy Judith Delfino Tiziana Della Croce John DeMeo Denise des Arts-Loup Stéphanie des

Arts-Loup William Devine **DeWITT** Miriam Di Ninni Danielle DiAntonio Carlos Dias Theodore Diehl **DIMIER** ♥♥ **DIOR** Mauro DiRoberto Nicole Domon Julie Dorin Marissa Drew Franck Dubarry

DUBEY & SCHALDENBRAND Carole Duboise Pierre Duboise Chrysline Dubuisson Jean-Frederic Dufour Nai-Ling Dunand Fanny Duval Anouk Duvillard **EBEL** ♥♥♥ **EBERHARD & C** ♥♥♥

Arnd Einhorn **ELINI** Guy Ellia Joëlle Esculier Robin Scheer Ettinger **EUROPEAN COMPANY WATCH** Joel Evequoz **F.P. JOURNE** Missy Farren Laurent Favre Raquel Feas Ben Feigenbaum Michael

Feldbausch Benedicte Ferlet Maryellen Fink Don FitzHenry Barry Fitzpatrick Denis Flageollet Bernard Fleury Stephen Forsey Lydie Foulon **FRANC VILA** ♥♥♥ **FRANCK MULLER** ♥♥♥ **HAUTLENCE**

FREDERIQUE CONSTANT Martin Frei Mireille Frick Monica Friedmann Samuel Friedmann Thierry Fritsch Vicky Fruchtman Sam Gabbas Tomasso Galli Jean Paul Galliard Mara Galzignato Pasquale

Gangi Annabelle Garcia Frédéric Gasser Xavier Gauderlot Kelly Gaussa John "JP" Geoghegan **GEORGES V** ♥♥♥ **GERALD GENTA** ♥♥♥ **GEVRIL** Christine Giotto **GIRARD-PERREGAUX** Jean-Paul

Girardin Lionel Giraud Anne-Charlotte Gonet Jasmine Gokbilgin **GOLDPFEIL** Christina Golze Fabrice Gonet Jasmine Gorre Borja Tani Gossenberger Debbie Gourdon Chantal Graff **GRAHAM** Bruno

Grande Julien Grandjean Ken Grazi Michael Graziadei **GREUBEL FORSEY** Robert Greubel Efraim Grinberg Gedalio "Gerry" Grinberg Kimberly Grogan Florie Gruber Fawaz Gruosi Caroline

Gruosi-Scheufele Ricardo Guadalupe **GUCCI** Natacha Guinnard **GUY ELLIA** ♥♥♥ **H. MOSER** Pierre Halimi Stephanie Halimi Ann Sofie Hansson Carole Harari **HARRY WINSTON** ♥♥♥ **HUBLOT** Sylvie

Marc A. Hayek Nicolas G. Hayek **HD3** Heinz J. Heimann **HERMÈS** Natacha Hertz Samantha Hickey Kelly Hodrick Patrik Hoffmann Catia Hofmann Steven Holtzman Marc Hruschka **HUBLOT** Sylvie

Humbert-Droz Harriet Hunter Susanne Hurni Thierry Huron Jorg Hysek **I&MT** Frances Ibarra Blair Max Imgrüth **INVICTA** ♥♥♥ **IWC** Ronald Jackson **JACOB & CO** Jean-Marc Jacot

JAEGER-LECOULTRE Simone Jaisli **JAQUET DROZ** ♥♥♥ **JEAN DUNAND** ♥♥♥ **JEAN-MAIRET & GILLMAN** César Jean-Mairet **JEANRICHARD** Ann Jesson Cédric Johner Christine Johner

François-Paul Journe Bruno Jufer Marc Junod Katherine Kane Hratch Kaprelian Nicolas Kawiak Jonathan Keller Knych Keller Jim Kennedy Georges Kern Nora Khadir John M. King Rachel

Konikiewicz Nathalie Kottelat Pierre Koukjian Michael Kowalski Peter Kramer Karl Kreiser **KRIËGER** Fabian Krone Masako Kumakura Stephanie Labeille Nina Lagdameo Maresa Laino Eyal

Lalo Gany Lalo Jérôme Lambert Catherine Lamy Angela Landone Gerd-Rüdiger Lange Stephanie Lebadezet Thérèse Legerer Frédéric Lejosne Marine Lemonnier Philippe Leopold-Metzger

LEONARD ♥♥♥ **LEROY** Marion Lescat **LEVIEV** Lev Leviev Guy Leymarie Caroline Lisker **LOCMAN** ♥♥♥ **LONGINES** Eric Loth **LOUIS MOINET** Anne-Charlotte Loupi Dr. Gino "Luigi"

Macaluso Umberto Macchi Massimo Machi Jean Bernard Maeder Larry Magen Gianluca Maina Brigitte Makhzani Jean-Louis Merandet Philippe C. Merk Katrin Meusinger **MEYERS** Georges-Henri Meylan

JORDI Mathilde Michel Pascal Michel **MICHELE** Nathalie Micheletto Richard Mille Linda Miller Igal Mizrahi Vincent Moesch Laure Monney **MONTBLANC** Scott Montemurro

Barbara Monti Kate Montini Diana Moran Scarlett Moreno Thomas Morf Hildegard Moser Scott Moskovitz **MOVADO** Sarah Mugnier Frederic Muller Josefine Müller Carlo

Munari Roberto Muniz Roland G. Murphy Amy Naim Thierry Nataf Franck Neveu Lisa Newman Cécile Neyaga Hân Nguyen Jean-Christophe Niarquin Peter Nicholson

Juliette North Julie O'Daly Paul O'Neil **OCEANAUT** Dr. Ludwig Oechslin **OLIVIER ROUX** Jon Omer Eric Oppliger Isabelle Oppliger Paola Orlando Stacie Orloff Thierry

Oulevay Elodie Pacault Steven Pachtinger Erdme Pailloux **PANERAI** ♥♥♥ **PARMIGIANI FLEURIER** Michel Parmigiani Eleonore Paschoud **PATEK PHILIPPE** Alvina

Patel **PAUL PICOT** Mary Peck Fran Pennella Yolande Peroulaz **PERRELET** Sarah Perriard Vincent Perriard Emmanuel Perrin Mario Peserico Léa Petersell **PHILIP**

STEIN TESLAR Dennis Phillips **PIAGET** Corinne Piaget-Blanc **PIERRE DEROCHE** ♥♥♥ **PIERRE KUNZ** Laurent Pierrugues Lisa Pilkington **POIRAY** ♥♥♥

POTGER-PIETRI Gaëlle Praz Simone Prévalet Heather Prizer Dan Prouty Alexis Przybylski **QUINTING** Philippe Rabin Pascal Raffy **RAYMOND WEIL** Michèle

Reichenbach Deborah Reiter Celine Rey **RGM** ♥♥♥ **RICHARD MILLE** Bernard Richards Kristine Riediger Veronika Riggauer Cinette Robert Juliane

Robert-Grandpierre Hoda Roche Gérald Roden **ROGER DUBUIS** Barbara Rogers **ROLEX** ♥♥♥ **ROMAIN JEROME** Scott Rosen Carlos Rosillo Vanessa

Rota **ROTARY** Béatrice Rouhier Olivier Roux Emilie Roy Anton Rubianto Jennifer Rubianto Natalia Rubio Simonetta Ruggeri Sylvie Rumo

S.COIFMAN ♥♥♥ **SALVATORE FERRAGAMO** Zanetta Sampson Jonathon San Pedro Claude Sanz Yacine Sar Alexis Sarkissian Pascal Savoy

Denise Scala **SCATOLA DEL TEMPO** Karl-Friedrich Scheufele René Schmidlin Elisabeth Schneider Theodore Schneider Stéphane Schuler

Sandrine Segato Nicole Segundo Monica Sese Melanie Seymour Paul Sheldon Randi Shinske Laetitia Sidler Natalia Signoroni Barbara

Simonian Greg Simonian John Simonian Anthony Siragusa Karin Soller Anouk Sorensen Peter Stas Daphné Stauffer Jasmine

Steele Rina Stein Will Stein Michael Steinhauser Henry Stern Jutta Stienen Olivier Stip Ron Stoll Michele Streker Denise Studer

Matthias Studer **STUHRLING ORIGINAL** Ed Sudyha William Sullivan Carra Sutherland Alain Swierk Sandrine-Lise Taboada

Dominique Tadion **TAG HEUER** Mélanie Tanner Florence Tauriac Sara Teass **TECHNOMARINE** Cristina Thévenaz

Isabelle Thomas Maud Tiberti **TIFFANY & CO** Maria Teresa Tiu Julien Tornare Olivia Tornare Juan-Carlos Torres

Clemence Toulouze Beatriz Rossel Tür **ULYSSE NARDIN** ♥♥♥ **UNIVERSAL GENEVE** Valérie Ursenbacher

URWERK Carla Uzel Béatrice Vaccaro **VACHERON CONSTANTIN** ♥♥♥ **VALENTINO** Katidja Valy **VAN**

CLEEF & ARPELS Thomas van der Kallen Harris Vaughn **VERSACE** ♥♥♥ **VERTU** Michelle Veyna

Anne-Laure Vibert Sarah Vicklund Franc Vila Patricia Villanueva **VINCENT BERARD** Eric Viscont

Caroline Vogt **VOLNA** Pierre-Frédéric Von Kaenel Walter von Känel Gabriella von Malaisé

Béatrice Vuille-Willemetz Jay Vullings Jean-Hugues Walther Stephane Waser

Anne-Lise Weistroff **WEMPE** Sara Wermus **WESTIME** ♥♥♥ **WINGS OF TIME**

David Witkover Wendy Witte Ronald Wolfgang Muriele Wormser

Tenten Wu Michael Wunderman Severin Wunderman **WYLER**

GENEVE David Yurman Sybil Yurman Federica Zamprogna

David Zanetta **ZANNETTI** Riccardo Zanetti Jack

Zemer Ori Zemer Sandy Zemer **ZENITH**

Claudette Zerbe Paul Ziff Daniel

Zimmermann Alexandra Zoller

♥♥♥♥

Caroline Childers

Ten years already?!

How time flies! I would like to take
this opportunity to extend my heartfelt thanks and love
to everyone who has shared their keen knowledge
of the watchmaking industry and supported me
in countless ways over the last ten years
of Watches International—
I feel younger than ever!

THE WATCH. RECONSTRUCTED.

WHAT OTHER WATCH HAS A 3.3 MM THICK SAPPHIRE CRYSTAL? WHAT OTHER WATCH HAS 7 SIDE SCREWS FOR GREATER STRUCTURAL STRENGTH? WHAT OTHER WATCH HAS A DISTINCT 3 LEVEL DIAL? WHAT OTHER WATCH HAS A CASE MADE OF 53 ELEMENTS THAT STANDS 16.7 MM TALL? WHAT OTHER WATCH HAS A FORMULA FOR THE ULTIMATE CONSTRUCTION?

VALENTINO

ROSE

DIAL IN MOTHER-OF-PEARL WITH ROSE PATTERN
AND DIAMONDS; STAINLESS STEEL CASE WITH
WHITE DIAMONDS, SAPPHIRE CRYSTAL,
STRAP IN SATIN.

Salvatore Ferragamo

TIMEPIECES

GANCINO
184 DIAMONDS AND STAINLESS STEEL
SILK SATIN STRAP

Letter from the Editor in Chief

Crisis and Conquests

To evoke the world markets and their characteristics with the Swiss clock- and watchmakers is an amusing exercise. The Russians are rarely satisfied with a standard product, but always request adjustments closer to their grandiose tastes. The Middle Eastern customers love very large, stunning timepieces, but preferably containing a quartz movement. The Southeast Asian clients are fine experts, and sometimes extremely demanding. Americans are conservative and have not yet discovered completely the variety offered by the luxury watch industry. Not to be condescending, but this observation is essential: the day when the Swiss clock- and watchmakers have finally demonstrated to the world that a watch represents much more than an object that gives the time, this day will mark the beginning of a true conquest.

One speaks about the maturity of a market when the production rate is high compared to the market potential. Between January and October 2008, Switzerland exported 2.8 million watches (all categories) to the United States, a country with more than 300 million citizens. The Swiss watchmaking industry managed to reach 0.95% of the population. In China, that rate goes down to 0.08%! It is conservative to say that these outlets and many others still hold exceptional sales growth prospects.

The effort to become established is considerable. The current crisis will eliminate the weakest branches of production. This is a welcome cleansing, but this will not improve the market. To attract new customers, companies must show significant creativity. The creativity with their products must appeal to a broader range customers and the creativity in the message must indoctrinate a certain watchmaking culture that is currently bypassing hundreds of thousands of potential consumers. The clock- and watchmakers must communicate more often and more effectively. Only the most dynamic companies will flourish.

Michel Jeannot

RICHARD MILLE

OFFICIAL TIMEKEEPER

GPHG Asia

Trailblazer award 2008

WINNER

**Grand Prix d'Horlogerie
de Genève**

Golden Hand • 2007

A RACING MACHINE ON THE WRIST

THE ORIGINAL ANNUAL OF THE WORLD'S FINEST WRISTWATCHES

TOURBILLON INTERNATIONAL
A MODERN LUXURY MEDIA, LLC COMPANY
ADMINISTRATION, ADVERTISING SALES, EDITORIAL, BOOK SALES

11 West 25th Street, 8th Floor, New York, NY 10010
Tel: +1 (212) 627-7732   Fax: +1 (312) 274-8418
sales@tourbillon-watches.com

CHAIRMAN AND CEO
Michael Kong

VICE CHAIRMAN
Stephen Kong

COO
Michael Lipson

PUBLISHER
Caroline Childers

EDITOR IN CHIEF
Michel Jeannot

EDITOR
Elizabeth Kindt

ASSOCIATE EDITOR
Claire Loeb

CONTRIBUTING EDITORS
Lynn Braz • Fabrice Eschmann • Scott Hickey
Louis Nardin • Elise Nussbaum

TRANSLATIONS
Susan Jacquet • Jeffrey Kostelecky
Caroline Ruiz

ART DIRECTOR
Mutsumi Hyuga

INTERNATIONAL ART DIRECTOR OF PRE-PRESS AND PRODUCTION
Franca Vitali - Grafica Effe

PRINT PROCUREMENT DIRECTOR
Sean Bertram

COORDINATION
Caroline Pita

SENIOR VICE PRESIDENT OF FINANCE
John Pietrolungo

DIRECTOR OF DISTRIBUTION
Eric Holden

WEBMASTER
Marcel Choukroun

WEB DISTRIBUTION
www.modernluxury.com/watches

PHOTOGRAPHERS
Photographic Archives
Property of Tourbillon International,
a Modern Luxury Media, LLC company

DANIEL ROTH

MASTERPIECES IN THE ART OF WATCHMAKING

20th

1989-2009
20th anniversary

8-DAY TOURBILLON
PERPETUAL CALENDAR

Double-face Daniel Roth tourbillon movement,
entirely decorated by hand. Off-centred hours
and minutes, three-arm small seconds hand
on the tourbillon axis, 200-hour power reserve
in a window and perpetual calendar on
the reverse side of the movement. Upper dial
in tinted sapphire crystal and openworked
inner dial in sapphire crystal and gold.

"**Time**
does not have the same
appeal for everyone.

WILLIAM SHAKESPEARE

ZENITH

SWISS WATCH MANUFACTURE

SINCE 1865

CHRONOMASTER

"Whatever does not destroy me makes me stronger.

FRIEDRICH NIETZSCHE

WESTIME
Los Angeles & Beverly Hills, CA

Champions of the new vanguard

THIS PAGE
RM 011 Automatic Flyback Chronograph
(Richard Mille)

FACING PAGE
Westime boutique on Rodeo Drive in Beverly
Hills.

A trailblazer in bringing mechanical art for the wrist to its zenith, Westime continues to break new ground in offering not just the widest range of high-concept watches, but the most revolutionary of brands, too.

Nearly 20 years ago, Westime was founded on a vision of a renaissance in watchmaking, and today, that vision is a reality. Three brands stand powerfully for the new watchmaking vanguard: Greubel Forsey, Richard Mille and URWERK.

Says Barbara Simonian, co-founder of Westime, "These brands represent two key values for Westime—they are incredibly sophisticated and their revolutionary approach to haute horlogerie sets them apart. We believe strongly in the potential of these brands to not only succeed aesthetically, but with our clients as well, who are strongly drawn to innovation, creativity and uniqueness."

Indeed, that they do: URWERK, the masters of kinetic sculpture; Greubel Forsey, the tourbillon revolutionaries; and Richard Mille, the master of materials which redefined the vocabulary of luxury. Initial reactions from collectors were a combination of hesitancy but also fascination, Simonian recalls. "Each brand draws its own particular response, and at first, there was a lot of 'What???' and even 'Why so much?'. But there was also a lot of 'Wow!'. There was definitely skepticism at first. But since these brands were introduced, there has been a real groundswell of enthusiasm, and we all now understand that horological design can be incredibly dynamic, and that watches can express powerful technical and aesthetic visions that have never been seen before. The avant-garde has become a huge success!"

BRANDS CARRIED

A. Lange & Söhne	Franck Muller	Milus
Audemars Piguet	Gérald Genta	Omega
Baume & Mercier	Girard-Perregaux	Parmigiani Fleurier
Bell & Ross	Glashütte	Richard Mille
Blancpain	Greubel Forsey	Roland Iten
Bovet	Guy Ellia	Mechanical Luxury
Breguet	Hamilton	Swiss Army
Breitling	Harry Winston	TAG Heuer
Chanel	HAUTLENCE	TAG Heuer Meridiist
Chopard	HD3	Tissot
Concord	Hermès	URWERK
Corum	Hublot	Vacheron Constantin
DeWitt	Ikepod	Vincent Berard
Dimier	IWC	Vertu
Dior Phones	Longines	Wyler Genève
Ebel	MB&F	Zenith
Eberhard	MCT	

PRIDE AND PLEASURE

"Watch lovers who are drawn to these pieces are strongly driven to be distinctive. Many of them are aficionados of modern art as well, and simply see these timepieces as a natural extension of their interest in sophisticated design," says Simonian. There is also a certain discreet pleasure in the fact that on their wrist is a timepiece that costs more than most luxury automobiles!

A watch may be a work of art, but it is also fundamentally a machine whose proper care can be a further extension of the joy and pride of ownership—and Westime considers it its duty to offer unsurpassed service before, during and after acquisition.

Besides knowledgeable sales staff, Westime has skilled in-house watchmakers on hand to service timepieces as necessary, and to perform various pressure and water-resistance tests to ensure the watches function optimally. "We believe fine timepieces should be a source of pleasure, not frustration, to our clients. Should a watch require service, we strive to ensure that it is done as expeditiously as possible and with the highest level of skill. Of course, our close relationship with the unique and sophisticated brands, whom it is our privilege to represent, helps ensure the quality communication and impeccable service our clients have come to expect."

THIS PAGE UR-202 Turbine Automatic (URWERK)

FACING PAGE Westime boutique on West Pico Blvd., Los Angeles.

STORE LOCATIONS

10800 West Pico Blvd., #197 • Los Angeles, CA 90064
tel: 310-470-1388 • fax: 310-475-0628

254 North Rodeo Drive • Beverly Hills, CA 90210
tel: 310-271-0000 • fax: 310-271-3091

www.westimewatches.com

Summary

BR 01 INSTRUMENT TOURBILLON PHANTOM Ø 46 MM · Regulator · Power reserve 120 hours · Trust index · Carbon fiber bridges
Titanium case with special carbon finish · Limited edition to 18 pieces · Information: Bell & Ross Inc. +1.888.307.7887 . www.bellross.com

Web Site Directory

AUDEMARS PIGUET	www.audemarspiguet.com	LOUIS MOINET	www.louismoinet.com
B.R.M	www.brm-manufacture.com	MCT	www.mctwatches.com
BAUME & MERCIER	www.baume-et-mercier.com	MONTBLANC MONTRE	www.montblanc.com
BELL & ROSS	www.bellross.com	MOVADO	www.movado.com
BERTOLUCCI	www.bertolucciwatches.com	PANERAI	www.panerai.com
BOUCHERON	www.boucheron.com	PARMIGIANI FLEURIER	www.parmigiani.ch
BOVET FLEURIER SA	www.bovet.com	PATEK PHILIPPE	www.patek.com
BVLGARI	www.bulgari.com	PIAGET	www.piaget.com
CARL F. BUCHERER	www.carl-f-bucherer.com	RAYMOND WEIL S.A.	www.raymondweil.com
CARTIER	www.cartier.com	RICHARD MILLE	www.richardmille.com
CHANEL	www.chanel.com	ROLEX	www.rolex.com
CHOPARD	www.chopard.com	ROMAIN JEROME	www.romainjerome.ch
CHRONOSWISS	www.chronoswiss.de	SALVATORE FERRAGAMO	www.ferragamo.com
CLERC	www.clercwatches.com	STÜHRLING ORIGINAL	www.stuhrling.com
CONCORD	www.concord.ch	TAG HEUER	www.tagheuer.com
CORUM	www.corum.ch	ULYSSE NARDIN	www.ulysse-nardin.com
CUERVO Y SOBRINOS	www.h-moser.com	UNIVERSAL GENÈVE	www.universal.ch
DANIEL ROTH	www.danielroth.com	URWERK	www.urwerk.com
DAVID YURMAN	www.davidyurman.com	VACHERON CONSTANTIN	www.vacheron-constantin.com
de GRISOGONO	www.degrisogono.com	VALENTINO	www.valentino.com
DeWITT	www.dewitt.ch	VERSACE	www.versace.com
DIMIER	www.bovet.com	VINCENT BERARD	www.vincentberard.ch
DIOR WATCHES	www.dior.com	ZANNETTI	www.zannettiwatches.com
EBEL	www.ebel.com	ZENITH	www.zenith-watches.com
F. P. JOURNE	www.fpjourne.com		
FRANC VILA	www.francvila.com		
GERALD GENTA	www.geraldgenta.com		
GREUBEL FORSEY	www.greubelforsey.com	RELATED SITES	
GUY ELLIA	www.guyellia.com	BaselWorld	www.baselworld.com
H. MOSER & CIE.	www.h-moser.com	SIHH	www.sihh.ch
HUBLOT	www.hublot.com	LVMH Group	www.lvmh.fr
INVICTA	www.invictawatches.com	Richemont Group	www.richemont.com
IWC	www.iwc.com	Swatch Gourp	www.swatchgroup.com
JACOB & CO.	www.jacobandco.com		
KRIEGER	www.kriegerwatch.com		
LEVIEV	www.leviev.com	Auctions	www.christies.com
LONGINES	www.longines.com		www.sothebys.com

BVLGARI

Celebrating 125 years

BVLGARI.COM

THE NEW *DIAGONO* CALIBRO 303 WATCH

INTEGRATED CHRONOGRAPH WITH COLUMN WHEEL MECHANISM
MANUFACTURE MOVEMENT WITH AUTOMATIC WINDING AND DATE, CALIBER BVL 303, 45-HOURS POWER RESERVE, 37 JEWELS,
21'600 VPH, COMPRISING 303 ELEMENTS. STEEL CASE WITH 18-CT WHITE GOLD BEZEL.
ANTIRE-FLECTIVE SAPPHIRE GLASS AND TRANSPARENT BACK CASE. THREE LAYERS DIAL WITH SATINÉ SOLEIL
AND VERTICAL TREATMENTS. APPLIED FACETED INDEXES. IN-HOUSE MANUFACTURED STEEL BRACELET.

Hublot: "Fusion em passion of extraordin

Eccentric, inspired, clashing, nonconformist, daring, and hardworking: there are not enough adjectives to describe Jean-Claude Biver. As the head of Hublot since 2004, this CEO gave new life to the brand to transform it into an internationally recognized icon.

A primary contributor to this success, the Big Bang model has been repeatedly redesigned to incorporate the concept of fusion between ideas and materials that were previously thought to be incompatible. Integrated into the LVMH group last year, Hublot adds two key victories to its prize list: unbelievable growth coupled with the undeniable role of pioneer.

Since its inception, Hublot has brilliantly mastered the science of astounding customers. In 1980, Carlo Croco, who established the brand, began breaking all of the rules of the luxury watch industry. For the first time in history, he combined the elements of precious substances such as gold with common elements like rubber in the same watch. This daring creativity would make indignant the traditional watchmakers who used only high-end materials, but it would also mark the beginning of a new era, freeing watchmakers of traditional constraints to conduct all kinds of new experiments. Hublot can pride itself on breaking free of the conventional constraints. Just like the original pioneers who discovered new territories, Hublot makes it possible for the watch industry to enter the 21st century.

odies the
ury unions."

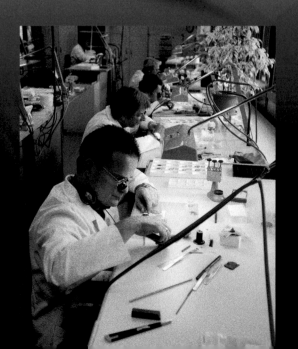

As a sponsor of the UEFA Cup, Hublot gave a special watch to all of the referees who officiated the tournament.

The Mag Bang has components in its casing and movement built from Hublonium, an alloy that is extremely hard and lightweight, exclusive to Hublot.

The Bullet Bang holds several elements made of Cermet, a new alloy that combines ceramics and metals.

A CONCEPT: FUSION

Biver gained leadership of Hublot in 2004 and immediately saw its unlimited potential. The brand had been was under-exploited to that point, and Biver decided to make it shine by utilizing its fundamental essence: fusion. As the central concept of Hublot, fusion creates alliances that had been considered contradictory. The new CEO chose to explore every facet of this miraculous formula. "Fusion is, for example, the alliance between traditional watchmaking and the latest technologies. This is clearly limitless. It embodies the passion of these extraordinary unions, which are like a freeway: once you are on it, you don't want to stop. My role was to rediscover and give new life to the Hublot DNA—to make it a new religion with its own commandments. And that is what I did."

In order to awaken Hublot, an experienced person was needed to lead the return to the forefront of the technology race. Known for his colorful vocabulary, his visionary ideas and his sharp intuition, Biver accepted the challenge. He had already resuscitated Blancpain before implementing strategic changes at Omega. When he arrived at Hublot, this exuberant executive from Luxemburg immersed himself in the DNA of Hublot. The first creative ideas came to him quickly and, following his legendary enthusiasm, he pressed his small development team to adopt an accelerated work tempo that is still in place today. Biver is like a constantly erupting volcano. Eternally aware and active, he starts his days at 3:00 a.m. to benefit from the early morning calm. By doing so, he carries out the advice of his former boss, Swiss Minister Jean-Pascal Delamuraz, who said, "As a leader, you must set the example by being the first one in the office." This is also why Biver never stays up late.

IN THE LIMELIGHT

Hublot and Biver—the two names have become so synonymous that the CEO is personally involved in the promotion of the brand. Always present in the media, he has earned his image as an exceptional communicator. Rather than maintaining a low profile like some watchmaking executives, he chose the opposite alternative: to be visible and call attention to himself. His characteristic energy that changed Hublot shines through during regularly scheduled press conferences while his charismatic personality promotes the brand. "In the United States, for example, the watchmaking culture is not yet completely anchored. Therefore, our role is to expose Americans to the emotional, artistic, exceptional aspect of luxury watches." He understands that before he can sell a watch, he must create the desire for one—another mission for him to fulfill.

Already cited as an example in marketing classes, Biver has an amazing ability to anticipate trends, determine new consumer lifestyles and invent new business models to relate to them. Before him, the watch industry did not participate in the soccer world, preferring the perfect grasses of the golf greens. He scored a goal by distributing watches to the players of the Hublot-sponsored soccer teams in their locker rooms. But the true stroke of genius was realized with the creation of the partnership between Hublot and the Union of European Football Associations at the 2008 European Soccer Cup. He would later acknowledge that when he signed the advertising contract worth several million francs, Biver knew it was a big gamble. However, his confidence in his business model and the company's development did not allow him to hesitate. His certainty was soon confirmed by the sales results exceeding forecasts. Seeing these results, the director decided to donate the soccer fields to "Football Against Racism in Europe" and kept only the Hublot name on the player billboard. In addition, Hublot sponsored the national Spanish soccer team, winner of the tournament. This was a double win for Hublot, concluding an exceptional marketing achievement.

Big Bang Classic

Big Bang All Black

Big Bang Cappuccino Gold

One Million Dollar Big Bang

BULL'S-EYE: THE BIG BANG

From the beginning, the Hublot models have been characterized by a bezel fixed in place by six screws, an invariable aesthetic code. From this original style, Biver would draw the Big Bang, the all-conquering watch that would make the brand known universally in record time. Indeed, with its large case size composed of several elements, its sharpened forms and its mechanical movement, the Big Bang offers an infinite number of variations and a masculine look that is totally in fashion today. Bezel, crown, or dial—each part can be fabricated using a different material. The Big Bang perfectly incarnates the concept of fusion. This philosophy is based on respect for watchmaking tradition, but also innovation in a search of new watchmaking materials. For example, Hublot's designers created several basic models in carbon, tungsten, titanium or composite resin. As a pioneer in the use of ceramics, Hublot is always on the lookout for any innovation. This is illustrated with the Bullet Bang model whose case components are made of Cermet, a bronze-colored alloy composed of metals and ceramics. Previously, the Nyon-based brand (in Switzerland, on the edges of Lake Léman) had even developed its own alloy, Hublonium, recognized for its hardness and light weight. Mag Bang, the first model to integrate this alloy, incorporates this exclusive material in the movement and case.

Without renouncing its resolutely technical and masculine identity, the Big Bang has several variations that reinforce its image of watchmaking chameleon. One of most the spectacular is the One Million Dollar Big Bang with its complete diamond setting. A masterpiece of craftsmanship, the model has been a soaring success with its diamond paving adjusted to one one-hundredth of a millimeter. The Big Bang Cappuccino Gold also represents an important stage in the development of the brand: its chocolate color has set the trend for other brown watches. Moreover, it exists in a smaller version for women—41mm—a version that has become very popular since its introduction. Winner of the Grand Prix d'Horologie de Genève 2005 in the Design category, Big Bang All Black marked the advent of the more purely designed watches, as it displays a completely black motif.

PHASE OF CONSOLIDATION

The conjunction between a high-profile executive and very powerful timepiece radically changed the image of Hublot. Like the cataclysm to which we attribute the creation of the universe, this brand seized the forefront of the watchmaking scene like no other. "In the beginning, we wanted to be noticed," comments Biver. "We needed to create a firework display to make noise, get attention and announce our return. The Big Bang achieved this revival. Its name was synonymous with creative explosion, corresponded completely to the spirit of the moment, and perfectly represented the positioning of the brand between past and future, like a window in space and time." After several boisterous years, Hublot started to develop more classic models. "Hublot is moving into a phase of consolidation. In its own way, it has entered an age of reason where the excesses of youth have not been renounced, but which will establish the brand for the duration." In fact, this new course was illustrated by the presentation of the Big Bang Classic model. A version of the iconic Big Bang, this new arrival affirms the brand's character with high-tech materials and All Black versions, but it also prevails with a pedigreed sobriety, with a fine case and display of the elementary functions such as the hours, minutes and seconds. This is truly stripped-down asceticism, when we consider that the technical side has always had prime importance in the Big Bang models, with the chronograph complication as a main attraction.

LIMITED SERIES

Interpreting the watch not as a tool intended to keep time—cell phones and computers have become more accurate and more ubiquitous—but as "an object conveying the personality of its owner, a social indicator," Biver creatively developed this idea of a different marketing strategy resulting with the concept of the limited series. Hublot thus became one of the brands most prolific in numbered series models. The signing of a contract sponsoring the Hublot Gold Cup Gstaad, the partnership with the sailing club (Real Club Nautico de Palma) and the sponsoring of a charitable organization (Ayrton Senna Foundation) each resulted in the creation of a limited edition line.

LEFT The 250-piece limited edition Big Bang honors the partnership between Hublot and the Polo Club of Gstaad.

CENTER Special Model Big-Bang "Copa del Rey" celebrates the bonds between Hublot and Real Club Nautico de Palma in Spain.

RIGHT Limited Edition in the honor of the Ayrton Senna Foundation.

WINNING STRATEGIES

Cultivating his image as the leader moving away from the beaten path, Biver readily declares that he has a farm and makes his own cheese. He also proves himself a well-informed entrepreneur. To respond to the recent strong labor demand within this industry, he decided to engage retired watchmakers. In addition to supporting production, these retired workers help to transfer to apprentices the detailed watchmaking knowledge that books alone cannot teach. The explosion of orders related to the success of the company resulted in the construction of a new building planned to be operational in 2009.

IN THE ARMS OF LVMH

From 2004 to 2008, Hublot transitioned from corporate sales of 29 million Swiss francs to 250 million francs and the brand became an attractive investment for a group looking to enlarge its investment portfolio. The French luxury group LVMH—already entrenched in the watch industry with Zenith, TAG Heuer, and Dior watches—purchased Hublot in 2008 for a sum estimated at 500 million Swiss francs. From that point on, Hublot has had new facilities at its disposal for provisioning and distribution.

The brand has become a symbol. Hublot has already developed its strategy to peacefully progress through these uncertain times. "The economic slowdown we see today in the luxury watch industry and the world economy does not represent a threat because we have prepared ourselves by reducing our investments and by distributing them over the long term." Confident in the future and full of communicative enthusiasm, Biver progresses according to three principles: health, job satisfaction, and emotional balance. This winning formula is proven by the results, and certainly not contradicted by the three prizes brought home by Hublot at the end of 2008 in Geneva, Paris and Bahrain.

FACING PAGE

TOP   Front view of the new Hublot factory while under construction.

BOTTOM   Bright colors are also a favorite of the brand, as demonstrated with the Big Bang Orange Carat.

THIS PAGE

ABOVE   Jean-Claude Biver, CEO of Hublot.

FAR LEFT   Fusion Man, the first flying man who used a special wing equipped with four micro-scopic engines, receives support from Hublot.

LEFT   Hublot joined the high-end ski manufac-turer Zai to create watch models named after the ski company.

"Reflet XL" Watch

B
1858 2008
150 ANS

"Reflet XL"
Steel and pink gold watch
limited edition

BOUCHERON

PARIS

"Today, *Corum* places watchmaking expertise at the top of its priorities."

In 2006, this up-and-coming brand developed a strategic approach based on four clearly defined collections. At the same time, it totally revamped its catalog and reduced its number of models from 1,000 to 150. The final step of this complete overhaul was to increase the value of its merchandise by creating limited edition series and consolidating its experience toward fewer elite timepieces. The CEO of Corum, Antonio Calce, considers the strategy and the challenges of the brand.

LEFT Antonio Calce, CEO of Corum.

ABOVE The Corum headquarters in La Chaux-de-Fonds in Switzerland.

This new model symbolizes the work achieved by the brand since its reinvention. Let me elaborate. First, it embodies an innovative product created by Corum in 1966. This reinforces the legitimacy of the brand and underscores its sense of innovation, since Romvlvs was the first watch to represent time with engraved Roman numerals on its bezel. Next, it symbolizes my venture to integrate the brand's jobs and tools. Indeed, since 2005, Corum has actively developed its human capital in order to manage a complete and integrated expertise in our workforce. By including a perpetual calendar complication in the Romvlvs collection, Corum has sent a strong signal to its distribution network and its customers: it has returned to the membership of exclusive luxury brands. On this model, the caliber's exceptional technical performance is met with extraordinary finishings. Each component is manually crafted and decorated, creating skeleton movements whose quality is the equal of any in the luxury watchmaking industry. The watchmaking masters and engravers dedicate ten working days to each piece to assemble the caliber and ensure this level of finishing. Today, Corum places watchmaking expertise at the top of its priorities.

Corum is an exclusive brand. We quietly produce fewer than 20,000 watches per year. We are not a brand who produces volume. Moreover, limiting production to twenty-five pieces makes it possible to create value and exclusivity in the product. When Corum launched this model at the BaselWorld fair in 2008, it proved its undeniable return to the haute horology scene, in particular through the Admiral's Cup Tourbillon. Today, we see only advantages in the creation of very limited editions. The perpetual calendar constitutes the height of watchmaking art. Consequently, we consider that the costs generated by a reduced production are not actually costs, but an investment that is transformed into the added value we offer our customers.

Yes, all of the orders were placed at Basel, but they are not all delivered yet.

TOP Romvlvs Perpetual Calendar illustrates the Corum will to develop top-level watchmaking expertise.

ABOVE The fruit of intense artisanal labor, the Romvlvs Perpetual Calendar movement shows all of the characteris-

How did your distribution perceive this product?

In general, the 2008 model received an excellent reception from our markets and distribution network because we put into practice what we had previously announced. Since 2005, a strategic effort was undertaken to reposition the brand and this endeavor was communicated to our markets and our retailers. The year 2008 marked the tangible application of our strategy in our products. Implemented according to the four key collections which structure the brand, namely the Admiral's Cup, the Romvlvs, the Golden Bridge and the Artisans, these new models exemplify the brand's effort to reveal its expertise and define its stature as an exclusive watchmaking brand. We kept our promises and we determined that our newly discovered values brought us closer to our distribution network.

None of the 2006 models are still produced in 2008. Is that correct? Why make such a drastic change?

Corum is known as a brand with overflowing audacity and creativity. It is enough to examine its history and the unrestrained rate and rhythm with which our innovations were launched.

But this inventiveness must evolve within a framework—trying to overdo it will kill everything. So we put the product at the center of our work and we strive to create the greatest consistency. It was the results of a strategic audit that led us to preserve the four key pillars that I mentioned earlier. In addition, we streamlined our catalog and reduced our collection from one thousand to one hundred and fifty. It was a difficult exercise and a risky bet. But today, the brand has gained cohesion and clarity and consequently has become stronger. Corum has found its historical legitimacy and now sees its sales growing substantially. Moreover, we are lucky not to be a single product brand, but based on several different and complementary products. All are closely related to the history of the brand with the Artisans collection introduced before the arrival of Admiral's Cup in 1960, of Romvlvs in 1966, and the Golden Bridge in 1980.

This change was accompanied by a significant rise on the scale of luxury. Aren't you afraid to lose your traditional customers in this venture?

The rise in range is the logical result of our formal efforts to find the historical positioning of the brand. The integration of jobs, the development of production equipment, and emphasis on human capital are clearly the result of investments implemented by Corum. Moreover, the reduction in the number of references and the centralization of our image through the four key pillars are clearly linked to the exclusive nature of the brand. From that point on, those steps were performed in the logical progression of the brand. This repositioning has reconnected us with our historical customers, proof that Corum is again in perfect harmony with its DNA.

TOP LEFT   The Romvlvs Retrograde Annual Calendar is the brand's first model to feature this complication.

TOP RIGHT   Romvlvs Chronograph.

RIGHT   The Admiral's Cup Challenge 44 Split-Seconds.

BOTTOM RIGHT Admiral's Cup Tourbillon 48.

In the future, you want to focus on vertically integrating the jobs of the watch industry. How do you hope to arrive there?

This is our priority in terms of investment because it is essential for us to integrate the jobs necessary to create, manufacture and produce a watch. This consolidation is essential for any brand that wants to ensure its independence, to be proactive and entirely control the development processes from the first sketch to the finished product. This approach aims to create long-term value. Human capital represents the key element of our company and it takes time to develop. This imperative consists of initially ensuring that the foundations are good and solid before assembling the organization. So we are consolidating our expertise and our team to enable them to grow in the future. Of course, we are aware of the current difficulty in recruiting craftsmen and watchmakers that meets the watchmaking industry today. Unfortunately, this is getting more difficult as time progresses, but we count on our key people to increase the capability and efficiency of our teams.

You've refocused on the four historical pillars that made Corum: the Admiral's Cup, the Romvlvs, the Golden Bridge and the Artisans. Won't Corum surprise us again with true novelties?

We are lucky to have four collections that offer unique territories of unlimited play. Each has a very precise positioning and targets specific customers. I believe that this will strengthen our creativity. Being daring and inventive does not make us mad scientists. Today, I can only tell you one thing, come ask me this exact question at the end of March and at that time I am convinced the model I will present to you will answer your request well beyond your expectations.

What has been your sales progression over the last five years?

We do not normally discuss our sales numbers. However, during the past three years, we realized a progression of more than twenty percent and our profitability also increased.

Do you envision relaunching the Admiral's Cup Regatta? If so, how?

This legendary race, which was last sailed in 2003, is inextricably linked with our Admiral's Cup collection of watches. Legends can sometimes become so strong that they exceed reality. Since the beginning of its history, Corum has been lucky to be associated with sailing, even becoming a pioneer in this field. If this discipline still proudly

carries the colors of Corum, we are conscious of the potential that still remains for us to put forward in this field.

How does 2009 look for Corum?

For us, as for all watchmaking brands, the year truly starts with the watchmaking fairs. We have worked very hard to reposition the brand products on a new level. Now comes the rebranding. In spite of the financial tightening of the current markets, we decided to stay the course, maintaining the limited production that positions us in a privileged segment of the market. Our strategy was planned for the long term, so we will move forward with our planned projects and we are convinced that our determination will enable us to achieve our goals. I am looking forward to being in Basel and sharing the fruit of our work with the public, our retailers and our markets.

TOP Sparkling with a thousand lights, this Golden Bridge model is completely pavé.

ABOVE Designed for ladies, the Admiral's Cup Competition 40 features a bezel paved with white diamonds.

RIGHT Pavé version of Admiral's Cup Tourbillon 48.

INSTRUMENTO
novantatre
ANNUAL CALENDAR

de GRISOGONO
GENEVE

"An F.P.Journe watch is not necessarily easy to explain."

François-Paul Journe

first specialized in the restoration of antique pieces before taking on the fabrication of his first watches in his spare time. Immersed in the culture of haute horology, the artisan wanted to make his pieces more accessible in order to share his passion. The solution: founding his own brand.

TOP RIGHT   Journe at his worktable.

BOTTOM   The Chronomètre à Résonance.

60

Convention dictates that we speak of Swiss horology, but the facts show that even if the most prestigious manufactures are located there, many of those who work in them hail from other horizons. This is the case of Journe, who was born in France. Following the example of many of his compatriots, he emigrated to join the global epicenter of haute horology. In his bags were solid experience and recognized expertise. He honed his horological knowledge in Paris before making the leap.

His company, F.P. Journe, has been located in the heart of Geneva since 2000. It will soon be 10 years since Journe dove into making wristwatches, and F.P. Journe, which he founded at the same time, naturally grew along with his spectacular technical advancements. His arrival in Geneva would lead, a few years later, to an expansion of his means of production, since F.P. Journe had enough space to create a true manufacture, complete with its own equipment fleet.

A constant inventor fascinated by the masters who have left their marks on horological history, Journe pushes the limits of tradition while treating it with the utmost respect. Among the extraordinary creations that strew his path, we must mention the Sonnerie Souveraine—which contains a grande and a petite sonnerie, as well as a minute repeater, and whose hammer is directly visible on the dial—a thoroughly original staging and Journe's "most beautiful creation yet"; and the Chronomètre à Résonance, with its unprecedented movement based on the interaction between two escapement systems, permitting self-regulation of the working of the conjoined movements housed inside the watch.

The Sonnerie Souverain.

A PRIZEWINNER

The power and perfection of Journe's creations did not take long to capture the admiration and respect of connoisseurs. Born in Marseille, Journe earned his watchmaking degree in Paris in 1976. First working with his uncle before setting up shop independently on Saint-Germain des Prés, the watchmaker developed his skill by repairing old models in the hushed environment of watch lovers. After five years of work, he put the final touches on a tourbillon chronograph pocket watch. An admirer of Abraham-Louis Breguet, one of the giants in watchmaking history (and inventor of the tourbillon, among other things) Journe threw himself into the creation of an automatic pocket watch inspired by the famous Marie-Antoinette, a legendary watch that the great master was working on just before his death.

The year 1987 marked the debut of recognition by Journe's peers and by several institutions that would only grow over the years. That was the year that Journe won the Prix de la Vocation from the Fondation Bleustein Blanchet, which he considered a precious encouragement. Two years later, the watchmakers' convention in Madrid awarded him their Balancier d'Or prize. In 1994, Switzerland and its horological community adopted Journe, awarding him with the best watchmaker Prix Gaïa from Institut l'Homme et le Temps. Then the fame of the products themselves began to surpass that of the man. Journe's watches have regularly inspired the admiration of the jury at the Grand Prix d'Horlogerie de Genève, which has given him several awards. In 2002, the special jury prize went to the Octa Calendrier Annuel. In 2003, Journe won the prize for best men's watch for the Octa Lune. In 2004, he garnered the watchmaker's highest prize, Aiguille d'Or (Golden Hand), for his dead-seconds Tourbillon Souverain. The following year, the Chronomètre Souverain

TOP LEFT   The Octa Lune.

TOP RIGHT   François-Paul Journe's first pocket-watch tourbillon.

ABOVE   The Tourbillon Souverain with dead seconds won the Aiguille d'Or at the Grand Prix de Genève.

BOTTOM LEFT   The Chronomètre Souverain.

BOTTOM RIGHT   The Centigraphe Souverain can calculate speeds up to 360,000 kilometers per hour. This watch also won the Aiguille d'Or at the Grand Prix d'Horlogerie de Genève 2008.

won the men's watch prize, while in 2006, the Sonnerie Souveraine showed the way back to the Aiguille d'Or. Most recently, in 2008, the Centigraphe Souverain allowed Journe to walk away with the Aiguille d'Or one more time. A masterpiece protected by two patents, this timepiece allows the wearer to calculate speeds of up to 360,000 kilometers per hour, through a display featuring a tacho-metric scale and a time scale. In a second quirk of the Centigraphe Souverain, its chronograph—accurate to one one-hundredth of a second—has been isolated from the movement so as not to influence its functioning. After an indispensable testing period, the Centigraphe Souverain made its first deliveries in the summer of 2008.

TALENT AND A STRONG PERSONALITY

Demanding of himself and of his collaborators, talented, and gifted with a strong personality that makes him among the most charismatic players in the field, Journe leads his company with an acute sense of the industry. For example, when arranging dis-tribution, he concentrated on a network of 50 points of sale. His challenge: weaving long-term relationships based on trust. For this, he makes sure to surround himself with the best of the best—after all, as he says, "an F.P. Journe watch is not necessarily easy to explain." Journe currently has five F.P. Journe boutiques based in Tokyo, Hong Kong, Geneva, Boca Raton, Fl. and Paris. New York will follow "once we've found the right place," Singapore will surely open in July, and Beijing is also under consideration.

PRECIOUS SERVICE

The slowdown that began to affect the watch industry at the end of 2008 does not worry Journe. "The crisis will clean out all the opportunists," he says. "The growth in this industry over the last several years has led to an explosion of brands without the slightest legitimacy. They claimed to belong to the tradition of haute horology, but usually just focused on the look of the products. I think they have done a wrong to all the houses that have persistently worked over the years to push back the techni-cal as well as visual boundaries. I also give a lot of thought to the idea of service that goes along with my products."

By "service," Journe means the effort expended by brands the period after the sale. The commitment to honor past orders is the main impetus that led Journe to forgo introducing any new models in 2009. "My motto is 'flawless performance.' That is why I go step by step, even slowly, when I have to. Right now, I am working to make some products even more reliable and deliver them to my customers." This straight trajectory has guided the watchmaker since the beginning on a road paved with success.

TOP F.P. Journe's manufacture, located in the heart of Geneva.

BOTTOM Journe's collaborators.

MOVADO
THE ART OF DESIGN

movado calendomatic™
from the red label™ collection. fine 25-jewel
swiss automatic movement with custom-designed
red "m" rotor. unique calendar ring with date magnifier.
stainless steel case. black museum® dial. exhibition case-back.
alligator strap. www.movado.com/redlabel

Telling Time

A Retrospective on the Life and Times of Gerry Grinberg: Founder and Chairman of Movado Group, Inc.

THE FIRST TIME

The earliest recorded Western philosophy of time was expounded by the ancient Egyptian thinker Ptahhotep (c. 2650-2600 BC) who said, "Do not lessen the time of following desire, for the wasting of time is an abomination to the spirit."

Born in Cuba in 1931, Gedalio "Gerry" Grinberg grew up in a family active in the jewelry trade and worked in the family jewelry store for a time, later studying economics at Havana University. At age 15, he began what was destined to become a distinguished career in the watch industry. It started through a request from a friend's father to procure an alarm clock (a scarce commodity in Cuba) for his shoe store. Grinberg utilized his resourcefulness to obtain a Westclox.

Always fascinated by watches, Grinberg changed course slightly and became a supplier for watches. The first watch Grinberg distributed was produced in the United States, a gold-plated Speidel bracelet watch for ladies. Grinberg worked on his own, selling 30 to 40 watches a month and making a modest profit through word-of-mouth clientele. He was hired shortly thereafter by a local distributer of Sheffield watches and started selling to retail stores.

With an intuitive gift for mathematics and marketing, Grinberg established the foundation from which he would build the North American Watch Company—a leading manufacturer, marketer and distributor of luxury watches—and forerunner of what was to become the Movado Group.

EARLY YEARS

Navigating through Cuban watch circles, Grinberg partnered with Fabien Weiss, one of his father's suppliers and the most successful watch dealer in Cuba. Weiss was a distributor of Switzerland's most successful brand at the time, Omega, in addition to other significant Swiss brands.

Chosen as Weiss' successor, Grinberg learned how to run a business and began his mastery of marketing through the tutelage of Adolph Vallat, Managing Director of Omega in Switzerland and, by all accounts, one of the great watch marketers of the 20th century.

Grinberg implemented Vallat's system back in Cuba and realized its success as he saw sales increase. During one of his visits to Cuba, Vallat suggested that Weiss and Grinberg add another Swiss watch, Piaget, to their existing brands. In the early 1950s, Piaget was primarily involved with the manufacture of watch movements for Omega. The Piaget family decided to produce finished watches under its own name, developing Piaget into a true brand. Weiss and Grinberg became the official distributers of Piaget in Cuba.

TIME IS OF THE ESSENCE

Business was flourishing in Cuba up until the onset of Castro's Revolution. During an afternoon lunch, Grinberg and several colleagues were interrogated, threatened and accused of having CIA connections by members of Castro's secret police. Although later released, Grinberg made the decision to flee Cuba for Miami, realizing that he had no future in his homeland under Fidel Castro's regime. His departure was successful and aided by a fortuitous encounter with a friend who was, unbeknownst to Grinberg, an officer in the regime.

Times were challenging in Miami and Grinberg engaged in various business ventures to earn a living for his wife and their two young children. An opportunity was presented to accompany Fabien and Jose Weiss, who had also fled Cuba for Miami, to New York City to open a Piaget agency. The International Sales Manager for Piaget, Camille Pilet, offered them exclusive sales rights in the USA and Puerto Rico. Together with the Weisses, Grinberg took the offer and opened the New York office of Piaget in 1961.

The Piaget brand was virtually unknown in the USA when Grinberg launched his luxury watch business in 1961 from a one-room office at 610 Fifth Avenue. Grinberg attempted to sell his inventory of Piaget watches from store to store but, with no brand recognition and an average price of one-thousand dollars, the watches were virtually non-sellable. The demand for luxury timepieces had not yet been founded in Manhattan's competitive marketplace.

1947 Horwitt Museum watch.

Through his tenacity and visionary prowess, Grinberg realized two significant turning points that altered the course of history. A negotiation with the *The New Yorker* resulted in the placement of a small advertisement for Piaget in the magazine. The copy, authored by Grinberg, referred to the Piaget timepiece as "the most expensive watch in the world."

The second turning point was the relationship forged with Claude Arpels, head of Van Cleef & Arpels. Piaget had developed a collection of watches with colored stone dials and the opportunity to feature these watches in Van Cleef's window resulted in the doubling of Piaget watch sales in a year's time.

Through his alliance with Van Cleef & Arpels, Grinberg gained access to high-fashion magazines and advertising venues to continue touting Piaget as "the most expensive watch in the world." Grinberg was also able to convince other leading retailers such as Neiman Marcus and Tiffany & Co. to carry the Piaget product line. The times were shifting towards a status conscious consumer and Piaget was well positioned to address the demands of this newly created market segment.

Piaget sales grew from $165,000 in 1961 to almost $40 million in the late 1980s. An ingenious marketer, Grinberg had changed the way Americans viewed watches. Grinberg founded the North American Watch Company with the vision of importing and distributing other fine watch brands.

WINNING TIMES

In time, Grinberg added Corum Watch to his growing portfolio of brands. Specializing in the manufacture of high-grade watches, Corum became a part of North American Watch and the brand began to earn a reputation for creating unique and very unusual designs. Then in 1969, North American Watch acquired the Swiss watchmaker Concord.

Swiss watchmakers first developed the quartz watch, an integrated circuit with a battery-powered quartz crystal that oscillated at thousands of vibrations per second. The resulting watch was more accurate than the meticulously handcrafted mechanical watches the Swiss were so famed for making. The technology quickly spread to other countries, resulting in the production of low-cost watches, cutting deeply into the Swiss market share.

Grinberg played a pivotal role in convincing the Swiss to embrace the new technology and battle for quartz supremacy. In January 1979 the Concord Delirium was unveiled and touted as one of the most important watches of the 20th century—it was an ultra-thin and ultra-accurate quartz watch that marked a turning point in the Swiss quartz crisis, proving that Switzerland could compete with the Japanese in the new quartz technology that was sweeping the watch world.

With Piaget, Corum and the acquisition of Concord in 1969, Grinberg had emerged as a major Swiss-watch distributor in the US.

THE ART OF DESIGN

An older Swiss watch company dating back to 1881, Movado was admired as an innovator of technological sophistication and design. The small workshop in the Swiss mountains grew so quickly that by 1897 it had become one of the largest watch manufacturers in all of Switzerland. The company was named Movado in 1905—meaning "always in motion" in the international language of Esperanto.

In 1947, the American artist Nathan George Horwitt designed the stark, black, numberless dial watch, becoming the first artist to explore the concept of time as design. The single-dot watch dial that would earn world renown as the Movado Museum Watch was so minimalistic that critics claimed it had no design at all. In 1960, Horwitt's watch finally garnered some attention when the Museum of Modern Art added it into its permanent collection. It became known from that day forward as the Museum Watch.

Gedalio Grinberg had always been fascinated by Movado and he strongly admired the Museum Watch Design. North American Watch eventually acquired the brand in 1983. A new product line and advertising campaign were developed surrounding the Museum Watch. The campaign was geared to attract a younger consumer who was culturally and artistically enriched.

This winning formula resulted in sales increases—at the time of Movado's acquisition in 1983, sales were $4 million; by 1987 they had increased to $50 million. Movado became the flagship of North American Watch Company and resulted in the organization being renamed the Movado Group in 1996.

The most intriguing and innovative watches developed by Movado after 1983 were a series of watches designed by world-renowned artists. The concept was developed through Grinberg's friendship with Andy Warhol. The collaboration resulted in "The Warhol Times/5" design, a bracelet of five self-contained watchcases with dials featuring cityscapes of New York City. This was the first timepiece in a series of watches designed in partnership with prominent contemporary artists.

THE ART OF SUCCESS

"Watches measure time and I have always been fascinated by what a person does with their time," said Grinberg.

Today, the Movado Group encompasses nine distinct watch brands that address a multitude of lifestyles. In addition to Movado, the Group's portfolio includes luxury watch brands Concord and Ebel, the entry-level Swiss watch brand ESQ Swiss and through licensing agreements, Coach Watches, Tommy Hilfiger Watches, HUGO BOSS Watches, Lacoste Watches and Juicy Couture Timepieces.

A sophisticated marketer and arts enthusiast, Grinberg realized the marketing potential of associating Movado and the Museum Watch with cultural pursuits. Throughout Grinberg's tenure the Company has proudly sponsored some of the country's most prestigious cultural institutions: Lincoln Center, American Ballet Theatre, and Miami City Ballet among many others.

In 2003, Gerry Grinberg was named the first Lifetime Achievement Award recipient by the Jewelry Industry Council, the promotional arm of the jewelry and watch industry. Grinberg was hailed by the Council as "a visionary in the watch industry for recognizing the potential cachet of luxury watches and marketing them accordingly."

Grinberg possesses a deep and abiding appreciation for the United States. His experience in Cuba and success here has made him an outspoken advocate for the American way. "This is the best country in the world, no question about that," he once said when profiled on CNN's "Pinnacle." "Here I am a Cuban from a Jewish background, with an accent, and I never feel like a foreigner in this country. It is a country of opportunity. What happened to me here could not happen anywhere else in the world."

When Gedalio "Gerry" Grinberg retired as chairman of the Movado Group Inc. in January 2009, his son Efraim became the firm's new chairman.

As a postscript to this Retrospective, it is with deep sadness that we communicate the passing of Gedalio "Gerry" Grinberg, Founder and Chairman of the Movado Group, Inc. Mr. Grinberg passed away on January 4, 2009.

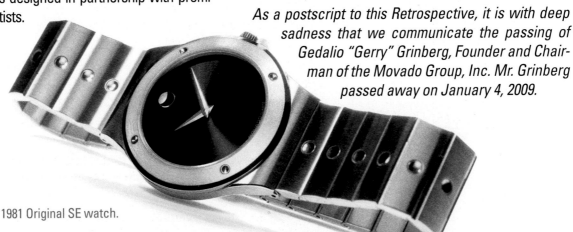

1981 Original SE watch.

EBEL

THE ARCHITECTS OF TIME

1911 TEKTON

Ebel Caliber 139 – Automatic Chronograph with unique functions display, multi-level skeleton dial, hand-stitched alligator strap.

THE ULTIMATE IN ENGINEERED DESIGN
A prestigious chronograph of sophisticated design, engineered with architectural vision.
From a bold new collection powered exclusively by COSC-certified Ebel manufacture movements.
Water resistant to 20 atm. www.ebel.com or call 800 920 3153.

"Demand exceeding Panerai's supply is a sign of quality."

Angelo Bonati has been expertly directing Officine Panerai since 1997. This Italian brand, whose watches are manufactured in Switzerland, is an international sensation with its own group of fans. Since 2005, the brand has developed and produced its own movements as the foundation for its top-of-the-line Manifattura collection. In addition, Bonati promises to develop a new project each year.

Angelo Bonati, CEO of Panerai, at the Classic Yachts Challenge in Imperia, Italy.

There are very few watchmaking brands that can legitimately claim a clear and coherent line through the years. Panerai is one of these rare brands. Originally from Florence, this brand has 158 years of rich history and became world renowned in 1993. For a long period of time, this brand performed secret work for the Italian Navy where it developed the famous Radiomir, a luminescent mixture making it possible to read orders in the darkness of the depths. Panerai finally seduced the public with authentic pedigreed watches, recognizable among thousands. The brand combines Italian elegance and Swiss expertise, and has become an incredible world success on its solid foundation. Though Panerai's competitor brands constantly vary their design aesthetic, Bonati sees no need to do so. He prefers to invest fully in a long-term strategy to propel the brand to the higher realms of the watch industry: the development of in-house movements and the growth of its sales network.

A COVERT EXISTENCE

In 1850, Giovanni Panerai established the company in Florence, Italy. The brand worked in the shadow of the Italian Royal Navy, providing numerous precision measuring instruments. It was only in 1936 that it developed its first watch, an innovative prototype equipped with a Rolex movement and intended for a secret Italian Special Forces military unit. It was the beginning of an extraordinary saga, which would lead Panerai to develop the Radiomir (1938), the Mare Nostrum (1943), and the Luminor (1949). In 1997, Panerai was purchased by the Vendôme (now Richemont) Group and its collections quickly became legendary all around the world.

The Luminor collection has a special lever bridge that compresses the crown against the case middle of the watch to improve its water resistance. This bridge, as well as the luminescent dials treated with tritium (not radium, the original material) today comprises part of the brand's DNA. "We have been lucky in that, for years, demand has exceeded the supply," states Bonati. "And it is not due to marketing, but a sign of quality."

Flush with this success, Panerai took an important turn in 2005. That was the year that the brand's technical research center for materials and movements in Neuchâtel, Switzerland, released P.2002, the first movement developed and produced entirely in-house. Two years later it was followed the P.2003, P.2004 and P.2005. These four calibers are the foundation of the new top-of-the-line Manifattura collection. Ten patents crown their realization. In addition to a permanent double time zone, all of them have an impressive power reserve ranging between six and ten days, thanks to three double barrels. "The idea is that from now on, Panerai will develop a new movement every year," specifies Angelo Bonati.

TOP   By definition the brand of the sea, Panerai sponsors the Classic Yachts Challenge in Imperia, Italy.

CENTER   Panerai supports the Shell Ferrari Historic Challenge, a competition that includes Ferrari and Maserati models produced between 1930 and 1980.

BOTTOM   Mike Horn carried the antimagnetic Panerai Luminor Arktos model to the North Pole during his 20,000-kilometer tour between 2002 and 2004.

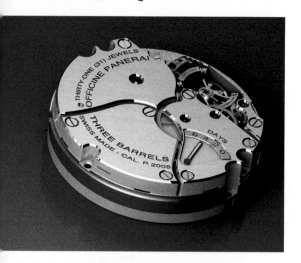

AN IN-HOUSE TOURBILLON

The P.2005 caliber, with its entirely redesigned, patented tourbillon, is the most complicated of the four in-house movements. It is distinguished from other tourbillons by its axis of rotation in the case—it is parallel with the base of the movement (the axis is perpendicular in traditional models)—and its speed of rotation is two revolutions per minute (compared to the usual one revolution per minute).

This caliber powers the all-new Luminor 1950 Titanium Tourbillon GMT 47 MM. Its case, made of grade-2 titanium (a material that is extremely light but very difficult to work with), retains the unique angular shape that has made the Luminor models so recognizable for more than sixty years. This 239-part manual-winding movement has a power reserve of six days, which is monitored through the sapphire crystal caseback via a needle positioned in a circular arc.

The tourbillon is also visible through the caseback. Following the example of a few rare, refined models, the Luminor 1950 does not exhibit this complication on the dial. However, its presence is announced by a discreet detail: on the subdial at 9:00 beside the perpetually moving second hand, a small white circular indicator linked to the tourbillon turns twice as quickly as its neighbor, which makes only one full rotation per minute. Another subdial, at 3:00, has one hand that completes a full rotation every 24 hours; with its AM and PM display, it specifies the hour of day or night indicated by the GMT hand at the center of the dial.

But Panerai could not limit its P.2005 caliber to just one model. The diving watch, with which the brand entered the world of horology, is also equipped with this exceptional caliber. The Radiomir Tourbillon GMT 48 MM revisits the aesthetic of the legendary watch, designed 70 years ago for the Italian Navy. Designed in two versions—75 watches produced with the platinum case and 125 watches manufactured with the titanium case—it features the same functions as the Luminor 1950.

THIS PAGE

TOP   The P.2005 tourbillon movement.

CENTER LEFT   The caseback of the Panerai Luminor 1950 Tourbillon GMT.

CENTER RIGHT   Panerai Luminor 1950 Tourbillon GMT.

BOTTOM LEFT   Panerai Luminor 1950 Titanium Tourbillon GMT 47 MM.

BOTTOM RIGHT   Panerai Radiomir Platinum Tourbillon GMT.

FACING PAGE

TOP   The P.2004 chronograph movement.

CENTER RIGHT   The Panerai Luminor 1950 Ceramic 8 Days Chrono Monopusher GMT.

CENTER LEFT   Panerai Luminor 1950 8 Days Chrono Monopusher Titanium.

BOTTOM FAR RIGHT   The Panerai Luminor Chrono Daylight 44 MM Titanium, with the exclusive OP XII movement.

BOTTOM LEFT   In June 2002, Panerai presented historical archives and rare precision objects in a premier public historical exposition in Florence.

BOTTOM CENTER AND RIGHT   Bottega d' Arte Panerai, the brand's first boutique, opened in Florence in October 2001.

AN EXCEPTIONAL CHRONOGRAPH

The little sibling of the P.2005 caliber, the P.2004, is the first chronograph produced by Panerai. It is characterized by a monopusher construction, relying on only one button on the left side of the case to perform all functions: departure, stop and return to zero. With manual winding and 321 parts, the P.2004 is also reinforced with a column-wheel friction engagement—a component that makes the reputation of the highest quality chronographs—and is equipped with three spring barrels that provide a power reserve of eight days.

This movement powers the splendid Luminor 1950 8 Day Chrono Monopusher GMT 44 MM, which is available in a ceramic or titanium case. For the ceramic case, the traditional production method of molding and machining has been replaced by a process of isostatic pressure that creates an extremely hard material up to five times harder than steel. The grade-5 titanium case is hypoallergenic, heat-resistant and anticorrosive; this last is a principal requirement for any watch in regular contact with seawater. Each model has a chronograph minute counter at 3:00, a linear power-reserve indicator at 6:00, and a small seconds counter at 9:00. The small seconds counter includes a small triangular hand indicating whether the second time-zone display is indicating day or night.

Panerai introduced its latest Luminor innovation at the exclusive Salon International de la Haute Horlogerie (SIHH 2009) in Geneva. As traditional as it is modern, the new Luminor Chrono Daylight 44 MM Titanium has a surprising blue dial rather than the usual black. The indicators and numerals have a luminescent coating, as do the hands. Two pushers, positioned on either side of the bridge with its characteristic lever, control the functions of the chronograph, whose minutes, hours, and seconds are visible, respectively, at 3:00, 6:00 and 9:00. This timepiece with its exclusive COSC-certified automatic movement provides a date-stamp at 5:00 and a tachometer on the bezel.

Such energy can only reflect exceptional world success. Some 450 carefully selected shops already represent the brand on five continents. In the last few years, Panerai has begun opening its own boutiques. "For us, it is very important," explains Bonati. "It enables us to convey our true image, and brings us closer the final customer." Florence, Hong Kong, Portofino, Tokyo, Beverly Hills and New York are all home to Panerai boutiques. Other shops have opened in Buenos Aires and Madrid, and Shanghai boasts two. "And we are on the verge of opening two new stores in the Middle East at the beginning of 2009," concludes Bonati.

Perpetual fascination

L.U.C Lunar One. Chopard brings the universe to the wrist in a stellar model precisely reproducing the phases of the moon and following the celestial patterns governing our division of time into days, nights, weeks, months and leap years.

An exquisitely balanced dial highlights the poetry and romance of a starlit sky portraying the orbital moon-phase display, complementing the perpetual calendar functions including a 24-hour scale. These aesthetically appealing and useful indications are powered by a chronometer-certified self-winding movement bearing the "Poinçon de Genève" quality hallmark.

L.U.C
MANUFACTURE DE HAUTE HORLOGERIE
LOUIS-ULYSSE CHOPARD

 L.U.C Lunar One: available in two limited and numbered series of 250 in platinum and 18-carat rose gold with two dial versions featuring either Roman or Arabic numerals.

ZENITH
SWISS WATCH MANUFACTURE
SINCE 1865

The Eternal
Ascension of
ZENITH

For a few years, ZENITH has exhibited an extraordinary vitality.

After opening up dials to reveal the mysteries of its mechanics and developing a whole range of ladies' watches, the brand from Le Locle has dazzled watch connoisseurs by releasing, in 2008, its Defy Tourbillon Zero-G, whose oscillating rotor remains horizontal, no matter what.

ZENITH: a name, a history, a future. There are no better three words to sum up the identity of this legendary brand. Created in 1865 by Georges Favre-Jacot and named ZENITH in 1911, the manufacture is one of a rare breed that has never stopped making its own movements. In 1969, the brand released the world's first automatic chronograph with a central rotor, the famous El Primero. Far from resting on its laurels, ZENITH lives up to its glorious past by presenting sensation after sensation in the world of high-end watchmaking. Its latest performance: the Tourbillon Zero-G, foundation of the Defy collection, created in 2006.

When Georges Favre-Jacot opened his workshops in Le Locle, he was only 22 years old. Visionary and genius inventor, he was the first to create the very idea of a manufacture. Success came quickly—ten years later, the business had more than 1,000 employees. Up until his death in 1917, Favre-Jacot never stopped innovating, keeping up with the most avant-garde trends. At the beginning of the 20th century, unlike his competitors, he did not hesitate to create Art Nouveau cases, explicitly inspired by Alphonse Mucha's *Seasons* series.

TOP LEFT   Thierry Nataf, President and CEO of ZENITH International.

TOP RIGHT   The ZENITH manufacture in Le Locle, founded in 1865.

LEFT   The automatic El Primero 4031 movement with a minute repeater, chronograph and date.

EL PRIMERO: THE MOTOR

When the name ZENITH is mentioned today, however, most connoisseurs immediately think of the fabulous story of the El Primero movement. Introduced in 1969, it was the first automatic chronograph movement with a central rotor. During the same period, the trio of Breitling/Büren/Heuer-Leonidas introduced its own automatic chronograph movement, this one with an off-center mini-rotor. But the El Primero, beating at 36,000 vibrations per hour, was—and remains—the fastest chronograph, guaranteeing time measurement to one-tenth of a second. After the mechanical watch crisis of the 1980s, several other brands utilized it in their own watches. Rolex would make it the power behind its famous Daytona chronograph before the Geneva-based company developed its own movement at the turn of the 21st century. To celebrate the El Primero's 40th anniversary, ZENITH is planning to present an updated version of the 1969 model. "The New Vintage 1969 is directly inspired by the original model," says Thierry Nataf. "It is produced in three limited editions of 250 pieces each and will be available only in the year 2009. The three series are differentiated by the material of their cases, crafted in gold, steel or titanium, to elegantly celebrate three eras: past, present and future."

The 2001 arrival of Nataf, named to lead the company after its purchase by LVMH in 1999, rang in the rebirth of the El Primero movement. The lively new chief executive decided to explore the house's prize jewel in several versions, adding new complications to the base chronograph. But that's not all. "For three years, I have been working to reinvent the style of our watches to give them a truly distinct character and a mechanical signature," Nataf explains. "Whatever the collection, I keep in mind ZENITH's aesthetic and technical values. With us, even the mechanics are styled and a lot of care is poured into the details, bringing a real resonance to each collection and affirming our uniqueness. 'Being first' could be the signature on all our creations."

Beyond the limits of time and fashion, the Academy collection incorporates the most prestigious complications. Tourbillon, minute repeater or even perpetual calendar, all the highest-level technical specialties take their places in this collection for extraordinary men. For example, the Academy Open Minute Repeater model, which is in the multi-complications collection, joins the minute-repeater mechanism with the

El Primero base. It was a world-first that required the perfecting of a system in which the sonnerie could work around the axes of the chronograph.

For measuring very short amounts of time, the iconic ChronoMaster collection benefits from the El Primero movement. "It is one of the brand's oldest collections," explains Nataf. "It has appeared in catalogs since 1865 and draws its name from Master of Chronos—Master of Time. When I arrived, I decided to open up the dial to reveal the interior of the movement. The ChronoMaster Open collection sprang from that impulse, showing the beats of the escapement. This idea rapidly became almost a calling card for the brand; a perfect combination between tradition and modernity." Home to many different models, the line added one more in 2008: an unusual complication that combined date, tourbillon, day/night indicator, and moonphase. This ChronoMaster Tourbillon Moonphase Day & Night is produced in a limited edition.

TOP LEFT   Academy Open Repetition Minutes.

TOP RIGHT   ChronoMaster Tourbillon Moonphase Day & Night.

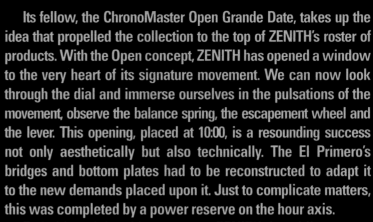

Its fellow, the ChronoMaster Open Grande Date, takes up the idea that propelled the collection to the top of ZENITH's roster of products. With the Open concept, ZENITH has opened a window to the very heart of its signature movement. We can now look through the dial and immerse ourselves in the pulsations of the movement, observe the balance spring, the escapement wheel and the lever. This opening, placed at 10:00, is a resounding success not only aesthetically but also technically. The El Primero's bridges and bottom plates had to be reconstructed to adapt it to the new demands placed upon it. Just to complicate matters, this was completed by a power reserve on the hour axis.

Emboldened by this success, ZENITH is adding open-worked windows to more and more of its best-known collections: Class, Port-Royal and Defy. Characterized by its simplicity and sobriety, the Class line is steeped in the classic aesthetic of the 1950s. It gained several new models in 2008, including the Class Open Multicity. Displaying the time in 24 cities around the globe through a rotating disk indexed to the hour hand, it is available in two versions. The first, with a diameter of 46mm, contains the El Primero, and the 44mm version is equipped with the Elite, another manufacture movement. In the Port-Royal category, which associates the watches with urban, rectangular architecture, the Mega Port-Royal Open Grande Date Concept is a monument to the avant-garde. An impressively sized case in black titanium houses the new motor El Primero 4039 C, which contains 331 pieces, some of them visible through a window in the dial.

THE 21ST-CENTURY DEFY

One might think that with all these successes and innovations, the brand would be satisfied. However, it lacked an unequivocally sporty watch in its repertoire. That is why, in 2006, ZENITH launched a collection that has certainly been much talked about these last few months: Defy. Alliance of creation and performance, it attains unprecedented combinations of effect and materials. ZENITHium© (an alloy of titanium, niobium and aluminum) is three times more resistant to shocks than steel and was specially developed in-house for this very avant-garde line, available in Xtreme and Classic versions.

The huge splash made by this collection was due also in part to the 2008 launch of the incredible Defy Tourbillon Zero-G, which means zero gravity. Equipped with a gyroscopic tourbillon cage, the system is completely unprecedented. The oscillator is always kept in a horizontal position, guaranteeing optimal amplitude to the balance spring. The coordination is assured by a second gear train that refers back to the axes of the escapement, and by a differential gear train that compensates for all the relative movements of the caliber's fundamental elements. The cage alone contains 166 components, ten gear wheels and six ball bearings.

The Xtreme version has a dial composed of Hesalite glass, carbon and aluminum fibers, a case in blackened titanium that is water resistant to 1,000 meters, a blackened titanium bezel, a protected crown, a helium valve and a titanium bracelet with Kevlar inserts to stand up to high temperatures. The Classic model boasts a rose-gold case and a sophisticated dial, structured on several levels. Of course, both versions are available for ladies in a case that measures 43mm instead of 46.5mm.

HER WATCH

Over the last few years, women have earned a considerable place at ZENITH. In 2003, the brand offered them a collection in their own image: the Star, which followed in the footsteps of Baby Doll (with star-shaped openings in the dial), Queen of Love (heart-shaped openings), Star Rock and Starissime (which paid tribute to jewelry). The latter would give birth to the "haute couture" line, which paid homage to all of these divine divas. Sales in the ladies' segment continue to grow, reaching at least a third of total production, but ZENITH is doing even more for women. With the "his watch for her" concept, the brand offers women their own versions of watches ordinarily designed for men. As women have made strides in a masculine world with the pleasure that comes from breaking taboos, ZENITH has designed feminine alter egos, smaller or set with diamonds, for models in the Class, Chrono-Master and Defy collections. To the question of what awaits ZENITH in the year 2009, Nataf exclaims, "we've been doing the same thing since 1865, following our motto: always higher, always stronger in the ultimate quest for perfection."

FACING PAGE
TOP LEFT   ChronoMaster Open Grande Date.

TOP RIGHT   The El Primero 4039 movement, which powers the ChronoMaster Open Grande Date model.

BOTTOM LEFT   Mega Port Royal Open Grande Date Concept.

BOTTOM CENTER   Defy Xtreme Open Sea.

BOTTOM RIGHT   The Defy Xtreme Collection universe.

THIS PAGE

LEFT   Starissime Open Minute Repeater.

RIGHT   Star Open Love.

PIAGET POLO
FortyFive

TITANIUM CASE

SAPPHIRE CASE BACK

880P AUTOMATIC FLYBACK CHRONOGRAPH

PIAGET MANUFACTURE MOVEMENT

DUAL TIME ZONE

DOUBLE BARREL

BALANCE WITH SCREWS

100 METERS WATER RESISTANT

RUBBER STRAP

PIAGET

Striptease!

The art of revealing

a timepiece's mechanism is as old as the watch industry. The traditional exposure of the movements was first introduced on pocket watches and the beautiful days of wristwatch skeletonization began between the end of World War II and the 1970s. But this process, which requires great expertise, was lost with modern and less expensive production methods. Only one thing does not vary—the passion of the dedicated aficionado for fully visible mechanics.

TOP
Corum: Romvlvs Perpetual Calendar

ABOVE AND LEFT
Piaget: Altiplano Squelette

Veni Vidi Da Vinci!

IWC
SCHAFFHAUSEN
SINCE 1868

TAG HEUER MONACO CALIBRE 12 CHRONOGRAPH GULF LIMITED EDITION

The new version of the timeless, legendary Monaco chronograph is a tribute to the famous car driven by Steve McQueen in the 1970 film, Le Mans. The watch has a classic yet daring design and is equipped with a TAG Heuer Calibre 12 : a gray dial is enlivened by bands of orange and blue. It is available with a bracelet in grey meteorite alligator.

The MONACO Calibre 12 Chronograph in the Gulf Limited Edition will delight car-racing specialists and confirmed lovers of design and innovation.

It may be timid, letting us observe only its tourbillon through an openwork dial. It may be sensual, inviting us to imagine a slightly more generous view of its anatomy from behind a semi-transparent dial. Or it may be a straightforward exhibitionist, abandoning the masquerade to offer itself lasciviously to the mesmerized voyeur. Whatever the style, the luxury watch never tires of stripping down, a recent fashion statement in the wake of new horological technologies. High-tech materials and coatings lend themselves particularly well to this purpose, but they are not always necessary for strippeddown watches. The transparency of watches is also a trend that supplements, though it does not replace, the ancestral and very expensive art of skeletonization. Some might say that the watch that drops its dress most quickly is not always that which has the most to show.

Bovet: Fleurier Minute Repeater Tourbillon

Daniel Roth: Tourbillon Lumière

Going back to the origins of watchmaking, the traditional technique of exposure is only as good as the engraver's skills. The technique consists of removing the maximum amount of material from the bottom plate, pendulum, barrel bridge and many other components. The repeated strokes of the file leave a metal structure just sufficient to house the screws, springs, and jewels. This frame is then decorated with intricate engravings. This very complex art, which requires incredible expertise and whose difficulty increases with the number of complications the watch includes, leads to the highest esteem in the watch industry.

Maxi Marine Diver Chronograph - 8006-102-3A/92

Self-winding movement. Water-resistant to 200 m.

18 ct rose gold case, rubber strap with rose gold elements.

Available on gold bracelet.

GΞ | GUY ELLIA

Arije **Paris**

Doux Joaillier **Courchevel**   Zegg & Cerlati **Monaco**   Doux Joaillier **Saint Tropez**   Carat & Time **Saint Barthelemy**

Piantelli **London**   Avakian **Geneva**   Hubner **Vienna**   Diamond Time **Athens**   Steltman **Den Haag**

Lydion Mucevher **Antalya**   Azal **Dubaï**   Harvey Nichols **Dubaï**   Louvre **Moscow**   Crystal **Kiev**

Sincere **Kuala Lumpur**   Sincere **Singapore**   Cellini **New York**   Westime **Los Angeles**

«JUMBO» CHRONO

Art has a price

Skeletonization became very fashionable in the mid 20th century and certain brands had made a specialty of it. "At that time, skeletonization was a method of proving that one excelled at the art of watchmaking," explains Jean-Frederic Dufour, Director of Product Development at Chopard. "The more one removed material, the more prestigious it was. The idea being to say: with all these holes you see, it still works!"

But art has a price, and this one is very expensive. "A regular movement that would normally cost 150 Swiss francs, would cost 2,000 Swiss francs or more after completing this process," says Jean-Hugues Walther, Director of La Montre Extra-plate located in Fleurier (Val-de-Travers), Switzerland, which specializes in skeletonization. The arrival of electro-erosion, an electrochemical method that enables automated cutting of metal, will definitely change the traditional process.

Parmigiani Fleurier:
Kalpa XL Tourbillon

Guy Ellia:
Repetition Minute Zephyr

INSPIRED BY THE PAST, BUILT FOR THE FUTURE.

LUMINOR 1950 TOURBILLON GMT.
Hand-wound mechanical Tourbillon
movement P.2005 calibre, three spring
barrels, second time zone with 12/24 hr
indicator, 6-day power reserve.
Steel case 47 mm Ø. Steel buckle.

PANERAI
LABORATORIO DI IDEE.

www.panerai.com   Toll Free 1-877-PANERAI

Elegance is an attitude

"It's time to give a little bit of your time to others."

Andre Agassi

Longines supports The Andre Agassi Charitable Foundation

LONGINES®

GrandeVitesse

Elegance is an attitude

Aishwarya Rai

Aishwarya Rai

LONGINES®

Beautiful visible mechanics

Today, only a few major brands like Patek Philippe, Vacheron Constantin, Audemars Piguet, Corum and a few others still produce a limited number of skeleton watches intended for selected customers. In the majority of cases, the work is entrusted to specialized companies that are dedicated to the art of skeletonization. "But there are fewer and fewer requests for this," says Walther.

Among the latest achievements, the Patek Philippe Ref. 5180 is one of most remarkable. Respecting both the letter and the spirit of this practice, the manufacturer has created a jewel of watchmaking tradition. All of the bridges, framework and rotors are hand engraved, accentuating the lace effect of the components.

In another style, Maurice Lacroix's Masterpiece Squelette incarnates the other aspect of skeletonization: the one carried out by electro-erosion. Keeping in mind the rules of traditional skeletonization while conferring a resolutely modern appearance, Maurice Lacroix applied a treatment to the PVD surface with a tantalum color.

Chronoswiss: Grand Opus Chronograph

Patek Philippe: Montre Squelette Ref. 5180

Dior

DIOR CHRISTAL

Automatic movement
Sapphire crystal & diamonds

Alfredo Häberli, Industrial Designer.
Creating smart simplicity with passion.

But if the propensity for traditional transparency has been lost, the passion of admirers of beautiful visible mechanics has not ebbed. One of the first people to have understood this was Richard Mille at the beginning of the 21st century. "My concept rests on three principles: the best technology, the best of the watchmaking tradition and a passion for 3D pieces. When you emphasize all three of those in a movement, you can't not show it!"

The result of this train of thought made history in the watch industry. Created in 2001, the Richard Mille brand became legendary in a few years. He was among the first to use materials like carbon fiber, aluminum and ceramic bearings. Inspired by F1 engines, his creations revolutionized the sector with their new architectures, conspicuously displayed through a window.

Richard Mille: RM 016

Journey of initiation

Debuting in 2006, The RM 012 is a spectacular example. The exterior was replaced by a tubular structure of Invar (non-corrosive stainless steel). Extremely complex, this construction required two years of development and four prototypes. Richard Mille even delayed the release for one year to completely review the surface treatments and finishings. "Observing one of my watches is truly a journey of initiation," says Richard Mille. "I like the way it mimics a tracking shot: from afar, this object has a strong identity and big personality. When you get closer, you discern the mechanics under various angles, and finally through a magnifying glass you enter the magical universe, where the light is different for each viewing angle."

Richard Mille: RM 012

The trend was born. Several top-of-the-line brands followed in Mille's wake. Among them was Chopard: since 1996, the manufacturer has created its own movements in its factory in Fleurier. Its calibers equip the new L.U.C line, a classic collection which will mark the watchmaker's revival. The inside of the L.U.C watch is already partially visible thanks to a sapphire caseback, but now the L.U.C mechanisms will be revealed from the dial side as well.

Since 2001, the L.U.C Tech collection has presented pieces with largely openwork dials, enabling views of the wheels' actions. But the movement is not completely "skeletonized," save the opening on the tourbillon (when there is one), comparable to a partial exposure. "We practice a kind of modern skeletonization, not on the level of the engine, but of the exterior," Dufour explains. "Ferrari, with its Modena and F430 models, has already put its engines in view the same way, by covering the engine with Plexiglas instead of metal. It is an object of art that evokes an emotion. These are the watches of the 21st century!"

Cartier: Tank Americaine
Flying Tourbillon

Chopard: L.U.C
Tourbillon Tech Twist

The Admiral's Cup Challenge 48 "Black Flag" Limited Edition timepiece features the exclusive Corum CO753 automatic chronograph COSC certified chronometer movement in a black titanium case with rubber accents and locking pushers. www.corum.ch

Visual game

Vacheron Constantin has not been left behind. Already a specialist in traditional skeletonization, the Geneva-based manufacture offers a new variation on transparency with its latest creation, Quai de l'Ile. The sapphire dial is rendered semi-transparent by a film that is applied to the back and featuring printed symbols using "security printing" methods used on banknotes and passports. This surface creates a first level, which opens onto a second level, the wheels and the bridges. Visual play between the subtle inscriptions on the dial and the refinement of the mechanism has seduced many admirers.

Vacheron Constantin: Quai de l'Ile
Day-Date Power Reserve

FRANC VILA
— esprit unique —

A very contemporary return to traditional high-end standards

FVa9 "El Bandido" Complete Calendar and Moon Phase Chronograph

Limited Edition 88 pieces

Due to the very limited production of these timepieces, there may be slight variances in the details of each watch.

"Not only mine, but a part of me"

SERENA
polished stainless steel
on natural calf leather strap
56 full cut finest diamonds
(0.71 carat)

www.bertolucci-watches.com
Phone: +41 22 756 95 00

STRIA
18 carat rose gold
on white satin strap
162 full cut finest diamonds
(0.70 carat)

B
BERTOLUCCI
Mediterranean inspiration, Swiss craftsmanship

The dial of the Quai de l'Ile confers upon it, almost paradoxically, its very strong identity, just like a traditional dial embodies the face of the watch. Other brands, such as Zenith with its ChronoMaster Open Grande Date, chose a halfway position by revealing some of the parts of the watch while preserving a true dial, with openwork in certain places. An advocate of this solution, Andre Hartje, responsible for product development and client relationships for the Cadralux company, insists: "One can open the dial only insofar as one has something to show. But, the dial remains the most visible part of the watch. One can open up a quarter of its surface, but not more."

This is advice that Bernhard Lederer, founder of the Blu brand, obviously does not follow. For his last creation, the Majesty Tourbillon MT3, he simply did without a dial. The result, more poetic than technical, reveals three superimposed tourbillons revolving in a case reserved entirely for them. The two barrels and the wheels are laid out under the principle platform supporting the first tourbillon. A spectacular glass with antireflective treatment (to such a degree that one wonders whether there is a glass at all!) as well as transparent walls invites complete immersion into the mechanism that is guaranteed to astonish!

Jacob & Co.: Napoleon Quadra

Zenith: ChronoMaster Open Grande Date

B.R.M

Bernard Richards Manufacture

CT-48-AR

www.brm-manufacture.com
Tel 1 214 235 91 27

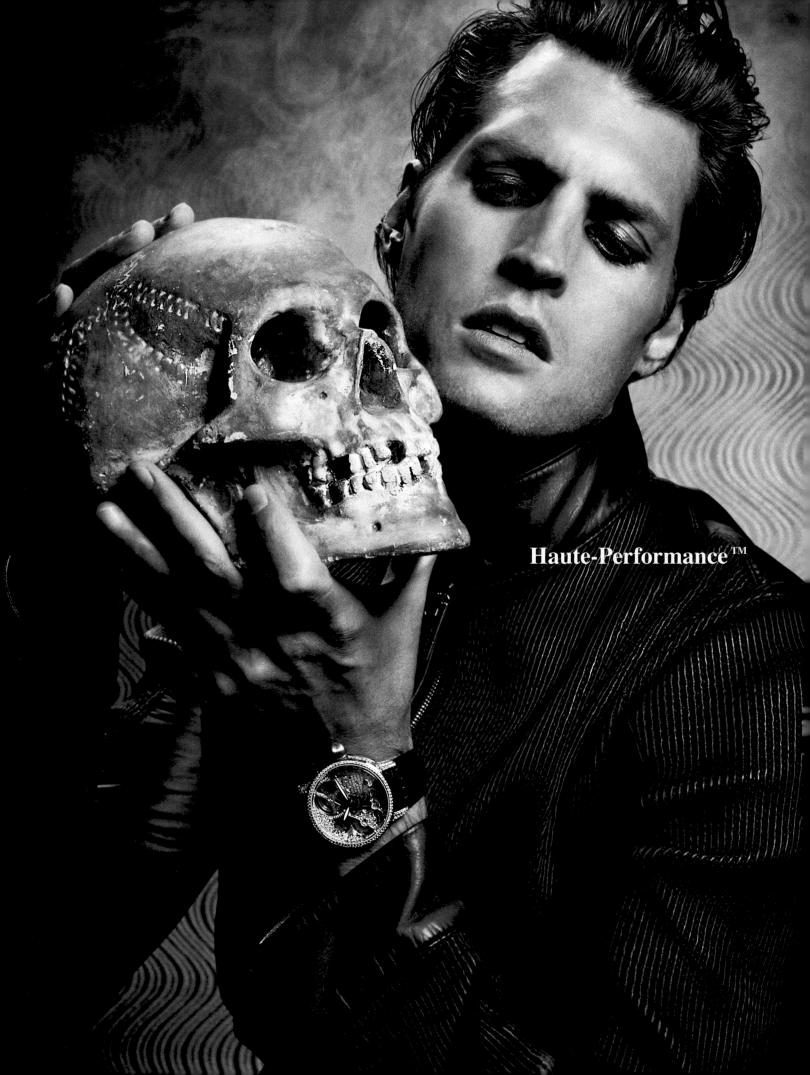

Haute-Performance™

KRIËGER®
CHRONOMÈTRES SUISSES

Romaine Jerome: Cabestan

Size of the engine

Corum: Golden Bridge

New developments in machining techniques and research into new materials have enabled the watch industry to show more for less expense in the last few years. This is a natural progression, but it could not have taken place without the extraordinary passion of luxury watch clients during this decade. Quite well informed and fascinated by mechanics, today's customers are not the same as yesterday's. Instead of an opaque body, the clients prefer to see the different aspects of the movement. And the brands agree. There is a risk that this irresistible inclination to reveal the components of their watches may condemn the ancestral art of the exposure, that it will be seen as too expensive and obsolete.

"No! One will not replace the other!" counters and reassures Marc-Aurèle Rochat, Director of Development at Arola, a company specializing in skeletonization. "There are cycles and trends as in the fashion world. The miniskirt has never replaced the evening gown!"

Squelette XL
automatic - rose gold

ZANNETTI
HANDMADE WATCHES

00186 Rome/ITALY - Via Monte d'Oro, 23A - Tel. +39/06.6819.2566 Fax +39/06.6875.027
www.zannettiwatches.com - mail: info@zannettiwatches.it

ZANNETTI
RomA
EST. 1982

NEW YORK | PARIS
11 WEST 25TH STREET | 14 RUE TOLBIAC
NEW YORK, NY 10010 | 75013 PARIS
(T) 212.243.3500 (F) 212.243.3535 | (T) +33.1.44.06.08.70 (F) +33.1.44.06.07.39
info@frenchwaytravel.com | robin@frenchwaytravel.com

www.FrenchwayTravel.com

AUDEMARS PIGUET
Exceptional Complications

A true Combier, or native of the Joux Valley, Georges-Henri Meylan has devoted more than 20 years to the service of Audemars Piguet. Now he has handed his mandate as CEO over to Philippe C. Merk. Meylan's vision and love of fine workmanship made a brilliant contribution to keeping the brand on the road to prosperity. As a family company, Audemars Piguet ranks among the most highly regarded and representative brands of Swiss watchmaking.

Meylan is devoted to the Joux Valley. The former general manager and director diligently gave of his patriotism while he was in charge of Audemars Piguet's fortunes until the end of last year. At the peak of his career, the long-distance navigator decided to hand over the helm to Merk, Maurice Lacroix's former CEO, and turn a page in his logbook. Meylan's dedication has ensured the healthy development of the Le Brassus manufacturing company while maintaining its independence as a family business. Father of three and a keen golfer—a game that recharges his batteries—Meylan joined Audemars Piguet in 1985 as operations director before being promoted to the sole directorship of the group in 1997.

During his tenure, annual sales rose tenfold from CHF50 million to CHF500 million. This success can be attributed not only to the quality of the products but also to the launch of new collections, especially for women, and to an astute communications strategy. Who today would deny Audemars Piguet's legitimate membership of the sail after it sponsored the double victory of Switzerland's Team Alinghi in the last two America's Cup races?

FAR LEFT Georges-Henri Meylan worked for Audemars Piguet for 20 years before retiring. Under Meylan's management, the firm multiplied its turnover by 10 to reach CHF500 million in 2008.

CENTER Philippe C. Merk replaced Meylan as CEO of Audemars Piguet on January 1, 2009.

ABOVE The Royal Oak Carbon Concept tourbillon and chronograph has a caseband constructed of forged carbon, a light, shock-resistant material requiring a revolutionary technology mastered only by Audemars Piguet.

The iconic Royal Oak collection has been updated with several new cutting-edge models.

ROYAL OAK: THE WATCH YOU HAVE TO HAVE

The Royal Oak model is considered iconic for Audemars Piguet. However, its introduction in 1972 caused uproar among purists: A steel watch sold at a luxury price? The brand's answer was that precious metals are not the only factor in the value of a watch; the style and the technical quality count for as much. In 2002, Audemars Piguet produced a concept version of the model for its 30th anniversary. Its overwhelming success encouraged its designers to explore further. The result was the 2008 Royal Oak Carbon Concept tourbillon and chronograph. It incorporates the revolutionary technology of forged carbon, the manufacturing process of which is mastered solely by Audemars

Piguet. The Royal Oak Carbon Concept's caseband is made of this light, shock-resistant material and the dashingly futuristic model uses such groundbreaking materials as ceramics, amorphous carbon and anodically inactivated aluminum. With its highly technical functions like the linear chronograph and the tourbillon, it became sought-after by enthusiasts. Stylistically, the Royal Oak Carbon Concept tourbillon and chronograph reveals vision, with hitherto unknown indications, among other systems. For example, the power-reserve indication, the winding-crown position indicator and the chronograph minute-counter act both as bridges and as display aids.

PERPETUAL CALENDAR

Audemars Piguet does honor to its reputation as a manufacturer of luxury watches by unveiling the Jules Audemars 30th anniversary perpetual calendar. The brand reissued its first extra-thin perpetual calendar, launched in 1978, as a limited edition of 90 watches. With a Tuscan-blue dial and a platinum case, the refined exterior of this timepiece reflects the technicality of the movement, which dependably displays the days, dates and months until 2100 without the slightest adjustment.

For the Millenary collection, the manufacturing company took its cue from the world of music with the Millenary Pianoforte watch. Although it makes no sound, this newcomer features piano keys. Surrounding an off-center dial in mother-of-pearl they suggest that this watch shall have music wherever it goes, even when dressed in diamonds.

ROSE-COLORED GLASSES

For women, Audemars Piguet brings out the rose-colored glasses, first with the Lady Royal Oak Offshore chronograph in pink gold and then with the Royal Oak Offshore Ladycat chronograph featuring several elements such as the hands, numerals, pushers and gem-set bezel in a vivid fuchsia, inspired from the color codes of the Ladycat sailing boat, sponsored by the manufacture. The classically inspired model from the Jules Audemars Collection, which has a manually wound movement, and the Millenary Black & White collection complete the palette of novelties.

Finally, Audemars Piguet has established a new showcase for its collections in its new Geneva boutique in the Place de la Fusterie, a step away from the city's Rue du Rhône luxury shopping street. Embodying the values of the brand, the space was designed to guarantee the visitor a unique horological experience.

FACING PAGE

TOP LEFT   The Royal Oak Offshore Survivor chronograph was launched in November 2008.

TOP RIGHT   This Royal Oak Offshore Grand Prix Singapore chronograph was released in September 2008.

BOTTOM LEFT   With its Tuscan-blue dial and platinum case, the sophisticated exterior of the Jules Audemars 30th anniversary perpetual calendar echoes the technicality of the movement, which accurately displays the days, dates and months without the any adjustment until 2100.

THIS PAGE

TOP (*from left to right*)   Ambassador Jarno Trulli on a visit to the Audemars Piguet factory; Audemars Piguet ambassadress Anggun attended the SIHH 2008 wearing the Carnet de Bal high jewelry set, and the Millenary Précieuse Gourmande ring and earrings; Ambassadress Michelle Yeoh wore the Millenary Sortilège necklace and Millenary Pianoforte watch during the SIHH 2008; On the behalf of Audemars Piguet, CEO Georges-Henri Meylan accepted two awards at the Grand Prix d'Horlogerie de Genève 2008: Favorite Jewelry Watch and Favorite Full Calendar Watch.

ABOVE LEFT   The classically inspired Jules Audemars collection for women encases an exclusive hand-wound movement.

ABOVE RIGHT   The Millenary Pianoforte watch features piano keys arranged around a dial that is clad partially in mother-of-pearl.

RIGHT   The Royal Oak Offshore Ladycat chronograph features some elements in bright fuchsia, such as the hands, numerals and even the rubber-molded chronograph pushers.

ROYAL OAK CARBON CONCEPT TOURBILLON AND CHRONOGRAPH REF. 26265FO.OO.D002CR.01

Movement: mechanical manual-winding Audemars Piguet Caliber 2326/2848 with tourbillon and chronograph; up to 237 hours' power reserve; 34 jewels; 384 parts; 21,600 vph; hand-polished beveling; sides hand-drawn with a file; matte surface; sapphire-blasted carbon mainplate; anodized aluminum bridges.

Functions: hours, minutes; linear chronograph minute counter with central sweep seconds hand; power-reserve indicator; selection indicator.

Case: forged carbon (carbon nano-fibers treated with high pressure and temperature); Ø 44mm; ceramic bezel; black PVD-coated titanium caseback ring; ceramics pushers and crown; water resistant to 100 meters.

Dial: display integrated onto the movement; graduated dial ring with luminescent hour markers and white minute markers; luminescent openworked hour and minute hands.

Strap: black crocodile leather; titanium AP folding clasp.

Suggested price: $225,800

ROYAL OAK CHRONOGRAPH REF. 26300ST.OO.1110ST.06

Movement: mechanical automatic-winding Audemars Piguet Caliber 2385 with chronograph; up to 40 hours' power reserve; 37 jewels; 21,600 vph; Côtes de Genève decorative pattern and circular graining; all parts decorated by hand.

Functions: hours, minutes, small seconds; chronograph with central seconds hand, 30-minute and 12-hour counters; date.

Case: stainless steel; Ø 39mm; caseback engraved with the *Royal Oak* logo; water resistant to 50 meters.

Dial: silvered with "Grande tapisserie" pattern; bi-color counters; applied luminescent white-gold index; luminescent white-gold hour and minute hands; red central chronograph seconds hand.

Bracelet: stainless steel; AP folding clasp.

Suggested price: $19,000

Also available: with dark blue or brown dial.

ROYAL OAK CHRONOGRAPH REF. 26022OR.OO.D098CR.01

Movement: mechanical automatic-winding Audemars Piguet Caliber 2385 with chronograph; up to 40 hours' power reserve; 37 jewels; 21,600 vph; Côtes de Genève decorative pattern and circular graining; all parts decorated by hand.

Functions: hours, minutes; small seconds; chronograph with central seconds hand, 30-minute and 12-hour counters; date.

Case: 18K pink gold; Ø 39mm; caseback engraved with the *Royal Oak* logo; water resistant to 50 meters.

Dial: silvered with "Grande tapisserie" pattern; bi-color counters; applied luminescent pink-gold index; luminescent pink-gold hour and minute hands; pink-gold central chronograph seconds hand.

Strap: brown crocodile leather; 18K pink-gold AP folding clasp.

Suggested price: $32,400

Also available: with brown dial.

ROYAL OAK PERPETUAL CALENDAR REF. 26252OR.OO.D092CR.01

Movement: mechanical automatic-winding Audemars Piguet Caliber 2120/2802; up to 40 hours' power reserve; 38 jewels; 355 parts; 19,800 vph; Côtes de Genève decorative pattern and circular graining; all parts decorated by hand.

Functions: hours, minutes; moonphases; perpetual calendar with indication of day, date, month, leap year.

Case: 18K pink gold; Ø 39mm; sapphire crystal caseback; water resistant to 20 meters.

Dial: brown with "Grande tapisserie" pattern; applied luminescent pink-gold index; luminescent pink-gold hour and minute hands.

Strap: brown crocodile leather; 18K pink-gold AP folding clasp.

Suggested price: $59,800

Also available: with silvered dial.

LADY ROYAL OAK   REF. 67601OR.ZZ.D080CA.01

Movement: quartz 2712 caliber.
Functions: hours, minutes; date.
Case: 18K pink gold; Ø 33mm; pink-gold bezel set with 32 brilliant-cut diamonds; crown set with a translucent cabochon-cut sapphire; caseback engraved with the *Lady Royal Oak* logo; water resistant to 50 meters.
Dial: brown with "Grande tapisserie" pattern; applied pink-gold faceted index; pink-gold faceted hour and minute hands.
Strap: brown rubber; 18K pink-gold AP folding clasp.
Suggested price: $19,100
Also available: with silvered dial on white rubber strap.

ROYAL OAK   REF. 77321OR.ZZ.1230OR.01

Movement: mechanical automatic-winding Audemars Piguet Caliber 2140; up to 40 hours' power reserve; 31 jewels; 28,800 vph; circular-grained and sandblasted mainplate; countersunk holes; circular-grained bridges adorned with Côtes de Genève motif; all parts decorated by hand.
Functions: hours, minutes, central seconds hand; date.
Case: 18K pink gold; Ø 33mm; pink-gold bezel set with 32 brilliant-cut diamonds; crown set with a translucent cabochon-cut sapphire; caseback engraved with the *Lady Royal Oak* logo; water resistant to 50 meters.
Dial: silvered with "Grande tapisserie" pattern; applied pink-gold faceted index; pink-gold faceted hour and minute hands; pink-gold central seconds hand.
Bracelet: 18K pink gold; AP folding clasp.
Suggested price: $32,100

ROYAL OAK OFFSHORE SAFARI CHRONOGRAPH   REF. 26020ST.OO.D091CR.01

Movement: mechanical automatic-winding Audemars Piguet Caliber 2326/2840 with chronograph; 54 jewels; 370 parts; 28,800 vph; Côtes de Genève decorative pattern and circular graining; all parts decorated by hand.
Functions: hours, minutes, small seconds; chronograph with sweep seconds hand, 30-minute and 12-hour counters; date.
Case: stainless steel; Ø 45mm; caseback engraved with the *Royal Oak Offshore* inscription; protected against magnetic fields; water resistant to 100 meters.
Dial: silvered guilloché with "Extra Grande Tapisserie" motif; luminescent hands and hour markers; black central chronograph seconds hand.
Strap: Hornback crocodile leather; stainless steel AP folding clasp.
Suggested price: $20,600

ROYAL OAK OFFSHORE LADYCAT CHRONOGRAPH   REF. 26266SK.ZZ.D069CA.01

Movement: mechanical automatic-winding Audemars Piguet Caliber 2385 with chronograph; up to 40 hours' power reserve; 37 jewels; 21,600 vph; Côtes de Genève decorative pattern and circular graining; all parts decorated by hand.
Functions: hours, minutes, small seconds; chronograph with central seconds hand, 30-minute and 12-hour counters; date.
Case: stainless steel; Ø 37mm; rubber-molded steel bezel set with 32 brilliant-cut diamonds; rubber-molded steel crown and pushers; caseback engraved with the *Royal Oak Offshore* inscription; water resistant to 50 meters.
Dial: black with "Mega tapisserie" pattern; silver-colored counters; applied hour markers; fuchsia hour and minute hands; fuchsia central chronograph seconds hand.
Strap: pink rubber; stainless steel AP folding clasp.
Suggested price: $25,500

LADY ROYAL OAK OFFSHORE CHRONOGRAPH   REF. 26092OK.ZZ.D010CA.01

Movement: mechanical automatic-winding Audemars Piguet Caliber 2385 with chronograph; up to 40 hours' power reserve; 37 jewels; 21,600 vph; Côtes de Genève decorative pattern and circular graining; all parts decorated by hand. Functions: hours, minutes, small seconds; chronograph with central seconds hand, 30-minute and 12-hour counters; date.
Case: 18K pink gold; Ø 37mm; entirely set with 323 brilliant-cut diamonds;

white rubber-molded pink-gold bezel set with 32 brilliant-cut diamonds; rubber-molded pink-gold crown and pushers; caseback engraved with the *Royal Oak Offshore* inscription; water resistant to 50 meters.
Dial: white mother-of-pearl with "Mega tapisserie" pattern; white mother-of-pearl subdials; 8 diamond hour markers; luminescent pink-gold hour and minute hands; black central chronograph seconds hand.
Strap: white vulcanized rubber; 18K pink-gold AP folding clasp set with brilliant-cut diamonds.
Suggested price: $80,500

MILLENARY WATCH WITH DEADBEAT SECONDS   REF. 26091OR.OO.D0803CR.01

Movement: mechanical manual-winding Audemars Piguet Caliber 2905 with Audemars Piguet escapement; 7-day power reserve; 31 jewels; 233 parts; 21,600 vph; Côtes de Genève decorative pattern and circular graining; all parts decorated by hand.
Functions: hours, minutes; dead-beat seconds.
Case: 18K pink gold; Ø 47mm; sapphire crystal caseback; water resistant to 20 meters.

Dial: open on the movement; silver-colored off-centered dial; applied blued numerals; blued openworked lozenge hands.
Strap: brown crocodile leather; 18K pink-gold AP folding clasp.
Suggested price: $171,800

MILLENARY TRADITION D'EXCELLENCE PERPETUAL CALENDAR   REF. 26066PT.OO.D028CR.01

Movement: mechanical manual-winding Audemars Piguet Caliber 2899, with Audemars Piguet escapement; 7-day power reserve; 42 jewels; 323 parts; 21,600 vph; Côtes de Genève decorative pattern and circular graining; all parts decorated by hand.
Functions: hours, minutes; dead-beat seconds; day, date, month and leap year indications; power-reserve indication.

Case: 950 platinum; Ø 47mm; sapphire crystal caseback; water resistant to 20 meters.
Dial: gold plate placed on the movement; applied blue Arabic numerals; blued openworked hands.
Strap: large square-scale hand-sewn blue crocodile leather; 950 platinum AP folding clasp.
Note: limited edition of 20 pieces; fifth piece in the Tradition d'Excellence collection.
Suggested price: $364,100

MILLENARY MC12 TOURBILLON AND CHRONOGRAPH   REF. 26069PT.OO.D028CR.01

Movement: mechanical manual-winding Audemars Piguet Caliber 2884 with tourbillon and chronograph; carbon mainplate; 10-day power reserve; 30 jewels; 336 parts; 21,600 vph; anodized aluminum bridges; all parts decorated by hand.
Functions: hours, minutes; chronograph; power-reserve indication.
Case: 950 platinum; Ø 47mm; sapphire crystal caseback; water resistant to 20 meters.

Dial: openworked dial; carbon 30-minute counter at 12; pearly and blue paintings; applied gold Maserati trident; blued and luminescent hands; red center seconds hand.
Strap: large square-scale hand-sewn blue crocodile leather; 950 platinum AP folding clasp.
Note: limited edition of 150 pieces.
Suggested price: $267,900

MILLENARY STARLIT SKY REF. 77316BC.ZZ.D007SU.01

Movement: mechanical automatic-winding Audemars Piguet Caliber 3123/3908; mainplate in aventurine; up to 62 hours' power reserve; 45 jewels; 21,600 vph; all parts decorated by hand.
Functions: hours, minutes, small seconds; power-reserve indicator; moonphases; date. **Case:** 18K white gold; Ø 39.5mm; set with brilliant-cut diamonds; bezel and lugs set with brilliant-cut diamonds; sapphire crystal caseback; water resistant to 20 meters.
Dial: featuring diamond-pavé zone and midnight blue zone adorned with 6 diamonds; applied Roman numerals; white-gold hour and minute hands; pink-gold center seconds hand; pink-gold counter hands.
Strap: midnight blue brushed satin; 18K white-gold folding clasp set with brilliant-cut diamonds.
Suggested price: $44,000
Also available: in 18K white gold set with brilliant-cut diamonds, off-centered midnight blue disc and half-moon zone in white mother-of-pearl on midnight blue brushed-satin strap with 18K white-gold folding clasp set with brilliant-cut diamonds.

MILLENARY STARLIT SKY REF. 77315OR.ZZ.D013SU.01

Movement: mechanical automatic-winding Audemars Piguet Caliber 3123/3908; up to 62 hours' power reserve; 45 jewels; 21,600 vph; all parts decorated by hand.
Functions: hours, minutes, small seconds; power-reserve indicator; moonphases; date.
Case: 18K pink gold; Ø 39.5mm; bezel and lugs set with brilliant-cut diamonds; sapphire crystal caseback; water resistant to 20 meters.
Dial: white mother-of-pearl off-centered disc; light blue Arabic numerals; half-moon zone in white mother-of-pearl; applied Roman numerals; pink-gold hour and minute hands; blue center seconds hand; blue counter hands.
Strap: white brushed satin; 18K pink-gold clasp set with brilliant-cut diamonds.
Suggested price: $37,200

LADY MILLENARY REF. 77301ST.ZZ.D015CR.01

Movement: mechanical automatic-winding Audemars Piguet Caliber 2325; up to 40 hours' power reserve; 32 jewels; 28,800 vph; Côtes de Genève decorative pattern and circular graining; all parts decorated by hand.
Functions: hours, minutes, central seconds.
Case: stainless steel; 39.5x35.5mm; bezel set with 66 brilliant-cut diamonds; crown set with a translucent sapphire cabochon; caseback engraved with the *Millenary* logo; water resistant to 20 meters.
Dial: black with "flinqué" motif bearing white Roman numerals; snailed black offset disc with white Arabic numerals; faceted hour and minute hands.
Strap: black crocodile leather; stainless steel AP folding clasp.
Suggested price: $13,400
Also available: with white dial on white crocodile leather strap.

MILLENARY PIANOFORTE REF. 15325BC.OO.D600CR.01

Movement: mechanical automatic-winding Audemars Piguet Caliber 3120; 40 jewels; 278 parts; 22K gold oscillating weight; 21,600 vph; variable inertia balance; Côtes de Genève decorative pattern and circular graining; all parts decorated by hand.
Functions: hours, minutes, center seconds; date.
Case: 18K white gold; 45x40mm; sapphire crystal caseback; water resistant to 20 meters.
Dial: two-zone dial in white mother-of-pearl with black piano-motif minute circle; off-centered hour zone with applied white gold Roman numerals; skeleton hands; wine-colored center seconds hand.
Strap: black crocodile leather; 18K white-gold AP folding clasp.
Note: limited edition of 500 pieces.
Suggested price: $31,500
Also available: with case, bezel and lugs set with brilliant-cut diamonds, diamond-pavé dial on black crocodile leather strap, limited edition of 250 pieces.

JULES AUDEMARS JUMPING HOUR MINUTE REPEATER   REF. 26151PT.OO.D028CR.01

Movement: mechanical manual-winding Audemars Piguet Caliber 2907; 35 jewels; 412 parts; 21,600 vph; Côtes de Genève decorative pattern and circular graining; all parts decorated by hand.
Functions: hours, minutes, small seconds; minute-repeater mechanism striking the hours, quarters and minutes on request.
Case: 950 platinum; Ø 43mm; sapphire crystal caseback.

Dial: opaline dial with applied blued numerals; flame-blued "Poire Paris" minute hand.
Strap: black crocodile leather; 950 platinum AP folding clasp.
Suggested price: $244,600
Also available: in 18K pink gold with opaline dial on brown crocodile leather strap.

JULES AUDEMARS 30TH ANNIVERSARY PERPETUAL CALENDAR   REF. 26000PT.OO.D028CR.01

Movement: mechanical automatic-winding, ultra-thin Audemars Piguet Caliber 2120/2802; up to 40 hours' power reserve; 38 jewels; 355 parts; 19,800 vph; Côtes de Genève decorative pattern and circular graining; all parts decorated by hand.
Functions: hours, minutes; moonphases; perpetual calendar with indication of day, date, month, leap year.

Case: 950 platinum; Ø 41mm; sapphire crystal caseback; water resistant to 20 meters.
Dial: Tuscany blue; applied 18K white-gold hour markers; 18K white-gold hour and minute hands.
Strap: blue crocodile leather; 950 platinum AP folding clasp.
Note: limited edition of 90 pieces.
Suggested price: $99,300

JULES AUDEMARS MINUTE REPEATER TOURBILLON CHRONOGRAPH   REF. 26050OR.OO.D002CR.01

Movement: mechanical manual-winding Audemars Piguet Caliber 2874 with tourbillon and chronograph; 38 jewels; 665 parts; 21,600 vph; Côtes de Genève decorative pattern and circular graining; all parts decorated by hand.
Functions: hours, minutes; minute-repeater mechanism striking the hours, quarters and minutes on request; chronograph with 30-minute counter; small seconds along the tourbillon axis.

Case: 18K pink gold; Ø 43mm; sapphire crystal caseback.
Dial: black guilloché with "spiral" motif; applied gold hour markers; gold leaf-type hands.
Strap: large square-scale hand-sewn black crocodile leather; 18K pink-gold AP folding clasp.
Suggested price: $341,600
Also available: in 950 platinum with silvered dial on black crocodile leather strap with 950 platinum AP folding clasp.

JULES AUDEMARS SKELETON EQUATION OF TIME   REF. 26053PT.OO.D002CR.01

Movement: mechanical automatic-winding skeleton Audemars Piguet Caliber 2120/2808; 41 jewels; 423 parts; 21K gold oscillating weight; 19,800 vph; Côtes de Genève decorative pattern and circular graining; all parts decorated by hand.
Functions: hours, minutes; sunrise and sunset times; equation of time; moonphases; perpetual calendar with indication of day, date, month, leap year.

Case: 950 platinum; Ø 43mm; sapphire crystal caseback; water resistant to 20 meters.
Dial: sapphire dial with printed counters.
Strap: black crocodile leather; 950 platinum AP folding clasp.
Suggested price: $154,900
Also available: in non-skeleton versions; in 18K yellow gold with silvered dial on brown crocodile leather strap; in 18K white gold with silvered dial on black crocodile leather strap; in 18K pink gold with black dial on black crocodile leather strap.

LADIES' JULES AUDEMARS TOURBILLON   REF. 26084OR.ZZ.D016CR.01

Movement: mechanical manual-winding Audemars Piguet Caliber 2906 with tourbillon; 19 jewels; 197 parts; 21,600 vph; bridges engraved with "dancing spiral" motifs; all parts decorated by hand.
Functions: hours, minutes.
Case: 18K pink gold; Ø 39mm; bezel set with 56 brilliant-cut diamonds; water resistant to 20 meters.
Dial: white mother-of-pearl; hand-engraved with a "spiral" flinqué motif; applied numerals; diamond hour markers.
Strap: glossy-silky hand-sewn white crocodile leather; 18K pink-gold AP folding clasp.
Suggested price: $122,400
Also available: in 18K white gold on violet crocodile leather strap with 18K white-gold AP folding clasp.

LADIES' JULES AUDEMARS TOURBILLON CHRONOGRAPH   REF. 26083BC.ZZ.D001GA.01

Movement: mechanical manual-winding Audemars Piguet Caliber 2889 with tourbillon and chronograph; 25 jewels; 286 parts; 21,600 vph; Côtes de Genève decorative pattern and circular graining; all parts decorated by hand.
Functions: hours, minutes; chronograph.
Case: 18K white gold; Ø 39mm; set with 251 brilliant-cut diamonds; bezel set with 68 baguette-cut diamonds; water resistant to 20 meters.
Dial: diamonds and white mother-of-pearl; polished hour markers and Roman numerals.
Strap: black galuchat; 18K white-gold AP folding clasp.
Suggested price: $237,400
Also available: on pearly white hand-sewn crocodile leather strap.

MINUTE REPEATER WITH PERPETUAL CALENDAR SQUARE PIECE   REF. 26052BC.OO.D092CR.01

Movement: mechanical manual-winding Audemars Piguet Caliber 2855; 29 jewels; 18,000 vph; Côtes de Genève decorative pattern and circular graining; all parts decorated by hand.
Functions: hours, minutes; minute-repeater mechanism striking the hours, quarters and minutes on request; moonphases; perpetual calendar with indication of day, date, month, leap year.
Case: 18K white gold; Ø 50mm; sapphire crystal caseback.
Dial: opaline with applied pink-gold numerals; pink-gold hour and minute hands.
Strap: brown crocodile leather; 18K white-gold AP folding clasp.
Note: limited production.

EDWARD PIGUET LARGE DATE TOURBILLON   REF. 26009OR.OO.D088CR.01

Movement: mechanical manual-winding Audemars Piguet Caliber 2886 with tourbillon; 23 jewels; 222 parts; 21,600 vph; Côtes de Genève decorative pattern and circular graining; all parts decorated by hand.
Functions: hours, minutes; small seconds on the tourbillon axis; date.
Case: 18K pink gold; sapphire crystal caseback; water resistant to 20 meters.
Dial: three-dimensional; silvered; gold applique featuring sunburst guilloché motif; oversized large date aperture; gold leaf-type hands.
Strap: large square-scale hand-sewn brown crocodile leather; 18K pink-gold AP folding clasp.
Suggested price: $168,100
Also available: in 18K white gold with silvered dial on black crocodile leather strap with 18K white-gold AP folding clasp.

B.R.M
On the Mark

French company B.R.M (Bernard Richards Manufacture) builds luxury watches as it would a racecar: with outstanding mechanics under the hood and intentionally "imperfect" finishings such as crude brushing and polishing on the body.

The brand fuses founder Bernard Richards's life-long adulation for motor sports and precision engineering into every detail of every high-end watch that it produces. The brand's watchmakers craft with the same high-tech materials used in racecar construction, checkered flags are emulated on the straps and piston-shaped modular cases, and engine parts inspire even the models' names.

In 2008, B.R.M teamed up with U.S.-based Ecosse Moto Works to design and build the ultimate gift set: a titanium EcosseHeretic motorcycle and matching Ecosse watch.

The collaboration with Ecosse Moto Works seemed a natural one—both companies are imbibed with a competitive spirit, a unique character and a flair for distinctive designs—and the ten resulting motorcycle/watch sets are superb fruits of those qualities plus high-tech machination meshing perfectly.

The ultra-precise accessory for an ultra-precise machine, Ecosse's 48mm titanium case is fitted on a reversible strap: one side is black rubber, the other is black leather with orange stitching matching the Ecosse-Heretic's seat. The automatic chronograph's brushed titanium bezel recalls the motorcycle's brushed titanium chassis, both watch and bike expose their inner mechanics, and both are engraved with a shared serial number.

> B.R.M teamed up with Ecosse Moto Works to design and build the ultimate package: an EcosseHeretic motorcycle and matching watch.

A new addition to B.R.M's fleet is the CT-48 chronograph. This striking timepiece is based on the same engineering principles as the R50 and Birotor models and also is powered by the proprietary Precitime movement with Isolastic System® shock absorption. The 48mm case is water resistant to 100 meters and features the brand's offset horns and a carbon-fiber dial bearing a tachymeter.

Also unveiled recently is the TR-Tourbillon. Available in titanium, rose gold, or black PVD-coated titanium with rose-gold elements, the watch's dial is completely skeletonized and fitted between two sapphire crystals. Its Precitime movement is suspended on carbon-fiber triangle bridges and equipped an automatic tourbillon with a 1.45-minute rotation, and Isolastic System® shock absorbers.

B.R.M's racing watches can be personalized on request, both in color and materials.

FACING PAGE
The matching titanium Ecosse chronograph and EcosseHeretic motorcycle were created as special sets for ten privileged collectors.

THIS PAGE
TOP Crafted in stainless steel and titanium with black PVD, CT-48 is also available with orange or yellow accents on its skeletonized carbon-fiber dial and strap. The watch's mechanics are visible through a sapphire crystal caseback.

RIGHT CENTER Developed in-house, the Precitime caliber is visible through sapphire crystal slats in the Birotor's caseside.

RIGHT The Ø 52mm TR-Tourbillon (TR1) is shown here in a titanium case with stainless steel crown and lugs, and on an alligator leather strap. It is also available in rose gold (TR3 OR), or black PVD-coated titanium with rose-gold lugs, crown, crown protection, rotor weights and screws (TR2 TN OR).

TR - TOURBILLON　　　　　　REF. TR1

Movement: Precitime; suspended on triangle bridges in carbon fiber; shock absorbers with cone-shaped spring, Isolastic System® (certified); differential automatic tourbillon, rotation: 1.45 minutes; tourbillon bar in carbon fiber set on Isolastic System; protection bush of the escapement axis set on Isolastic System; titanium tourbillon cage; Arcap plate and bridges assembled movement with bolts; BRM balance with ruby gyroscopic effect; double ceramic rotor bearings; aluminum Fortale HR rotors; tantalum rotor weights.
Case: titanium; 52mm; polished stainless steel lugs; stainless steel crown moved to 2 for better comfort; sapphire crystal front and back; water resistant up to 100 meters.
Dial: skeleton.
Strap: alligator.
Also available: 48mm.

BIROTOR　　　　　　REF. BRT3N

Movement: Precitime; suspended on triangles in carbon fiber; shock absorbers with cone-shaped spring, Isolastic System® (certified); differential automatic Birotor mechanics; Arcap plate and bridges; 6-sided bolts; lightened motor structure; B.R.M pendulum with gyroscopic effect; double ceramic rotor bearings; Fortale HR rotor hubs; tantalum rotor bob weights.
Functions: bipolar time system with double crowns (certified).

Case: titanium with black PVD; clear; 40x48mm; 18K rose-gold, ergonomic lugs with 3 adjustable positions (certified); 18K rose-gold crown transfer for better comfort; curvilinear double sapphire crystal glass; water resistant to 30 meters.
Dial: skeleton.
Strap: alligator leather.
Also available: titanium and steel (clear case); rose gold (clear case); on leather Winner checkerboard strap

CT 48

Movement: Precitime based on ETA Vajoux 7753; suspended on triangles in carbon fiber; shock absorber with cone-shaped spring, Isolastic System® (certified); Fortale HR rotor hubs ; tantalum rotor bob weight.
Functions: chronograph; tachymeter.
Case: polished stainless steel, titanium with black PVD; scratchproof sapphire crystal front and back; water resistant up to 100 meters.

Dial: carbon-fiber skeleton dial.
Strap: black leather with red stitching.

R50T　　　　　　REF. R50TN

Movement: automatic Precitime A07161; engine caliber; 28,800 vph; 48-hour power reserve; 24 rubies.
Functions: hours, minutes, seconds; power reserve at 6.
Case: titanium and black PVD-treated case; Ø 50mm; stainless steel lugs and crown; scratchproof crystal sapphire front and back.
Dial: skeleton; orange ultra-light hands.

Strap: black leather.
Also available: in rose-gold case; rose-gold and black PVD-treated case; red or yellow hands.
Note: 3-year warranty.

V18

Movement: round, automatic Swiss chronograph 7753 ETA Valjoux; round, 7.9mm thick; 28,800 vph; 46-hour power reserve; 27 rubies; ultra-slim stainless steel specific screws.
Functions: 60-second chronograph function; 30-minute and 12-hour registers; calendar in window.
Case: gray-and-black checkered grade-2 titanium case; Ø 48mm; extra-hard black PVD case protection; ultra-slim stainless steel lugs 18/8; start/stop chronograph button at 2; chronograph reset button at 4; date corrector at 10; scratchproof sapphire crystal front and back; water resistant up to 100 meters.
Dial: applied carbon-aluminum; super light, red and black hands.
Strap: black rubber.
Also available: on leather strap.
Note: 3-year warranty.

V12   REF. V12-44-BN

Movement: automatic 7753 ETA Valjoux chronograph; round, 7.9mm thick; 28,800 vph; 46-hour power reserve; 27 rubies.
Functions: 12-hour and 30-minute countdown registers; 60-second chronograph function; calendar window.
Case: brushed, black case; Ø 44mm; start/stop button at 2; chronograph reset button at 4; date corrector at 10; double-face scratchproof sapphire crystal; extra-hard PVD-treatment protection; water resistant to 100 meters.
Dial: black; white ultra-light hands.
Strap: black rubber.
Also available: brushed or polished case; gray, black, red or yellow hands; carbon or fiberglass dial with various designs.
Note: 3-year warranty.

GP44   REF. GP-44-109

Movement: automatic 7753 ETA Valjoux chronograph; round, 7.9mm thick; 28,800 vph; 27 rubies.
Functions: 12-hour and 30-minute countdown registers; 60-second chronograph function; calendar window.
Case: gray; grade-2 titanium; Ø 44mm; ultra-slim 18/8 stainless steel lugs; start/stop button at 2; chronograph reset button at 4; date corrector at 10; double-face scratchproof sapphire crystal; extra-hard PVD-treatment protection; water resistant to 100 meters.
Dial: black; ultra-light hands.
Strap: black genuine rubber.
Also available: gray case / gray dial; black case / black dial.
Note: 3-year warranty.

V8 COMPETITION

Movement: automatic 7753 ETA Valjoux chronograph; round, 7.9mm thick; 28,800 vph; 27 rubies.
Functions: 12-hour and 30-minute countdown registers; calendar window.
Case: black PVD-treated titanium; Ø 44mm; engraved with V8 COMPETITION; brushed ultra-slim 18/8 stainless steel or titanium lugs; start/stop button at 2; chronograph reset button at 4; date corrector at 10; double-face scratchproof sapphire crystal; water resistant to 100 meters.
Dial: carbon with white or orange tracings; yellow ultra-light hands.
Strap: leather Winner checkerboard strap.
Also available: gray, white, red, or orange hands.
Note: 3-year warranty.

BAUME & MERCIER
Time for a Lovely Lady

Baume & Mercier has brought forth a new watch just for women. Named Iléa, she demurely revealed that she has all the right curves in all the right places at this year's SIHH watch show in Geneva.

While most brands are thinking big, male and complicated, Baume & Mercier has chosen a different set of key words for Iléa's coming of age: purity, emotion, simplicity. Indeed, she exudes feminine virtues, starting with her name, which stands for Intimate, Luxuriant, Elegant and Active. Her look epitomizes the ultimate incarnation of woman as both mysterious and radiant. This new watch was thus developed as the perfect expression of time controlled by women in a display of mechanical poetry.

THIS PAGE
RIGHT   Dials in the new Iléa collection bear patterns of convex lines.

FAR RIGHT The collection includes versions with plain, partially set or fully set bezels.

FACING PAGE
Baume & Mercier's quintessentially feminine Iléa collection pays tribute to women who manage to be radiant, elegant, active and secretive all at the same time.

Iléa: Intimate, Luxuriant, Elegant and Active.

Round and elegant, Iléa shows off a finely sculpted outline where the steel of the case and bracelet seem gently to embrace the heart of the watch. The simple beauty of this model lies in the purity of its forms and volumes, perfectly matched by the serenely harmonious dial that can be opalescent, mother-of-pearl or even set with diamonds. It displays a rare horological decoration: an engine-turned convex pattern. The engraved vertical lines curve out towards the edges until they bracket the dial to create the illusion of volume, emphasized by an oval flange. Particular care has been taken for the structure of the bezel. Depending on the model, the bezel can be set entirely with diamonds or just on the sides at 9:00 and 3:00. In the latter case, the line of diamonds links one lug of the case to its opposite number, mimicking the curved lines of the dial. Baume & Mercier has chosen to downplay the functions with indications limited to the hours, minutes, seconds, and the date at 6:00.

Iléa fills out a Baume & Mercier catalogue that is already well endowed with such models as the Riviera, Classima, Diamant and Hampton models. The company, established in 1830 and now belonging to the Richemont Group, is thus equipped for healthy growth according to the resolve of the founding Baume brothers to make only fine quality watches.

WILLIAM BAUME ULTRA-THIN   REF. M0A08794

Movement: mechanical manual-winding extra-flat caliber.
Functions: hours, minutes.
Case: 18K pink-gold three-piece case; Ø 41mm, thickness: 6.1mm; flat sapphire crystal; back fastened by 6 screws; water resistant to 3atm.
Dial: silvered; brushed with a circular pattern; center disc with a guilloché "old-basket" pattern; black Roman numerals and applied pink-gold bâton markers, luminescent at quarters; black minute track; pink-gold leaf-style hands.
Strap: hand-stitched alligator leather; pink-gold clasp.
Suggested price: $12,900
Note: limited edition of 178 pieces.

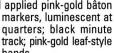
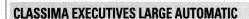

WILLIAM BAUME RETROGRADE   REF. M0A08795

Movement: mechanical automatic-winding ETA 2892-A2 caliber; decorated with a circular-graining pattern; skeleton rotor.
Functions: hours, minutes; retrograde small seconds at 6; large date at 12.
Case: 18K pink-gold three-piece case; Ø 41mm, thickness: 9.75mm; polished and brushed finish; flat sapphire crystal; back fastened by 6 screws, displaying the movement through a sapphire crystal; water resistant to 3atm.
Dial: silvered; brushed with a sun pattern; center disc with a guilloché "old-basket" pattern, hollowed small-second sector; black Roman numerals and applied pink-gold bâton markers, luminescent at quarters; black minute track; pink-gold leaf-style hands; serpentine-shaped small-seconds hand.
Strap: hand-stitched alligator leather; pink-gold clasp.
Suggested price: $13,900
Note: limited edition of 178 pieces.

CLASSIMA EXECUTIVES LARGE AUTOMATIC   REF. M0A08789

Movement: mechanical automatic-winding Soprod 2824-BV caliber.
Functions: hours, minutes, seconds.
Case: 18K pink-gold three-piece case; Ø 39mm, thickness: 9.2mm; polished finish; flat sapphire crystal; snap-on back with ligné engraving and a small sapphire-crystal bull's eye on the balance; water resistant to 3atm.
Dial: matte black; center disc with guilloché vertical-lines pattern; aperture on the balance; logo at 12; applied pink-gold-plated bâton markers and Roman numerals at 3, 6 and 9; pink-gold-plated minute track on the flange.
Strap: black alligator leather; pink-gold clasp.
Suggested price: $5,490
Also available: Ø 42mm: in stainless steel with black or silvered dial.

CLASSIMA EXECUTIVES LARGE GMT   REF. M0A08788

Movement: mechanical automatic-winding BM 11893-2 caliber (ETA 2893-2 base).
Functions: hours, minutes, seconds; date at 3; 24-hour dual time with arrow-tip center hand and dedicated scale.
Case: 18K yellow-gold three-piece case; Ø 39mm, thickness: 8.9mm; polished finish; flat sapphire crystal; snap-on back; water resistant to 3atm.
Dial: silvered; grained; center disc with guilloché vertical-lines pattern; applied gilded bâton markers (logo at 12) and Roman numerals at 6 and 9; gilded leaf-style hands; black minute track.
Strap: black alligator leather; yellow-gold clasp.
Suggested price: $4,990
Also available: Ø 42mm: in stainless steel with matte white dial on alligator-leather strap or bracelet.

CLASSIMA EXECUTIVES SKELETON REF. M0A08786

Movement: mechanical manual-winding skeleton caliber; 17 jewels.
Functions: hours, minutes, small seconds at 6.
Case: stainless steel three-piece case; Ø 42mm, thickness: 9.9mm; polished finish; flat sapphire crystal; snap-on back displaying the movement through a sapphire crystal; water resistant to 3atm.
Dial: silvered; grained; center disc with guilloché vertical-lines pattern and an aperture; logo at 12; applied rhodium-plated bâton markers and Roman numerals at 3 and 9; minute track with black 5-minute graduation; leaf-style hands in blued steel.
Strap: dark brown alligator leather; steel clasp.
Suggested price: $4,990

RIVIERA SPORTY XL REF. M0A08779

Movement: mechanical automatic-winding ETA 2892-A2 caliber.
Functions: hours, minutes, seconds; date at 6.
Case: stainless steel three-piece case in octagon shape; Ø 40mm, thickness: 11.6mm; polished finish; flat sapphire crystal; counterclockwise-turning bezel with a blue aluminum ring, luminescent pointer and silvered minute track for the calculation of diving times; screw-down crown; screw-on back; water resistant to 20atm.
Dial: silvered, brushed with a sun pattern; luminescent applied rhodium-plated round markers, 12 as black Roman numeral; black minute track on the flange; luminescent Dauphine hands in blued steel.
Bracelet: polished and brushed stainless steel; double fold-over steel clasp with 2 safety pushers.
Suggested price: $2,990
Also available: with black ring and dial on black rubber strap or steel bracelet; in stainless steel and yellow gold with black ring and black or silvered dial on steel and yellow-gold bracelet.

RIVIERA SPORTY XL REF. M0A08780

Movement: mechanical automatic-winding ETA 2892-A2 caliber.
Functions: hours, minutes, seconds; date at 6.
Case: stainless steel three-piece case in octagon shape; Ø 40mm, thickness: 11.6mm; polished finish; flat sapphire crystal; counterclockwise-turning bezel with an aluminum ring; luminescent pointer and silvered minute track for the calculation of diving times; screw-down crown; screw-on back; water resistant to 20atm.
Dial: matte black; luminescent, applied rhodium-plated round markers; 12 as luminescent silver Roman numeral; silver minute track on the flange; luminescent rhodium-plated Dauphine hands.
Strap: black rubber; double fold-over steel clasp with 2 safety pushers.
Suggested price: $2,790
Also available: on steel bracelet; with blue ring and silvered dial on steel bracelet; in stainless steel and yellow gold with black ring and black or silvered dial on steel and yellow-gold bracelet.

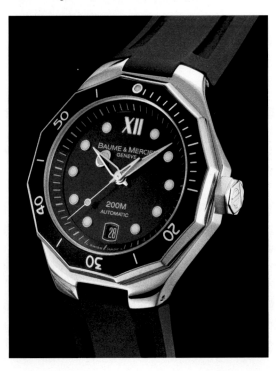

RIVIERA SPORTY CHRONOGRAPH XXL REF. M0A08797

Movement: mechanical automatic-winding ETA 7750 caliber.
Functions: hours, minutes, small seconds; date at 3; chronograph with 3 counters: hour at 6; small seconds at 9; minute at 12.
Case: stainless steel three-piece case in octagonal shape; Ø 43mm, thickness: 15.5mm; polished and brushed finish; flat sapphire crystal; counterclockwise-turning ring with a black aluminum ring, orange luminescent pointer and silvered minute track for the calculation of diving times; screw-down crown; rectangular pushers; screw-on back; water resistant to 20atm.
Dial: matte black; hollowed subdials decorated with circular beads; orange luminescent, silver Roman numerals; orange luminescent, rhodium-plated Dauphine hands; minute track, tachometer on the flange.
Strap: black with orange stitches, satin liner with blue stitches; double fold-over steel through clasp.
Suggested price: $3,990

BELL & ROSS
Defying the Ordinary

In the early 1990s, a team of designers and specialists of aircraft controls joined forces to work on the same project: to be part of the great Swiss watch making tradition while meeting the demands of professionals facing extreme situations.

THE SEARCH FOR THE EXTREME

There are trades that lead you to bear extreme temperatures, undergo violent accelerations, or resist dangerous pressures. Bell & Ross studies these extreme situations with those who experience them: pilots, divers, astronauts and bomb disposal experts—professionals for whom a watch must not only be a tool to serve them in their missions, but an ally at all moments.

To ensure that a watch perfectly meets the expectations of its users, Bell & Ross gathers men with complementary know-how. United around a unique project—to create a utility watch—master watchmakers, engineers, designers and professional users have combined their expertise and experience. Their sole motto: The essential is never compromised by the superfluous.

Over the years and with each new success, Bell & Ross has built a selective network of 500 points of sale in 50 countries worldwide. Bell & Ross has thus become a point of reference in the exclusive world of professionals, collectors and fine Swiss watchmaking.

Designed for professionals who demand tools with optimum reliability, Bell & Ross watches correspond to four fundamental principles: Readability, Functionality, Precision, Water Resistance.

Since 1996, Bell & Ross manufactures in its own production unit in La Chaux-de-Fonds, Switzerland. It is there that all the master watchmakers develop, assemble and carry out the ultimate adjustments to Bell & Ross watches.

Regardless of the watch's mechanical complexity, the art is revealed in the precision of the measurements, the rigor of the controls and the care given to each work-stage.

WATCHMAKING REFERENCES

BR 01 TOURBILLON The Instrument watch Grande Complication: a tourbillon, a regulator, a power-reserve Indicator and a precision indicator. Bell & Ross joined forces with leading Swiss master watchmakers to create an exceptional movement in a state-of-the-art timepiece.

VINTAGE JUMPING HOUR The first watch with a jumping hour and power reserve. A masterpiece of ingenuity, this watch is the fruit of the collaboration between Bell & Ross and Swiss master watchmaker Vincent Calabrese. It combines the complexity of a mechanical movement with the simplicity of a new reading system.

HYDROMAX 11 100 M Holds the world water-resistance record. By introducing a liquid into the case, this watch possesses perfect water resistance and masters incomparable readability. It can withstand a pressure of 1,110 bar, or a depth of 11,100 meters.

Bell & Ross's watches are designed with the help of men who dare to risk and demand the best in professional-grade timepieces.

BELGIAN GRAND PRIX

Bell & Ross takes flight with the BR 01 Instrument collection for pilots. In their search for the ideal professional watch and armed with their experience in the aeronautic and military fields, in-house engineers, master watchmakers, designers and professional users pooled their knowledge to create a unique, revolutionary concept: the BR 01 Instrument. Aeronautic instrumentation is the absolute reference for readability, reliability and performance. Bell & Ross replicates a plane's clock as accurately as possible in a size proportionate to the wrist.

The new BR 02 Instrument collection is to divers as the BR 01 series is to pilots. Extreme resistance to crushing underwater pressure, precision and easy legibility are all very important features and divers are provided with via helium release valves, precisely rotating internal unidirectional bezels, and bold, highly luminous dials to aid them in their missions. BR 02 Instruments are available in stainless steel, 18-karat pink gold, or a combination of carbon-coated steel and pink gold.

LEFT A professional user tests the water resistance and functions of this new BR 02 Instrument for divers.

BELOW LEFT A mechanical automatic movement powers the 44mm BR 02 Instrument Blacktop Pro dial from within a carbon-coated steel case. Its black dial with large photoluminescent index marks in framed by a unidirectional, cranted interior bezel with screw-in crown at 2:00. Water resistant to 1,000 meters, this BR 02 is available on rubber or heavy-duty synthetic fabric strap.

BELOW The 44mm BR 02 Instrument Steel houses a mechanical automatic movement beneath a black dial with numerals, hands and index marks treated with white photoluminescence to optimize nighttime reading. Fitted on a rubber or heavy-duty synthetic fabric strap, the stainless steel case is topped with a unidirectional, cranted interior bezel with screw-in crown at 2:00, and is water resistant to 1,000 meters.

BR 01 TOURBILLON PHANTOM

Movement: tourbillon movement with carbon-fiber mainplates and black-gold tourbillon carriage associated to three additional complications; 120-hour power reserve.
Functions: regulator at 12 (dissociating hour counter at 12 and main central hand for the minutes); trust index at 3; power-reserve indicator at 9.
Case: virtually non-scratchable titanium case with DLC (Diamond Like Carbon); water resistant to 100 meters.
Dial: black carbon fiber; numerals, hands and indexes with photo-luminescent coating to optimize nighttime reading.
Strap: rubber.
Suggested price: $148,000

BR 01 GRAND MINUTEUR TOURBILLON

Movement: mechanical manual-winding; pink-gold anodized aluminum bridges; 3-day power reserve.
Functions: hours, minutes, small second counter; minuteur with flyback function (back to zero and fast boosting of the measure of time, 2 graduations of 60 minutes and 10/10th of hours); power-reserve indicator.
Case: XXL 44x50mm; satin-polished pink gold; screw-in crown; antireflective sapphire crystal and caseback; water resistant to 100 meters.
Dial: black; hands and indexes covered with photo-luminescent coating to optimize nighttime reading.
Strap: rubber or alligator.
Suggested price: $250,000

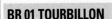

BR 01 TOURBILLON

Movement: mechanical manual-winding BR 01 Tourbillon with carbon-fiber mainplates and black-gold tourbillon carriage; 120-hour power reserve.
Functions: hour counter at 12, central minutes; power-reserve indicator at 9; trust index at 3.
Case: XXL Ø 46mm; glass-bead-blasted titanium with DLC (Diamond Like Carbon); virtually non-scratchable coating (4,000 vickers); screw-in crown; antireflective sapphire crystal and caseback; water resistant to 100 meters.
Dial: black carbon fiber; hands and indexes with photo-luminescent coating to optimize nighttime reading.
Strap: black rubber.
Suggested price: $131,000

BR 01 TOURBILLON PINK GOLD

Movement: mechanical manual-winding BR 01 Tourbillon with carbon-fiber mainplates and black-gold tourbillon carriage; 120-hour power reserve.
Functions: hour counter at 12, central minutes; power-reserve indicator at 9; trust index at 3.
Case: XXL Ø 46mm; pink gold; screw-in crown; antireflective sapphire crystal and caseback; water resistant to 100 meters.
Dial: black carbon fiber; hands and indexes with photo-luminescent coating to optimize nighttime reading.
Strap: black alligator leather.
Suggested price: $184,000

BR 01-92 RED

Movement: automatic mechanical ETA 2892.
Functions: hours, minutes, seconds.
Case: XXL Ø 46mm; glass-bead-blasted 316L steel finished with black carbon-powder coating; screw-in crown; antireflective sapphire crystal; water resistant to 100 meters.
Dial: black; numerals, index markers and hands covered with a red photo-luminescent coating to optimize nighttime reading.
Strap: rubber or heavy-duty synthetic fabric.
Suggested price: $4,500

BR 01-94 RED

Movement: automatic mechanical ETA 2892.
Functions: hours, minutes, seconds; date.
Case: XXL Ø 46mm; glass-bead-blasted 316L steel finished with black carbon-powder coating; screw-in crown; antireflective sapphire crystal; water resistant to 100 meters.
Dial: black; numerals, index markers and hands covered with a red photo-luminescent coating to optimize nighttime reading.
Strap: rubber or heavy-duty synthetic fabric.
Suggested price: $6,500

BR 01-94 PRO TITANIUM

Movement: mechanical automatic.
Functions: hours, minutes, seconds; 3-counter chronograph (12-hour, 30-minute and 60-second); date.
Case: XL Ø 46mm; satin-finished grade-2 titanium; screw-in crown; antireflective sapphire crystal; water resistant to 100 meters.
Dial: gray; numerals and hands coated with white SuperLumiNova® photo-luminescent coating to optimize nighttime reading.
Strap: rubber.
Suggested price: $8,000

BR 03-92 PHANTOM

Movement: automatic mechanical ETA 2892.
Functions: hours, minutes, seconds; date.
Case: Ø 42mm; glass-bead-blasted 316L steel finished with black carbon-powder coating; antireflective sapphire crystal; water resistant to 100 meters.
Dial: black; numerals, indexes and hands are coated with a photo-luminescent finish to optimize nighttime reading.
Strap: rubber or heavy-duty synthetic fabric.
Suggested price: $4,000

BR 02-92 PINK GOLD

Movement: mechanical automatic.
Functions: hours, minutes, seconds; date.
Case: Ø 44mm; solid 18K (5N) brushed pink gold; unidirectional, toothed-interior bezel graduated to 60 minutes with photoluminescent reference point; screw-in crowns; decompression valve for deep-sea diving; antireflective sapphire crystal; water resistant to 300 meters. **Dial:** carbon fiber; numerals and hands coated in photoluminescence to optimize nighttime reading; gold applique indexes.
Strap: rubber.
Suggested price: $22,000

BR 02 INSTRUMENT PINK GOLD + CARBON

Movement: mechanical automatic.
Functions: hours, minutes, seconds; date.
Case: Ø 44mm; pink gold and steel with black carbon-powder-coating finish; water resistant to 1,000 meters.
Dial: black dial; numerals and hands coated in photoluminescence to optimize nighttime reading; gold applique indexes.
Strap: rubber.
Suggested price: $9,900

BR 02 CARBON CHRONO

Movement: mechanical automatic.
Functions: hours, minutes, seconds; date; 2-counter chronograph with 30- and 60-minute totalizers.
Case: Ø 44mm; satin-polished stainless steel or glass-bead-blasted 316L steel finished with black "vacuum carbon"; screw-in pushpieces, crowns and caseback; antireflective sapphire crystal; decompression valve for deep-sea diving; unidirectional, cranted interior bezel graduated to 60 minutes with photoluminescent reference point; antireflective sapphire crystal; water resistant to 500 meters.
Dials: black; numerals, index and hands covered in photo-luminescent coating to optimize nighttime reading.
Strap: rubber or heavy-duty synthetic fabric.
Suggested price: $7,000

BR 02 CHRONO STEEL

Movement: mechanical automatic.
Functions: hours, minutes, seconds; date; 2-counter chronograph with 30- and 60-minute totalizers,
Case: Ø 44mm; satin-polished stainless steel or glass-bead-blasted 316L steel finished with black "vacuum carbon"; screw-in pushpieces, crowns and caseback; antireflective sapphire crystal; decompression valve for deep-sea diving; unidirectional, cranted interior bezel graduated to 60 minutes with photoluminescent reference point; water resistant to 500 meters.
Dial: black; numerals, indexes and hands covered with photoluminescent coating to optimize nighttime reading.
Strap: rubber or heavy-duty synthetic fabric.
Suggested price: $6,500

VINTAGE 126XL EDICION LIMITADA

Movement: mechanical automatic; Côtes de Genève decoration; 40-hour power reserve.
Functions: hours, minutes, seconds; big date for 1 calendar year with indication of day and month; 2-counter chronograph: 30- minute and 60-second.
Case: Ø 42.5mm; polished satin-finished 18K pink gold; antireflective sapphire crystal and flat sapphire caseback; screw-in crown and caseback; water resistant to 200 meters.
Dial: brown with gold-plated counters; gold-plated hands and photo-luminescent index markers to optimize nighttime reading.
Strap: leather.
Suggested price: $19,900
Note: limited edition 99 pieces.

VINTAGE 126 YELLOW-GOLD PEARL

Movement: self-winding ETA 2894; high-quality finish; rhodium-plated or gold movement with Côtes de Genève engraved winding rotor; 28,800 vph; 28 rubies; approx. 42-hour power reserve; pearled plate and bridge; hardened steel screws; high-precision settings.
Functions: hours, minutes, seconds; 2-counter chronograph: 60-second and 30-minutes accumulators; date with rapid date correction. Second hand stops when time is set.
Case: polished 18K yellow gold; curved, antireflective sapphire crystal; sapphire crystal caseback crown and back are screwed in order to ensure perfect water resistance to 200 meters.
Dial: pearl with anti-reflective and anti-UV treatment; hands and indexes coated in luminescent paint to optimize nighttime reading.
Strap: crocodile leather.
Suggested price: $9,600

VINTAGE 123 JUMPING HOUR PLATINUM

Movement: mechanical automatic-winding; quality finishing; 28,800 vph; 40-hour power reserve; 30 jewels; high-precision setting in 5 positions; rhodium-treated, decorated and engraved plates, oscillating weight and bridges; bluish screws.
Functions: hours, minutes; power reserve.
Case: satin-finished 950 platinum; screw-in crown; antireflective sapphire crystal; screw-on, flat caseback in sapphire crystal; water resistant to 100 meters.
Dial: hand-chased 18K gold.
Strap: full-skin alligator.
Suggested price: $30,000
Note: limited edition 99 pieces.

VINTAGE 123 JUMPING HOUR PLATINUM DOUBLE SUBDIAL

Movement: mechanical automatic-winding; quality finishing; 28,800 vph; 40-hour power reserve; 30 jewels; high-precision setting in 5 positions; rhodium-treated, decorated and engraved plates, oscillating weight and bridges; bluish screws.
Functions: hours, minutes; power reserve.
Case: satin-finished 950 platinum; screw-in crown; antireflective sapphire crystal; screw-on, flat caseback in sapphire crystal; water resistant to 100 meters.
Dial: gray; double subdial: hour subdial at top of dial, power-reserve subdial in an arc at bottom of dial.
Strap: full-skin alligator.
Suggested price: $30,000
Note: limited edition 99 pieces.

BERTOLUCCI
Italian Artistry, Swiss Tradition

The figurative marriage of Italian sensibility and Swiss craftsmanship was a natural one for Bertolucci. After all, the seeds of the company were planted in the literal marriage between Remo Bertolucci, born and raised on the Italian Riviera in Tuscany, and his one true love, the daughter and granddaughter of Swiss watchmakers and heir to time-honored tradition.

When Remo Bertolucci moved to Switzerland to join his wife's family at their manufacture, the wheels were set in motion for the creation of what would one day be a major representative of the Mediterranean spirit in the universe of haute horology. The watches produced by today's Bertolucci are judged like diamonds, according to the brand's unique four C's: creativity, curves, comfort and construction.

Curves are the main focus of the Serena garbo collection, which evokes the rounded contours of a pebble being continually washed ashore by the Mediterranean. Also taking as inspiration the voluptuous vigor and sophistication of Latin women, the Serena garbo is available with luxurious touches such as a diamond-set bezel, a mother-of-pearl dial, or a leather strap with saddle stitching. The concepts behind the Serena garbo collection are so versatile that Bertolucci has also created a Serena garbo Gent Chronograph—with all the supreme confidence of the rest of the collection but a masculine personality.

The understated, elegant simplicity of the Serena collection lends itself to complete comfort, appropriate as it is for any occasion. The clean contours and concentric ovals of the dial and bezel suit its self-assured combination of femininity, simplicity and modernity. An icon for the brand, the Serena collection also features a witty visual trick in which the fine leather strap appears to pass through the case.

ABOVE This Serena garbo (Ref. 303.55.41.1B1) is decorated with white mother-of-pearl guilloché dial in a steel case and alternated steel bracelet.

LEFT This classic and chic Serena (Ref. 323.51.41.88. 10M.233) is crafted in a steel case set with 120 diamonds set (1.56 carats) with white opaline and mother-of-pearl dial, fitted on a natural calf strap.

Bertolucci judges its watches by its own unique set of 4 C's: creativity, curves, comfort, and construction.

The newest classic collection from Bertolucci, the Stria is creatively reminiscent of the magic of the Mediterranean. The lightly rippled design of the case, and the dial's slightly off-center position call to mind a perfect seashell found just under the surface of the waves, sunlight dancing across its undulations. The jeweled Stria is adorned with diamonds that highlight the shimmering beauty of the Italian Riviera.

And when Stria merges with the magic of kaleidoscope, Bertolucci has drawn upon the arts of watch-making and jewellery to surprise you with the exclusive creation Stria Luce, the most glamorous jewel of this season…A glittering cover dresses the pure and timeless lines of Stria by the richness of gold and the sparkle of precious stones. Paying tribute to the enchanting colours and lights of Mediterranean coasts, the jeweller cover rotates to give life to the delicate ripples of shell, showing through a firework of precious stones specially hand cut in cabochon. Once again, Bertolucci innovates in stones cutting and setting to explore new avenues in creation and the hand made jewellery work gives birth to the strong inspiration of Stria Luce which will transport prestigious women in the magical universe of the Italian Riviera.

Classic Italian exuberance makes a comeback in Bertolucci's Ouni collection, inspired by sea urchins and bedecked with a fantastic array of colored stones. The profusion of warm colored stones reflects the wealth of colors, motifs and materials to be found in the Mediterranean.

TOP RIGHT Crafted in 18K rose gold, this Stria (Ref. 723.50.67.3.301.R00) features 162 diamonds set (0.70 carat) with white guilloché mother-of-pearl dial fitted on a white satin strap.

BOTTOM LEFT Bearing 331 diamonds (1.47 carats), this stunning Stria Luce (Ref. HJ173.50.67. 88.TACP.301.R01) is fitted in a rose-gold case and 14 precious stones (amethyst, peridot, topaze, citrine), specially cut by hand in a cabochon shape (14.45 carats), on a black satin strap.

BOTTOM RIGHT This Ouni Lady (Ref. HJ113.51. 68.88.SRY.60C.2L8) is highlighted with a yellow-gold case set with 36 diamonds (0.29 carat) and 89 sapphires and spessartites (20.1 carats). Set with a yellow mother-of-pearl dial with purple-varnished calf strap.

SERENA GARBO LADY   REF. 303.51.41.8.1B6.366

Movement: Swiss Watch Quartz, caliber ETA 5½x6¾ 976.001; 3-year battery life.
Functions: hours, minutes; time-setting crown at 3.
Case: stainless steel; Ø 36.5mm, thickness: 9mm; full-cut diamonds in FGH color and VVS clarity; set with 50 diamonds (1.29 carats); curved sapphire crystal with antireflective treatment; caseback screwed on with 4 screws; water resistant to 3atm.
Dial: dark brown shell-guilloché; 12 white, printed Bertolucci Roman numerals; white, printed applied rhodium Bertolucci "B" at 12; polished rhodium leaf-shaped hands, plated with anthracite.
Strap: dark brown calf and alligator leather; stainless steel folding clasp; rose-gold-plated cover for the steel and gold models; fitted and secured by a 4-screw ring (back bezel) allowing interchangeability.

SERENA GARBO LADY   REF. 303.55.47P.88.3B1

Movement: Swiss Watch Quartz, caliber ETA 5½x6¾ 976.001; 3-year battery life.
Functions: hours, minutes; time-setting crown at 3.
Case: stainless steel case and caseback; 18K 5N rose-gold bezel with plated crown; Ø 36.5mm, thickness: 9mm; full-cut diamonds in FGH color and VVS clarity; diamonds set with 180 diamonds (2.02 carats); curved sapphire crystal with antireflective treatment; caseback screwed on with 4 screws; water resistant to 3atm.
Dial: white natural mother-of-pearl shell guilloché; 12 anthracite printed Bertolucci Roman numerals; applied rhodium anthracite Bertolucci "B" printed at 12; polished rose-gold leaf-shaped hands, plated with anthracite.
Bracelet: 18K 5N rose-gold bracelet (central row) bracelet; polished stainless steel lateral rows; folding buckle, rose-gold-plated clasp cover, fitted and secured by a 4-screw ring (back bezel) allowing interchangeability.

SERENA MEDIUM   REF. 313.51.68.8.2BM.233L

Movement: swiss quartz caliber ETA 5½x6¾ 976.001; 3-year battery life.
Functions: hours, minutes; time setting crown at 3.
Case: 18K 3N yellow gold; full cut diamonds in FGH color and VVS clarity; ø 24.50x35mm, thickness: 7mm; set with 76 diamonds (0.67 carat); screw-on caseback with 4-screws; curved sapphire crystal with anti-reflective treatment; water resistance to 3atm.
Dial: white natural mother-of-pearl; 12-black printed Bertolucci Roman figures; index B of Bertolucci gold-plated applied at 12; BERTOLUCCI at 12 and Serena at 6 black-printed; dauphine polished yellow-gold-plated hands.
Strap: natural brown calf leather strap with ivory stitch; 18K 3N yellow-gold double folding clasp; fitted and secured by a 4-screws ring (back bezel) allowing interchangeability.

SERENA   REF. 323.55.41.8.10M

Movement: Swiss Quartz, caliber ETA 8¼ 256.041; 3-year battery life.
Functions: hours; minutes; date; time-setting crown at 3.
Case: stainless steel; 29.1x40mm, thickness: 8.3mm; full-cut diamonds in FGH color, VVS clarity; set with 56 diamonds (0.71 carat); curved sapphire crystal with antireflective treatment; caseback screwed on with 4 screws; water resistant to 3atm.
Dial: white-silvered opaline with white natural mother-of-pearl center; calendar date at 6; 11 indexes (8 sticks+3 double sticks); printed anthracite interior minute track; applied rhodium Bertolucci "B" at 12; printed anthracite SERENA at 6; polished rhodium Dauphine hands.
Bracelet: alternating fine-brushed and polished stainless steel bracelet; folding buckle; fitted and secured by a 4-screw ring (back bezel) allowing interchangeability.

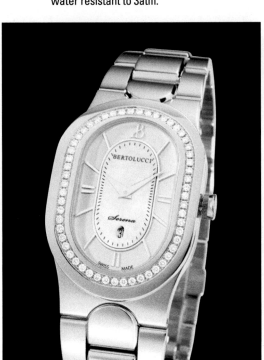

SERENA GARBO GENT CHRONOGRAPH   REF. 393.55.42.10D

Movement: Swiss Chronograph Quartz, caliber ISA 11½ 8162/220; 3-year battery life.
Functions: hours, minutes, seconds; day; date-setting crown at 3; minute and second chronograph; pushbuttons: start/stop at 2, reset at 4. **Case:** stainless steel case and pushbuttons; black PVD bezel, crown and back bezel; Ø 41mm, thickness: 11.5mm; shiny black PVD finishing; curved sapphire crystal with antireflective treatment; caseback screwed on with 4 screws; water resistant to 3atm. **Dial:** black opalin; vertical guilloché with an inner steel

flange; calendar date at 6; sunray guilloché subcounter with silver metallic ring at 6; 2 matte elliptical subcounters at 2:30 and 10:30 with anthracite, silver and blue printings; silver printed BERTOLUCCI at 12; printed anthracite day track on the ring; printed anthracite minute track on the flange; 9 trapezoid luminescent rhodium-plated indexes; polished H. & M. Dauphine skeleton hands, rhodium plated with luminescent SuperLumiNova inlay; S. bâton hand partially painted metallic blue; subcounter arrow-shaped hands at 2:30 and 10:30 painted white and blue; subcounter at 6 with rhodium-plated lozenge hand.
Bracelet: alternating fine-brushed stainless steel and polished black PVD; folding buckle; fitted and secured by a 4-screw ring (back bezel) allowing interchangeability.

STRIA   REF. 723.50.41.8.15D.R01

Movement: Swiss Watch Quartz, caliber ETA 4⅞ E01.701; 3-year battery life.
Functions: hours, minutes; time-setting by a corrector on the caseback.
Case: stainless steel; Ø 39.7mm, thickness 7.8mm; full-cut diamonds in FGH color and VVS clarity; shell pattern set with 274 diamonds (1.26 carats); domed sapphire crystal with antireflective treatment; caseback screwed on with 4-screws; water resistant to 3atm.
Dial: black opaline; hour track in snail décor mixing diamonds and gold printed points; silver printed BERTOLUCCI at 12; snail décor with 10 diamonds (0.03 carat); applied rhodium Bertolucci "B" at 12; rhodium Dauphine hands, polished and fine-brushed.
Strap: black technologic satin strap; stainless steel pin buckle.

VOGLIA   REF. 923.54.41.2.123

Movement: Swiss Quartz, caliber ETA 5 ½ 976.001; 3-year battery life.
Functions: hours, minutes; time-setting crown at 3.
Case: 923 stainless steel; 24x37mm, thickness: 8.2mm; full-cut diamonds in FGH color and VVS clarity; set with 116 diamonds (0.70 carat); curved sapphire crystal, metalized with antireflective treatment; caseback screwed on with 4 screws; water resistant to 3atm.
Dial: black lacquered; silver printed BERTOLUCCI at 12; applied rhodium-plated Bertolucci "B" at 12; rhodium stick applied at 6; polished, skeleton rhodium-plated Dauphine hands.
Bracelet: polished black ceramic bracelet; folding stainless steel buckle.

OUNI LADY   REF. HJ113.51.69.88.BSRSA.608G.009

Movement: Swiss Watch Quartz, caliber ETA 4⅞ E01.701; 3-year battery life.
Functions: hours, minutes; time-setting corrector on the caseback.
Case: 18K white gold; Ø 36mm, thickness: 14.5mm; full-cut pink sapphires, rubies and amethysts; set with 89 red beryls and pink sapphires, orange spessartites and amethysts (21.81 carats); domed sapphire crystal with antireflective treatment; flange set with 36 diamonds (0.29 carat); caseback screwed on with 4 screws; water resistant to 3atm.
Dial: red natural mother-of-pearl; 12-point rhodium-plated indexes; applied rhodium-plated Bertolucci "B" at 12; polished rhodium-plated bâton hands.
Bracelet: red-varnished calf leather; 18K white-gold folding clasp.

BOUCHERON
Creative Timekeeping Through the Ages

Boucheron has always been fantastically ahead of its time. Before there was an Art Nouveau movement, there was Boucheron's founder, Frédéric, creating elaborate haute jewelry and watches with naturalistic details—details that would later become the quintessential symbols of Art Nouveau, details that elevated his work to a fine art. When Frédéric debuted his first timepiece at the 1867 World Fair in Paris, he was already a world-renowned jeweler. That this watch—a chatelaine—won a gold medal at the Fair and was heralded "intriguing and incredible" foreshadowed Boucheron's place in the story of watchmaking.

Christened "the jeweler of time," Boucheron was 28 years old when he opened his first boutique in 1858. Boucheron's 151-year history is a history of firsts. From the beginning, Boucheron collaborated with Switzerland's most prominent horologers, creating timepieces that combined technological mastery with resplendent jewels, crafted in a variety of case shapes—round, square, baguette and rectangular. In 1880, Boucheron launched the inaugural line of watch bracelets, which caught the attention of sophisticated women around the world and gave birth to today's *de rigueur* wristwatch.

As the first jeweler to open a boutique on Paris's Place Vendôme in 1893, Boucheron is credited with creating the cachet of the "most beautiful square in the world." That accomplishment is immortalized in the design of the watches themselves—the hands on a Boucheron timepiece are often depicted as obelisks in honor of the Napoleonic bronze column that is Place Vendôme's defining feature. The Reflet watch, first introduced in 1946, features diamonds inset in the shape of Place Vendôme and the date positioned to reflect Boucheron's placement on the square. It is rumored that Boucheron chose the location because it was the sunniest on the Place, and the bright light would show off his diamonds to their best advantage.

Mysterious glamour defines Boucheron's flagship store on Place Vendôme. The Countess of Castiglione, mistress to Napoleon III and one of the most beautiful and notorious women of her time, kept an apartment at 26 Place Vendôme. When her youth faded, she spent her later years as a recluse and, upon her death in 1893, ceded her residence—and spirit—to Boucheron.

Since 1867, Boucheron's timepieces have married its inimitable *savoir-faire* and sublime artistry in jewelry with the horological expertise of the oldest luxury Swiss watchmakers. Among Boucheron's innovations—the ultra-thin diamond and emerald pendant watch created for the Maharajah of Baroda in 1910.

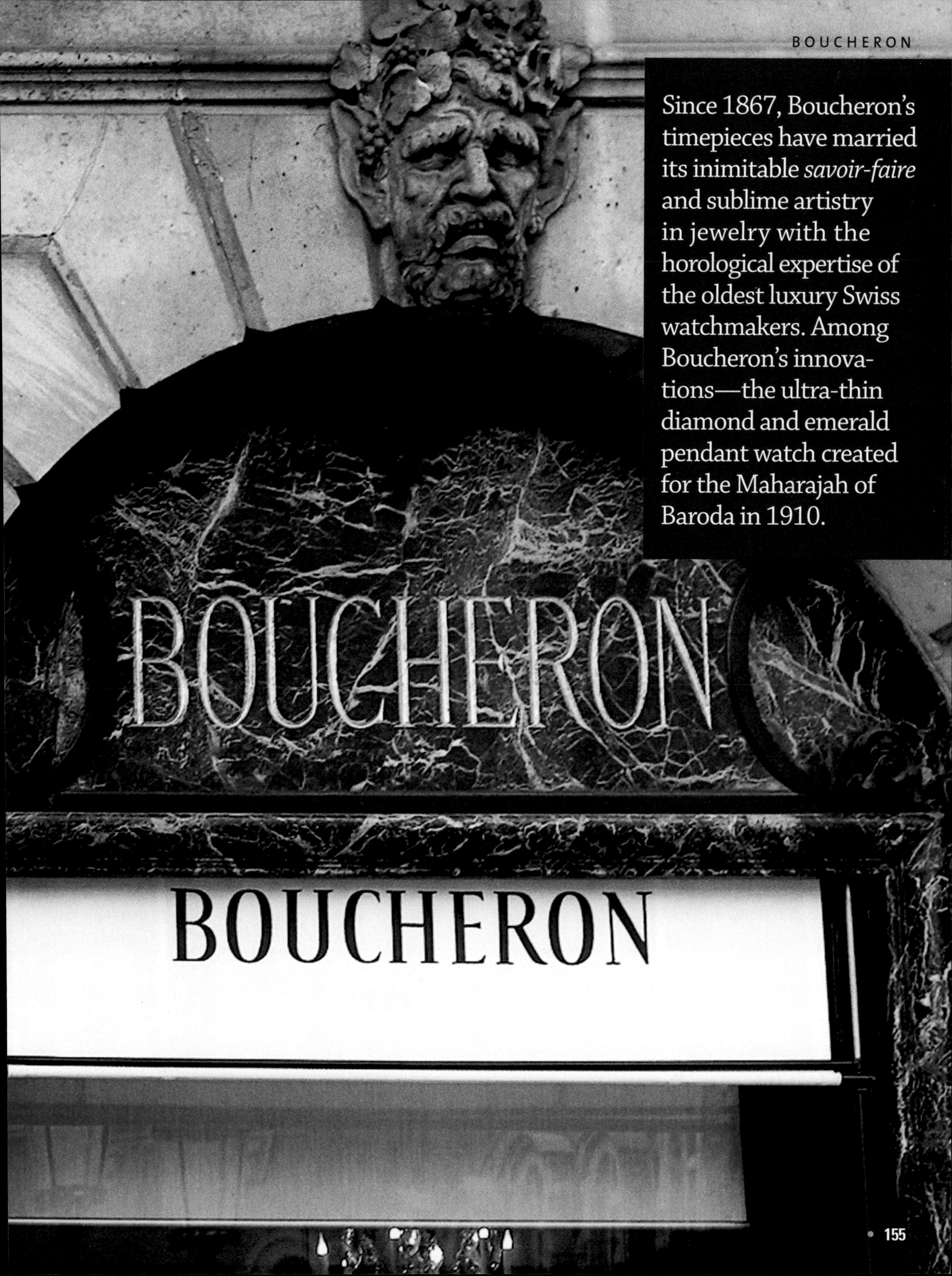

BOUCHERON

BOUCHERON

Louis Boucheron, Frédéric's son, took the reins of the company in 1902. In 1928, India's Maharajah of Patiala arrived at 26 Place Vendôme with six cases full of diamonds, emeralds, rubies and sapphires, requesting that Louis create from them 149 pieces of jewelry fit for a king. The Shah of Iran named Boucheron the Curator and Guardian of Iran's Imperial Treasure in 1930. Luminaries have always counted themselves among Boucheron's devotees—including Sarah Bernhardt, Greta Garbo, Rita Hayworth, Queen Rania of Jordan, Julianne Moore, Penelope Cruz, Michele Yeoh and Nicole Kidman.

Boucheron's latest first underscores the company's progressive, yet storied, reputation—Boucheron is the first French jeweler to offer its haute horology and jewelry for purchase through its own Internet store. Launched in Europe in 2007, Boucheron.com is now open for business in the U.S. as well.

THE TIMELESS REFLET

Relaunched in 1989, the iconic Reflet watch with its interchangeable straps has been updated several times, yet remains essentially the same as its original 1946 design. The 2009 Reflet XL Cruise features an over-sized wooden dial, nautically reminiscent of a Mediterranean yacht. The 2009 Reflet XL Seconde Folle features complications developed by Girard-Perregaux, whose founder, Constant Girard, first collaborated with Frédéric Boucheron to create the 1867 World Fair watch. On these models as well as others in the Reflet line, the Boucheron name is placed vertically on the face, again recalling the famous Place Vendôme obelisk, with Boucheron's address etched, at the crown or at 6:00.

TOP LEFT   Reflet XL Seconde Folle: New in 2009, the second hand of this watch has been replaced by a disc at 7:00. The timepiece features an exclusive complication developed in collaboration with Girard-Perregaux.

TOP RIGHT   A new release for 2009, the limited edition Reflet XL Cruise features the mechanical self-winding GP4000 caliber. It displays hours, minutes, seconds and date. The wooden deck dial is paired with an alligator strap.

BOTTOM LEFT   The sumptuous Reflet XL Jewelry features channel-set diamonds surrounding the dial and marking 12:00 and 6:00.

BOTTOM RIGHT   Reflet Medium: As a signature Boucheron watch that has enjoyed tremendous success for over 60 years, the Reflet is available in a choice of interchangeable straps.

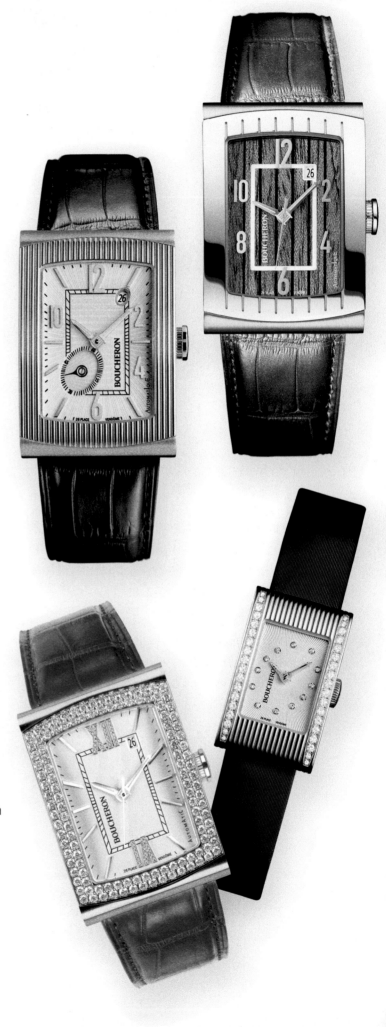

CREATIVE TIMEKEEPING

Audacious and innovative—yet always glamorous Boucheron continues to create some of haute horology's most unique designs. The limited edition bestiary watches, available in white or rose gold or steel, feature cobras, frogs, bats and other mysterious creatures rendered in multi-dimensional detail. On the 2008 Snake Tourbillon, a diamond-set white-gold snake slithers sensually around the diamond-set tourbillon carriage and a cabochon emerald. Echoing the snake theme, bridges are snake-shaped, the strap fashioned from natural python leather. A nocturnal landscape of white gold and diamonds laced with rubies and sapphires is turned upside down as a draped bat's wing sprawls across the face of the 2009 automatic Bat MEC watch. Fancy-colored diamond feathers fan around the hands of time on another bold Boucheron creation—the 2009 Feather MEC. Boucheron's bestiary timepieces dare to accomplish the seemingly impossible, expressing extraordinary ingenuity that sumptuously harkens back to the illustrious watch-maker's original Art Nouveau themes.

TOP LEFT Bat MEC: This amazing 2009 timepiece features blue sapphires, violet sapphires, rubies and diamond, with a midnight blue python bracelet.

TOP CENTER As part of the 2009 multi-gemmed creations, the sizable MEC watches feature an automatic movement. The Feather MEC is comprised of diamonds and blue, violet and yellow sapphires.

TOP RIGHT The Snake Tourbillon is fashioned from diamonds with emeralds highlighting the eyes and dangling from the white-gold case.

BOTTOM RIGHT The RM018 Hommage à Boucheron combines the best of jewelry design with Richard Mille's revolutionary ingenuity.

RICHARD MILLE COLLABORATION

In 2008 Boucheron began its highly acclaimed liaison with Swiss watchmaker Richard Mille. To commemorate the company's recent 150th anniversary, Boucheron launched the Hommage à Boucheron—one-of-a-kind, limited edition, technical marvels embellished with precious and semi-precious stones set in 18-karat white gold. Recent innovations to the Richard Mille line include creating the interior mechanical complications with precious stones—a feat that is another Boucheron first. Thirty of these incredible watches will be produced over the next five years, with each one already pre-ordered.

RONDE AUTOMATIC WATCH   REF.WA010308

Movement: mechanical automatic movement Girard-Perregaux: GP4000.
Functions: hours, minutes, seconds; date at 1.
Case: steel; Ø 39mm, thickness: 8.9mm; steel bezel set like three gadroons; 237 diamonds (total 1.69 carats); fluted crown with "26 Place Vendôme Paris" engraving; polished "Pointe de diamant" pattern on the caseback with 6 screws; sapphire crystal with antireflective treatment on the inner side of the glass; water resistant to 30 meters.
Dial: black gadroons with sunray effect; diamonds set applied indexes; nickel-plated hour and minute hands; vertical BOUCHERON mark at 7; "26 Place Vendôme" printed at 6; special "Automatique" mark between 4 and 5.
Strap: black alligator strap with black alligator lining; steel "Pointe de diamant" pin buckle.
Also available: pink-gold case with silver dial.

CARRÉE AUTOMATIC WATCH   REF.WA011307

Movement: mechanical automatic movement Girard-Perregaux: GP4000.
Functions: hours, minutes, seconds; date at 1.
Case: 18K 5N pink gold; 33.5x42mm, thickness: 8.8mm; pink-gold bezel set like three gadroons with 213 diamonds (total 2.4 carats); fluted crown with 26 "Place Vendôme Paris" engraving; polished "Pointe de diamant" pattern on the caseback with 6 screws; sapphire crystal with antireflective treatment on the inner side of the glass; water resistant to 30 meters.
Dial: silver gadroons with sunray effect; diamonds set applied indexes; 3N gold hour and minute hands; vertical BOUCHERON mark at 7; "26 Place Vendôme" printed at 6; special "Automatique" mark between 4 and 5
Strap: brown alligator strap with brown alligator lining; 18K 5N pink-gold folding buckle with BOUCHERON mark.
Also available: steel case with black dial.

RONDE AUTOMATIC WATCH IN PINK GOLD   REF.WA010304

Movement: mechanical automatic movement Girard-Perregaux: GP4000.
Functions: hours, minutes, seconds; date at 1.
Case: 18K 5N pink gold; Ø 39mm; thickness: 8.9mm; fluted crown with "26 Place Vendôme Paris" engraving; polished "Pointe de diamant" pattern on the caseback with 6 screws; sapphire crystal with antireflective treatment on the inner side of the glass; water resistant to 30 meters.
Dial: silver gadroons with sunray effect; roman numerals indexes; 3N gold-plated hour and minute hands; vertical BOUCHERON mark at 7, "26 Place Vendôme" printed at 6, special "Automatique" mark between 4 and 5..
Strap: black alligator strap with black alligator lining; 18K 5N pink-gold buckle with "Pointe de diamant" pattern.
Also available: steel case with silver dial.

REFLET XL AUTOMATIC WATCH   REF.WA009204

Movement: mechanical automatic movement.
Functions: hours, minutes, seconds; date at 1.
Case: polished 18K 5N pink gold; polished bezel with vertical gadroons; 45x31.5mm, thickness: 9.75mm, fine brushed middle case; fine brushed caseback with polished angles; elliptic sapphire crystal opening, BOUCHERON mark; serial number and BOUCHERON historical stamp engraving; pink-gold-crown 5N with "26 Place Vendôme Paris" engraving; sapphire crystal with antireflective treatment on the inner side of the glass; water resistant to 50 meters.
Dial: stamped silver dial with 4N pink-gold Roman numerals and applied indexes; 4N pink-gold hour and minute hands; vertical BOUCHERON mark at 7; anthracite minute scale; "26 Place Vendôme" printed at 6; special "Automatique" mark between 4 and 5.
Strap: sold with two straps chosen in the assortment.
Also available: steel case with silver dial; steel case with black dial and steel and pink-gold case with silver dial.

REFLET MEDIUM WATCH   REF.WA009405

Movement: quartz movement.
Functions: hours, minutes.
Case: polished 18K 3N yellow gold; vertical gadroons; 34x21mm, thickness: 6.5mm; bezel set with 36 diamonds (total 0.57 carat); caseback with "Pointe de diamant" pattern; specific cartouches with BOUCHERON signature, serial number and BOUCHERON historical stamp; fluted crown with "26 Place Vendôme Paris" engraving; sapphire crystal with antireflective treatment on the inner side of the glass; water resistant to 30 meters.
Dial: silver dial with vertical gadroons pattern; vertically set with 30 diamonds (total 0.13 carat);18K 3N yellow-gold hour and minute hands; vertical BOUCHERON mark at 7.
Strap: sold with two straps chosen in the assortment.
Also available: yellow-gold bracelet.

REFLET SMALL WATCH IN STEEL   REF.WA009502

Movement: quartz movement.
Functions: hours, minutes.
Case: polished stainless steel; vertical gadroons; 29.5x18mm, thickness: 6.4mm; caseback with "Pointe de diamant" pattern; specific cartouches with BOUCHERON signature; serial number and BOUCHERON historical stamp; crown with "26 Place Vendôme Paris" engraving; sapphire crystal with antireflective treatment on the inner side of the glass; water resistant to 30 meters.
Dial: silver dial with vertical gadroons pattern; 4 diamonds indexes (total 0.04 carat); nickel-plated hour and minute hands; vertical BOUCHERON mark at 7.
Strap: sold with two straps chosen in the assortment.
Also available: diamond set case and in medium size; steel bracelet.

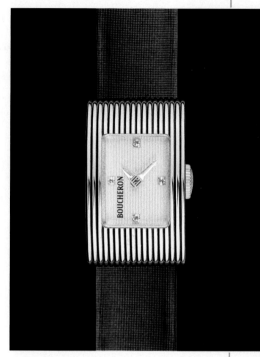

MEC XL AUTOMATIC CHRONOGRAPH   REF.WA006213

Movement: mechanical automatic chronograph movement.
Functions: hours, minutes, seconds; date at 4:30.
Case: steel; 41x45.5mm, thickness: 13.15mm; steel bezel set with 124 diamonds (total: 2.59 carats); sapphire crystal with antireflective treatment on the inner side of the glass; sapphire caseback; screwed-in crown; water resistant to 100 meters.
Dial: silver dial with "Pointe de diamant" pattern set with 68 diamonds (total: 0.32 carat); rhodium-plated applied Arabic numerals and indexes; rhodium-plated hour and minute hands; horizontal BOUCHERON mark at 12.
Strap: sold with a black alligator strap; steel folding buckle set with 41 diamonds (total: 0.23 carat).
Also available: pink-gold case with silver dial.

MEC COBRA WATCH SEMI-PAVED DIAMONDS SNAKE   REF.WA006345

Movement: mechanical automatic movement.
Functions: hours, minutes, seconds.
Case: 18K 5N pink gold; 42x38mm, thickness: 11.05mm; sapphire crystal with antireflective treatment on the inner side of the glass; pink-gold 5N snake set with 88 diamonds (total: 1.04 carats) and one emerald (total: 0.02 carat) sapphire caseback with snake design on the glass; fixing screws for the snake made of pink gold; pink-gold crown; water resistant to 50 meters.
Dial: white mother-of-pearl dial with sunray gadroons; white roman numerals indexes; 5N pink-gold-plated hour and minute hands; vertical BOUCHERON mark at 7; "26 Place Vendôme" printed at 6; Automatic mark between 4 and 5.
Strap: sold with beige python strap; 18K 5N pink-gold folding buckle with BOUCHERON mark.
Also available: steel case with white-gold snake set with diamonds and one emerald; steel case with white-gold snake set with blue sapphires and one ruby.

BOVET
Visionary Artistry

The Château de Môtiers, high above Edouard Bovet's hometown of Fleurier, represents everything that makes BOVET unique in the world of watchmaking.

Steeped in tradition, the château houses a thoroughly modern watchmaking atelier: the Artisan Haute Horlogerie Watchmaking Workshop. Over 10 expert watchmakers work in the atelier, assembling BOVET's timepieces. The château will also house artisans, engravers and miniature painters who turn BOVET's timepieces into small masterpieces. As the artistic center of BOVET, the château's Diesse Tower will house a museum dedicated to BOVET, featuring an exquisite collection of BOVET's archives of 19th-century pocket watches.

"The essential is invisible to the naked eye," says Pascal Raffy, CEO and owner of BOVET. His recognition of the roots of connoisseurship "the discernment that goes far beyond ornamentation to the very heart of a timepiece" has breathed new life into a company that was on its last legs just a few years ago. In less than six years, BOVET has gone from producing

ABOVE Drawing of a tourbillon, one of the many horological complications in BOVET's repertoire.

BELOW Built eight centuries ago, the Château de Môtiers offers a view of the village of Fleurier, where the BOVET story began.

two complications to 20 complicated movements, with every component being worked and reworked until it meets the highest possible standards. The interior of the watch is by no means the only element beloved by aficionados of BOVET—the brand is world-renowned for the miniature paintings it boasts on enamel or mother-of-pearl, its engraved champlevés and Fleurisanne detailing, not to mention the pearls and precious stones with which the pieces are set. BOVET represents a marriage of the highest level between horological skill and the most luxurious expression of the decorative arts on a BOVET watch, any surface is fair game to become a canvas for luminous artistic expression.

In March of 2007, Raffy moved the headquarters of BOVET to the Château de Môtiers, ancestral home of the Bovet clan. The château maintains the highest standards of watchmaking technology, one of which is the insistence that artisans work in a carefully controlled climate, hermetically sealed to keep an optimal temperature and a minimal amount of dust in the air. At the same time, the brand still holds true to its originality and devotion to age-old, irreplaceable skill; this dual emphasis on tradition and modernity means that the guiding force of BOVET continues to be, as Raffy calls it, the "eye for detail that governs good taste."

> BOVET artisans work in a carefully controlled climate, hermetically sealed to keep an optimal temperature and minimal amounts of dust in the air.

TOP LEFT Housed in the Château de Môtiers, BOVET's Artisan Haute Horlogerie Watchmaking Workshop provides a serene setting for creating marvels of craftsmanship.

TOP RIGHT This 18-karat gold enameled "Mille Fleurs" is set with split pearls, was crafted by Bovet Frères circa 1840. The cover is decorated with polychrome champlevé enamel floral and leafy pattern. The movement contains a Chinese duplex escapement, and the piece is a scarce quarter number on the edge of the cuvette.

FLEURIER 39MM RAINBOW DIAL

Movement: quartz movement caliber 10BQ01; 10 lines; 7 rubies; 32,768 vph; 2-year power reserve.
Functions: hours, minutes.
Case: 18K rose-gold Fleurier case; 39mm; bow, bezel and lug set with 108 brilliant-cut diamonds; 1.8 carats in total; antireflective sapphire crystal; crown and strap-bolts; set with cabochon sapphires; water resistant to 30 meters.
Dial: white mother-of-pearl; rainbow colored numerals; Serpentine hands.
Strap: hand-stitched alligator leather; gold ardillon buckle.
Suggested price: $26,200

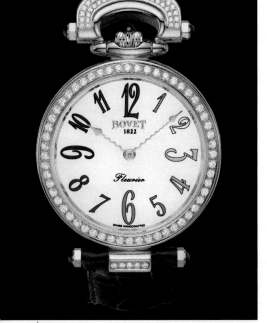

FLEURIER CLASSICAL 42

Movement: self-winding caliber 13BA04; 13¼ lines; 23 rubies; 28,800 vph; 48-hour power reserve.
Functions: hours, minutes, seconds; twin barrels; 22K gold winding rotor with openings in *Fleurisanne* shape; bridges beveled and decorated in *Fleurisanne* style; steel screws with angled edges; polished by hand and blued by fire.
Case: 18K rose-gold Fleurier case; 42mm; anti-reflective sapphire crystal for the curved top glass and flat bottom glass; gold crown at 12 set with sapphire cabochon; water resistant to 30 meters.
Dial: chocolate-brown "sun" lacquered guilloché; rose-gold applied indexes; seconds counter at 6; Serpentine hands.
Strap: hand-stitched alligator leather; gold-folding buckle.
Suggested price: $29,900

FLEURIER 34MM PEARLS DIAMOND 8

Movement: quartz movement caliber 8BQ01; Côtes de Genève surface-finish on bridges; screws angled and blued by fire.
Functions: hours, minutes.
Case: 18K rose-gold Fleurier case; 34mm; bow, bezel and bracelet links set with 492 brilliant-cut diamonds; 4.29 carats in total; antireflective sapphire crystal for the curved top glass and flat bottom glass; caseback fastened by 6 gold screws; gold crown at 12 set with briolette-cut diamond; water resistant to 30 meters.
Dial: hand guilloché white mother-of-pearl; number "8" set with diamonds; 11 brilliant-cut diamonds indexes; Serpentine hands.
Bracelet: 110 pearls; folding buckle in 18K gold.
Suggested price: $60,500
Also available: white gold, black or chocolate-brown pearls and black or chocolate-brown guilloché dial.

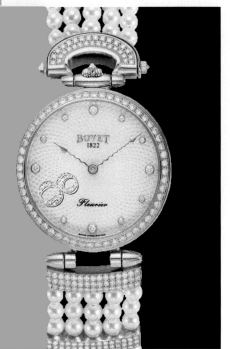

FLEURIER CLASSICAL 42

Movement: self-winding caliber 13BA04; 13¼ lines; 23 rubies; 28,800 vph; 48-hour power reserve.
Functions: hours, minutes, seconds; twin barrels; 22K gold winding rotor with openings in *Fleurisanne* shape; bridges beveled and decorated in *Fleurisanne* style; steel screws with angled edges, polished by hand and blued by fire.
Case: 18K white-gold Fleurier case; 42mm; anti reflective sapphire crystal for the curved top glass and flat bottom glass; gold crown at 12 set with cabochon sapphire; water resistant to 30 meters.
Dial: blued "sun" lacquered guilloché with white-gold applied indexes; seconds counter at 6; Serpentine hands.
Strap: hand-stitched alligator leather; gold folding buckle.
Suggested price: $33,400
Also available: black "sun" lacquered guilloché dial.

FLEURIER JUMPING HOURS *FLEURISANNE*

Movement: self-winding caliber 13BA04; 13¼ lines; 23 rubies; 28,800 vph; 48-hour power reserve.
Functions: jumping hours (blackened disk); minutes indicated by rotating white triangle on the outside ring; twin barrels; 22K gold winding rotor with openings in *Fleurisanne* shape; bridges beveled and decorated in *Fleurisanne* style; steel screws with angled edges, polished by hand and blued by fire.

Case: 18K rose-gold Fleurier case; 42mm; antireflective sapphire crystal for the curved top glass and flat bottom glass; caseback fastened by 6 gold screws; gold crown at 12 and strap-bolts set with cabochon sapphires; water resistant to 30 meters.
Dial: openwork on engraved bridges in *Fleurisanne* style; blackened hour disc with SuperLumiNova numbers; minutes on inner bezel indicated by a SuperLumiNova rotating triangle.
Strap: hand-stitched alligator leather; gold folding buckle.
Suggested price: $45,800
Also available: white gold; non-engraved bridges; blackened bridges.

FLEURIER SELF-WINDING 7-DAY TOURBILLON – LIMITED EDITION

Movement: self-winding caliber 13BA05; 133/4 lines; 47 rubies; 21,600 vph; 7-day (168-hour) power reserve.
Functions: hours, minutes; tourbillon; fully engraved by hand in *Fleurisanne* style; twin barrels; steel tourbillon "lotus flower" cage with 1 revolution per minute; 22K gold winding rotor with openings in *Fleurisanne* shape; bridges angled and hand-engraved in *Fleurisanne* style; steel screws with angled edges, polished by hand and blued by fire.

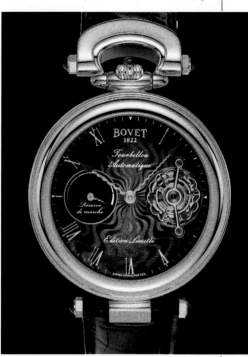

Case: 18K rose-gold Fleurier case; 42mm; antireflective sapphire crystal for the curved top glass and flat bottom glass; caseback fastened by 6 gold screws; gold crown at 12; strap-bolts set with cabochon sapphires; water resistant to 30 meters.
Dial: brown guilloché; applied Roman numerals; power reserve counter in onyx; Serpentine hands.
Strap: hand-stitched alligator leather; gold folding buckle.
Suggested price: $129,100
Also available: green, black, blue guilloché dial; fully hand-engraved *Fleurisanne* dial; jewelry pavé.

FLEURIER PERPETUAL CALENDAR RETROGRADE MOONPHASE

Movement: self-winding Caliber 13BA04; 13 1/4 lignes; 23 rubies; 28,800 vph; 48-hour power reserve; twin barrels; steel tourbillon "lotus flower" cage with 1 revolution per minute; 22K gold winding rotor with openings in *Fleurisanne* shape; bridges beveled and decorated in *Fleurisanne* style; steel screws with angled edges, polished by hand and blued by fire.
Functions: hours, minutes; leap years; day, month, retrograde date; moonphase.

Case: 18K white-gold; Fleurier case; 42mm; antireflective sapphire crystal for the curved top glass and flat bottom glass; caseback fastened by 6 gold screws; gold crown at 12 and strap-bolts set with cabochon sapphires; water resistant to 30 meters.
Dial: blue guilloché with applied Roman numerals; onyx sky; Serpentine hands.
Strap: hand-stitched alligator leather; gold folding buckle.
Suggested price: $66,700
Also available: with black, brown or green guilloché dial; with GMT.

SELF-WINDING 7-DAY TOURBILLON DOUBLE TIME ZONE ORBIS MUNDI – LIMITED EDITION

Movement: self-winding caliber 13BA05; 133/4 lines; 47 rubies; 21,600 vph; 7-day (168-hour) power reserve. **Functions:** local time with hours, minutes, second; time zone with hours: 24 cities synchronized to second time zone; seconds on tourbillon; night/day; twin barrels; steel tourbillon "lotus flower" cage with 1 revolution per minute; 22K gold winding rotor with openings in *Fleurisanne* shape; bridges angled and hand-engraved in *Fleurisanne* style; steel screws with angled edges, polished by hand and blued by fire. **Case:** 18K red-gold Fleurier case; 46mm; antireflective sapphire crystal for the curved top glass and flat bottom glass; caseback fastened by 6 gold screws; gold crown at 12 and strap-bolts set with cabochon sapphires; water resistant to 30 meters. **Dial:** black anthracite guilloché; black lacquered local time-zone and second time-zone counters with applied indexes; Serpentine hands with tips in white SuperLumiNova.

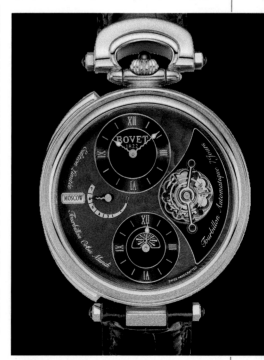

Strap: hand-stitched alligator leather; gold folding buckle.
Suggested price: $166,700
Also available: white gold; limited edition of 39 pieces per precious metal.

SELF-WINDING 7-DAY TOURBILLON WITH JUMPING HOURS – LIMITED EDITION

Movement: self-winding caliber 13BA05; 13¾ lines; 47 rubies; 21,600 vph; 7-day (168-hour) power reserve. **Functions:** jumping hours on blackened disk with SuperLumiNova numbers; minutes on inner bezel black ring indicated by rotating white SuperLumiNova triangle; seconds on tourbillon cage; twin barrels; steel tourbillon "lotus flower" cage with 1 revolution per minute; 22K gold winding rotor with openings in *Fleurisanne* shape; bridges angled and hand-engraved in *Fleurisanne* style; steel screws with angled edges, polished by hand and blued by fire. **Case:** 18K rose-gold Fleurier case; 47mm; anti-reflective sapphire crystal for the curved top glass and flat bottom glass; caseback fastened by 6 gold screws; gold crown at 12 and strap-bolts set with cabochon sapphires; water resistant to 30 meters. **Dial:** openwork on engraved bridges in *Fleurisanne* style. **Strap:** hand-stitched alligator leather; gold folding buckle.
Suggested price: $166,700
Also available: white gold.
Note: limited edition of 50 pieces per precious metal.

MINUTE REPEATER WITH TOURBILLON, TRIPLE TIME ZONE AND AUTOMATE

Movement: hand-wound caliber 13BM02; 13¼ lines; 53 rubies; 18,000 vph; 40-hour power reserve. **Functions:** hours, minutes from central hands; 2 independent time zones, subdials at 3 and 9 with city indications in windows; 24 indexed cities at 3 and 16 at 9; minute repeater: hours, quarters and minutes striking on demand; engraved by hand in *Fleurisanne* style; balance spring with Breguet overcoil; cathedral chiming gongs in steel blued by fire, ratchet wheels with hand-chamfered wolf's teeth; chamfered steel tourbillon cage with 1 revolution per minute; steel screws with angled edges, polished by hand and blued by fire. **Case:** 18K rose-gold Fleurier case; 46mm; antireflective sapphire crystal for the curved top glass and flat bottom glass; caseback fastened by 6 gold screws; gold crown at 12 and strap-bolts set with cabochon sapphires; water resistant to 10 meters. **Dial:** black; hand-made guilloché; applied indexes; time-zone counters in black enamel with guilloché centers; rectangular windows at 3 and 9; aperture at 6 on automaton bells; Serpentine hands. **Strap:** hand-stitched alligator leather; gold-folding buckle.
Suggested price: upon request (2009 collection)
Also available: white gold.

FLEURIER MINUTE REPEATER TOURBILLON WITH REVERSED HAND FITTING

Movement: hand-wound caliber 12BM06; 12¼ lines; 39 rubies; 18,000 vph; 52-hour power reserve.
Functions: hours, minutes from central hands; minute repeater: hours, quarters and minutes striking on demand; blackened and fully engraved by hand in *Fleurisanne* style; balance spring with Breguet overcoil; cathedral chiming gongs in steel blued by fire; ratchet wheels with hand-chamfered wolf's teeth; chamfered steel tourbillon cage with 1 revolution per minute; steel screws with angled edges, polished by hand and blued by fire. **Case:** blackened 18K rose-gold Fleurier case; 44mm; bow in 18K rose gold; blackened bezel with rose-gold applied Roman numerals; lug with 18K rose-gold strap bolts; anti-reflective sapphire crystal for the curved top glass and flat bottom glass; caseback fastened by 6 gold screws; gold crown at 12 set with cabochon sapphire; water resistant to 10 meters. **Dial:** openwork; Serpentine hands. **Strap:** hand-stitched alligator leather; gold-folding buckle.
Suggested price: upon request (2009 collection)
Also available: white gold.

FLEURIER BUTTERFLY TOURBILLON

Movement: hand-wound caliber 12BM05; 12¼ lines; 19 rubies; 21,600 vph; 110-hour power reserve.
Functions: hours, minutes; tourbillon; blackened and engraved by hand in *Fleurisanne* style; butterfly shaped bridges set with 76 baguette-cut diamonds (0.64 carats); chamfered steel tourbillon cage with 1 revolution per minute; steel screws with angled edges, polished by hand and blued by fire. **Case:** blackened 18K rose-gold Fleurier case; 44mm; partly blackened 18K rose-gold bow; 18K rose-gold lug; rose-gold applied Roman numerals; antireflective sapphire crystal for the curved top glass and flat bottom glass; caseback fastened by 6-gold screws; gold crown at 12, set with cabochon sapphire; water resistant to 30 meters. **Dial:** openwork; Serpentine hands. **Strap:** hand-stitched alligator leather; gold folding buckle.
Suggested price: upon request (2009 collection)
Also available: white gold.

SPORTSTER SAGUARO CHRONOGRAPH METEORITE

Movement: self-winding caliber 11BA01; 13¼ lines; 28 rubies; 28,800 vph; COSC-certified chronograph; 42-hour power reserve.
Functions: hours, minutes, seconds; big date; chronograph; finished in Côtes de Genève; 22K gold rotor blued by fire; steel screws with angled edges, polished by hand and blued by fire.
Case: 18K rose-gold Sportster case; 46mm; antireflective sapphire crystal for the curved top glass and flat bottom glass; 18K rose-gold crown, pushers and inner bezel; inner bezel with pulsometer indication; water resistant to 300 meters.
Dial: black iron meteorite with applied rose-gold Art Deco numerals; iron meteorite counters; red SuperLumiNova dots.
Strap: rubber; gold ardillon buckle.
Suggested price: $35, 000 (2009 collection)
Also available: white iron meteorite dial; ivory-color enamel dial.

SPORTSTER SAGUARO CHRONOGRAPH METEORITE

Movement: self-winding caliber 11BA01; 13¼ lines; 28 rubies; 28,800 vph; COSC-chronometer certificate; 42-hour power reserve.
Functions: hours, minutes, seconds; big date; chronograph; finished in Côtes de Genève; steel rotor blued by fire; steel screws with angled edges, polished by hand and blued by fire.
Case: steel Sportster case; 18K rose-gold 46mm; bow, crown and pushers; antireflective sapphire crystal for the curved top glass and flat bottom glass; inner bezel with pulsometer indication; water resistant to 300 meters.
Dial: white-iron meteorite with rose-gold applied Art Deco numerals; iron meteorite counters; black SuperLumiNova dots.
Strap: rubber; gold ardillon buckle.
Suggested price: $17,900 (2009 collection)
Also available: full steel; rose gold.

SPORTSTER SAGUARO CHRONOGRAPH METEORITE

Movement: self-winding caliber 11BA01; 13¼ lines; 28 rubies; 28,800 vph; COSC- certified chronograph; 42-hour power reserve.
Functions: hours, minutes, seconds; big date; chronograph; finished in Côtes de Genève; 22K blackened gold rotor; steel screws with angled edges, polished by hand and blued by fire.
Case: black PVD steel Sportster case; 46mm; 18K rose-gold bow, crown and pushers; antireflective sapphire crystal for the curved top glass and flat bottom glass; inner bezel with pulsometer indication; water resistant to 300 meters.
Dial: rose-gold colored iron meteorite; black applied Art Deco numerals; iron meteorite counters; white SuperLumiNova dots.
Strap: rubber; gold ardillon buckle.
Suggested price: $21,300 (2009 collection)
Also available: black pvd; 18K rose-gold bow, crown and pushers; black iron meteorite dial; carbon dial; black enamel dial.

SPORTSTER SAGUARO CHRONOGRAPH

Movement: self-winding caliber 11BA01; 13¼ lines; 28 rubies; 28,800 vph; COSC-certified chronograph; 42-hour power reserve.
Functions: hours, minutes, seconds; big date; chronograph; finished in Côtes de Genève; 22K blackened gold rotor; steel screws with angled edges, polished by hand and blued by fire.
Case: black PVD steel Sportster case; 46mm; antireflective sapphire crystal for the curved top glass and flat bottom glass; 18K rose-gold crown, pushers and inner bezel; inner bezel with pulsometer indication; water resistant to 300 meters.
Dial: black enamel with rose-gold applied Art Deco numerals; white SuperLumiNova dots.
Strap: rubber; gold ardillon buckle.
Suggested price: $19,600

BVLGARI
Autonomy and Artistry

Driven by a deep need to exert absolute control over its watchmaking process, Bulgari continues to increase its ability to produce everything from complicated movements to sophisticated gem-set dials and cases. Being an independent watch manufacture gives Bulgari the freedom to create innovative timepieces that combine Swiss precision with Italian design.

To celebrate the 20-year anniversary of its Diagono last year, Bulgari updated this line of sports watches with several handcrafted complications. Along with the new mechanical modifications, Bulgari also unveiled redesigned dials, pushbuttons, lugs and more for the Diagono collection. The most prominent change, however, is to the signature engraved double-logo bezel, which now features a new, flat profile along with a 45-degree beveled edge.

Introduced in 2008 to commemorate the anniversary, the Diagono Calibro 303 Chronograph embodies the collection's bold new direction.

Its sophisticated chronograph movement—dubbed BVL 303 after the number of components used to create it—undergoes a very time-consuming production process. The chronograph mechanism employs a column wheel to control its counters, using a vertically mounted pinion to prevent jumping during start-up, stopping and resetting.

Beyond the Diagono Calibro 303's list of impressive technical achievements, Bulgari pays equal attention to its level of visual artistry. The watch's 43mm stainless steel case—comprised of 75 different elements—uses the newly designed bezel in polished white gold to outline the multilevel dial. The watchmaker uses a trio of different finishing techniques to create the dial's rich detail: satiné soleil decoration on the metal base; a vertical treatment on the gray-colored top half; and circular trimmed counters.

Designed to commemorate the Diagono collection's 20-year anniversary, the Calibro 303 Chronograph includes redesigned details like the chronograph pushers, large screws on the lugs and the signature double-logo bezel, which now features a flat profile. The multilevel dial and automatic movement are both decorated by hand.

Bulgari's growing manufacturing capabilities enable the brand to create complicated and jeweled timepieces that demonstrate the brand's mastery of the watchmaking art.

While the Diagono Calibro 303 proudly breaks new ground in the world of sports watches, its innovation does not come at the expense of Bulgari's commitment to traditional Swiss watchmaking.

The roots of Bulgari's storied haute joaillerie watches date back more than 80 years to the age of Art Deco, when the watchmaker's bejeweled, serpent-shaped timepieces were seen slithering around the arms of chic socialites. Through the years, the company unveiled other seductive designs, such as the *Bulgari Bulgari*, Rettangolo and Ergon.

That storied tradition lives on as Bulgari beguiles women with a new generation of eclectic and alluring watch creations enriched with diamonds and precious gems. The Assioma D provides a sparkling example of the brand's remarkable "invisible" gem-setting technique.

A reinterpretation of the circle and square design of Bulgari's Assioma, the Assioma D pays tribute to the beauty and purity of diamonds. In fact, it takes one of Bulgari's master gem setters more than two months to complete work on a single watch. The Assioma D's dial, as well as its white-gold case and bracelet, can be dressed entirely in white diamonds, or in white diamonds with blue sapphire or red ruby accents.

The *Via dei Condotti* collection, unveiled in spring 2008, takes its name from the famed street in Rome where Bulgari's flagship store is located. Three diamond-set models are available, including a gorgeous diamond-shaped timepiece decorated with baguettes or brilliants, and a model that features two bezels (one round, the other crescent-shaped) set with graduated stones.

Powered by its growing manufacturing capabilities and dedication to superior craftsmanship, Bulgari's collections of complicated mechanical and luxurious jewelry timepieces skillfully demonstrate its mastery of the watchmaking art.

ABOVE This *Bulgari Bulgari's* dial was manufactured in house with two curved levels designed with vertical guilloché and satiné soleil treatments.

BELOW LEFT The bezel of this timepiece from the *Via dei Condotti* Collection is adorned with round brilliants that graduate in size as they wrap around the black dial. Positioned opposite the crown, Bulgari adds a crescent-shaped bezel also set with round brilliants.

BELOW RIGHT Part of Bulgari's *Via dei Condotti*, the case of this model is rotated, giving the watch a diamond shape. The white-gold case can be set with baguettes or two rows of round brilliants.

ASSIOMA MUTICOMPLICATION SQUELETTE   REF. AA48PLTBSK

Movement: mechanical automatic-winding BVL 416 caliber; manufactured by Bulgari, with tourbillon device; 64-hour power reserve; 39 jewels; 28,800 vph; 416 components; hand-finished, black-gold burnished, pillar-plate decorated with a circular graining pattern; bridges brushed, day and date disks brushed with a circular pattern; beveled; skeleton rotor in brushed 18K white gold with hand-polished bevels and logo engraved on an applied 18K yellow-gold ring. Functions: hour, minute; 24-hour dual time; perpetual calendar (date, day, month, four-year cycle). **Case:** 950 platinum; bridge-

shaped lugs, flared middle with brand name engraved on the upper faces, back; in curved rectangular shape; total length: 48mm, polished finish; anti-reflective curved sapphire crystal; platinum crown; 4 correctors on the middle; back fastened by 6 screws displays the movement through a sapphire crystal; water resistant to 3atm. **Dial:** four-level stepped, perforated; black-gold-plated crowns brushed with a horizontal pattern; arms with a nickel-palladium covering; black oxidized minute-track ring; pink-gold-plated skeleton bâton hands. **Indications:** month at 3; date and four-year cycle (with red hand) at 6; day of the week at 9; 24-hour dual time at 12. **Strap:** pre-curved rebordé black alligator strap; platinum triple-fold-over clasp; also available on bracelet with triple-fold-over clasp.
Note: limited edition of 20 numbered pieces.

ASSIOMA HEURES RETROGRADE   REF. AA48GLHR

Movement: manufactured in house; mechanical automatic-winding Caliber BVL 261; 45-hour power reserve; 44 jewels; 28,800 vph; consisting of 261 pieces; finished and decorated by hand; black-gold back with perlage treatment; skeletonized rotor with engraved ring; Ø 25.6mm, thickness: 4.78mm.
Functions: 240°-retrograde hours and minutes, small seconds; AM/PM indication.
Case: curved, polished 18K yellow gold; bridge-shaped lugs, flared middle with brand

name engraved on the upper faces, back, in curved rectangular shape, total length: 48mm, polished finish; curved, anti-reflective scratch-resistant sapphire crystal; 18K yellow-gold crown; snap-on back, displaying the movement through a sapphire crystal; water resistant to 3atm.
Dial: manufactured in house; opalin silver central and external decorations; satin-finished anthracite hour/minute area and small second; opalin silver cartouche; hand-applied indexes.
Indications: AM/PM indication and small second at 6.
Strap: pre-curved rebordé brown alligator strap; 18K yellow-gold triple-fold-over buckle.
Also available: in pink or white gold with alligator strap.
Note: limited edition of 99 numbered pieces; limited-edition number engraved on the case side.

ASSIOMA   REF. AA48BGLDCH

Movement: mechanical movement with automatic-winding; 42-hour power reserve; 37 jewels; 28,800 vph (4HZ).
Functions: hour, minute, second; date between 4 and 5; chronograph with 3 counters; small second at 3; hour counter at 6; minute counter at 9.
Case: polished 18K yellow gold; 48mm; curved antireflective scratch-resistant sapphire crystal; water resistant to 3atm.

Dial: black with fine vertical treatment and 3-anthracite; black counters with azuré treatment; hand-applied yellow-gold plated; diamond treated indexes.
Strap: pre-curved; rebordé black alligator strap with 3-blades; 18K yellow-gold folding buckle.
Also available: stainless steel case and bracelet; stainless steel case with black alligator strap.

ASSIOMA PRECIOUS   REF. AAW36D2BL/12

Movement: quartz.
Functions: hours, minutes.
Case: curved, polished 18K white-gold case set with round brilliant-cut diamonds; 36mm; curved, antireflective scratch-resistant sapphire crystal; water resistant to 3atm.
Dial: light blue mother-of-pearl dial with diamonds on indexes.

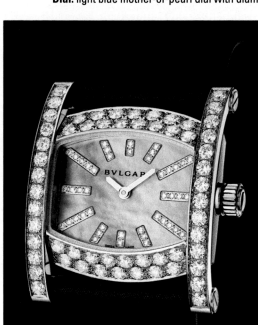

Strap: black technological satin strap; 18K white-gold buckle set with round brilliant-cut diamonds.

BVLGARI-BVLGARI   REF. BB38WGGDAUTO

Movement: mechanical automatic-winding B77 caliber; 42-hour power reserve; 21 jewels; 28,800 vph; decorated with Côtes de Genève and circular-graining patterns; rotor with engraved logo.
Functions: hour, minute, second; date.
Case: 18K yellow-gold case; Ø 38mm; polished finish, brand-name engraved on the bezel; flat, antireflective sapphire crystal; yellow-gold crown; brushed back; water resistant to 3atm.
Dial: silvered; Clous de Paris pattern; grained minute ring; applied gilded indexes; Arabic numerals 6 and 12; gilded hands.
Indications: date at 3.
Bracelet: manufactured in house; polished and brushed yellow gold; invisible triple-fold-over yellow-gold clasp.

BVLGARI-BVLGARI   REF. BB42WGLDCH

Movement: mechanical automatic-winding B130 caliber; 42-hour power reserve; 37 jewels; 28,800 vph; decorated with Côtes de Genève and circular-graining patterns; rotor with engraved logo.
Functions: hour, minute, small seconds; date; chronograph with hour, minute and second.
Case: 18K yellow-gold two-piece case; Ø 42mm; polished finish, brand-name engraved on the bezel; antireflective curved sapphire crystal; brushed back fastened by 6 screws; water resistant to 3atm.
Dial: silvered; Clous de Paris pattern; grained minute ring; subdials decorated with a circular-graining pattern and grained crowns; applied gilded bâton markers, 12 as Arabic numeral; luminescent gilded bâton hands.
Indications: small seconds at 3; date between 4 and 5; hour counter at 6; minute counter at 9; center second; minute track with luminescent dots.
Strap: hand-sewn alligator strap; fold-over yellow-gold clasp with circular buckle with engraved brand name.
Also available: in stainless steel with silvered or black dial and alligator leather strap or bracelet; in pink gold with black or brown dial and alligator leather strap. 199 numbered pieces for each dial color.

BVLGARI-BVLGARI RESERVE DE MARCHE   REF. BBP41BGL

Movement: extra-flat manufactured; manual-winding BVL131; double-barrel 72-hour power reserve; 21 jewels; 21,600 vph; consisting of 131 pieces; decorated by hand with Côtes de Genève; perlage and satiné soleil treatments; Ø 25.6mm, thickness: 2.8mm.
Functions: hours, minutes, seconds; power reserve.
Case: curved, polished 18K pink gold; Ø 41mm; curved, antireflective scratch-resistant sapphire crystal; water resistant to 30 meters.
Dial: manufactured in house; curved with 2 levels; vertical guilloché, satiné soleil and vertical treatment; hand-applied gold-plated indexes; satiné soleil power-reserve area.
Indications: power reserve.
Strap: hand-sewn brown alligator strap; 18K pink-gold triple-fold-over buckle.
Also available: in white gold.

BVLGAR-BVLGARI   REF. BB42BSSDCH

Movement: mechanical automatic-winding B130 caliber; 2894-2 base, modified exclusively for Bulgari with first-quality components; 42-hour power reserve; 37 jewels; 28,800 vph; decorated with Côtes de Genève and circular-graining patterns; rotor with engraved logo.
Functions: hour, minute, small second; date; chronograph with hour, minute and second.
Case: stainless steel case; Ø 42mm; polished finish; antireflective curved sapphire crystal; bezel with engraved brand name; brushed back fastened by 6 screws; water resistant to 3atm.
Dial: black; Clous de Paris pattern; grained minute ring; subdials decorated with circular beads and grained crowns; silver-color prints; applied rhodium-plated bâton markers; luminescent rhodium-plated bâton hands.
Indications: small second at 3; date between 4 and 5; hour counter at 6; minute counter at 9; center second counter; minute track with luminescent dots.
Bracelet: manufactured in house; brushed and polished stainless steel; recessed steel triple-fold-over clasp.
Also available: with silvered dial; on leather strap; in yellow gold with silvered dial on leather strap; in pink gold with black or brown dial on leather strap.

DIAGONO CALIBRO 303   REF. DG42C14SWGSDCH

Movement: manufacture mechanical chronograph with column wheel; automatic-winding BVL 303 caliber; 45-hour power reserve; 37 jewels; 21,600 vph (3HZ).
Functions: hour, minute, small second; date; chronograph with 3 counters; minute counter at 3; small second and date at 6; hour counter at 9.
Case: 42mm steel case with transparent back; antireflective scratch-resistant sapphire crystal; 18K white-gold bezel; water resistant to 10atm (100 meters).
Dial: manufactured dial with three level, satiné soleil; vertical treatments; hand-applied faceted indexes; azuré counters and luminescent 18K pink-gold plated hands.
Strap: in-house manufactured steel bracelet.

DIAGONO PHASES DE LUNE   REF. DGP42BGLDMP

Movement: automatic-winding BVL 347 caliber in-house manufacture; 44-hour power reserve; 46 jewels; 28,800 vph (4HZ).
Functions: hour, minute, small second, day and date retrograde (150°) with exclusive moon phase indication (European Patent Pending); window with raising or descending arrow and bidirectional hand at 6.
Case: 42mm 18K pink-gold case with transparent back; antireflective scratch-resistant sapphire crystal; water resistant to 5atm.
Dial: black oxydized manufactured in-house; four-layer dial with radial and azuré treatments; hand-applied counter with satiné circulaire treatment; diamond edges and faceted indexes; skeleton pink-gold plated hands.
Strap: brown alligator strap with 18K pink-gold two-blade folding buckle.
Note: limited edition of 350 pieces engraved on the case side.

DIAGONO   REF: DG42C6SVDCH

Movement: chronograph with mechanical movement and automatic-winding B130 caliber; 42-hour power reserve; 37 jewels; 28,800 vph (4HZ).
Functions: hour, minute, second; date between 4 and 5; chronograph with 3 counters; small second at 3; hour counter at 6; minute counter at 9.
Case: 42mm stainless steel and rubber case; antireflective scratch-resistant sapphire crystal; satin finished caseback; water resistant to 10atm.
Dial: silver dial with embossed treatment; raised indexes; azuré chronograph counter- and luminescent skeleton rhodium-plated hands.
Strap: vulcanized black rubber strap with steel links and ardillon buckle.
Also available: black dial.

DIAGONO PROFESSIONAL   REF: DP42C14GVDGMT

Movement: mechanical movement with automatic-winding B151 caliber; 42-hour power reserve; 21 jewels; 28,800 vph (4HZ); COSC-certified chronometer.
Functions: hour, minute, second; date at 6; simultaneous display of 3 time zones; central home time hand.
Case: 42mm 18K yellow-gold case; satin finished caseback; bidirectional-rotating bezel with 24-hour scale; antireflective scratch-resistant sapphire crystal; water resistant to 10atm.
Dial: Ardoise dial with planisphere pattern; hand-applied and luminescent faceted 18K yellow-gold plated indexes; and luminescent 18K yellow-gold plated hands; red date hand at 6 and central red home time hand.
Strap: vulcanized black rubber strap with 18K yellow-gold links and ardillon buckle.
Also available: stainless steel; steel bracelet.

PARENTESI
REF: PAW35WD2DL

Movement: quartz.
Functions: hours, minutes.
Case: curved and polished 18K white gold; 35mm; set with round brilliant cut diamonds; 18K white-gold crown set with one rose cut diamond; scratch-resistant sapphire crystal; water resistant to 3atm.
Dial: white.
Strap: black technological satin strap with 18K white-gold ardillon buckle set with round brilliant cut diamonds.
Also available: 18K yellow gold.

ASSIOMA D
REF. AAP31BGD1G

Movement: quartz.
Functions: hours, minutes.
Case: polished, curved 18K pink gold; 31mm; set with round brilliant-cut diamonds; curved scratch-resistant sapphire crystal with antireflective effect.
Dial: black dial with gold-plated numerals 12 and 6; gold-plated hands.
Bracelet: 18K pink-gold bracelet with double treatment, completely polished internal and satin-finished external links.
Also available: 26mm (small model).

ASTRALE
REF. AE36D2CBL

Movement: quartz.
Functions: hours, minutes.
Case: polished 18K yellow gold; set with diamonds and colored gemstones; 36mm; scratch-resistant sapphire crystal.
Dial: black dial.
Strap: black technological satin strap; 18K yellow-gold triple-fold-over buckle.
Also available: white gold.

ASSIOMA D STEEL AND DIAMONDS
REF: AA35C6SDS

Movement: quartz.
Functions: hours, minutes
Case: curved stainless steel; 35mm; set with round brilliant-cut diamonds; curved scratch-resistant sapphire crystal with antireflective effect; water resistant to 3atm.
Dial: argenté; "clou de Paris" treatment; raised indexes and numerals.
Bracelet: stainless steel bracelet; double treatment satin finished and polished.
Also available: Argenté dial without diamonds; black dial with or without diamonds in size 26.

CARL F. BUCHERER
Innovative Independence

Completely independent, Carl F. Bucherer is a rarity among luxury watch manufactures. By catering only to its own desires—and those of its clientele—Carl F. Bucherer enjoys the freedom to create exquisite high-end timepieces that embody its followers' ideal of authenticity: practical functionality and mechanical complications nestled within striking designs.

Carl Friedrich Bucherer established his jewelry and watch shop in Lucerne, Switzerland in 1888. By 1919, this spirited entrepreneur was armed with a profound knowledge of watchmaking and, equally important, an acute appreciation of his clientele's demands and desires in a well-crafted timepiece. Bucherer's instincts served him well that year when he unveiled his first proprietary collection of expressive, high-quality Swiss watches.

Presently, third-generation watchmaker/horologist Jörg G. Bucherer manages the brand named for his grandfather with the same values of innovation and impeccable technique that Carl Friedrich adhered to ninety years ago—while keeping the brand fresh and relevant in today's global marketplace. Selective distribution in key international markets is critical to maintaining Carl F. Bucherer's elite status among the luxury sector. Trusted trading partners in Germany, Hong Kong, Japan, North America, and Taiwan were chosen very carefully as support affiliates to the brand's Swiss headquarters and production facility in Lengnau, near Biel; each is an independent establishment within the parent Bucherer Montres S.A., entrusted with choosing points of sale within its market that meet Carl F. Bucherer's high standards of service and quality products. Markets not represented by an affiliate are serviced by highly qualified agencies selected by Carl F. Bucherer.

In house, Jörg G. Bucherer and CEO Thomas Morf lead a team of 85 employees intent on maintaining individualism, independence and—since 2008—its status as a movement manufacture.

Carl Friedrich's spirit of expressive, high-quality watchmaking is very much alive in the brand's GMT Patravi collection. Boasting "the most complex watchcase in the world" that is constructed with more than 70 components, the TravelTec FourX combines titanium, palladium, ceramic and caoutchou—a vulcanized, naturally grown rubber favored for its powerful grip and flexibility.

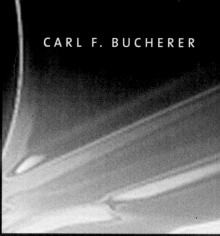

Jörg G. Bucherer manages the brand with the same values of innovation and impeccable technique to which his grandfather adhered while keeping the brand fresh in today's global marketplace.

After a decade of rewarding cooperation with the esteemed Techniques Horlogères Appliquées SA from Ste Croix in the Jura region, Carl F. Bucherer acquired the renowned movement producer and fully integrated its operations into the Bucherer Montres S.A. family.

The first movement designed and built entirely in-house by Carl F. Bucherer Technologies S.A., giving the brand its official claim to "manufacture," is the automatic CFB A1000 caliber. Because Carl F. Bucherer Technologies S.A. serves as the brand's think tank, research and development department, as well as production facility, CFB A1000 benefited from each division's expertise and the combined result is truly original.

The movement's patent-pending peripheral winding rotor revolves around its edge, the most unusual type of rotor arrangement. The brand redesigned this arrangement, adding the efficient Dynamic Shock Absorption (DSA) system, bidirectional winding, and the Central Dual Adjusting System (CDAS).

The DSA system employs DLC-coated rollers (Diamond-Like Carbon for vastly improved strength and reliability) and ceramic ball bearings, which make the system virtually maintenance free. The roller and ball bearing units are mounted on rocking bars that are positioned by springs, and the transmission wheel that transfers kinetic energy to the winding mechanism is further reinforced with two Incabloc shock absorbers to prevent the axis from snapping under extreme impact.

CFB A1000 is capable of receiving energy when the rotor is turned in either direction and the rotor's movements are polarized by a low-loss winding system. The rotor's clutch wheels require no lubrication and are maintenance free.

The movement's Glucydur balance and flat "Etastable" spring pair up with the Swiss club-tooth lever escapement to create another patented innovation: Central Dual Adjusting System. An intelligent precision adjustment system with central control that requires a special key to access, the balance and escapement require just one adjustment and then the system is secured into position to protect it from shocks. CDAS's balance and stem are mounted on bearings by two Incabloc shock-absorber systems.

Currently offering hour, minute and small seconds, this 30mm caliber is packed with high-tech features that give it a solid foundation upon which subsequent functions can be added, including date, day and power-reserve indicators.

TOP LEFT The 44.6mm Patravi Brown Wave Chrono-Grade (left) features a unique combination of flyback chronograph, large date, annual calendar, power-reserve indication and retrograde hour totalizator. The COSC-certified, unisex T-Graph (right) is powered by the brand's exclusive CFB 1960.1 caliber and is also available in stainless steel.

TOP RIGHT Carl F. Bucherer creates equally intriguing timepieces for women. The 38x26.5mm, 18-karat white-gold Alacria Royal is available in three regal versions, each lavished with 606 diamonds and 304 sapphires or rubies. The Alacria Royal is limited to just 25 pieces of each adaptation.

BELOW CFB A1000 caliber is designed and decorated exquisitely. The multilevel bridges and bars are finished with alternating matte and brushed surfaces and diamond-cut facets.

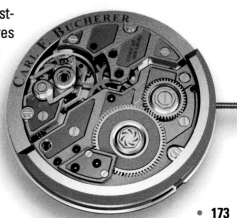

PATRAVI TRAVELTEC FOURX   REF. 00.10620.21.93.01

Movement: automatic CFB 1901.1 caliber chronometer; Ø 28.6mm, height: 7.3mm; 39 jewels; 42-hour power reserve.
Functions: chronograph; date; three time zones.
Case: palladium 950; Ø 46.6mm, height: 15.5mm; ceramic bezel; skeleton dial; rubber screw-down crown and pusher; titanium mono-pusher; sapphire crystal with antireflective coating on both sides; water resistant to 50 meters.
Strap: rubber strap with titanium buckle.
Suggested price: $52,900
Also available: 18K rose-gold and in stainless steel; with various dial combinations.

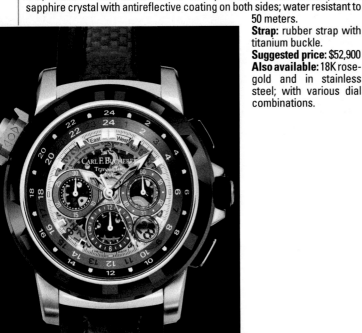

PATRAVI T-GRAPH   REF. 00.10615.03.93.01

Movement: automatic CFB 1960.1 caliber chronometer; Ø 30mm, height: 7.3mm; 47 jewels; 42-hour power reserve.
Functions: big date; chronograph; power-reserve indicator.
Case: 18K rose gold; 39x42mm, height: 13.8mm; screw-down crown; sapphire crystal with antireflective coating on both sides; water resistant to 50 meters.

Dial: brown with super-imposed indexes; luminescent plated hands and indexes.
Strap: brown Louisiana alligator leather; 18K rose-gold folding clasp.
Suggested price: $25,900
Also available: 18K rose-gold bracelet and in stainless steel; with various dial combinations.

PATRAVI TRAVELGRAPH   REF. 00.10618.08.53.01

Movement: automatic CFB 1901 caliber; Ø 28.6mm, height: 7.3mm; 39 jewels; 42-hour power reserve.
Functions: GMT chronograph; second time zone; date indication.
Case: Ø 42mm; screw-down crown; sapphire crystal with antireflective coating on both sides; water resistant to 50 meters.
Dial: blue with superimposed indexes; luminescent plated hands and indexes.
Strap: calf leather with folding clasp.
Suggested price: $6,900
Also available: stainless steel bracelet; rubber strap; with various dial combinations.

PATRAVI CHRONODATE   REF. 00.10619.03.33.01

Movement: automatic CFB 1957.1 caliber chronometer; Ø 30mm, height: 7.3mm; 49 jewels; 42-hour power reserve.
Functions: chronograph; big date indication; annual calendar.
Case: 18K rose gold; Ø 42mm; screwed crown; sapphire crystal with antireflective coating on both sides; water resistant to 50 meters.
Strap: handsawn Louisiana alligator leather strap; 18K rose-gold folding clasp.
Suggested price: $24,500
Also available: 18K rose-gold bracelet.

PATRAVI CHRONOGRADE — REF. 00.10623.08.63.21

Movement: automatic CFB 1902 caliber; Ø 30mm, height: 7.3mm; 51 jewels; 42-hour power reserve.
Functions: chronograph; flyback; retrograde indicator; big date indication; annual calendar; bidirectional power-reserve display.
Case: stainless steel; 44.6x14.1mm; screw-down crown; sapphire crystal with antireflective coating on both sides; water resistant to 50 meters.
Bracelet: stainless steel.
Suggested price: $13,600
Also available: calfskin strap with stainless steel folding clasp; 18K rose gold.

PATRAVI T-24 — REF. 00.10612.08.74.21

Movement: automatic CFB 1953 caliber; Ø 25.6mm, thickness: 5.1mm; 28 jewels; 42-hour power reserve.
Functions: second time zone; date indication; power-reserve display.
Case: stainless steel, 41.2x36mm, thickness: 11.1mm; screw-down crown; sapphire crystal with antireflective coating on both sides; water resistant to 50 meters.
Dial: mother-of-pearl.
Bracelet: stainless steel.
Suggested price: $7,700
Also available: alligator leather strap; 18K rose gold on alligator or stingray strap; with or without diamond bezel and various dial color combinations.

MANERO PERPETUAL — REF. 00.10902.03.16.01

Movement: automatic CFB 1955.1 caliber chronometer; 25.6mm, height: 5.2mm; 21 jewels; 42-hour power reserve.
Functions: perpetual calendar; date, day of the week, month indication; leap year; moonphase.
Case: 18K rose gold; Ø 40mm, thickness: 11.5mm; sapphire crystal with anti-reflective coating on both sides; water resistant to 30 meters.
Strap: alligator leather strap with 18K rose-gold pin buckle.
Suggest price: $33,000
Also available: 18K rose-gold bracelet with or without diamond bezel.

MANERO MONOGRAPH — REF. 00.10904.03.97.11

Movement: manual-wound CFB 1962 caliber; Ø 24.6mm, height: 4.2mm; 21 jewels; 42-hour power reserve.
Functions: chronograph with single pushbutton; 30-minute counters.
Case: 18K rose gold; Ø 35mm, height: 10.5mm; set with 50 diamonds FC TW 1.05 carat; domed sapphire crystal with antireflective coating on both sides; water resistant to 30 meters.
Dial: set with 62 diamonds FC TW 0.2 carat.
Strap: water snake/lizard skin strap with 18K rose-gold pin buckle.
Suggested price: $49,500
Also available: 18K rose-gold bracelet; stainless steel; with or without diamond bezel and various dial combinations.

CARTIER
Prince of the Watchmakers

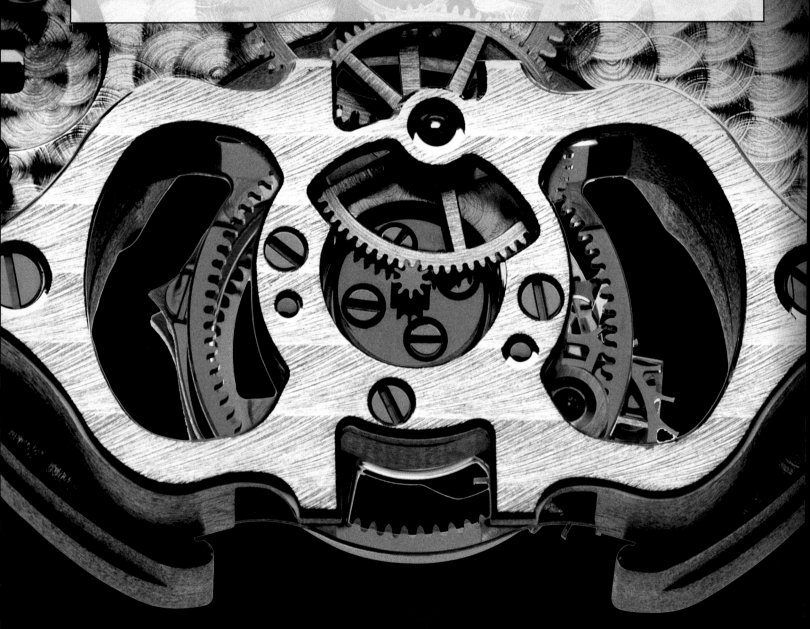

Cartier continuously affirms itself as a major watchmaking brand by employing extremely talented craftsmen to produce world-class timepieces. Thanks to these artisans, Cartier designs extraordinary watches combining magic and beauty with unparalleled creativity such as the Ballon Bleu Tourbillon Volant model.

n 1902, England's Edward VII proclaimed Cartier "jeweler of kings, king of jewelers." In 2008, Bernard Fornas, CEO of Cartier International, added "prince of watchmakers" to Cartier's list of monikers. Indeed, this very bold statement is validated by the brand's custom of releasing breathtaking innovations. The development of these creations takes place in Meyrin, a suburb of Geneva, where Cartier has an exclusive group devoted to luxury watchmaking and other intricate pieces. Ten people collaborated to produce luxury movements under the unique Poinçon de Genève. This label is applied only to flawless pieces of perfection.

The Ballon Bleu Tourbillon Volant represents the powerful rise of Cartier in the precision watch industry.

It is an understatement to say that the Ballon Bleu model revolutionized the Cartier catalogue. Presented in the shape of a river rock, the crown of this watch is decorated with a sapphire cabochon on its side. In 2007, this new model marked the advent of a new era in the watch-making history of Cartier.

One year later, the brand has already developed an intricate new version, called the Ballon Bleu Tourbillon Volant. Equipped with the flying tourbillon at 6:00 and the stamp of the prestigious Poinçon de Genève, it has a promising future with collectors fond of the precision watch industry. The handcrafted gauge is composed of 142 parts and offers the highest quality. This watch has a perfect appearance, thanks to the flawlessly finished bars, angles, polish, gloss, and the Côtes de Genève decoration. This attention to detail is also found in the racket of the flying tourbillon. Sculpted as a "C" for Cartier, the tourbillon indicates the seconds as it completes one revolution per minute. The movement is wound manually and indicates the date, hour, minutes and seconds. The frame around the dial is a brushed, slate-gray color and is seated in a 46mm pink-gold case with a sapphire bottom. In addition to its attention to this extravagant model, the brand also offers a smaller version of the original model on a leather strap. This version has a Ø 42mm case and displays the hours, minutes, seconds and date.

THREE FACES

The Santos Triple 100 comes with three different dial options: a conventional dial, a checkerboard pattern of white diamonds and black sapphires, or an encrusted head of a tiger requiring 40 hours of workmanship. This masterpiece of technology developed in house required a new patent application. Thanks to a system of micro wheels, it actuates the mobile prisms in 18-karat gray gold making it possible to display the various faces. Equipped with two reservoirs offering 72 hours of power reserve, the entire skeleton is visible through the gray-gold case completely encrusted with white diamonds and a bottom sapphire. This prestigious masterpiece combines the dual universes of Cartier: the watch industry and the jewelry industry. Only 20 of the Santos Triple 100 watches were produced and their gems weigh a total of 7.6 carats.

THIS PAGE   Thanks to an exclusive mechanism developed in house, the Santos 100 Triple has interchanging dials that can display the choice of a traditional dial, a checkerboard pattern of black sapphires and white diamonds, or a gem-set head of a tiger.

FACING PAGE
TOP LEFT   The Cirque Animalier De Cartier collection's acrobatic elephant balances on a pink-gold circus ball.

TOP RIGHT   The Cirque Animalier De Cartier collection's panda is made with black sapphires, white diamonds and emerald eyes.

BOTTOM   The Montre Froissée of the Cartier Libre collection opens on the side like fanned rays of light.

WATCHES IN THE CIRCUS RING

The panda, elephant and tiger—these three animals are the stars of the Cirque Animalier De Cartier collection. With true creative insight, the brand has carved each animal and paved it with precious gemstones: the panda is designed with black sapphires, diamonds and emeralds; the tiger comes alive via yellow diamonds, onyx and emeralds; and the elephant, balanced on a pink-gold ball with stars, is covered entirely in diamonds.

DIVERSE

Reserved for women, the Cartier Libre collection keeps its promise with diverse models that are each uniquely elegant. The Montre Perles de Cartier has four circles with an off-center dial and displays only the hours and minutes. The principal dial is decorated with two large pearls, one in its center and the other slightly off to the side. The La Montre Nœud displays a square knot modeled after the Japanese obis, the traditional belt of the kimonos. With a horizontal display, its case is covered entirely with white diamonds. As for the Montre Froissée, it symbolizes folds of fabric, its case displaying rays composed of diamonds. Montre Froissée has a triangular dial with only the "3" as a Roman numeral.

TANK AMERICAINE FLYING TOURBILLON WG   REF. W2620007

Movement: mechanical manual-winding 9452 MC Cartier workshop-crafted caliber with the Geneva Hallmark; flying tourbillon with seconds indicated by the C-shaped index assembly.
Functions: hours, minutes, seconds.
Case: 18K white gold; octagonal crown set with a faceted sapphire; sapphire caseback; water resistant to 3atm.

Dial: slate-colored galvanic dial with guilloché finish; sun satin-finished grid with black Roman numerals; sword-shaped blued steel hands.
Strap: alligator leather strap.
Also available: in 18K rose gold.

SANTOS 100 SKELETON   REF. W2020018

Movement: mechanical manual-winding caliber 9611 MC Cartier workshop-crafted with skeleton bridges shaped as Roman numerals.
Functions: hours, minutes.
Case: palladium; palladium octagonal crown set with a faceted sapphire.
Dial: skeleton bridges of the movement are shaped as Roman numerals; sword-shaped blued steel hands.

Strap: alligator leather strap.

BALLON BLEU DE CARTIER CHRONOGRAPH YG   REF. W6920008

Movement: mechanical automatic-winding caliber 8101 MC Cartier workshop-crafted chronograph movement.
Functions: hours, minutes, seconds; date; 2 chronograph counters.
Case: 18K yellow gold; 44mm; 18K yellow-gold fluted crown set with a blue cabochon sapphire; water resistant to 3atm.
Dial: silvered opaline dial; guilloché and lacquered; 12 black Roman numerals;

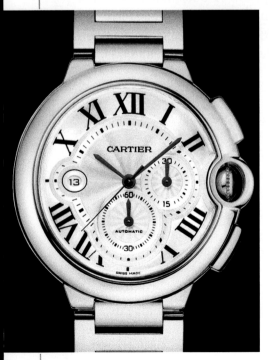

calendar with aperture at 9; sword-shaped blued steel hands.
Bracelet: 18K yellow-gold bracelet; triple deployant clasp.
Also available: in 18K rose or white gold; on leather strap; with diamonds.

PASHA DE CARTIER 42MM CHRONOGRAPH STEEL   REF. W3108555

Movement: mechanical workshop-crafted automatic-winding 8100 MC Cartier workshop-crafted caliber.
Functions: hours, minutes, seconds; 3-counter chronograph; date.
Case: stainless steel; Ø 42mm; stainless steel crown protected by a screw-on crown cover set with a spinel and with a safety fastener; stainless steel pushers; flat sapphire crystal; caseback fastened by 8 screws, displaying

the movement through a sapphire crystal; water resistant to 3atm.
Dial: grained opaline silvered; central square guilloché soleil; hollowed subdials; black printed markers and numeral 12; printed minute track; blued steel lozenge hands.
Strap: semi-matte alligator leather strap; stainless steel adjustable deployant buckle.
Suggested price: $11,300
Also available: in 18K rose or yellow gold; on strap or bracelet.

TANK AMERICAINE XL RG — REF. W2609856

Movement: mechanical automatic-winding 191 MC extra-thin workshop-crafted caliber (GP 3100 base); 27 jewels; 28,800 vph; 50-hour power reserve; Cartier's double interlaced C decoration.
Functions: hours, minutes, seconds; date.
Case: 18K pink gold; curved rectangle shape; 52x31.4mm, thickness: 12.5mm; polished and brushed finish; curved sapphire glass; open back with a sapphire crystal; 18K pink-gold octagonal crown set with a faceted sapphire; water resistant to 3atm.
Dial: silvered opaline; guilloché; Roman numerals and minute track; sword-shaped blued steel hands.
Strap: semi-matte alligator leather strap; 18K pink-gold adjustable deployant buckle.
Suggested price: $16,750
Also available: in small or large size; 18K yellow or white gold.

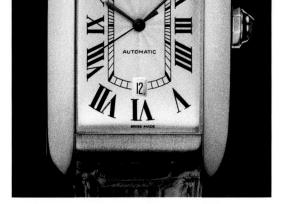

BALLON BLEU DE CARTIER LM RG — REF. W6900651

Movement: automatic-winding Cartier caliber 049.
Functions: hours, minutes, seconds; date.
Case: 18K rose gold; 42mm; 18K rose-gold fluted crown set with a blue cabochon sapphire; water resistant to 3atm.
Dial: silvered opaline dial; guilloché and lacquered; 12 black Roman numerals; calendar with aperture at 3; sword-shaped blued steel hands.
Strap: alligator leather strap; rose-gold fold-over through clasp.
Suggested price: $17,300
Also available: in small or medium size; with or without brilliants; on metal bracelet.

PASHA SEATIMER CHRONOGRAPH RG — REF. W301980M

Movement: automatic-winding Cartier caliber 8630; 27 jewels; 28,800 vph, 42-hour power reserve; 247 parts.
Functions: hours, minutes, seconds; date; 3-counter chronograph; rotating 18K rose-gold diving bezel.
Case: 18K rose gold; Ø 42.5mm; black ceramic clou de Paris-motif ring; 18K rose-gold screw-down crown and chronograph pushpieces decorated with a clou de Paris motif and shaped black ceramic; scratch-proof sapphire crystal; water resistant to 10atm.
Dial: varnished matte black dial; luminescent and rhodiumized hands; four white Arabic numerals, luminescent 12.
Bracelet: 18K pink-gold H-shaped links and black rubber central links; 18K pink-gold triple-safety deployant clasp.
Suggested price: $41,400
Also available: with diamonds; in 18K yellow gold.

ROADSTER CHRONO YG — REF. W62021Y2

Movement: automatic-winding Cartier 8510 caliber; 37 jewels; 28,800vph; 42-hour power reserve.
Functions: hours, minutes, seconds; date; 3 chronograph counters.
Case: 18K yellow gold; water resistant to 3atm.
Dial: white rhodium dial with sunray effect; silvered opaline flange; black minute-circle; luminescent coating; Roman numerals; black oxidized steel hand with luminescent coating.
Bracelet: 18K yellow-gold bracelet.
Suggested price: $34,450
Also available: in stainless steel or steel and gold; on alligator leather strap and 18K yellow gold adjustable deployant buckle.

BALLON BLEU DE CARTIER LM STEEL   REF. W69012Z4

Movement: automatic-winding Cartier caliber 049.
Functions: hours, minutes, seconds; date.
Case: stainless steel; 42mm; stainless steel fluted crown set with a synthetic spinel cabochon; sapphire crystal; water resistant to 3atm.
Dial: silvered opaline dial; guilloché and lacquered; 12 black Roman numerals; calendar with aperture at 3; sword-shaped blued steel hands.

Bracelet: stainless steel bracelet; triple deployant clasp.
Also available: in stainless steel and 18K gold; in 18K rose, white or yellow gold; in small or medium size; with or without brilliants.

SANTOS 100 LM RG/ADLC   REF. W2020009

Movement: automatic-winding Cartier caliber 049.
Functions: hours, minutes, seconds.
Case: ADLC coated steel case; 18K rose-gold bezel; ADLC coated steel crews; 51x38mm; 18K rose-gold octagonal crown set with a faceted spinel; sapphire crystal; water resistant to 10atm.
Dial: 12 Roman numerals; sword-shaped metal hands with luminescent coating.
Strap: black fabric strap.
Also available: In ADLC coated stainless steel case with stainless steel bezel.

NEW BAIGNOIRE LM WG   REF. WB520009

Movement: mechanical manual-winding 430 MC workshop-crafted caliber.
Functions: hours, minutes.
Case: 18K white gold; set with round-cut diamonds; 18K white-gold octagonal crown set with a diamond; water resistant to 3atm.
Dial: silvered opaline dial; guilloché and lacquered; 12 black Roman numerals; sword-shaped blued steel hands.
Strap: dark gray toile brossée strap.
Also available: in 18K yellow or rose gold; in small model; without diamonds.

TANK AMERICAINE SM WG   REF. WB7073L1

Movement: Cartier caliber 157 quartz movement.
Functions: hours, minutes.
Case: 18K white gold; case set with round-cut diamonds; 18K white-gold octagonal crown set with a diamond; water resistant to 3atm.
Dial: silver-grained; Roman numerals and minute track; sword-shaped blued steel hands.

Bracelet: 18K white-gold bracelet; 18K white-gold clasp.
Suggested price: $33,875
Also available: in 18K yellow gold and 18K pink gold.

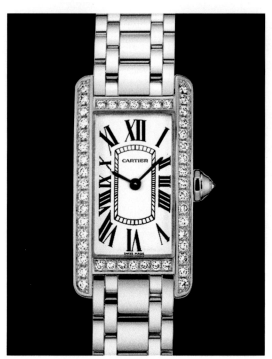

PANTHERE SECRETE YG REF. WG500131

Movement: Cartier caliber 056 quartz movement.
Functions: hours, minutes.
Case: 18K yellow-gold secret case; with round-cut diamonds, emeralds and black lacquer; sliding panther's head reveals the dial.
Dial: silvered, lacquered sunburst; 12 black Roman numerals; sword-shaped blued steel hands.
Strap: black fabric strap.
Also available: in 18K white gold.

BAIGNOIRE S WG REF. WJ306004

Movement: mechanical manual-winding 8970 MC workshop-crafted caliber.
Functions: hours, minutes.
Case: 18K white gold; set with round cut diamonds; 18K white-gold circular grained crown set with a diamond; water resistant to 3atm.
Dial: silvered, lacquered sunburst; 12 black Roman numerals; sword-shaped blued steel hands.
Strap: white fabric strap.
Also available: 18K rose gold with diamonds; in 18K white gold with diamonds and pink sapphires (special limited edition for the US).

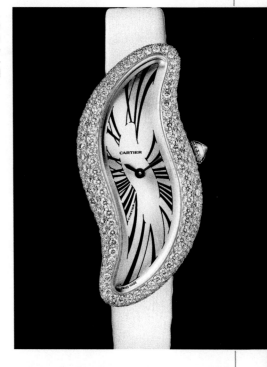

BALLON BLEU DE CARTIER MM YG REF. WE9004Z3

Movement: automatic-winding Cartier caliber 076.
Functions: hours, minutes, seconds.
Case: 18K yellow gold; 36.5mm; set with round-cut diamonds; 18K yellow-gold fluted crown set with a blue cabochon sapphire; water resistant to 3atm.
Dial: silvered opaline dial; guilloché and lacquered; 12 black Roman numerals; sword-shaped blued steel hands.
Bracelet: 18K yellow-gold bracelet; triple deployant clasp.
Suggested price: $39,175
Also available: in stainless steel or stainless steel and 18K gold or 18K rose or white gold; in small or large model; with or without brilliants; on leather strap.

LA DOÑA LM YG REF. WE600204

Movement: Cartier caliber 690 quartz movement.
Functions: hours, minutes.
Case: 18K yellow-gold case set with round-cut diamonds; 18K yellow-gold octagonal crown set with a diamond; sapphire crystal; water resistant to 3atm.
Dial: silver-grained dial with sunburst décor; 12 black Roman numerals.
Bracelet: 18K yellow-gold bracelet; 18K yellow-gold clasp.
Suggested price: $39,425
Also available: in small or mini size, with or without brilliants; in 18K rose or white gold; on leather strap.

CHANEL
A Unique Universe of Fine Jewelry and Watches

Inspired by Mademoiselle Chanel's creations, the brand's watches bring a new dimension to luxury watchmaking.

Gabrielle Chanel once said, "Fashion goes out of fashion, but style never." The CHANEL style is unparalleled, built through a subtle alchemy of never-before-used materials and colors suffused with emotions. The style grew and established itself through an idiosyncratic and avant-garde vision. It endures through its ability to continually reinvent itself.

Naturally, the spirit of Gabrielle Chanel is found in the watches' designs. To do away with the superfluous, go straight for the essentials and aim for simplicity while observing the CHANEL codes when it comes to design. As for technology, always champion the quality of the products.

This is how these unique watches, made in Switzerland and in compliance with the strictest rules governing the age-old tradition of watchmaking, have come into being.

The craftsmen of the "watchmaking valleys" have given Switzerland its reputation that dates back three centuries. At the center of the watch valley, a veritable "silicon valley" of European watchmaking, La Chaux-de-Fonds lives in time with watches.

J12 COLLECTION

The J12 watch for both men and women combines technological design and innovations. Its name is inspired by the world of yacht racing and its curves by a famous racing car. The ceramic case is paired with a ceramic bracelet of 48 links for aeration and absolute comfort. It is equipped with a curved, ergonomic case and a patented automatic folding buckle.

Borrowed from state-of-the-art technology, ceramic has extraordinary characteristics: non-oxidizing, scratch-resistant, and hardness just below that of diamonds. (On the international Mohs scale, diamonds have the highest

score of 10, ceramic registers at 9, while steel and gold are respectively just at 5 and 2.5). And so, the diamond is the only material used with extreme precision to work, form and polish each ceramic component to achieve the perfect aesthetic appearance demanded by the creator. Produced in deep black or immaculate white, the J12 is available in several versions encompassing classic to jeweled.

J12 CALIBER 3125

J12 Caliber 3125 is, for CHANEL, a return to authenticity with a Fine Watchmaking automatic movement with three hands, paying homage to the very roots of traditional watchmaking.

In order to create this new movement, CHANEL naturally turned to one of the most prestigious fine Swiss watchmakers, Audemars Piguet. The result of this partnership is the J12 Caliber 3125 in 18-karat yellow gold and black ceramic bringing together an association of graphic perfection and mechanical excellence. The movement of this watch is based on the Caliber AP 3120 and is equipped with a new balance bridge and a 22-karat gold rotor, clad in black ceramic and designed by CHANEL.

> I chose the diamond because its density represents the greatest value for the smallest size.
>
> *- Mademoiselle Chanel*

J12 EDITIONS EXCLUSIVES

Right from her first Fine Jewelry collection, Gabrielle Chanel revealed a penchant for fine gemstones, particularly diamonds. "If I chose diamonds it's because they represent highest value in the smallest volume."

The Editions Exclusives collection draws together the rarest of J12 timepieces. The watchmaking perfection achieved by the different movements and fine gemstones—diamonds, rubies, emeralds and sapphires—makes them the true ambassadors of CHANEL Jewelry Watchmaking expertise.

Through the Editions Exclusives collection, the J12 reveals itself more than ever before as a watchmaking icon for the new millennium.

PREMIÈRE COLLECTION

1987: Première, the first CHANEL watch. Its octagonal watchcase is reminiscent of both the N°5 bottle stopper and the outline of Place Vendôme in Paris.

2008: Ceramic—avant-garde yet elegant—this smooth and lustrous material luxuriously envelops the Première. In retaining the octagonal watchcase, this model gracefully revives the refined and feminine silhouette of dainty watches from the 1930s.

Produced in both black and white ceramic, this new Première is available in ceramic with steel and diamonds or ceramic with 18-karat white gold and diamonds.

TIMELESS COLLECTION

Coco Chanel herself inspired five collections of jewelry watches: Camélia, 1932, Mademoiselle, Matelassée and Chocolat.

The Camélia collection, which symbolizes purity, is adorned with diamonds, blue sapphires and pink sapphires. Camélia was Coco Chanel's favorite flower.

The 1932 collection is inspired by the Art Deco spirit, an alliance of structure and femininity. The 1932 is available in different models, paved in combinations of black and white diamonds.

With its large square case, slender Roman numerals and its plain and uncluttered shape, the Mademoiselle line conveys a strong character in the spirit of the 1930s. The Mademoiselle Pearls—with its bracelet of five strings of Akoya pearls mounted on five gold wire strands—is designed as a tribute to Coco Chanel.

The design of the Matelassée watch is inspired by one of CHANEL's timeless designs, quilting, which still today adorns the most celebrated bags in the world.

Firmly rooted in the CHANEL universe, the Chocolat watch merges luxury with seduction and brings a breath of fresh air to the world of traditional watchmaking. With avant-garde allure and a digital display specially designed for CHANEL, it is available in steel, steel and diamonds, or white gold and diamonds.

FACING PAGE
J12 Caliber 3125, a new J12, is cased in 18-karat yellow gold and ceramic and equipped with an automatic-winding mechanical movement. The CHANEL-AP 3125 was developed in collaboration with the manufacturer Audemars Piguet.

THIS PAGE
TOP This Première, housed in an 18-karat white-gold case with diamonds, is fitted on a bracelet of articulated 18-karat white-gold and ceramic links set with diamonds.

BOTTOM CHANEL workshops in La Chaux-de-Fonds, Switzerland.

J12 JOAILLERIE   REF. H1671

Movement: Swiss automatic, tourbillon mechanical movement CHANEL 05-T1.
Functions: hours, minutes, seconds; tourbillon.
Case: 38mm; black ceramic; white-gold bezel set with 46 baguette-cut diamonds (4.55 carats, F/G VVS1); water resistant to 5atm.
Dial: lacquered black.
Bracelet: black ceramic; white-gold triple-folding buckle; adjustable standard size.

Also available: white ceramic.
Suggested price: upon request.
Note: limited edition of 12 pieces.

J12 JOAILLERIE   REF. H2137

Movement: Swiss automatic; COSC certified.
Functions: hours, minutes, seconds; date; chronograph.
Case: 41mm; black ceramic; pink-gold bezel set with 48 baguette-cut diamonds (4.8 carats, F/G VVS1); water resistant to 10atm.
Dial: lacquered black; 264 brilliant-cut diamonds (0.6 carat, F/G VVS1) and 9 diamond indicators.

Bracelet: black ceramic; triple-folding buckle; adjustable standard size.
Also available: white ceramic.
Suggested price: $80,000
Note: limited edition of 100 pieces.

J12 HAUTE JOAILLERIE   REF. H2008

Movement: Swiss automatic.
Functions: hours, minutes, seconds.
Case: 38mm; white gold set with 74 baguette-cut diamonds (4.95 carats, F/G VVS1); white-gold bezel set with 46 baguette-cut diamonds (4.4 carats, F/G VVS1); water resistant to 5atm.
Dial: black ceramic center; 84 baguette-cut diamonds (2 carats, F/G VVS1) and 12 baguette-cut black ceramic indicators.
Bracelet: white gold set with 502 baguette-cut diamonds (29.25 carats, F/G VVS1); triple-folding buckle; adjustable standard size.
Also available: 33mm (high-precision Swiss quartz movement); 42mm (Swiss automatic movement).
Suggested price: upon request.
Note: limited edition of 12 pieces.

J12 JOAILLERIE   REF. H2029

Movement: Swiss automatic.
Functions: hours, minutes, seconds.
Case: 38mm; white ceramic; white-gold bezel set with 46 baguette-cut diamonds (4.40 carats, F/G VVS); water resistant to 10atm.
Dial: white ceramic center; 84 baguette-cut diamonds (2 carats, F/G VVS) and 12 black baguette-cut ceramic indicators.

Bracelet: white ceramic; triple-folding buckle; adjustable standard size.
Also available: 33mm (Swiss automatic movement); 42mm (Swiss automatic movement).
Suggested price: $99,750

J12 GMT   REF. H2012

Movement: Swiss automatic.
Functions: hours, minutes, seconds; date; GMT (Greenwich Mean Time) with two times zones (second time zone displayed on the 24-hour bezel).
Case: 42mm; black ceramic; water resistant to 10atm.
Dial: black lacquered.
Bracelet: black ceramic; triple-folding buckle; adjustable standard size.
Also available: white ceramic (limited edition).
Suggested price: $5,800

J12 DIAMONDS   REF. H0950

Movement: Swiss automatic.
Functions: hours, minutes, seconds; date.
Case: black ceramic; steel bezel set with diamonds (F/G VVS); water resistant to 20atm.
Bracelet: black ceramic; triple-folding buckle; adjustable standard size.
Also available: high-precision Swiss; 41mm (chronograph, COSC certified).
Suggested price: $12,900

J12 DIAMONDS   REF. H1422

Movement: Swiss automatic.
Functions: hours, minutes, seconds; date.
Case: 38mm; white ceramic; steel bezel set with 118 diamonds (1.60 carats, F/G VVS); water resistant to 20atm.
Dial: white lacquered.
Bracelet: white ceramic; central steel links set with 312 diamonds (4.22 carats, F/G VVS); triple-folding buckle; adjustable standard size.
Also available: 33mm (high-precision Swiss quartz); 41mm (chronograph, COSC certified).
Suggested price: $30,500

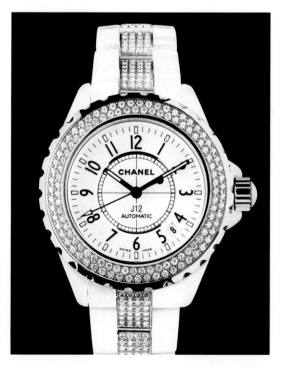

J12 PINK GOLD   REF. H2180

Movement: high-precision Swiss quartz.
Functions: hours, minutes; date.
Case: 38mm; white ceramic; pink-gold bezel; water resistant to 20atm.
Dial: white lacquered set with 11 diamond indicators; hands plated in pink gold.
Bracelet: white ceramic; triple-folding buckle; adjustable standard size.
Also available: 33mm (high-precision Swiss quartz).
Suggested price: $8,750

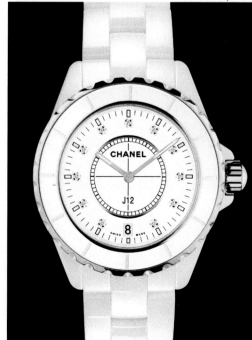

PREMIÈRE REF. H2147

Movement: high-precision Swiss quartz.
Functions: hours, minutes.
Case: 19.7mm; white gold set with 52 diamonds; water resistant to 3atm.
Dial: lacquered black.
Bracelet: black ceramic and white gold set with 216 diamonds (1.55 carats, F/G VVS); adjustable size.

Also available: steel case set with 52 diamonds, steel and black ceramic bracelet.
Suggested price: $24,850

PREMIÈRE REF. H0451

Movement: high-precision Swiss quartz.
Functions: hours, minutes.
Case: 26mm; steel; water resistant to 3atm.
Dial: lacquered black.
Bracelet: steel chain interwoven with black leather ribbons; steel clasp; several sizes.

Also available: white version on steel chain bracelet interwoven with white rubber ribbons.
Suggested price: $2,650

PREMIÈRE REF. H2146

Movement: high-precision Swiss quartz.
Functions: hours, minutes.
Case: 19.7mm; white gold set with 52 diamonds; water resistant to 3atm.
Dial: lacquered white.
Bracelet: white ceramic and white gold set with 216 diamonds (1.55 carats, F/G VVS); adjustable size.

Also available: steel case set with 52 diamonds, steel and white ceramic bracelet.
Suggested price: $24,850

PREMIÈRE PEARLS REF. H2032

Movement: high-precision Swiss quartz.
Functions: hours, minutes.
Case: 19mm; white gold; caseback pave-set with 136 diamonds (0.7 carats, F/G VVS); water resistant to 3atm.
Dial: pave-set with 34 baguette-cut diamonds (1.25 carats, F/G VVS).
Bracelet: 194 Akoya cultured pearls mounted on white-gold strands; clasp set with 110 diamonds; bracelet ends set with 38 diamonds; adjustable size.
Suggested price: $50,000

MADEMOISELLE PEARLS — REF. H1434

Movement: high-precision Swiss quartz.
Functions: hours, minutes.
Case: 22mm; white gold; water resistant to 3atm.
Dial: 168 diamonds (0.8 carats, F/G VVS).
Bracelet: Akoya cultured pearls mounted on 5 white-gold strands.
Also available: yellow gold with Roman numerals.
Suggested price: $23,500

CAMÉLIA — REF. H1348

Movement: high-precision Swiss quartz.
Functions: hours, minutes.
Case: 27mm; white-gold; petals pave-set with 147 diamonds (2.2 carats, F/G VVS); water resistant to 3atm.
Dial: mother of pearl; 4 diamond indicators.
Strap: black satin; white-gold buckle; adjustable standard size.
Also available: petals pave-set with blue sapphires around mother-of-pearl dial; petals pave-set with blue sapphires around dial pave-set with diamonds; petals pave-set with pink sapphires around mother-of-pearl dial.
Suggested price: $20,950

MATELASSÉE — REF. H0489

Movement: high-precision Swiss quartz.
Functions: hours, minutes.
Case: 19mm; steel case set with 32 diamonds; water resistant to 3atm.
Dial: black lacquered.
Bracelet: polished steel; triple-folding buckle; adjustable size.
Also available: steel case without diamonds on polished steel bracelet.
Suggested price: $5,650

1932 — REF. H1185

Movement: high-precision Swiss quartz.
Functions: hours, minutes.
Case: 28mm; white gold; bezel set with 101 diamonds (1.25 carats, F/G VVS); water resistant to 3atm.
Dial: mother of pearl; 4 diamond indicators.
Strap: black satin; white-gold buckle set with 44 diamonds; adjustable size.
Also available: dial pave-set with diamonds, two sections set with white diamonds, three sections set with black diamonds; black lacquered dial, three sections set with white diamonds.
Suggested price: $11,950

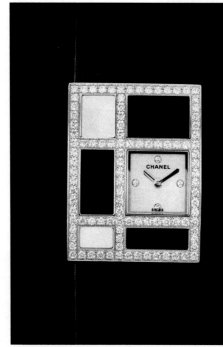

CHOPARD
Contemporary Expression of the L.U.C Tech Collection

Chopard demonstrates its watchmaking excellence through the new L.U.C collection. At its core, the L.U.C Tech line delivers unusual, futuristic versions of L.U.C's original models. With innovative openworked dials, modern materials, and purely cutting-edge mechanics, this series has no limits.

Since the development of the L.U.C collection powered exclusively by in-house mechanical movements, Chopard has been fully integrated into the exclusive circle of true luxury watch manufactures. Under the guidance of Karl-Friedrich Scheufele, co-president of Chopard, the prestigious L.U.C (named for founder Louis-Ulysse Chopard) employs the highest standards of techniques and finishes applied to high-end watchmaking. The introduction of this innovative, flawless collection established Chopard as a major player in the contemporary luxury watch industry in the 1990s; further cementing this position was Chopard's invitation to join the exclusive Foundation de la Haute Horlogerie in October 2008.

The introduction of the L.U.C collection established Chopard as a major player in the contemporary luxury watch industry more than a decade ago.

From within its universe of excellence, Chopard has created the limited edition L.U.C Tech Collection and has preserved the contemporary and fundamental principles of its original model while partially displaying their internal movements by alternating open and hidden zones, creating an interactive scenery and opening up one's eyes to the splendor of the internal mechanics.

Recently, Chopard has added to this high-tech collection 250 numbered, limited edition L.U.C Tech Twist watches made of pink gold. The model is characterized by its crown at 4:00 and its small second and date with arrow at 7:00. The L.U.C 96 TB self-winding mechanical movement is a treat for the eyes: its bridges are decorated with Côtes de Genève and gray engravings, and are admired through its transparent casing. This COSC-certified chronograph also boasts two stacked barrels (L.U.C "Twin"® Technology) and offers 65 hours of operation.

The L.U.C Tourbillon Tech Twist W.A.S. displays a matching configuration with its crown at 4:00. With four power reserves offering an uninterrupted operation of 216 hours, this exceptional timepiece has the exclusive "Winding Assistance System" consisting of a small crank facilitating the operation. A COSC-certified chronograph, this watch houses its tourbillon movement within an aluminum case—a Chopard

exclusive. Aesthetically, the L.U.C Tourbillon Tech Twist W.A.S. presents a vibrant, transparent dial cut with two bands in the form of horizontal waves; the movement's bridges, decorated by Côtes de Genève, can be seen beneath the wave motif. This L.U.C's tourbillon is animated at the 7:00 position while the power reserve is displayed at 1:00. Only 100 of these exclusive watches were produced.

The L.U.C Tech Strike One sounds a gong at the top of the hour. The ringing mechanism can be turned on or off and is located in only the top half of the watch. In addition, this model has a sun guilloché and displays the hour on the skeleton circumference. A COSC-certified chronograph, the mechanical L.U.C 96 SHT movement has automatic rewind utilizing a 22-karat gold oscillating weight, a 65-hour power reserve, and the L.U.C "Twin"® Technology with two stacked barrels. Just 100 of these Ø 40.5mm titanium L.U.C Tech Strike One watches are available.

L.U.C TONNEAU   REF. 162267-1001

Movement: automatic tonneau-shaped L.U.C 3.97 caliber; mounted and finished entirely by hand; bridges decorated with Côtes de Genève pattern; COSC-certified chronometer.
Functions: hour, minute; small seconds and date at 6.
Case: 18K white-gold three-piece case; 38.5x40mm, thickness: 10mm; curved sapphire crystal; white-gold crown; transparent sapphire crystal caseback attached by 8 screws, displaying the movement; water resistant to 3atm.
Dial: black; center guilloché with sun pattern; brushed hour ring; applied faceted white-gold pointed markers; printed railway minute track; white-gold Dauphine-style hands.
Strap: crocodile leather; white-gold clasp.
Note: limited edition of 1,860 pieces, dedicated to Louis-Ulysse Chopard who founded the firm in that year.
Also available: yellow gold.

L.U.C LUNAR ONE   REF. 161894-5001

Movement: mechanical automatic-winding L.U.C 96QP caliber; 65-hour power reserve; mounted, decorated and finished entirely by hand (Côtes de Genève decorated and beveled); COSC-certified chronometer; hallmarked with the Geneva Seal.
Functions: hour, minute, small seconds; 24 hour; perpetual calendar (date, day, month, year, moonphase).
Case: 18K rose-gold three-piece case; Ø 40.5mm, thickness: 11.6mm; antireflective curved sapphire crystal; 4 correctors on the middle; pink-gold crown; back fastened by 8 screws, displaying the movement through a sapphire crystal; water resistant to 3atm.
Dial: solid gold, argenté; guilloché by hand with a wave pattern at the center; brushed hour ring; guilloché subdials; printed minute track with luminescent dots; applied faceted pink-gold markers and Roman numerals; luminescent pink-gold Dauphine hands.
Indications: month and 4-year cycle at 3; moonphase and small seconds at 6; day of the week and 24-hour at 9; large date display with a double window at 12.
Strap: hand-stitched crocodile leather; pink-gold foldover clasp.
Note: limited edition of 250 numbered pieces.
Also available: with black/argenté dial; in platinum, 250 pieces.

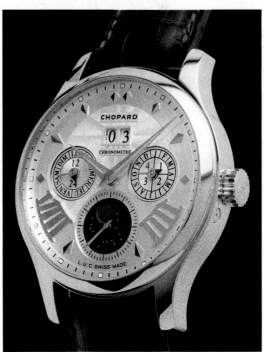

L.U.C TWIST   REF. 161888-1001

Movement: mechanical automatic-winding L.U.C 1.96 caliber; two barrels; 65-hour power reserve; mounted and finished entirely by hand; COSC-certified chronometer; hallmarked with the Geneva Seal.
Functions: hour, minute, small seconds at 7; date at 3.
Case: 18K white-gold three-piece case; Ø 41mm, thickness: 10.3mm; antireflective curved sapphire crystal; white-gold crown at 4 with case protection; back fastened by 6 screws, displaying the movement through a sapphire crystal; water resistant to 3atm.
Dial: solid gold, silvered; hand-guilloché jonquille center; black brushed subdial and hour ring; applied white-gold Arabic numerals; printed minute track; white-gold Dauphine hands.
Strap: crocodile leather; white-gold clasp.
Also available: in yellow gold.

L.U.C EXTRA PLATE   REF. 161902-1001

Movement: mechanical self-winding L.U.C 96HM caliber; equipped with two barrels; 65- to 70-hour power reserve; bridges decorated with Côtes de Genève pattern.
Functions: central hour, minute.
Case: white gold; thickness: 6.80mm, weight: 39g; antireflective sapphire crystal; water resistant to 3atm.
Dial: black dial with four Arabic numerals and applied baton hands; dauphine-style hour and minute hands.
Strap: crocodile leather; gold buckle.
Also available: yellow gold with white dial.

L.U.C TOURBILLON STEEL WINGS CLASSIC   REF. 161906-1001

Movement: mechanical manual-winding L.U.C 4T caliber; equipped with four barrels (two sets of two stacked barrels); L.U.C Quattro® Technology; 216-hour power reserve; patented Variner® balance with variable moment of inertia; bridges decorated with straight Côtes de Genève pattern; COSC-certified chronometer.
Functions: hour, minute; tourbillon; power-reserve indicator.
Case: white gold; sapphire crystal; water resistant to 3atm.
Dial: two-part, black, gold dial; black outer ring; white Arabic numerals and inner zone with sunburst engine-turned décor; dauphine-style hour and minute hands; arrow power-reserve and second hands.
Strap: crocodile leather strap; folding clasp.
Note: 100-piece limited, numbered edition in white gold.

L.U.C TECH REGULATEUR   REF. 168449-3001

Movement: mechanical manual-winding L.U.C 4RT caliber; equipped with four barrels meaning two sets of two stacked barrels; L.U.C Quattro® Technology; 216-hour power reserve; bridges decorated with horizontal Côtes de Genève pattern; COSC-certified chronometer.
Functions: hour subdial at 3; center minutes; semi-instantaneous date display at 6 (stop seconds function during time-setting); 2nd time zone at 9, adjustable via push-piece; power-reserve indicator at 12.
Case: polished steel; steel crown; steel time-zone corrector at 8; 3-position winding-stem; water resistant to 3atm.
Dial: skeleton dial; minute circle with applied Arabic numerals; blued-steel dauphine-style hour and minute hands; baton-style small seconds hand and arrow-style time-zone pointer.
Strap: hand-stitched crocodile leather strap; folding buckle.
Note: 250-piece limited, numbered edition in steel.

L.U.C PRO ONE GMT   REF. 168959-3001

Movement: mechanical self-winding L.U.C 4.96 Pro One caliber; two stacked barrels (L.U.C Twin® Technology); 65-hour power reserve; COSC-certified chronometer.
Functions: hour, minute, center seconds; date window; fixed 2nd time-zone hand.
Case: steel; antireflective sapphire crystal; screw-lock crown and screw-in caseback; water resistant to 30atm.
Dial: black dial; Super-LumiNova-coated arrow-style hands and hour markers for excellent nighttime readability.
Strap: hand-stitched crocodile leather strap; steel folding clasp.

MILLE MIGLIA GTXL POWER CONTROL   REF. 168457-3001

Movement: mechanical self-winding movement ETA A07.161; bidirectional winding mechanism; 46-hour power reserve; COSC-certified chronometer.
Functions: hour, minute, second; instantaneous date display at 3 (highlighted through a magnifying glass); power-reserve indicator at 6.
Case: steel; screw-down crown; scratchproof, cambered and glare-proofed sapphire crystal; water resistant to 10atm.
Dial: black; luminescent numeral and hands; black and silver-colored power-reserve indicator.
Strap: rubber strap.

CHRONOSWISS
Breaking New Ground

After celebrating its 25th anniversary last year, Chronoswiss looks to the future as it begins a new era. Next year, the pioneering watchmaker will celebrate another milestone when it becomes a true manufacture, developing and creating its own movements.

The process began in 2006, when the company consolidated its various departments into one building named Zeitpunkt, German for "point in time." Located near Munich, the facility will unveil Chronoswiss's first proprietary movement in 2010, heralding a new chapter in the brand's history.

This achievement must have been hard to imagine for Gerd-Rüdiger Lang when he launched Chronoswiss in 1983. At the time, quartz watches were rapidly eclipsing the mechanical watch industry. Despite the grim forecast, Lang persevered. His family-owned business enjoyed hard-fought success, earning the respect of collectors around the world with its high standards of quality and bold innovations.

One of those early improvements was the addition of a transparent caseback, which not only provided an enticing view of the movement's elegant machinations, but also distinguished it from other watch brands at the time. Today, the sapphire crystal caseback is ubiquitous in the world of high-end watchmaking.

But the glories of the past hold no sway over a restless spirit like Lang. Lang is busy preparing Chronoswiss for the future, including the appointment of a new general manager at the factory, Johann Baptist Lindner. Lindner served as Lang's financial advisor for many years and is an obvious perfect fit to lift operational pressure off the founder's shoulders for the next chapter in Chronoswiss history. Another leap forward is the recent launch of a new distribution platform, Chronoswiss of North America. Headed by Hartmut Kraft as an independent distribution partner, the group's goal is to raise the watchmaker's profile on the continent by introducing models that appeal to the unique sensibilities of North American collectors.

Before accepting this position, Kraft worked in Chronoswiss's German headquarters where he was involved in product development and instrumental in streamlining the company's factory. He will help reorganize distribution and maximize advertising in North America. He also will improve customer service by implementing

THIS PAGE Named Zeitpunkt, Chronoswiss's newly opened facility near Munich will produce watch movements that will define the company's future.

FACING PAGE Measuring only 7.6mm thick, Régulateur 24's svelte profile is possible thanks to its thin mechanical movement, modified by Chronoswiss's master watchmakers.

"Factory Signature Service," a program that requires all repairs to be performed at the Chronoswiss factory and returned to the client by a guaranteed time.

It's no coincidence that a regulator clock made by trailblazing clockmaker Siegmund Riefler is among the first things visitors see when they enter Zeitpunkt; the regulator's distinct way of telling time has become a signature style of Chronoswiss, which introduced its first regulator model more than 20 years ago. Today, the first Régulateur from 1988 is a rare collector's item, commanding many times its original price.

To mark the occasion of its anniversary celebration in 2008, Chronoswiss introduced Régulateur 24, of which the brand will produce only 3,000 pieces. At the heart of this exquisite watch is a very special mechanical movement, first introduced in the 1950s and modified by Chronoswiss. Selected for its thinness, the movement ensures that Régulateur 24 maintains a low profile (7.6mm) in keeping with modern tastes.

The watch's contemporary appeal carries over to the red-gold case, where visual drama is played out via the contrast of smooth bezel against brushed case band. Inside the 40mm round case, the Régulateur 24's solid silver dial is truly the star of the show. Its unusual 24-hour indicator is complemented by an off-center small seconds and central minute hand.

With the Régulateur 24, Chronoswiss honors its past; with the new manufacture facility, it's charting a course for the future.

> The regulator's distinct way of telling time is a signature style of Chronoswiss.

RÉGULATEUR 24 — REF. CH 1121 R

Movement: hand-wound Chronoswiss Caliber C.112; 13'''; Ø 29.40mm; 21,600 vph (3 Hz); 46-hour power reserve; 17 jewels; Glucydur balance; Incabloc shock absorber.
Functions: regulator with 24-hour indication.
Case: 18K red gold; solid 20 parts; Ø 40mm, height: 7.6mm; smooth bezel and brushed case band; special turnip-shaped crown; screw-in Autobloc System strap lugs; sapphire crystal; antireflective on the inside; screw-down caseback with full thread and one-sided antireflective sapphire crystal; water resistant to 3atm.
Dial: solid 925 silver; hand-finished pear-shaped blued steel Losange hands.
Limited edition: anniversary watch (3,000 pieces worldwide).

GRAND LUNAR — REF. CH 7541 L R

Movement: automatic Chronoswiss Caliber C.755; 13¼'''; Ø 30mm; 28,800 vph (4 Hz); 46-hour power reserve; 25 jewels; Incabloc shock absorber; skeletonized rotor; individually numbered.
Functions: hours, minutes, small seconds; analogue date; moonphase; center chronograph seconds, 12-hour counter, 30-minute counter.
Case: 18K red gold; 23 parts; Ø 41mm, height: 15mm; abraded, polished, screwed and fluted bezel; special turnip-shaped crown; screw-on lugs with patented Autobloc System; antireflective sapphire crystal on one surface; screw-in caseback with full-thread and pane of antireflective sapphire crystal; water resistant to 3atm.
Dial: guilloché; 925 sterling silver dial; printed Arabic numerals; minute-circle with ¼-second subdivisions; gold-plated steel Breguet Losange hands.

GRAND OPUS — REF. CH 7541 S R

Movement: automatic Chronoswiss Caliber C.741 S; 13¼'''; Ø 30mm; 28,800 vph (4 Hz); 46-hour power reserve; 25 jewels; Incabloc shock absorber; individually numbered; skeletonized movement.
Functions: hours, minutes, seconds; analogue date; center chronograph second, 12-hour register, 30-minute register.
Case: 18K red gold; 23 parts; Ø 41mm, height: 15mm; abraded, polished, screwed and fluted bezel; special turnip-shaped crown; sapphire crystal, antireflective on one surface; screw-in caseback with full-thread and pane of antireflective sapphire crystal; water resistant to 3atm.
Dial: skeletonized and beveled metal dial with printed Arabic numerals; minute-circle with ¼ second subdivisions; individually numbered; polished, blued steel Breguet Losange hands.

GRAND RÉGULATEUR — REF. CH 6721 R

Movement: hand-wound Chronoswiss Caliber C.673; 16½'''; Ø 36.6mm, height: 4.7mm; 18,000 vph (2.5 Hz); approx. 40-hour power reserve; 17 jewels; Glucydur balance; Nivarox 1 flat balance spring swan-neck precision regulator; Incabloc shock absorber; polished pallet, pallet-wheel and screws; circular grained plate; bridges with Geneva-brush polish; individually numbered.
Functions: hour, minute, second.
Case: 5N rose gold; 21 parts; Ø 44mm, height: 13.45mm; brushed and polished, screw-on bezel; special turnip-shaped crown; screw-on lugs with patented Autobloc System; one-sided antireflective sapphire crystal; screw-on caseback with full-thread and one-sided antireflective sapphire crystal; water resistant up to 3atm.
Dial: 925 sterling silver; guilloché-finish; blued steel Poire Losange hands.
Strap: Louisiana-crocodile; width at the case: 22mm; buckle: 18mm.
Also available: folding clasp or metal bracelet; steel (Ref. CH 6723).

IMPERATOR — REF. CH 2873 BK

Movement: ETA 2892-A2; 11½'''; Ø 25.60mm; height: 3.60mm; 28,800 vph (semi-oscillations) (4 Hz); 42-hour power reserve; 21 jewels, three-armed Glucydur balance; Nivarox 1 flat spring index pointer with eccentric; Incabloc shock absorber; polished pallets; pallet wheel and screws; bridges with Côte Genève polish and circular graining; skeletonized rotor.
Functions: hours, minutes, seconds and date.

Case: polished stainless steel; rectangular; width: 36.5mm, length: 56mm, height: 10mm; screw-on lugs with patented Autobloc System; crown at 12; sapphire crystal domed on both sides, antireflective on one; four screws for open sapphire crystal caseback, antireflective on one side; water resistant up to 3atm.
Dial: blued hands in Constance shape; spacious date window with three-day indication.

TIMEMASTER DATE NIGHTHAWK — REF. CH 7533 NH

Movement: automatic Chronoswiss Caliber C.751; 13¼'''; Ø 30mm, height 7.90mm; 28,800 vph (4 Hz); approx. 46-hour power reserve; 25 jewels; three-armed Glucydur balance; Nivarox 1 flat spring with precision eccentric-screw regulation; Incabloc shock absorber; polished pallet, pallet-wheel and screws; skeletonized and gold-plated rotor; circular-grained plate; bridges with Côtes de Genève; individually numbered. **Functions:** hours, minutes, seconds; center chronograph seconds, 30-minute counter, 12-hour-counter; centered analog date.

Case: stainless steel; 27 parts; Ø 44mm, height: 16mm; brushed and polished bezel with luminous marking; special turnip-shaped crown to ease watch winding when wearing gloves; screw-on lugs with patented Autobloc System; scratch-resistant; antireflective sapphire crystal; sapphire crystal caseback with full-thread; screw-on tube body; water resistant up to 10atm. **Dial:** Nighthawk black dial; luminous Super-LumiNova C3 (no radiation); metal hands with luminous SuperLumiNova C3 in fair blue and orange. **Strap:** water-resistant Walknappa strap; end width: 22mm; folding clasps; metal bracelets. **Also available:** matte black metal dial with luminous SuperLumiNova C3 (no radiation), metal hands, "modern" shape (CH 7533 BK); or metal dial with luminous SuperLumiNova C3 (no radiation), black numerals, metal hands, black-varnished, "modern" shape (CH 7533 LU).

TIMEMASTER 24 H GOOSE — REF. CH 6433 GO

Movement: hand-wound Chronoswiss Caliber C.674; 16½'''; Ø 36.6mm, height: 5.40mm; 18,000 vph; 24-hour display; 18 jewels; Glucydur with screws and Nivarox flat spring; Incabloc shock absorber; swan-neck precision regulator; approx. 48-hour power reserve; 24-hour modification exclusively Chronoswiss; individually numbered.
Function: hour, minute, second.
Case: stainless steel; 22 solid parts; Ø 44mm, height: 12.3mm; ground brushed and polished; bezel with luminous marking; special turnip-shaped crown to ease watch winding when wearing gloves; patented Autobloc System; scratch-resistant; antireflective sapphire glass; sapphire glass base with full thread; screw-on crown tube body; water resistant to 10atm.
Dial: matte black metal; 24-hour display; luminous SuperLumiNova C3 (no radiation) numerals in gray coloring; luminous metal hands with SuperLumiNova C3 (no radiation); "modern" shape.
Strap: water-resistant Walknappa strap; extended cowhide leather strap for professional use over the outfit with quick clasp; width of ends: 22mm.

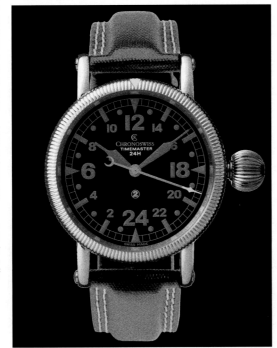

WRISTMASTER — REF. CH 2703

Movements: two independent, autonomously functioning automatic movements with independent displays. **Functions:** hours, minutes, central stop second; oversized minute and hour counters; date. **Case:** stainless steel; 84x42mm, height: 20mm; desk-shaped; bayonette clasp; fluted rotating bezels; screw-in lugs with patented Autobloc System; brushed and polished assembly plate and case; solid stainless steel crowns and buttons; sapphire crystals; antireflective on the inside; on back and front; water resistant to 3atm. **Dial:** solid metal dial; numerals with SuperLumiNova C3 (no radiation); metal hands with luminous SuperLumiNova C3 (no radiation).
Strap: solid crocodile skin or cowhide leather; board watch set in the form of a wristwatch.
Wristtimer Ref. CH 2803 (normal watch): hours, minutes, seconds, date; individually refined Chronoswiss Caliber, ETA 2892-A2 with automatic winding, date window at 6, 11 ½ ''', Ø 25.60mm, height: 3.60mm; 21 jewels; 28,800 vph; skeletonized rotor; Incabloc shock protection; fine adjustment for the index. **Wristcounter Ref. CH 7503** (stop watch): hours, minutes, central stop second and oversized minute and hour counters; Chronoswiss Caliber C. 751; 13 ¼'''; Ø 30mm, height: 7.90mm; 25 jewels; 28,800 vph (4 Hz); skeletonized rotor; Incabloc shock protection; fine adjustment for the index.

CLERC
Tradition of Innovation

At the Geneva-based Montres Clerc, fourth-generation watchmaker Gérald Clerc creates exceptional timepieces that reflect a delicate alchemy of creative vision, mechanical innovation and family tradition. Each Clerc watch is manufacture-made in a limited series and equipped with complications and original features defined by more than 130 years of watchmaking heritage.

Two years ago, Clerc launched Odyssey, an acclaimed collection that embodies his family's passion for refined horology.

The company invites women to join the adventure this year with the first Odyssey watches for ladies. The invitation comes as no surprise. Long before mechanical watches were en vogue for women, Clerc was the first company to offer a collection of self-winding ladies' pieces. The new Odyssey Lady models—Skeleton and Galaxy—are ornate works of mechanical art and expressions of authentic style.

The rose-gold case and inner bezel of Odyssey Lady Skeleton both are adorned with a constellation of twinkling diamonds that shine a spotlight on the watch's skeletonized movement. The exceptional decoration is visible through a sapphire crystal dial topped with diamond numerals and markers.

The second model is the rose-gold Odyssey Lady Galaxy. For the dial, the dark firmament of space is recast as mother-of-pearl and cloisonné, creating an iridescent field filled with celestial bodies of diamond pavé and brilliants.

Clerc chose to name the collection Odyssey because the word succinctly evokes the spirit of adventure that defines the epic journeys undertaken on Earth by Homer and in space by modern-day astronauts.

One of his biggest inspirations, Clerc says, is the optimism that surrounded the exploration of space in the '60s and '70s, a phenomenon he describes as humankind's wholehearted embrace of progress.

The Odyssey's case is visibly influenced by this quest for discovery, adopting the realm of aerospace design through its sleek shape, modern materials and patented structure.

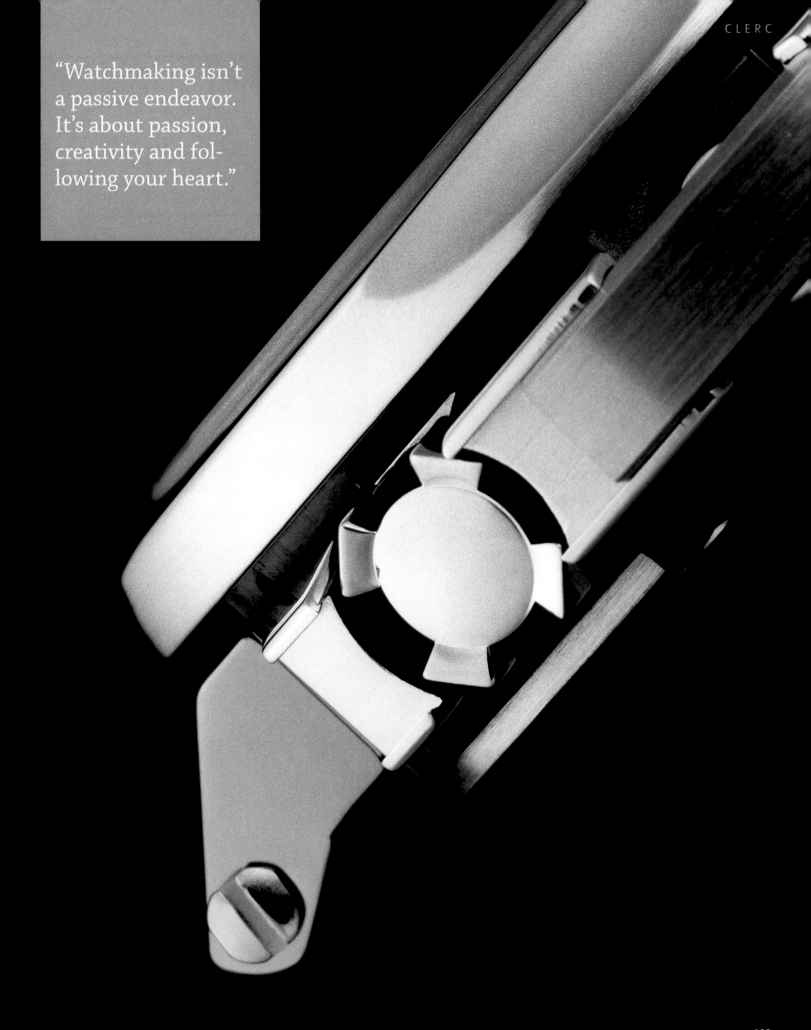

"Watchmaking isn't a passive endeavor. It's about passion, creativity and following your heart."

One element worthy of special mention is the lateral sliding protector used to guard Odyssey's crowns and pusher. This revolutionary system is the first of its kind.

The mechanism is part of the Odyssey's cutting-edge case. Assembled by hand, the complex arrangement of expertly finished pieces incorporates materials that range from the precious (grade-5 titanium, black titanium, red gold and palladium) to the progressive (ceramics, carbon and rubber).

An evolution of the brand's signature elegance, Clerc says the design for Odyssey was realized by making none of the usual compromises. "All too often, the details that make something truly unique are eliminated to accommodate the manufacturing process," says the creator and brand president. "With Odyssey, the goal was purity. By hewing closely to the original inspiration, the design maintains its integrity while clearly conveying the undiluted passion of the creative spark that brought the idea to life."

A mix of forward-thinking design and Old World craftsmanship, Odyssey heralds the emergence of a watchmaking trend that Clerc refers to as "futuristic haute horlogerie," a movement driven by a desire to express the modern age through technology.

ABOVE ODYSSEY: a Mechanical Work of Modern Art. Inspired by space research and exploration, the complex patented case structure blends high-technology materials. A world premiere lateral sliding protector guards the crowns and pusher The watch is powered by an exclusive self-winding 45-jewel double-barrel manufacture movement with 120 hours of power reserve. Individually numbered and hand-crafted in Switzerland. Ref. ODY122.

BELOW ODYSSEY combining 18-karat red gold with high-technology materials on vulcanized rubber strap. Ref. ODY311.

Hydroscaph honors that futuristic vision with a complex architecture developed by Clerc, his team of watchmakers and diving professionals. Working in concert and pooling centuries of knowledge, they created a powerful diving instrument that performs reliably and intuitively while confronting some of nature's most extreme conditions.

The result is the most sophisticated diving watch in the world, a mechanical sports watch crafted according to Swiss watchmaking tradition and instilled with the expertise of those who work in the underwater world.

Their influence on Hydroscaph can be seen in several features, including the inclusion of an automatic helium valve that allows the watch to bear water resistance to 1,000 meters. Another aspect that experienced divers will appreciate is the bezel, which is activated and locked into position by a special crown to prevent accidental movement underwater.

HYDROSCAPH: The Most Sophisticated Diving Instrument. Available with a choice of GMT 24-hour and power-reserve indicators or big jumping date with power-reserve indicator, automatic movements. Choice of grade-5 titanium, 18-karat red gold and black titanium, or carbon fiber and black titanium. Vulcanized rubber strap.

Clerc's insistence on the highest watchmaking standards ensures that the Hydroscaph's movement is crafted with a distinguished style befitting captains of industry. It employs an unconventional disc to indicate the status of the mainspring and includes a 24-hour second time zone to keep frequent travelers on schedule.

Thankfully, the technological steps forward are not at the expense of comfort. In fact, Hydroscaph is the first watch in the world to feature a lug mechanism—developed by Clerc—that adjusts to the wrist for a perfect fit.

When Gérald Clerc ascended to take the company's reins in 1997, he embarked upon a journey of discovery that would serve to expand the brand's understanding of complications. Today, the fruits of those labors have found their place among the company's limited edition collections in the form of tourbillons, second time-zone mechanisms and generous power reserves.

The mechanical and aesthetic innovations that enrich the watchmaker's timepieces express Clerc's uncompromising vision. "A watchmaker-designer shouldn't be influenced by expenses, trends in the mass market or confining demand," he says. "Watchmaking isn't a passive endeavor. It's about passion, creativity and following your heart whether you succeed or fail."

Following his heart is precisely what Clerc did in 1998. That year, he unveiled his first collection, debuting a new case shape that would soon become the brand's signature. The watchmaker achieved this unique octagonal shape by artfully combining a circle and square, an unprecedented shape in horology that Clerc patented. The design of the case reflects Clerc's deep appreciation for the art and science architecture.

Founded in Paris in 1874, the family watch firm quickly earned a reputation for its refined style and connections to iconic watch brands such as Jaeger-LeCoultre, Rolex and Vacheron Constantin. A century later, the brand shifted its focus exclusively to developing and producing its own manufacture watches.

From its earliest days, Clerc crafted only small batches of limited editions and pieces uniques, allowing watchmakers to lavish attention on every piece of the mechanical puzzle, from machining to finishing. This meticulous process has earned Clerc many high watchmaking honors, perhaps no other more prestigious than the Key of Geneva seal.

The appeal of Clerc's rarity continues to transcend generations, captivating the likes of Princess Grace of Monaco, Salvador Dali, Michael Douglas, and countless other devotees who identify with the spirit of originality shared by all of the company's timepieces.

The brand even played a role in international relations when Charles de Gaulle, the influential French leader, commissioned a globe-shaped timekeeper as a gift for Nikita Khrushchev, the Premier of the Soviet Union. This special piece featured the time in Paris and Moscow using two small clocks, one adorned with a sapphire representing the French capital and the other with a ruby for the Soviet capital.

THIS PAGE

ABOVE   Gerald Clerc, fourth-generation watchmaker.

RIGHT   This high-tech creation features unique adaptable lugs mechanism ensuring a perfect fit on the wrist.

FACING PAGE
The Hydroscaph is a powerful and complex futuristic diving instrument designed to withstand extreme conditions in confronting the elements. Developed in close cooperation with a team of professionals closely acquainted with the deep underwater world and its requirements, this prestige mechanical sports watch is water-resistant to 1,000 meters thanks to a helium valve and being fitted with a world-premiere crown-activated rotating bezel mechanism.

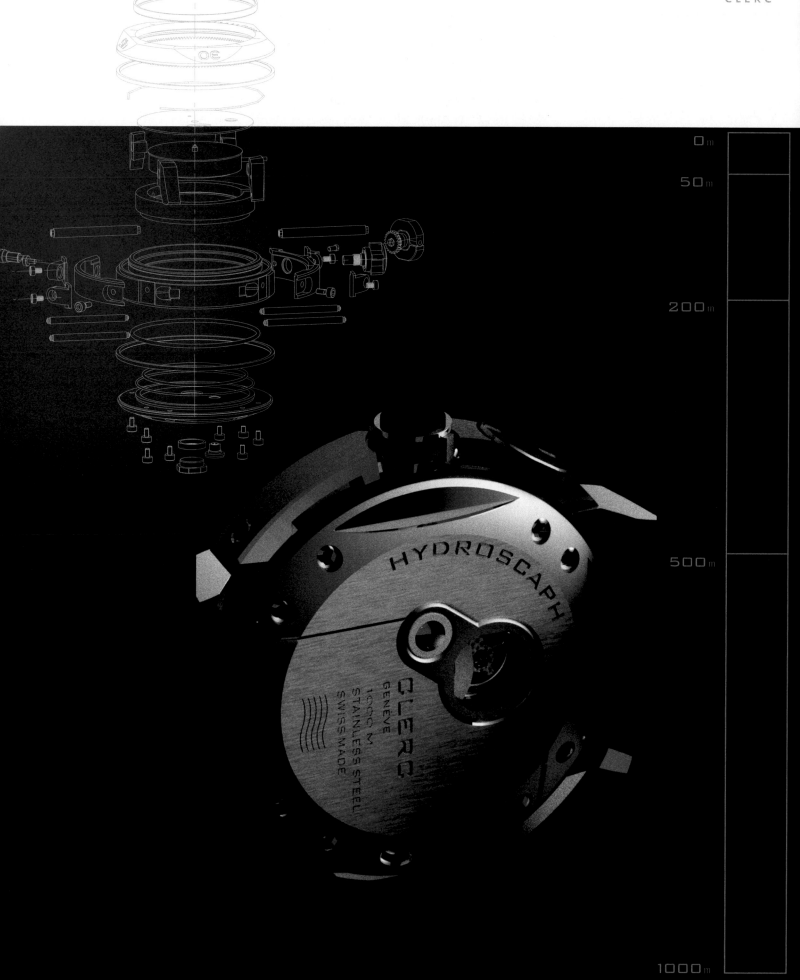

0 m

50 m

200 m

500 m

1000 m

CONCORD
On the Move

Introduced on the eve of the watchmaker's centennial, Concord's C1 Chronograph heralded a bold new direction for the brand. After 2007's reinvention, Concord continues to forge a new identity with a pair of complicated timepieces and several jewelry watches that build on the C1's foundation.

T he C1 Tourbillon Gravity is emblematic of Concord's new avant-garde vision. The tantalizing design relocates the tourbillon to the outside of the watch's white-gold case in a dramatic display of engineering and aesthetics. The tourbillon is mounted perpendicularly to the thick case (18.5mm), connecting to the movement internally with a pinion. Also making the journey away from the dial to outside the movement is the small seconds display, visible through a window on the side of the tourbillon.

The innovative construction leaves more room in the watch for other functions, including a flyback chronograph that measures minutes and hours with a single subdial. Engineers use the remaining space for a pair of functions used to optimize the watch's performance: one is an 84-hour power reserve, and the other is a trust index that warns against overwinding.

Made of machined metal, the multi-level dial is arranged dynamically. The offset hours and minutes are prominently displayed above the chronograph subdial, while the trust index and power-reserve indicator are positioned opposite one another. Concord will issue the C1 Tourbillon Gravity in a limited edition of 25 pieces.

Equally impressive is the speed in which the C1 Tourbillon Gravity was brought to life—one year. Concord developed the watch with BNB Concept, a complicated movement specialist. "We are propelled by the same audacity, the same strong convictions and the same drive, all of which enable us to produce an innovative and iconoclastic form of watchmaking," says Concord CEO Vincent Perriard.

C1 TOURBILLON GRAVITY

The tourbillon and small seconds display find an unusual home outside the C1 Tourbillon Gravity's large case. Concord will produce just 25 of these special timepieces.

FAR LEFT Blue-tinted sapphire crystal forms a C-shaped, dual time-zone display on the black engine-turned dial of the C1 World Timer.

RIGHT The 44mm stainless steel C1 Big Date with carbon-fiber dial includes a rotating disc to indicate the seconds.

BOTTOM LEFT The newly introduced C1 Chronograph High Jewelry offers diamond-paved versions in either white or rose gold while the C1 Pure is an all-white model that pairs a stainless steel case with a white rubber strap. Both the High Jewelry and Pure collections build upon Concord's popular C1 Chronograph technology.

BOTTOM RIGHT Vincent Perriard and Concord's first Champion ambassador, Bryan Colangelo.

> Concord and BNB Concept are propelled by the same audacity, strong convictions, and drive, which enable the partnership to produce an innovative and iconoclastic form of watchmaking.

The second complication introduced by Concord last year, the C1 World Timer, is for the globetrotting horological aficionado. The automatic movement displays time in a second time zone through a C-shaped opening that uses a pair of rotating indexes to indicate the city and its corresponding time. Simple to operate, a pusher at 2:00 is used to select one of the many destination cities.

The all-black, 47mm-diameter case is made of steel covered with Diamond-Like Carbon, a dense, scratch-resistant coating that combines the graphite and diamond forms of carbon.

Despite the black engine-turned dial's dark hue, it's eminently readable thanks to the blue-tinted opening for the city and time-zone indexes, along with a blue seconds hand and luminescent hour and minute hands.

From bold complications to haute joaillerie, Concord adds a trio of diamond versions to its signature C1 Chronograph collection.

The C1 Pure takes its name from an all-white design, from the rubber strap to the textured dial. C1 Pure's stainless steel case is set with 80 white diamonds, totaling nearly a full carat.

Concord offers two more diamond-set watches with rose- and white-gold versions of the C1 Chronograph High Jewelry. Both cases and dials are decorated with 184 white diamonds, including a dramatic paved section by the date display. Gems circle the edge of the dial and outline the chronograph's hour and minute subdials, as well as the small seconds disc.

The watchmaker concludes its centennial with the C1 Big Date, a stainless steel and black rubber watch that celebrates simple elegance. The carbon-fiber dial features the watch's namesake large date display offset by a rotating disc positioned at 6:00 that shows the seconds.

Concord is now launching a new line of limited edition timepieces called Champions. To represent this new line, the brand will select high-profile ambassadors who share Concord's uncompromising quest for performance. The first Concord Champion is Bryan Colangelo, president of the Toronto Raptors professional basketball team.

"Bryan is a natural choice for our new Champions program," says Vincent Perriard, president of Concord U.S. "He has a strong personality and is a trend-setter who embraces Concord's philosophy and vision."

As the watchmaker moves into its second century, Concord embraces a future marked by innovation and creativity.

C1 BIG DATE
REF. 0320011

Movement: mechanical automatic-winding Caliber 3532 La Joux-Perret (ETA 2892-A2, 11 1/2'''); Ø 26.2mm, 4.9mm thick; official COSC-certified chronometer; 90 components; 26 jewels; 28,800 vph; 44-hour power reserve; black PVD rotor with openworked C1 logo.
Functions: hours, minutes; small seconds on permanent turning disk at 6; big date window at 12. **Case:** stainless steel; Ø 44mm, thickness:

12.95mm; rubber-coated steel top ring, screwed in laterally, enhanced by 8 decorative elements on bezel; stainless steel, black rubber and composite screw-down crown with embossed C1 logo; 3.3mm-thick sapphire crystal, antireflective on both sides; open caseback with 8 screws; water resistant to 20atm.
Dial: black carbon fiber with silver edge; hour markers with Super-LumiNova material SLN C1; rhodium, lacquered Dauphine hour and minute hands with Super-LumiNova SLN C1, asymmetrically hollowed out.
Strap: black vulcanized rubber; stainless steel Concord folding deployment buckle.
Suggested price: $10,500

C1 BIRETROGRADE
REF. 0320045

Movement: mechanical self-winding Caliber 3535 La Joux-Perret 13 1/4''' (ETA 2892-A2, 11 1/2'''); (ETA 89 components; 29 jewels; 28,800 vph; 42-hour power reserve; skeletonized plate, pallet bridge, module plate and module bridge; circlular graining; black PVD treatment; snailed bevel; vertical Côtes de Genève; "C1" engraved in center. **Functions:** hours, minutes; retrograde date between 3 and 6; retrograde day between 6 and 9. **Case:** 18K 5N rose

gold; Ø 44mm, thickness: 14.6mm; protective ring with 8 rubber-coated rose-gold blocks; 3.3mm-thick sapphire crystal with antireflective treatment on both sides; exhibition caseback, rose gold embossed "Audace—Savoir Faire Avant-Garde"; black rubber and composite screw-down crown with embossed C1 logo; water resistant to 5atm.
Dial: black skeletized dial; 18K 5N rose-gold-plated polished hour markers; dauphine hands, assymmetrically hollowed out, lacquered, sandblasted, SuperLumiNova.
Strap: black vulcanized rubber strap; 18K 5N rose-gold deployment buckle with embossed CONCORD cover.
Note: 3-year warranty.
Suggested price: $60,000

C1 RETROGRADE
REF. 0320054

Movement: mechanical self-winding movement Caliber 9094 Soprod; 11 1/2'''; Ø 25.6mm, thickness: 5.25mm, height: 13.15mm; 150 components; 30 jewels; 28,800 vph; 42-hour power reserve; black PVD treatment; snailed bevel; vertical Côtes de Genève; "C1" engraved in center.
Functions: hours, minutes, and seconds; retrograde date at 3; retrograde day at 9; power reserve at 6.

Case: titanium; Ø -44mm, thickness: 13.15mm; protective ring coated in black rubber and fixed by 7 self-blocking screws; screw-down crown with C1 logo; 3.3mm-thick sapphire crystal, antireflective on both sides; exhibition caseback embossed "Audace—Savoir Faire—Avant-Garde"; water resistant to 20atm.
Dial: black ribbed; guilloché; dark gray date disc, lacquered and sandblasted; rhodium-plated polished hour markers with SuperLumiNova SLN C1; dauphine hands, asymmetrically hollowed out, lacquered, sandblasted, SuperLumiNova.
Strap: black vulcanized rubber; DLC-coated stainless steel deployment buckle with embossed CONCORD cover.
Note: 3-year warranty.
Suggested price: $20,600

C1 WORLDTIMER
REF. 0320048

Movement: mechanical self-winding GMT Worldtimer 201 Dubois-Dépraz (ETA 2892-A2, 11 1/2'''); Ø 26.2m, thickness: 5mm; 256 components; 21 jewels; 42-hour power reserve; black PVD treatment; snailed bevel; vertical Côtes de Genève; "C1" engraved in center.
Functions: hours, minutes, seconds; 24 time zones with cities at 9; date window with magnifying glass at 3. **Case:** black DLC-coated stainless steel; Ø 47mm,

thickness: 13.55mm; 53 elements; metal protective ring coated in black rubber and fixed by 7 self-blocking screws; screw-down crown with embossed C1 logo; 3.3mm-thick sapphire crystal, antireflective on both sides; screw-on caseback embossed "Audace—Savoir Faire—Avant-Garde"; water resistant to 20atm.
Dial: black; engine turned; wide opening for second time zone; rhodium-plated polished hour markers with SuperLumiNova SLN C1; dauphine hands, asymmetrically hollowed out, lacquered, sandblasted, SuperLumiNova.
Strap: black vulcanized rubber; DLC-coated stainless steel deployment buckle with embossed CONCORD cover.
Suggested price: $20,000

C1 PURE   REF. 0320028

Movement: mechanical self-winding Caliber A07.211 (ETA Valgranges); 16 ½'''; Ø 37.2mm, thickness: 7.9mm; height: 2.39mm; official COSC-certified chronograph;132 components; 25 jewels; 28,800 vph; 48-hour power reserve; rhodium treatment; snailed bevel; vertical Côtes de Genève; "C1" engraved in center. **Functions:** hours, minutes, central sweep seconds; small seconds on turning disc at 9; 30-minute counter at 12; 12-hour counter at 6; date window at 3. **Case:** stainless steel; Ø 44mm, thickness: 16.7mm; diamond-set bezel; pro-

tective ring with 8 blocks in white rubber-coated stainless steel; screw-down crown with embossed C1 logo; 80 VVS diamonds (52 x 1.6; 12 x 1.4; 16 x 0.8; TCW=0.99) set on the bezel and the case; 3.3mm-thick sapphire crystal, antireflective on both sides; exhibition caseback embossed "Audace—Savoir Faire—Avant-Garde"; water resistant to 20atm.
Dial: 3 layers; white; fiber-glass texture; rhodium-plated polished hour-markers with SuperLumi-Nova SLN C; chronograph seconds hand in bright blue Pantone 293 C; dauphine hands, asymmetri-cally hollowed out, in gray Pantone 430 U, lacquered, with SuperLumiNova.
Strap: white vulcanized rub-ber; deployment buckle in stainless steel with embossed CONCORD cover.
Note: 3-year warranty.
Suggested price: $19,700

C1 CHRONOGRAPH HIGH JEWELRY   REF. 0320026

Movement: mechanical self-winding Caliber A07.211 (ETA Valgranges); 16 1/2 '''; of-ficial COSC-certified chronograph; Ø 37.2mm, thickness: 7.9mm; 132 components; 25 jewels; 28,800 vph; 48-hour power reserve; black PVD treatment; snailed bevel; vertical Côtes de Genève; "C1" engraved in center. **Functions:** hours, minutes, cen-tral sweep seconds; small seconds on turning disc at 9; 30-minute counter at 12; 12-hour counter at 6; date window at 3. **Case:** white gold; Ø 44mm, thickness: 16.7mm;

53 elements; set with 184 diamonds (TCW=2.398); protective ring in white gold, fixed laterally by 7 self-blocking screws; 3.3mm-thick sapphire crystal, antireflective on both sides; exhibition caseback em-bossed "Audace—Savoir Faire—Avant-Garde"; wa-ter resistant to 5atm. **Dial:** ruthenium dial set with 259 diamonds (73 x 1.0; 140 x 0.9; 22 x 0.8; 24 x 0.7; TCW=0.825); hour-markers with Super-Lumi-Nova SLN C1; chronograph seconds hand in bright blue Pantone 293 C; dau-phine hands, asymmetrical-ly hollowed out, lacquered, SuperLumiNova SLN C1.
Strap: black vulcanized rubber; 18K white-gold deployment buckle set with 72 diamonds (0.6 ct) and embossed CONCORD cover.
Note: 3-year warranty.
Suggested price: $99,000

C1 CHRONOGRAPH   REF. 0320012

Movement: mechanical self-winding Caliber A07.211 (ETA Valgranges); 16 1/2 '''; Ø 37.2mm, thickness: 7.9mm; official COSC-certified chronograph; 25 jewels; 28,800 vph; 48-hour power reserve; black PVD treatment; snailed bevel; vertical Côtes de Genève; "C1" engraved in center. **Functions:** hours, minutes, central sweep seconds; small seconds on turning disc at 9; 30-minute counter at 12; 12-hour counter at 6; date window at 3. **Case:** 18K 5N rose gold; Ø 44mm, thick-ness: 16.7mm; 53 elements; metal protective ring coated in black rubber and fixed laterally by 7 self-blocking screws; screw-down crown with embossed C1 logo; 3.3mm-thick sapphire crys-tal, antireflective on both sides; exhibition case-back embossed "Au-dace—Savoir Faire—Avant-Garde"; water resistant to 20atm.

Dial: 3 layers; black carbon fiber; rhodium-plated polished hour-markers; chronograph seconds hand in bright blue Pantone 293 C; dauphine hands, asym-metrically hollowed out, lacquered, SuperLumi-Nova SLN C1.
Strap: black vulcanized rubber; 18K 5N rose-gold deployment buckle with embossed CONCORD cover.
Suggested price: $34,500

C1 CHRONOGRAPH   REF. 0320005

Movement: mechanical self-winding Caliber A07.211 Valgranges; 16 1/2 '''; Ø 37.2mm; thickness: 7.9mm; official COSC-certified chronometer; 25 jewels; 28,800 vph; 48-hour power reserve; black PVD treatment; snailed bevel; vertical Côtes de Genève; "C1" engraved in center. **Functions:** hours, minutes, central sweep seconds; small seconds on permanent turning disc at 9; 30-minute counter at 12; 12-hour coun-ter at 6; date window at 3; **Case:** stainless steel; Ø 44mm, thickness: 16.7mm; 53 elements; metal protective ring coated in black rubber and fixed laterally by 7 self-blocking screws; screw-down crown with embossed C1 logo; 3.3mm-thick sapphire crystal, antireflective on both sides; exhibition caseback embossed "Audace—Savoir Faire—Avant-Garde"; water resistant to 20atm.

Dial: 3 layers; black carbon fiber; rhodium-plated polished hour-markers with SuperLumiNova SLN C; dauphine hands, asym-metrically hollowed out, rhodium, lacquered, SuperLumiNova SLN C1; chronograph seconds hand in blue Pantone 287 U. **Strap:** black vulcanized rubber; stain-less steel deployment buckle with embossed CONCORD cover.
Suggested price: $12,900

CORUM
Spirit of Renewal

After more than 50 years, Corum continues to demonstrate its ability to craft daring watches balanced by an uncompromising commitment to quality. From its early days as the first-and-only watchmaker to create a wristwatch with a gold coin for a dial to its latest introduction of haute horlogerie timepieces such as the Romvlvs Retrograde Annual Calendar, Corum remains a benchmark for both style and substance.

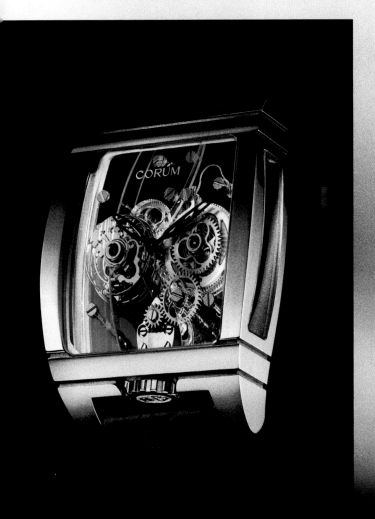

N early a decade ago, Corum focused its energy on what the company calls, the "four pillars" of its collection: Admiral's Cup, Romvlvs, Golden Bridge and Specialties.

Before examining the first two pillars, it's important to touch briefly upon the watches of the Golden Bridge and Specialties lines in order to get a complete portrait of the watchmaker.

To distinguish its Golden Bridge collection, Corum uses sapphire crystal on all four sides of the case to spotlight the watch's remarkable linear movement. A spectacular visual feat, it appears to float inside the case, anchored only by its namesake gold bridge.

Corum's other pillar, Specialties, encompasses complicated timepieces that push the envelope of haute horlogerie. Among the many standouts are the jewel-encrusted Billionaire Tourbillon and the Golden Tourbillon Panoramique, which features a tourbillon movement suspended between sapphire bridges.

THIS PAGE **Part of Corum's Specialties collection, the Golden Tourbillon Panoramique includes a sapphire tourbillon movement. The 38x53mm tonneau case, shown here in red gold, features the crown at 6:00.**

The four pillars of Corum's collection: Admiral's Cup, Golden Bridge, Romvlvs, and Specialties.

In 1957, two years after Corum was founded, the Royal Ocean Racing Club organized the first Admiral's Cup yachting regatta. Based at Cowes on England's Isle of Wight, the biennial Admiral's Cup was considered the unofficial world championship of offshore racing.

Corum shares a long association with the Admiral's Cup, introducing the first watch from its Admiral's Cup collection in 1960. Since then, the watchmaker has regularly unveiled new additions to this iconic line of sports watches, whose design has evolved over the years. Today, the Admiral's Cup is one of Corum's signature designs, immediately identifiable by its 12-sided case and bezel featuring 12 nautical pennants instead of traditional hour markers.

Corum adds a trio of timepieces, starting with the titanium Admiral's Cup Leap Second 48, which includes a split-seconds chronograph controlled by a pusher incorporated into the watch's crown. In addition to the chronograph's central seconds hands, the Admiral's Cup Leap Second 48 also features a jumping seconds counter positioned at 9:00 and a 30-minute counter opposite.

Corum offers a smaller chronograph model with the Admiral's Cup Challenge 44 Split-Seconds. In keeping with the watchmaker's dedication to using innovative materials, carbon fiber is used for the bezel atop the stainless steel case, as well as on the bracelet's center links.

The company also unveils the Admiral's Cup Competition 40, the first ladies' model in the collection. Corum presents two versions of this automatic timepiece, a red-gold model with mother-of-pearl dial and a stainless steel version paired with a white lacquered dial and diamond bezel.

Corum welcomed Ben Ainslie as its new brand ambassador in 2008. The 31-year-old English sailor won his third consecutive gold medal at the Beijing Olympics last year, making him the second-most decorated sailor in the history of the global competition. He will attempt his fourth gold in 2012, when the Olympics are held in his native country. Despite his youth, Ainslie has already won seven world championship titles and twice has been named World Sailor of the Year by the International Sailing Federation.

Ainslie began sailing at the age of eight, winning his first world championship at 16. A year later, Corum became the young sailor's first sponsor when he began his professional career. The partnership inspired Ainslie's love for fine timepieces, which has grown over the years.

Today, his sailing partner of choice is the Corum Admiral's Cup Tides, an indispensable sailing instrument for coastal regions with a twice-daily lunar cycle. The watch provides key information pertaining to: the lunar cycle and strength of the tides; an estimation of water levels; the strength of the currents; and the time of the tides.

Corum expands another of its signature collections by adding a pair of watches to its storied Romvlvs line, a design that features the hours engraved elegantly upon the bezel.

In a first for the company, Corum offers an annual calendar with an automatic movement—developed exclusively for the brand—that only requires a single annual correction. In tandem with the elegant mechanical engineering, the Romvlvs Retrograde Annual Calendar also offers an elaborately decorated movement paired with an equally handsome sunburst guilloché dial. The watch's annual calendar is expressed with a retrograde date along with day and month displays. Corum will produce this watch in a limited edition of 50 pieces.

Corum continues to demonstrate its mastery of the watchmaking art with the Romvlvs Perpetual Calendar. Visible through the caseback, the watch's hand-finished, skeletonized movement controls the date, day of the week, month and moonphases. It is one of the world's thinnest perpetual calendar movements. The complex mechanism will not require an adjustment until the year 2100. Corum pairs the polished red-gold case with a satin-brushed version of the Romvlvs' signature bezel. Even more rare than the Romvlvs Retrograde Annual Calendar, only 25 Romvlvs Perpetual Calendars will be issued.

Building on its solid pillars, Corum continues to create a solid foundation for its future.

ADMIRAL'S CUP TOURBILLON 48   REF. 372.931.55/0F01.0000

Movement: manually wound tourbillon CO372 (LJP 7912); 19 jewels; 90-hour power reserve.
Case: Ø 48mm; 18K red gold with vulcanized rubber detailing; open caseback.
Strap: crocodile.
Suggested price: $170,000

Also available: gray dial, diamonds on strap (10.48 carats); full-pavé diamond bracelet (19.68 carats).

ADMIRAL'S CUP TIDES 48   REF. 277.931.91/0371 AG32

Movement: CO277 (Dubois Dépraz 801/2892A2); 42-hour power reserve.
Functions: automatic tides with date indicator.
Case: Ø 48mm; 18K red gold with vulcanized rubber detailing.
Suggested price: $22,000
Also available: titanium with vulcanized rubber.

ADMIRAL'S CUP COMPETITION 48   REF. 947.931.05/V790 AA32

Movement: automatic CO947 (LJP 8235); COSC certified; 24 jewels; 42-hour power reserve.
Functions: day / date indicator; compass rose seconds subdial at 9.
Case: Ø 48mm; titanium with 18K red-gold detailing.
Dial: nautical pennants as hour markers.
Suggested price: $16,000

Also available: titanium on vulcanized rubber strap or bracelet; titanium and red gold on strap.

ADMIRAL'S CUP CHALLENGE 44   REF. 753.691.20/F371 AA92

Movement: automatic chronograph CO753 (Valjoux 7753); COSC certified; 27 jewels.
Case: Ø 44mm; stainless steel.
Strap: vulcanized rubber.
Suggested price: $5,900
Also available: stainless steel bracelet; 18K red gold on crocodile strap or gold bracelet; diamond bezel.

ADMIRAL'S CUP LEAP SECOND 48   REF. 895.931.91/0001 AN32

Movement: CO895 (La Joux Perret 8952); 40 jewels; 42-hour power reserve.
Functions: automatic split-seconds chronograph with jumping seconds.
Case: Ø 48mm; 18K red gold with vulcanized rubber detailing.
Dial: nautical pennants as hour markers.
Strap: crocodile leather.
Suggested price: $31,000
Also available: titanium on vulcanized rubber strap; red gold and rubber bracelet.

ADMIRAL'S CUP CHALLENGE 44 REGATTA (LIMITED EDITION)   REF. 986.694.55 V791 CG12

Movement: automatic split-second chronograph; CO986 (LJP 8601); 31 jewels; COSC certified.
Functions: center split-second hand; 30-minute counter at 3; 12-hour counter at 6; small seconds at 9.
Case: Ø 44mm; 18K red gold with vulcanized rubber detailing.
Suggested price: $32,000
Also available: vulcanized rubber strap.

ADMIRAL'S CUP CHALLENGE 44 SPLIT-SECONDS   REF. 986.691.11/V761 AN92

Movement: CO986 (LJP 8601); COSC certified; 31 jewels; 42-hour power reserve.
Functions: automatic split-seconds chronograph.
Case: Ø 44mm; stainless steel with carbon-fiber detailing.
Dial: nautical pennants as hour markers.
Suggested price: $11,000
Also available: 18K red gold on crocodile strap or 18K gold bracelet with carbon fiber.

ADMIRAL'S CUP COMPETITION 40   REF. 082.951.85/0089 PN34

Movement: CO082 (ETA 2892); 21 jewels; 42-hour power reserve.
Functions: automatic with date.
Case: Ø 40mm; 18K red gold with vulcanized rubber detailing; 0.92-carat diamond bezel.
Dial: nautical pennants as hour markers.
Strap: crocodile leather.
Suggested price: $21,000
Also available: stainless steel and diamond with vulcanized rubber strap.

ROMVLVS DUAL TIME   REF. 283.510.55 0001 BN56

Movement: automatic CO283 (Frédéric Piguet 5K60 base); 30 jewels; 72-hour power reserve.
Functions: second time zone (hour and minute) at 12; date at 3; small seconds at 6.
Case: Ø 41mm; 18K red gold; bezel engraved with 12 Roman numerals.
Suggested price: $18,000

Also available: 18K red-gold bracelet.

ROMVLVS CHRONOGRAPH   REF. 984.715.20/V810 BN77

Movement: CO984 (ETA 2894-2); COSC certified; 37 jewels; 42-hour power reserve.
Functions: date at 6.
Case: Ø 44mm; polished stainless steel; "Wave profile" case with satin-finished bezel bearing Roman numerals.
Suggested price: $5,900

Also available: crocodile strap.

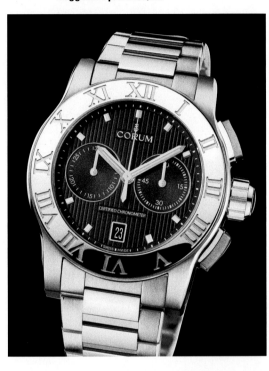

ROMVLVS RETROGRADE ANNUAL CALENDAR   REF. 502.510.55/0001 BN67

Movement: CO502 (VMF 5002/VMF 4001); 32 jewels; 55-hour power reserve.
Case: Ø 41mm; 18K red gold; open caseback.
Strap: crocodile.
Note: limited edition of 100 pieces.
Suggested price: $42,000

Also available: 18K white gold; diamond-set Roman numerals on bezel.

ROMVLVS PERPETUAL CALENDAR   REF. 183.510.55/0001 BN58

Movement: CO183 (FP71/DD 5100); 35 jewels; 45-hour power reserve.
Case: Ø 41mm; 18K red gold.
Functions: automatic perpetual calendar; date at 3; day at 9; moonphases at 6; month and year at 12.
Strap: crocodile.
Note: limited edition of 25 pieces.

Suggested price: $54,000

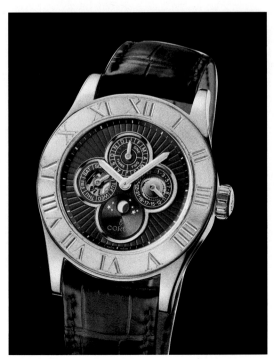

$20 GOLD COIN   REF. 082.355.56/0001 MU51

Movement: automatic CO082 (ETA 2892.A2); 21 jewels; 42-hour power reserve.
Case: Ø 36mm; vintage $20 "Double Eagle" gold coin, visible front and back.
Strap: hand-stitched crocodile strap.
Suggested price: $13,000
Also available: 18K gold bracelet.

GOLDEN BRIDGE   REF. 113.550.55/0001 0000R

Movement: unique, linear, manually wound mechanical caliber; 19 jewels; 40-hour power reserve.
Case: Ø 32x50.5mm; 18K red gold; sapphire crystal.
Suggested price: $24,000
Also available: 18K yellow or white gold on crocodile strap or bracelet; platinum on crocodile strap.

GOLDEN BRIDGE   REF. 113.553.69/0001 0000G

Movement: unique, linear, manually wound mechanical CO113 (VMF 700); 19 jewels; 40-hour power reserve.
Case: Ø 32x50.5mm; 18K white gold; sapphire crystal; 1.71 carats of diamonds.
Strap: crocodile.
Suggested price: $36,000

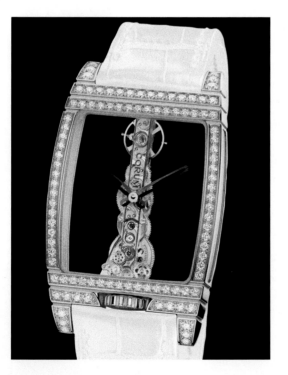

GOLDEN PANORAMIQUE TOURBILLON   REF. 382.850.55/0F02 0000

Movement: manual-winding CO382 (LJP 7951); tourbillon; 90-hour power reserve.
Case: Ø 38x53mm; 18K red gold; four transparent sapphire crystals; bridges and plate in transparent sapphire crystal; crown at 6.
Strap: crocodile leather with triple-folding clasp.
Suggested price: $171,000
Also available: black diamond, brown diamond, emerald, ruby or sapphire on crocodile strap of corresponding color.
Note: limited to five pieces in each variation.

CUERVO Y SOBRINOS
Spirit of Adventure

The Cuervo family's boutique on Havana's "Fifth Avenue" beguiled watch aficionados for 70 years before the business was closed amid the country's political strife in the late 1950s. From its new home in the Swiss Jura, Cuervo y Sobrinos made its long-awaited return in 2002, once again rejoining the elite ranks of the world's most prestigious watchmakers.

Despite the geographical shift, Havana's influence on Cuervo y Sobrinos has not waned. Indeed, today's collection features a number of timepieces inspired by movements and sketches recovered from the Cuervo family's old store. In another nod to the brand's heritage, each new Cuervo y Sobrinos is delivered in a humidor—created especially for the watchmaker—that is ready to store your prized Churchills and Panatelas.

After enjoying success last year as a limited edition with a carbon fiber dial, this year Cuervo y Sobrinos adds Prominente Chronograph to its standard collection. Living in two different worlds informs Prominente Chronograph's unique style, an elegant balance of the tropic's languid rhythms and the Swiss' demanding perfectionism.

Taking its design cues from the Art Deco movement, both the case and chronograph pushers share the same graceful lines. The guilloché dial serves as the backdrop for a trio of subdials, including the chronograph's minute and hour counters.

The watchmaker offers Prominente Chronograph's oblong case (31x52mm) in either stainless steel or rose gold. Each stands as a flawless expression of opulence, evoking the grandeur that defined Havana in 1882, the year Cuervo y Sobrinos was founded.

Prominente Chronograph's flared, oblong case reflects an Art Deco sensibility, giving this automatic timepiece its elegant character. Rose-gold and stainless steel versions are available with dials colored cream, black or white.

Cuervo y Sobrinos lets its rakish charm come to the fore with two treasures that bring to mind the buccaneers who prowled the West Indian waters off the coasts of Haiti and Cuba in the 17th century.

Designed to resonate with modern-day raconteurs and adventurers, the watchmaker offers a pair of limited edition variations: Torpedo Pirata Chronograph and Torpedo Pirata GMT. A confluence of rich details imparts these timepieces with a swashbuckling charm, including a grooved "cannonball" for the crown and a case shaped like a cannon's muzzle. Each is delivered in a "treasure chest" humidor housing a deck of cards for playing cutthroat with your mateys.

With these models, Cuervo y Sobrinos unveils a new case that includes several metal rings fitted between the case and bezel that are available in different configurations, each with a distinctive visual personality. The watchmaker currently offers two variations: bronze, titanium and steel, or rose gold, titanium and steel.

Each watch distinguishes itself through different functions. Pirata Chronograph uses cannon-shaped

Today's collection features a number of timepieces inspired by movements and sketches recovered from the Cuervo family's old store.

pushers to control the classic complication's hour, minute and central seconds counters. A date scale circles the black dial, which accommodates a moonphase at 3:00 opposite a small seconds that depicts the company's coat of arms.

For Pirata GMT, the black dial remains but the subdials disappear. Instead, the dial displays the hour in a second-time zone with a 24-hour ring. Its design references the watch's nautical inspiration, replacing the even numbers with anchors.

All but assured a future as an heirloom, each Cuervo y Sobrinos timepiece vividly recalls the past with the handiwork of gifted artisans and proclaims the future with transformative watchmaking.

LEFT The Cuervo y Sobrinos coat of arms is seen behind the small seconds of the limited edition Torpedo Pirata Chronograph. Cannon-shaped pushers control the watch's chronograph functions, while a grooved "cannonball" crown adjusts the time.

BELOW Torpedo Pirata GMT (and Pirata Chronograph) features a case (the first of its kind) that can be customized by changing the metal ring between the case and bezel. Cuervo y Sobrinos currently offers titanium, gold, burnished steel and bronze rings.

TORPEDO PIRATA CHRONOGRAPH - LIMITED EDITION   REF. 3050.1NLE

Movement: Valjoux 7750 with CYS 3050 caliber.
Functions: hours, minutes, small seconds; date; day of the week; 12-hours; 30-minutes; central seconds; chrono with moonphase.
Case: steel, titanium, bronze.
Dial: black.
Strap: black rubber with bronze stitching.

Also available: steel, titanium; 18K rose gold.
Price: $9,500

TORPEDO PIRATA GMT- LIMITED EDITION   REF. 3052.1NLE

Movement: ETA 2893-2 caliber.
Functions: hours, minutes, small seconds; date; second time zone.
Case: steel, titanium, bronze.
Dial: black.
Strap: black rubber with bronze stitching.
Also available: steel, titanium; 18K rose gold.

Price: $6,500

ROBUSTO TRI-CALENDAR LUNA   REF. 2804.1C

Movement: DP9000; base: ETA 2892.A2 caliber.
Functions: hours, minutes, seconds; date; day of the week; month; complete moonphase calendar.
Case: stainless.
Dial: cream.
Strap: crocodile.

Also available: 18K rose-gold case and guilloché; champagne, tobacco, black, argente dials; metal bracelet available.
Price: $4,900

ESPLENDIDOS 1882   REF. 2412.1C82

Movement: ETA 2824-2 caliber.
Functions: hours, minutes; date.
Case: stainless.
Dial: cream.
Strap: crocodile.
Also available: 18K rose gold; guilloché; black, silver, or gold dial; metal bracelet available.
Price: $3,600

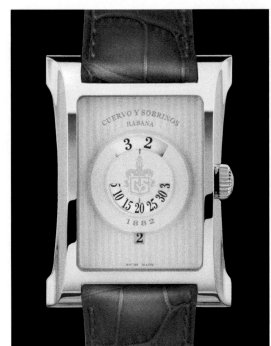

PROMINENTE CHRONOGRAPH   REF. 1014.8N

Movement: ETA2094 caliber.
Functions: hours, minutes, small seconds; date; 12-hours; 30-minutes and central seconds.
Case: 18K rose gold.
Dial: black guilloché.
Strap: crocodile.
Also available: steel; black, cream, white dials.
Limited edition: gold with tobacco guilloché dial; metal bracelet available.
Price: $18,200

ROBUSTO BUCEADOR (DIVE WATCH)   REF. 2806.1BIA

Movement: ETA 2824-2 caliber.
Functions: hours, minutes, seconds; date; internal rotating bezel for bottom time.
Case: stainless.
Dial: indigo blue.
Strap: indigo blue with orange stitching.
Also available: white and black dials with matching rubber straps; diamond or sapphire bezel; metal bracelet available.
Price: $3,400

ESPLENDIDOS RETROGRADE   REF. 2452.8C

Movement: Soprod 9094 caliber.
Functions: hours, minutes, seconds; power-reserve; day of week; retrograde date (backward hand).
Case: 18K rose gold.
Dial: cream guilloché.
Strap: crocodile.
Also available: black, tobacco, argente, copper, champagne dials; steel case; metal bracelet available.
Price: $13,700

PROMINENTE LADIES CONVERTIBLE   REF. 1011.8BSAR-S3

Movement: ETA 2671 caliber.
Functions: hours, minutes, seconds.
Case: 18K rose gold with full cut diamonds (1.99 carats).
Dial: gold.
Strap: python.
Also available: steel with diamonds.
Price: $16,500

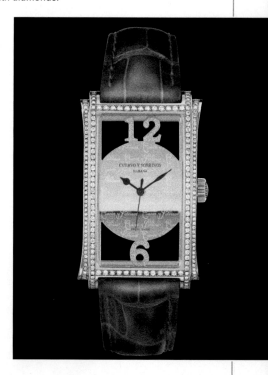

DANIEL ROTH
All the Right Moves

Daniel Roth is not afraid to dream big, offering a collection that adeptly demonstrates the company's mastery of grand complications and its penchant for creating world firsts. With its recent models, the Swiss watchmaker again captivates connoisseurs with timepieces that combine traditional techniques with groundbreaking designs.

One of the company's latest feats is an automaton watch, a timekeeper that features moving figures on the dial. This style of timepiece reached the heights of popularity in pocket watches during the late 17th century.

Daniel Roth takes this classic complication to a new level of complexity with Il Giocatore Veneziano: a dice-playing automaton wristwatch with minute repeater that represents the first-ever true automaton watch.

Historically, the automaton was animated by the watch mechanism. For the Il Giocatore Veneziano, that traditional system has been redesigned to include a movement dedicated exclusively to powering the automaton that is separate from the minute repeater mechanism. It took the master watchmakers at Daniel Roth three years to successfully achieve the exceptional DR 7300 caliber, a system new not only to Daniel Roth but to the entire world of watchmaking.

The idea for Il Giocatore Veneziano began with Gérald Roden, CEO of Daniel Roth, who envisioned an automaton that recalled Caravaggio's legendary painting, "The Card Players." Roden collaborated with acclaimed automaton specialist, François Junod, who helped make his vision a reality by creating a timepiece that features a 16th-century Venetian dice player who shakes two cups before lifting them to reveal the dice beneath.

Increasing the watch's already high level of complexity, Roden wanted the dice to fall in ever-changing combinations. To accomplish this, Il Giocatore Veneziano tosses seven different cycles of 72 combinations, resulting in 504 possible rolls of the dice.

Il Giocatore Vene-
ziano is the world's
most exceptional
automaton, thanks to
a separate movement
dedicated to provid-
ing its animation.

Daniel Roth's Il Giocatore
Veneziano is a unique
minute-repeater automaton
timepiece featuring a movement separate from the
minute-repeater mecha-
nism—a world's first. The
movement's complex design
provides 504 possible rolls of
the double dice.

TOP The details of Il Giocatore
Veneziano, including the Roman
numerals, moneybag and candle, are hand-painted and kiln-
dried in Daniel Roth's workshops.

BOTTOM Approximately
21.65 inches (550mm) tall, this
one-of-a-kind automaton clock
includes a moving body, hands,
head and blinking eyes. The
entire clock is controlled by a
system created by automaton
specialist, François Junod.

The advanced craftsmanship employed to create
Il Giocatore Veneziano exhibits Daniel Roth's attention to
detail in terms of its artistic vision and mechanical execution.

For instance, each hand-painted gold dial recalls the richness of chiaroscurist color used by Caravaggio. Other aspects
of the multilevel dial are painted by hand as well, including the
Daniel Roth logo, Roman numerals, moneybag and the candle
that flickers when the dice are shaken. The coins resting on
the dice player's table glow with applied gold.

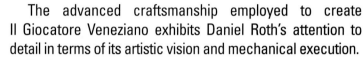

The artistry extends to
Il Giocatore Veneziano's
501-part movement, which
is entirely hand-finished
using traditional decora-
tion, including the nearly
lost art of hand-beveled
edges.

The DR 7300 move-
ment includes a minute-
repeater mechanism, visible through the watch's crystal
caseback. Activated by a sliding switch on the outer case,
the repeater strikes the hours, quarters and minutes on a
pair of cathedral gongs that resonate in a "sound box" hollowed into the mechanism.

Daniel Roth offers Il Giocatore Veneziano in the brand's
signature double-ellipse case (46x43x14.10mm) carved from
a single block of white or red gold. The watch is available in
a limited edition of 30 unique pieces.

The automaton inspired Daniel Roth to create a one-of-
a-kind automaton clock featuring the Venetian dice player.
Standing approximately 21.65 inches (or 550mm) tall, the
handmade clock sounds the hour, setting the automaton in
motion as he rolls his dice.

Daniel Roth is keeping a secret with another new limited edition model. From the front, the Tourbillon 8-Day Perpetual Calendar appears to be a handsome timepiece with a power-reserve indicator and an unusual three-arm seconds hand above the tourbillon.

Hidden on the flip side of the case, however, is a second dial with a perpetual calendar that indicates the day, month, and date, while automatically adjusting for leap year. At the top of the dial, Daniel Roth adds a moonphase that uses a realistic reproduction of the moon in its various phases, a rarity in watchmaking.

The Tourbillon 8-Day Perpetual Calendar's case is available in platinum, yellow gold or red gold. A button located at 6:00 releases the case, which flips over thanks to a hinge at 12:00.

Daniel Roth unveiled the first Papillon in 1999 during the watchmaker's 10-year anniversary. Last year, the brand debuted a new Papillon Chronographe version of this popular model.

The Papillon Chronographe houses an automatic Frédéric Piguet column-wheel chronograph movement in Daniel Roth's Ellipsocurvex case made of yellow, white or red gold. The dial, decorated with Côtes de Genève, includes a jump-hour window that separates the chronograph's 12-hour and 30-minute counters.

The most unusual feature of the watch's distinctive dial, however, is a patented pivoting double minute-hand mechanism. The lozenge-shaped minute hands are part of a disc rotating on a central axis. When one hand reaches 60 minutes, it pivots 90 degrees to retract while the other instantaneously pivots to open at zero minutes. This unique mechanism uses less energy and is more reliable than traditional retrograde minutes systems.

The latest innovations from Daniel Roth reaffirm the company's never-ending quest to reach the pinnacle of the watchmaking art.

TOP   The Tourbillon 8-Day Perpetual Calendar opens to reveal a second dial that includes a perpetual calendar and a rare, realistic moon-phase display. This limited edition timepiece is offered in platinum, red gold and yellow gold.

BOTTOM   The Papillon Chronograph employs a pivoting double minute-hand mechanism. When one lozenge-shaped hand reaches 60 minutes, it retracts while the other hand opens at zero minutes.

PERPETUAL CALENDAR EQUATION OF TIME   REF. 121.Y.60.721.CN.BD

Movement: automatic M143 on base DR114 caliber; 25.60x28.60mm; height: 2.98mm, (base); 26.50x29.50mm, height: 3mm (module); solid 18K gold guilloché rotor; 44-hour power reserve; hand beveled; Côtes de Genève finishing; 27 jewels; 28,800 vph; 3-arm Cupro-beryllium ring; flat balance-spring.
Functions: hours, minutes; perpetual calendar; day of the week; month; calendar; leap year; moonphases; time equation; end of month indicator.

Case: white gold 5N; 44x41x13mm; polished finishing; bezel set with 158 diamonds in 2-rows; crown: Ø 6mm, 32 teeth, not screwed; double elliptical case with two parts: upper with double-face antireflection treatment, lower with internal antireflection treatment; open caseback held by 6 pentagonal screws; water resistant to 3atm.
Dial: 18K gold mother-of-pearl.
Strap: black hand-stitched alligator leather; gold folding clasp.
Suggested price: $110,150
Note: each timepiece is delivered with an individual Functional Testing Certificate.
Also available: in pink gold or platinum.

TOURBILLON LUMIERE   REF. 200.Y.50.895.CB.BD

Movement: manual-winding DR 780 tourbillon, M054 caliber; 64-hour power reserve; Ø 31x34mm, height: 5.08mm; 22 jewels; 21,600 vph; flat-balance spring with screws.
Functions: hours, minutes.
Case: red gold 5N18; 44x41x10.5mm; crown: Ø 6mm; polished finishing; double elliptical case in two parts: upper with double-face antireflection treat-

ment, lower with internal antireflection treatment; 30.40x33.40mm sapphire crystal open caseback held by 6 pentagonal screws; water resistant to 3atm.
Dial: 18K gold; polished finishing.
Strap: brown hand-stitched double-face alligator leather.
Suggested price: $216,000
Note: each timepiece is delivered with an individual Functional Testing Certificate.

ATHYS II   REF. 109.Y.60.907.CN.BA

Movement: manual-winding DR206 caliber, base: FP 151; 43-hour power-reserve; Ø36.64x1.90mm; 20 jewels; 21600 vph; 2-arm Cupro-beryllium balance; bridges decorated with Côtes de Genève; concave chamfering and 2N gilt engraving on the barrel-bridge; circular-grained mainplate; hand-chamfered screws with countersunk polished and beveled slots, satin-brushed and drawn out with a file.

Functions: small seconds at 9.
Case: white gold 5N18; 41x44x6.20mm; sapphire crystal caseback; water resistant to 3atm.
Dial: black lacquered; Roman numeral hours; minute circle with Arabic numerals; second indication with sunray motif radiating from the axis of the 3-arm seconds hand.
Strap: black alligator leather; classical buckle.
Suggested price: $19,100
Also available: in 18K red gold.

ATHYS III   REF. 110.Y.50.101.CB.BA

Movement: DR 1301 caliber; 45-hour power reserve; Ø 25.60mm; module: 25.60x28.80mm, height: 5mm; 35 jewels; 28,800 vph; 3-arm Glucydur ring; flat-balance spring.
Functions: big date at 12 without separator between the 2 numerals; small second; moonphase; power-reserve indicator.
Case: 18K red gold; 44x41x9.20mm; sapphire crystal caseback; water resis-

tant to 3atm.
Dial: lacquered white.
Strap: brown alligator leather; classical buckle.
Suggested price: $21,700
Also available: in white gold.

ELLISPOCURVEX PAPILLON   REF. 318.Y.70.351.CM.BD

Movement: patented Daniel Roth movement, DR 115 caliber; 45-hour power reserve; Ø 25.60mm; height: 2.98mm; hand beveled; Côtes de Genève finishing; 35 jewels; 28,800 vph; 3-arm Glucydur ring; flat-balance spring.
Functions: jumping hours; 2 retractable minute hands.
Case: platinum sapphire crystal caseback; 44x41x13.55mm; water resistant to 3atm.
Dial: 3-part guilloché pattern.
Strap: dark blue hand-stitched alligator leather; gold folding clasp.
Suggested price: $49,300
Also available: in red gold and white gold.

PAPILLON CHRONOGRAPHE   REF. 319.Z.60.394.CM.BD

Movement: DR 2319 caliber; 45-hour power reserve; Ø 31.50mm, height: 5.50mm; hand beveled; Côtes de Genève finishing; 45 jewels; 21,600 vph; 3-arm Cupro-beryllium ring; flat-balance spring.
Functions: jumping hours; 2 retractable minute hands; chronograph.
Case: white gold; sapphire crystal caseback; 46x43x15.80mm; water resistant to 3atm.
Dial: silvered-colored or ruthenium silver dial; transparent counters and marking adorned with Côtes de Genève.
Strap: black hand-stitched alligator leather; gold folding clasp.
Also available: yellow gold or red gold.
Suggested price: $45,300

IL GIOCATORE VENEZIANO   REF. 310.Z.50.110.CB.BD

Movement: DR 3700 caliber; 48-hour power reserve; Ø 28mm (base), 35.8x33mm (module), height: 5.80mm; hand beveled; Côtes de Genève finishing; 49 jewels; 18,000 vph; 2-arm Glucydur ring; gold adjusting screw; flat-balance spring.
Case: red gold 5N18; open back with sapphire crystal; 46x43x14.10mm; water resistant to 3atm.
Dial: gold; hand painted.
Strap: brown hand-stitched alligator leather; gold folding clasp.
Suggested price: $452,100
Also available: in white gold.

8-DAY TOURBILLON PERPETUAL CALENDAR   REF. 220.Y.20.146.CN.BD

Movement: manually wound DR 5301 caliber; 200-hour power reserve; 31.50x34.50mm, height: 8.10mm; hand beveled; Côtes de Genève finishing; 24 jewels; 21,600 vph; balance with screws; 2-arm Glucydur; flat-balance spring. **Functions:** tourbillon; power-reserve indicator with disc; perpetual calendar; moonphase.
Case: yellow gold 2N18; flip-over case at 12; 43.35x40.35x14.60mm; water resistant to 3atm.
Dial: upper dial in tinted sapphire with applied gold numerals; lower dial in transparent sapphire crystal and gold.
Strap: chocolate-brown hand-stitched alligator leather; red-gold folding clasp.
Suggested price: $180,900
Also available: red gold 5N18 and platinum.
Note: possibility to personalize the inside.

DAVID YURMAN
A Family Affair

Blessed with the hands of a sculptor, David Yurman started his jewelry empire 30 years ago at the crossroads of craft and originality. His company blossomed into one of America's most recognizable luxury brands and today has grown to include a successful collection of fine watches for men and women.

THIS PAGE
Evan, David and Sybil Yurman.

FACING PAGE
The 43mm stainless steel case is equipped with an automatic movement with date. The watch comes with a black, silver or anthracite dial.

With Yurman and his wife Sybil presiding over the company from its Manhattan offices, the brand's success has been a family affair from the beginning. Just five years ago, the family circle expanded as the couple's son, Evan, joined them to direct men's design for the brand.

This year, David Yurman takes its watch collection in a bold new direction with the brand's first-ever round models. "This is a new chapter in David Yurman watchmaking," Evan says. "We are laying the groundwork for the future with watches that honor the past, but are technically and visually innovative."

"We've always bonded as a family through our shared creativity. It feels good working together, bringing our visions to life like this," adds David.

Defined by contrast, the new round case conveys a respect for tradition that is at odds with the modern aesthetic of the sophisticated design. The visual tension between the two opposing perspectives results in a dynamic timepiece. The debut collection encompasses three watches.

The timeless elegance of the basic steel model includes a galvanic dial (black, silver, or anthracite) decorated with guilloché. The second watch serves as a calendar for the wrist, providing the day, month, date and moonphase at a glance. For the final model, the case is enlarged from 43mm to 46mm to accommodate the watch's automatic chronograph movement.

David Yurman lays the groundwork for the future with innovative watches that honor the past.

While the round collection represents a new chapter for David Yurman, the company isn't turning the page on previous models. In fact, two recently introduced watches—one for men, the other for women—epitomize the signature David Yurman style that's sustained the brand's popularity through the years.

Distinguished by a red tip, the second time-zone indicator makes its presence known as it sweeps over the 24-hour scale at the edge of the dial. The automatic movement governing the GMT function and date display is an official COSC-certified chronometer.

The inspiration behind the ladies' Waverly is instantly recognizable to any fan of David Yurman's fine jewelry. The distinct bracelet references the brand's signature Cable design, an early Yurman creation. After capturing the public's consciousness more than 20 years ago, it continues to captivate the fashion elite.

As the David Yurman brand celebrates its time-honored tradition and excellence in watchmaking, the GMT and Waverly watches embody the success of the past, while the new round watches symbolize the promise of the future.

THIS PAGE
Inspired by the design of Belmont Shadow model from 2007, Stinger watches are introduced as the next generation of Yurman creation. Limited edition of 75 pieces are available with the red accents and diamond bezel; and 10 pieces with all black diamonds.

de GRISOGONO
15 Years of Sensational Creativity

A native of Florence, Italy, de GRISOGONO founder Fawaz Gruosi was introduced to the world of jewelry by a famous craftsman of the city. After working for other brands, he founded his own company in 1993. Since then, Gruosi, guided by his intuition, has become an icon in the jewelry and watch industry.

For the fifteen-year anniversary of his company, Gruosi set up an incredible, two-story BaselWorld 2008 stand with spacious interiors and a richly decorated glass staircase. This 30-ton metal display was designed and created in Italy.

According to de GRISOGONO, precious jewels are represented in a baroque style, rich in shapes, volumes, colors and materials. In 1995, Gruosi reintroduced black diamonds to the jewelry world and they have since become a cornerstone of his success. Always searching for new resources, Gruosi discovered a second family of milky white diamonds in 2000, which he called "Icy Diamonds." In 2003, he continued his advances by introducing the exotic leather of galuchat to de GRISOGONO's timepieces and inventing the gold caramel color "Browny Brown Gold" through the PVD (Physical Vapor Deposition) process in 2005.

The latest collection is marked by Haute Jewelry creations where coral takes pride of place. These pieces complete a jewelry line that offers more than 330 novelties, including the stunningly adaptable Bocca rings. This ingenious creativity was transformed into extremely precious jeweled watches: the Lipstick watch inspired by the shape of a tube of lipstick; the Be Eight in the shape of the numeral; the Piccolina mounted on a rigid bracelet; and the Boule Watch worn as a necklace.

A magnificent display, de GRISOGONO's BaselWorld 2008 stand was inaugurated for the 15ᵗʰ anniversary of the brand.

Since the year 2000, de GRISOGONO has been a true watchmaker. Its collections are dominated by the Instrumento family. These watches that are of a very modern character can be worn by men and women, and have mechanical movements with automatic rewind. The company chose to give the watches generic calibers, but individualizes them by adding many exclusive functions that require several patents. The quartz movements are reserved for some of the smaller, women's models. A few of these Instrumentino pieces and a few of the new Instrumentino Small models display the original moonphase.

FACING PAGE   The surprisingly light Boule Watch is worn as a pendant and is set with 772 brown diamonds, 109 black diamonds, and 103 white diamonds. This pink-gold piece is powered by a quartz movement with manual rewind.

THIS PAGE   Instrumentino Small is shown in pink gold with a black enameled dial and flat numerals. The quartz movement is equipped with a moonphase function.

The most astonishing feat of de GRISOGONO is the ability to create mechanical complications. In 2005, the Occhio Repetizione Minuti and the Power Breaker made lasting impressions in everyone's mind. In 2006, the FG One followed with impact of its own. In 2008, de GRISOGONO awed people with the Meccanico dG, the first watch to combine a mechanical movement with manual rewind and display of a first time zone and the digital posting of a second time zone. Made possible by a sophisticated system of 23 rotary segments necessary to process the hours and minutes every 24 hours, there are 651 components to the movement. Along with a large case and skeleton dial, the revolutionary movement gave rise to 177 futuristic, limited edition timepieces. The Otturatore, another outstanding innovation, evolved on its own. Its mechanical movement with manual rewind is comprised of four functions—small second, date, moonphase, and power reserve. These watches are built to the purchaser's specifications. This new concept, the result of extensive research for optimal legibility, rests on a mobile, bidirectional dial and is equipped with a notch that can be used to position the function as the wearer desires.

The de GRISOGONO boldness has generated remarkably constant growth for 15 years. Established in Geneva, the company's sales have grown 25% each year. At the end of 2007, the sales reached 135 million Swiss francs; 53% in jewelry and 47% in the watch industry. The staff grew to 180 employees and 17 de GRISOGONO boutiques. Last year, several new employees were hired and, by 2011, the brand expects to have a network of 300 worldwide distributors.

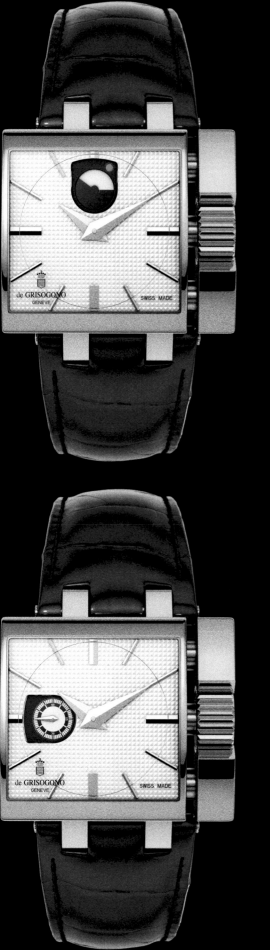

FACING PAGE
The Meccanico dG boasts
an exclusive manual-winding
movement of 651 components
with double spindle, and
analog and digital displays
with 23 moving segments.
This 56x48mm pink-gold piece
with a rubber case and open
dial displaying the movement
is fitted on a rubber bracelet.
This edition is limited to 177
watches.

THIS PAGE
Otturatore houses a mechanical
movement with manual
rewind holding 200 compo-
nents, more than 100 of which
are devoted to the displays:
small second, date, moon-
phase, and power reserve. The
pink-gold case's bidirectional
rotary center dial is decorated
with Clou de Paris.

FG ONE

REF. FG ONE N04

Movement: mechanical automatic movement.
Functions: jumping hour; retrograde minute and second; program hour; day and night indications on lower dial.
Case: 18K rose-gold two-piece case.
Dial: black dial.
Strap: black alligator strap.

GRANDE

REF. GRANDE N05

Movement: automatic movement.
Functions: large date at 6.
Case: polished 5N 18K rose-gold case; sapphire crystal caseback and lateral window; crown with de GRISOGONO crest; water resistant to 3atm.
Dial: brown guilloché dial; large date aperture at 3; pink-gold hands with SuperLumiNova; 9 pink-gold small indexes.

Strap: brown leather strap; de GRISOGONO 5N 18K rose-gold folding clasp.

MECCANICO dG

REF. MECCANICO N06

Movement: mechanical dual-time movement.
Functions: pink-gold analogical and digital displays.
Case: pink-gold case; pink-gold plates on the sides; exhibition caseback; water resistant 3atm.
Dial: metalized sapphire dial; PVD indexes.
Strap: natural rubber strap; pink-gold de GRISOGONO clasp.

INSTRUMENTO NOVANTATRE

REF. NOVANTATRE N07

Movement: mechanical automatic movement.
Functions: annual calendar; with date and month apertures; small seconds.
Case: polished 18K rose-gold two-piece case; sapphire crystal caseback; water resistant to 3atm.
Dial: brown dial; Arabic numerals and hands in polished 18K rose gold.

Strap: brown alligator strap; rose-gold fold-over clasp with de GRISOGONO crest.

OTTURATORE   REF. OTTURATORE N01

Movement: automatic movement.
Functions: seconds; date; power reserve; moonphase.
Case: 5N 18K rose-gold case.
Dial: silvery dial.
Strap: black alligator strap.

POWER BREAKER   REF. POWER BREAKER N04

Movement: automatic chronograph movement.
Functions: 2 counters.
Case: 5N 18K rose-gold case; crown engraved with de GRISOGONO crest and crown protection on upper part in 5N 18K rose-gold; integrated 18K rose-gold pushbuttons at 2 and 4; screwed caseback in 18K rose gold; water resistant to 3atm.
Dial: 2-level dial; lower level in satin-finished dark brown; 5N 18K rose-gold hour and minute hands with painted brown centers; steering wheel enhanced with 6 18K rose-gold screws.
Strap: dark brown or black rubber strap; 5N 18K rose-gold de GRISOGONO folding clasp.

INSTRUMENTINO SMALL   REF. TINO SMALL N02

Movement: quartz movement.
Functions: hours, minutes; moonphase.
Case: 5N 18K pink-gold; water resistant up to 3atm.
Dial: black lacquered dial; Arabic numerals index.
Bracelet: 5N 18K pink-gold bracelet; deployment clasp.

INSTRUMENTO N° UNO   REF. UNO DF N11

Movement: automatic movement.
Functions: dual time; large date aperture.
Case: polished 18K rose-gold case; crown set with a natural black diamond; sapphire crystal caseback; water resistant to 3atm.
Dial: rose-gold with black lacquered dial; polished 5N 18K rose-gold appliqué Arabic numerals.
Strap: genuine black alligator strap; polished 5N 18K rose-gold de GRISOGONO folding clasp.

DeWITT
Patently Superior

The history of DeWitt has a lineage unmatched by other watch brands, thanks in large part to its founder Jérôme de Witt, a fifth-generation descendant of the brother of Napoleon Bonaparte. This heritage means that DeWitt is poised for the future, yet uniquely sensitive to the traditions of the past.

N o stranger to technical innovation, DeWitt has obtained numerous patents for its advances in horological mastery, combining micro-mechanical achievements with a refined aesthetic appeal and avant-garde sophistication. The relatively young brand, with considerable accomplishments already under its belt, is headed to become a leader in the world of luxury watchmakingóby diving headfirst into complications.

It is a puzzle that has plagued watchmakers since the tourbillon was invented: how can one ensure a regular transmission of energy to the tourbillon, given that the barrel spring provides a decreasing amount of energy as it unwinds? After centuries of research into this quandary by watchmakers of all stripes, DeWitt devised the perfect solution in 2006 with its Tourbillon Force Constante, adding a mechanism to change the variable force emitting from the barrel spring into a steady source of energy. Now DeWitt surprises yet again with an innovation that relays energy to the power-reserve indicator. Rotating the crown and winding the barrel spring simultaneously drives a miniature chain that uses an intermediate wheel to slide the power-reserve indicator along a worm screw. The arrow shows the amount of energy left in the barrel spring.

> DeWitt surprises yet again with an innovation that relays energy to the power-reserve indicator.

THIS PAGE
This fascinating Academia Force Constante a Chaine is powered by a manual-wound movement featuring a patented constant force tourbillon. This model features a platinum case and dial with a sapphire crystal and black alligator strap.

FACING PAGE
TOP LEFT This rose-gold 750 Academia Night Chronograph is driven by a self-winding movement, visible through the sapphire crystal caseback, and topped with a black and white guilloché dial with SuperLumiNova application

TOP RIGHT The Academia Night Chronograph (pictured here in rose and white gold 750) is fitted on a black rubber strap.

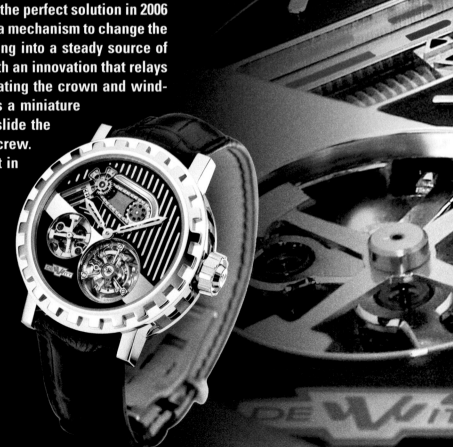

Bolstering DeWitt's well-earned reputation for originality, the brand breaks new ground with an expansion of the brand's successful Academia Chronograph Séquentiel line. Standing alone in the world of chronographs, known for its formal signature and sequential seconds counter, the Academia Night Chronograph continues the adventure, exploring the nocturnal world with nighttime readability. The new Night Chronograph is available in two versions: the first, crafted in rose and white gold, has an unusually dark black SuperLumiNova coating on the minute track and minute and second counters, all on a black dial. The second model boasts a case made entirely of 18-karat rose gold, with white SuperLumiNova printed on the minute and second counters. A self-winding mechanical movement powers both versions of the Night Chronograph.

ACADEMIA FORCE CONSTANTE A CHAINE   REF. AC.8050.20.1020

Movement: mechanical manual-wound manufactured by DeWitt caliber DW8050; Ø 30mm, thickness: 7.8mm; 72-hours with chain-driven device, indicator on worm screw power-reserve; 21,600 vph; 25 jewels.
Functions: tourbillon with constant force; special 4-arm Gyromax; flat balance-spring; water resistant to 30 meters.
Case: 950 platinum; Ø 43mm, thickness: 12mm; sapphire caseback.

Dial: Côtes de Genève finishing; folding clasp in 750 platinum.
Strap: black alligator.
Price: $280,000
Note: strictly limited edition to 50 pieces.

ACADEMIA TOURBILLON DIFFERENTIEL   REF. AC.8002.20.M958

Movement: mechanical manual-wound manufactured by DeWitt; 120-hours power reserve; Ø 30mm, height: 8.90mm; 21,600 vph; 24 jewels; Côtes de Genève-style blue, black and gray platinum bridge.
Functions: flat balance-spring; water resistant to 50 meters.
Case: 950 platinum; blue Cotes de Genève plate and bridge; rubber inserts; Ø 43mm, thickness: 12mm; sapphire caseback.

Dial: special patented IRM system power reserve indicator.
Strap: black alligator leather; 960 platinum folding clasp.
Price: $250,000
Note: strictly limited edition to 50 pieces.

ACADEMIA TOURBILLON DIFFERENTIEL   REF. AC.8002.53.M1052

Movement: mechanical manual-wound manufactured by DeWitt; 120-hours power reserve; Ø 30mm, height: 8.90mm; 21,600 vph; 24 jewels; Côtes de Genève-style blue, black or chocolate and gray platinum bridge.
Functions: flat balance-spring; water resistant to 50 meters.
Case: rose gold; 18K chocolate Cotes de Genève plate and bridge; Ø 43mm, thickness: 12mm; sapphire caseback.

Dial: special patented IRM system power reserve indicator.
Strap: brown alligator leather; pink-gold folding clasp.
Price: $220,000
Note: strictly limited edition to 250 pieces.

NEBULA   REF: AC.7021.35.M1001

Movement: mechanical self-winding DW 7021 caliber; 42-hour power reserve; Ø 25.6mm, height: 3.6mm; 28,800 vph; 21 jewels; black or gray Côtes de Genève motif.
Functions: perpetual calendar GMT; Glucydur balance; flat balance-spring; water resistant to 30 meters.
Case: rose gold and white gold, titanium; black ceramics; Ø 43mm, thickness: 12mm; sapphire caseback.

Dial: black and blue Silicium planetary nebula; Goldfluss moon disc; white mother-of-pearl moon; gray counters surrounded with rose gold.
Strap: black alligator leather; folding clasp in 750-rose gold.
Price: $94,000
Note: strictly limited edition to 99 pieces.

NEBULA
REF: AC.7021.34.M1000

Movement: mechanical self-winding DW 7021 caliber; 42-hour power reserve; Ø 25.6mm, height: 3.6mm; 28,800 vph; 21 jewels; black or gray Côtes de Genève motif.
Functions: perpetual calendar GMT; Glucydur balance; flat balance-spring; water resistant to 30 meters.
Case: white gold, titanium; black ceramics; Ø 43mm, thickness: 12mm; sapphire caseback.
Dial: blue Silicium planetary nebula; Goldfluss moon disc; white mother-of-pearl moon; gray counters surrounded with white gold.
Strap: black alligator leather; folding clasp in 750-white gold.
Price: $96,000
Note: strictly limited edition to 99 pieces.

ACADEMIA NIGHT CHRONOGRAPHE
REF. AC.6005.70A.M250

Movement: mechanical self-winding; 42-hour power reserve; Ø 30mm, thickness: 7.8mm; 28,800 vph; 27 jewels.
Functions: chronograph; 30-minute graduated counter; 3-arm Glucydur balance; flat spring-balance; water resistant to 50 meters.
Case: rose and white gold 750; rubber inserts; Ø 43mm, thickness: 13mm; sapphire crystal screw-on caseback.
Dial: black and white guilloché center; Arabic numerals in 18K rose gold, alternating white and black SuperLumiNova application; 21mm lug.
Strap: black rubber; 18K rose-gold folding clasp.
Price: $36,900
Note: strictly limited edition to 99 pieces.

ACADEMIA NIGHT CHRONOGRAPHE
REF. AC.6005.53.M255

Movement: mechanical self-winding; 42-hour power reserve; Ø 30mm, thickness: 7.8mm; 28,800 vph; 27 jewels.
Functions: chronograph; 30-minute graduated counter; 3-arm Glucydur balance; flat spring-balance; water resistant to 50 meters.
Case: rose gold 750; Ø 43mm, thickness: 13mm; sapphire crystal screw-on caseback.
Dial: black and white guilloché center; Arabic numerals in 18K rose gold, alternating white and black SuperLumiNova application; 21mm lug.
Strap: brown alligator leather; 18K rose-gold folding clasp.
Price: $36,900
Note: strictly limited edition to 250 pieces.

WX-1

Movement: mechanical hand-wound; 504-hour power reserve; vertical flying tourbillon; electronically driven pointed tool, or by hand; 21,600 vph.
Functions: hours, minutes displayed by rotating discs; Glucydur balance; flat spring-balance; water resistant to 30 meters.
Case: 18K rose gold; titanium and aluminum; thickness: 21.17mm, length: 72.51mm, width: 48.64mm; inter-horn width: 24mm; sapphire crystal screw-on caseback; black eloxed lithium-aluminum.
Strap: black rubber; 18K rose-gold buckle.
Price: $650,000
Note: strictly limited edition to 33 pieces.

DIMIER
Design Virtuoso

Pascal Raffy knows a brilliant idea when he hears one. A few years ago, a longtime collector asked him to create a special edition Bovet with the crown moved to 3:00 from its position at 12:00—one of the brand's design signatures. Not only did he grant the collector's request, Raffy launched an entire brand around the idea with Dimier 1738.

THIS PAGE
Pascal Raffy, President and CEO of Dimier.

FACING PAGE
TOP   The Dimier 1738 watch factory is nestled in the lush forests of the Swiss Jura. Home to a cadre of skilled artisans, the facility creates the complex movements in-house that are used to power the watchmaker's limited edition timepieces.

BOTTOM   The third installment of Dimier's Récital collection is a 48mm grand complication called Orbis Mundi. Its second time zone with day/night indicator is synchronized with the black disc featuring 24 destination cities. Both are adjusted easily via a pair of buttons on the case.

Raffy took over as president of Bovet eight years ago, rejuvenating the brand and captivating collectors with a procession of ever-more luxurious timepieces. Dimier began in 2006 when Raffy acquired a former supplier's factory in the town of Tramelan.

Today, the production facility is home to a number of the Jura region's top creative artisans. Each is dedicated to various aspects of haute horlogerie, such as the development and production of tourbillons, mechanical movements, mainsprings and more.

The workshop's vast capabilities free Dimier's creativity while ensuring its watches will always maintain a strict level of quality. As the factory grows steadily, its focus continues to be on producing calibers in-house for the next generation of Dimier watches.

More than just a point of pride, the facility in Tramelan elevates Dimier into an elite group of manufacture watchmakers; what makes the accomplishment all the more incredible is how quickly it happened. In less than a decade, Raffy has moved both Dimier and Bovet closer to autonomy. It's an achievement envied by more than a few watchmakers.

When Dimier released Récital 1 in 2007, it was the first of what would become consistent unveilings conducted by the watchmaker. Its newest limited edition models, the Récital 2 and the Récital 3 Orbis Mundi®, arrived in 2008.

Like its older sibling Bovet, Dimier respects exclusivity and limits production of each model to 50 watches each in platinum, red gold and white gold. And while it shares Bovet's refined visual aesthetic, the Dimier collection manages to carve out its own distinct identity based on designs that feature the crown in its traditional location a 3:00.

With the first few notes of its Récital collection, Dimier is transporting collectors into ecstatic reveries with superlative timepieces that balance Swiss tradition with audacious creativity. Based on the success of the Récital collection, one thing is certain: Raffy is conducting the business of watchmaking like a virtuoso intent on writing an horological opus.

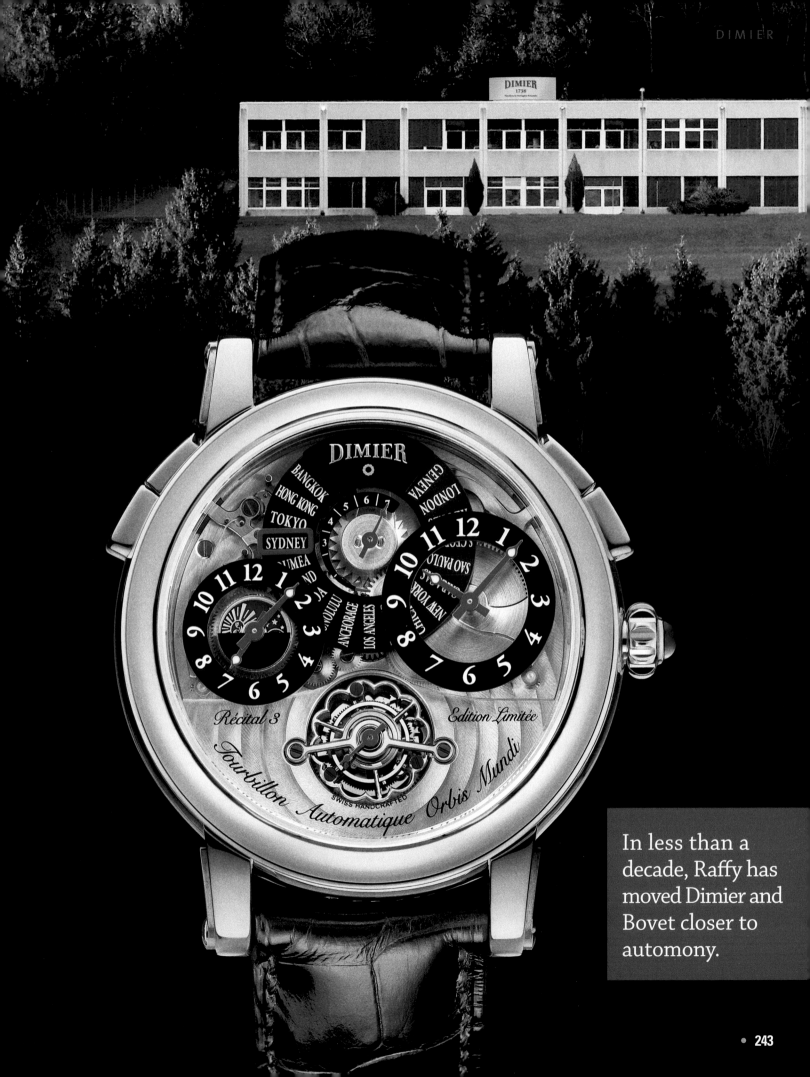

In less than a
decade, Raffy has
moved Dimier and
Bovet closer to
automony.

The third member in Dimier's Récital collection is a grand complication called Récital 3 Orbis Mundi.

The limited edition watch includes a transparent mineral rock crystal anchored over the top half of the dial. The round index for the minutes and hours is positioned opposite the indicators for the second time zone and day/night. A rotating disc adorned with the names of 24 cities is positioned at 12:00. When the button on the side of the case is engaged, the names advance, automatically adjusting the second time-zone indicator. Located in the center of the city disc, Dimier includes an indicator that monitors how much of Orbis Mundi's seven-day power reserve remains.

The cage of the 60-second tourbillon is decorated with an arabesque Lotus flower design. Blued screws anchor the design to the tourbillon and also secure the tourbillon's bridge. Adding another splash of color, a small red hand sits atop the tourbillon to track the seconds.

Complementing the technical achievements of Orbis Mundi's automatic tourbillon movement, the watch is decorated in the finest Swiss tradition. Instead of a traditional dial, the watch derives its visual personality from the movement's exposed bottom plate. Artists engraved it in the distinctive Côtes de Genève style, spreading ripples across the bottom plate as though the tourbillon were a pebble dropped into a pond.

Orbis Mundi is fitted with a sapphire crystal exhibition caseback and is water resistant to 3atm.

The company's name refers to the Dimier brothers, 19th-century watchmakers who ran a successful watchmaking business in Fleurier and later Geneva. In both cities, Charles-Louis and Auguste-Antoine Dimier were known for both the precision and artistry of their watches.

Both studied watchmaking in Geneva before starting their own factory in 1846. Auguste-Antoine stayed behind in Fleurier, working in the building that would later become the city's museum. Charles-Louis moved to China where he established an office in Shanghai. In fact, the ambitious brothers were among the first Swiss watchmakers to import watches to the Chinese market.

Today, the Dimier brand honors the brothers' technical prowess and bold vision with a collection of luxurious timepieces that share their deep dedication to the art of watchmaking.

LEFT Dedicated to exclusivity, Dimier will produce the Orbis Mundi in four 50-piece limited editions: platinum, red gold (shown here), white gold and white-gold PVD.

CENTER The Récital 3 DIMIER movement, caliber 13BA05, is an exquisite and refined self-winding movement with a seven-day power reserve.

RIGHT Brothers Charles-Louis (top) and Auguste-Antoine Dimier (bottom).

DIOR WATCHES
Unequalled Know-How and Creativity Since 1947

The French Haute Couture has its requirements for luxury, creation and know-how; Swiss watchmaking has its imperatives for reliability and precision.

EXPERTISE WRITTEN INTO THE DNA OF THE DIOR FASHION HOUSE

Since 1947, the Haute Couture Dior studios of Avenue Montaigne have housed the best workers able to achieve in only a few weeks the Couture challenges set for them by the ideas of creative geniuses, most recently, those of John Galliano.

Parisian like the Dior woman, the designer Victoire de Castellane, has in turn given birth to exclusively handmade jewelry in the Parisian workshops since 1999. Sewn together with knowledge, creativity and the highest of watchmaking standards, it follows that Dior watches had to come into the world in the international watchmaking cradle in Switzerland, at La Chaux-de-Fonds.

Created in the studios of Avenue Montaigne, developed by a team of watchmaking experts, each of its components tested in various ways, assembled within the production unit named Les Ateliers Horlogers Dior, Dior watches continue the logic of excellence embodied by the fashion house. Traditionally surrounded for its Couture division by the best embroiderers (Maison Lesage) or feather-workers (Maison Lemarié), Dior naturally turned to the Zenith Manufacture to develop its Irréductible movement specific to the limited editions of Chiffre Rouge.

In 2008, Dior entrusted the elaboration of its first Tourbillon caliber to Concepto and—following the same pattern of logic for the setting of its watches with precious stones—Dior turned to the Bunter House in Geneva.

It is along the same lines as with a Couture garment, beautiful right down to the details of its lining, that Dior watches seek their inspiration.

The casebacks with their graphic details and their tinted sapphire crystals reveal the hidden luxury of the automatic movements within the Christal and Chiffre Rouge.

FROM LEFT TO RIGHT:
I03 Chiffre Rouge; Les Ateliers Horlogers Dior in Switzerland; Creation of a Couture dress (photo: Sophie Carré); Ready-to-Wear Dior Homme Spring/Summer 2009 (photo: Patrick Stable); Bar suit; Beneath a Haute Couture dress.

A highly creative watchmaking thanks to Dior's three different universes.

Inventor of the famous "New Look" who turned around the Parisian style with long skirts made of numerous meters of fabric, and pinched waists when bodies were starting to free themselves, the Dior Style revolutionized fashion after the Second World War.

With a strong taste for extremes and for the highly creative, the famous fashion house offers a personality with three facets of three designer universes: Haute Couture and Ready-to-Wear, Men's Ready-to-Wear, and Jewellery.

CHRISTAL

A couture icon created by Galliano in Spring 2005, the Dior Christal timepiece incorporates sapphire crystal, normally used for the watch glass, as inserts on the bracelet and the bezel.

An innovative material, it can be colored infinitely and thus adapt itself to the baroque ideas of the designer.

In turn, dressed in the emblematic colors of the house, pure or set with diamonds, and on a steel or rubber bracelet, the Dior Christal watch also surprises with its Tourbillon caliber model in white gold set with baguette diamonds.

CHIFFRE ROUGE

Associating the formal vocabulary of Dior Homme and its values of excellence, Chiffre Rouge has served as a seal defining an identity since 2004. The initiated and the collectors recognize its technical performance, the accuracy and timelessness of its shape, and the authentic universe which elaborates its codes.

The principle of a luxury for oneself, exclusive and mysterious, is reaffirmed here with component materials of excellent quality.

The functional asymmetry of Chiffre Rouge's watch case renews the watchmaking design, with the larger right side encompassing all the controls (pushbuttons for the chronograph and the winding mechanism) and a bezel indented between 9:00 and 12:00 for an improved prehension. The pebble size, the smooth contours, the rounded surface, and the extreme flexibility of the bracelet make it a fluid and enveloping object.

Chiffre Rouge is available with an automatic movement and in steel and rubber versions in permanent collections; an Irréductible caliber developed by Zenith for Dior powers the limited-edition steel or solid gold versions.

LA D DE DIOR

A story created by de Castellane in autumn 2003, la D de Dior is inspired by a man's watch, a macho from the 1970s, which a woman thinks about continually.

Customary to exuberant creations transmitted from generation to generation through her work as a designer for Dior Jewellery, here de Castellane breaks her own codes by endowing her first watch with a pattern the exact opposite of her style. She wants it to be timeless, couture, with the guilloché effect on the bracelet and jewelry through the work done around the precious stones.

FROM LEFT TO RIGHT:
La D de Dior; "Incroyables et Merveilleuses Cerise" ring; High jewellery setting; Lady Dior bag; Dior Christal Tourbillon.

DIOR CHRISTAL TOURBILLON   REF. CD115960M001

Movement: Calibre Dior Tourbillon; manual winding; 80-hour power reserve.
Functions: hours, minutes.
Case: Ø 42mm; 18K white gold; bezel set with 54 baguette diamonds (3.62 carats) and 8 scratch-proof black sapphire crystal inserts; crown set with a rose-cut diamond (0.34 carat); water resistant to 50 meters.
Dial: transparent shaded gray sapphire crystal set with 43 baguette diamonds (0.96 carat).
Bracelet: 18K white gold set with 2 pyramid-cut scratch-proof black sapphire crystal ranks and 44 baguette diamonds on the central rank (10.90 carats).
Note: limited edition of 10 pieces.

DIOR CHRISTAL AMETHYST   REF. CD114560M001

Movement: ETA Swiss automatic; 42-hour power reserve.
Functions: hours, minutes, seconds.
Case: Ø 38mm; 18K white gold; bezel set with 84 baguette amethysts (3.18 carats); crown set with a rose-cut amethyst (0.15 carat); water resistant to 50 meters.
Dial: blue-gray mother-of-pearl marquetry set with 30 diamonds (0.08 carat) and 60 pink baguette sapphires (0.53 carat).
Bracelet: 18K white gold set with 1 pyramid-cut scratch-proof amethyst colored sapphire crystal central rank and 2 rows 108 baguette amethysts (13.50 carats).
Note: limited edition of 25 pieces.

DIOR CHRISTAL BLACK   REF. CD11431HM001

Movement: ETA Swiss chronograph quartz.
Functions: chronograph; hours, minutes, seconds; date.
Case: Ø 38mm; stainless steel; bezel and horns set with 108 diamonds (1.50 carats) and 14 scratch-proof black sapphire crystal inserts; water resistant to 50 meters.
Dial: black lacquered; set with 195 diamonds (0.56 carat).
Bracelet: stainless steel set with pyramid-cut scratch-proof black sapphire crystal and 606 diamonds (9.10 carats).
Note: limited edition of 100 pieces.

DIOR CHRISTAL AUTOMATIC BLUE   REF. CD114510M001

Movement: ETA Swiss automatic; 42-hours power reserve.
Functions: hours, minutes, seconds.
Case: Ø 38mm; stainless steel; bezel set with 88 diamonds (1.10 carats) and 16 scratch-proof blue sapphire crystal inserts; water resistant to 50 meters.
Dial: shaded blue mother-of-pearl; set with 36 diamonds (0.18 carat) of which 24 are luminous in the dark.
Bracelet: stainless steel set with pyramid-cut scratch-proof blue sapphire crystal and 108 diamonds (1.62 carats).
Note: limited edition of 500 pieces.

DIOR CHRISTAL AUTOMATIC BLACK   REF. CD113511M001

Movement: ETA Swiss automatic; 40-hour power reserve.
Functions: hours, minutes, seconds; date.
Case: Ø 33mm; stainless steel; bezel set with 80 diamonds (1 carat) and 16 scratch-proof black sapphire crystal inserts; water resistant to 50 meters.
Dial: black lacquered and silver; set with 97 diamonds (0.39 carat).
Bracelet: stainless steel set with 3 pyramid-cut scratch-proof black sapphire crystal ranks.

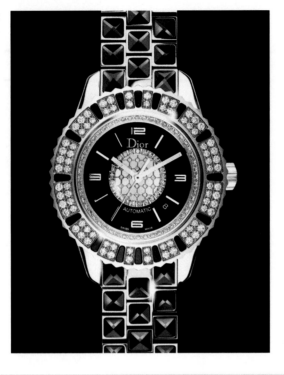

DIOR CHRISTAL AUTOMATIC WHITE   REF. CD113512M001

Movement: ETA Swiss automatic, 40-hour power reserve.
Functions: hours, minutes, seconds; date.
Case: Ø 33mm; stainless steel; bezel set with 80 diamonds (1 carat) and 16 scratch-proof white sapphire crystal inserts; water resistant to 50 meters.
Dial: white mother-of-pearl and silver; set with 97 diamonds (0.39 carat).
Bracelet: stainless steel set with 3 pyramid-cut scratch-proof white sapphire crystal ranks.

DIOR CHRISTAL BLACK   REF. CD11431CM001

Movement: ETA Swiss chronograph quartz.
Functions: chronograph; hours, minutes, seconds; date.
Case: Ø 38mm; stainless steel; bezel set with 76 diamonds (0.76 carat) and 14 scratch-proof black sapphire crystal inserts; water resistant to 50 meters.
Dial: black lacquered; set with 14 diamonds (0.07 carat).
Bracelet: stainless steel set with 3 pyramid-cut scratch-proof black sapphire crystal ranks.
Also available: Ø 28mm and Ø 33mm ETA Swiss quartz.

DIOR CHRISTAL WHITE   REF. CD114311R001

Movement: ETA Swiss chronograph quartz.
Functions: chronograph; hours, minutes, seconds; date.
Case: Ø 38mm; stainless steel; bezel set with 48 diamonds (0.24 carat) and 23 scratch-proof white sapphire crystal inserts; water resistant to 50 meters.
Dial: white lacquered.
Strap: genuine rubber and stainless steel set with 1 pyramid-cut scratch-proof white sapphire crystal rank.
Also available: Ø 28mm and Ø 33mm ETA Swiss quartz.

LA D DE DIOR MITZA — REF. CD043154A001

Movement: ETA Swiss quartz.
Functions: hours, minutes.
Case: Ø 38mm; 18K yellow gold; bezel set with 72 yellow sapphires (0.65 carat); water resistant to 30 meters.
Dial: golden and black lacquered set with 184 yellow sapphires (0.81 carat).
Strap: shiny black alligator.

Note: Limited edition of 99 pieces.

LA D DE DIOR — REF. CD043112M001

Movement: ETA Swiss quartz.
Functions: hours, minutes.
Case: Ø 38mm; stainless steel; bezel set with 72 diamonds (0.65 carat); water resistant to 30 meters.
Dial: blue-gray; set with 61 diamonds in spiral style (0.48 carat).
Bracelet: stainless steel.

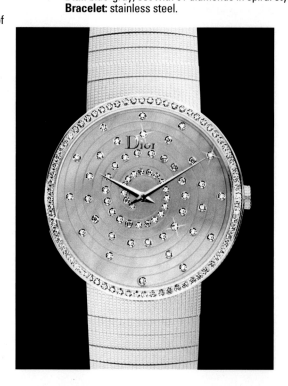

LA D DE DIOR — REF. CD041111A005

Movement: ETA Swiss quartz.
Functions: hours, minutes.
Case: Ø 33mm; stainless steel; bezel set with 60 diamonds (0.54 carat), water resistant to 30 meters.
Dial: black varnished; set with 153 diamonds (0.74 carat).
Strap: black genuine satin.

Note: limited edition of 99 pieces.

LA BABY D DE DIOR — REF. CD041111M003

Movement: ETA Swiss quartz.
Functions: hours, minutes.
Case: Ø 23mm; stainless steel; bezel set with 52 diamonds (0.26 carat), water resistant to 30 meters.
Dial: white mother-of-pearl; set with 12 diamond indexes (0.06 carat).
Bracelet: stainless steel.

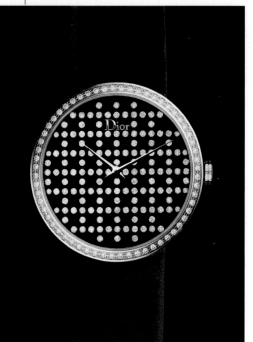

CHIFFRE ROUGE I03   REF. CD084850M001

Movement: automatic chronograph chronometer, calibre Irreductible by Zenith for Dior (COSC certified); oscillating weight in sapphire crystal and gold, 50-hour power reserve.
Functions: chronograph; hours, minutes, seconds, date.
Case: Ø 38mm; 18K yellow gold set with 25 diamonds (0.315 carat); transparent sapphire caseback; water resistant to 50 meters.
Dial: golden set with 4 princess-cut diamonds (0.06 carat).
Bracelet: 18K yellow gold.
Note: limited edition to 15 pieces.

CHIFFRE ROUGE I02   REF. CD084860M001

Movement: automatic chronograph chronometer, calibre Irreductible by Zenith for Dior; COSC certified; 50-hour power reserve.
Functions: chronograph; hours, minutes, seconds; date.
Case: Ø 38mm; 18K white gold set with 27 diamonds (0.24 carat); milk-white tinted sapphire caseback; water resistant to 50 meters.
Dial: white lacquered set with 4 baguette diamonds (0.12 carat).
Bracelet: 18K white gold.
Note: limited edition to 30 pieces.

CHIFFRE ROUGE A05   REF. CD084840R001

Movement: ETA Swiss automatic chronograph chronometer; COSC certified; 42-hour power reserve.
Functions: chronograph; hours, minutes, seconds; date; tachymeter.
Case: Ø 41mm; stainless steel molded with black rubber; water resistant to 50 meters.
Dial: black sun-brushed with tachymeter scale.
Bracelet: stainless steel molded with black rubber.

CHIFFRE ROUGE A03   REF. CD084510M001

Movement: ETA Swiss automatic; 42-hour power reserve.
Functions: hours, minutes, seconds; date.
Case: Ø 36mm; stainless steel; water resistant to 50 meters.
Dial: black sun-brushed.
Bracelet: stainless steel.

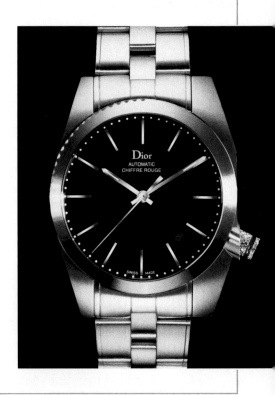

EBEL
Building on a Strong Foundation

Ebel achieves a rare status among watchmakers by creating timepieces that inspire devotion among both men and women. Nearly a century after Eugène Blum and Alice Lévy founded the company known as "The Architects of Time," Ebel continues to build upon its reputation, offering instantly recognizable watches that pulse with masculine brawn and sparkle with feminine charm.

Ebel expands its sophisticated 1911 collection with the newly introduced Tekton line, featuring two limited edition timekeepers designed for gentlemen with a passion for both European football and fine Swiss watchmaking. The watches are the result of partnerships with two elite football clubs—Bayern Munich of Germany and Arsenal of England. Ebel will be adding other clubs to this line in the coming years.

The automatic chronograph movement that powers these Tekton watches was developed and assembled in-house at Ebel's workshop in La Chaux-de-Fonds, Switzerland. Watchmakers numbered the caliber 245, which represents the two 45-minute halves of a football match. In fact, the dial features a retrograde 45-minute counter that shows the elapsed time, while the disc at 6:00 indicates the 15 minutes allotted for injury time in a match.

Collaborating with Ebel's watchmakers, each team selected the colors, materials and style of their respective watches. Bayern Munich opted for a dark design that's nearly all black, while Arsenal selected details that echo the team's colors. Visible through the football-motif caseback, the watch sports a COSC-certified, automatic movement emblazoned with the corresponding team's logo.

Both watches skillfully combine Ebel's technical expertise with the winning spirits of these prestigious football clubs.

The Arsenal 1911 Tekton Automatic Chronograph sports an Ebel proprietary caliber 245 with oscillating weight, visible through a football-shaped caseback.

Ebel teams with two of Europe's top football clubs for limited edition versions of its 1911 Tekton.

Both 1911 Tekton Automatic Chronographs include a 45-minute counter to measure the halves of a football match, as well as a 15-minute counter for the match's injury time. The Arsenal (top) version integrates the club's colors into the design, while the Bayern Munich version is nearly all black.

The spotlight continues to shine on the 1911 collection as Ebel presents new color options for its sporty 1911 Discovery line of automatic chronographs. The hexagonal stainless steel case is now available with an orange, blue or red tachometric scale on the watch's aluminum bezel.

Like the original 1911 Discovery that debuted in 2007, these new timepieces feature a COSC-certified movement that controls the chronograph's central seconds, as well as 30-minute and 12-hour indicators. The dial also includes a running seconds along with day and date displays. To allow readability in the dark, the hour markers and hands are coated with SuperLumiNova.

Several other features add to the 1911 Discovery's rugged appeal, including a water-resistant design that uses a screw-lock crown and pusher guards to ensure the watch's integrity to 10atm. Along with the movement's reliability and the design's durability, Ebel enhances the watch's visual charm by pairing the case with a bracelet distinguished by its polished and brushed finish or a "technofiber" strap made to keep up with the demands of active lifestyles.

Ebel pays tribute to the essence of femininity with Ray of Light, the latest addition to the watchmaker's popular Brasilia collection of fashion timepieces.

The iridescent white mother-of-pearl dial is studded with 10 square diamond hour markers, providing a luminous center from which a sunburst guilloché radiates. The sparkling beams spread out over the sleek rectangular case in the form of 36 diamonds arranged in what Ebel calls a "halo of sunbeams." The light show continues onto the dial with Roman numerals at 12 and 6, plus hour and minute hands, all of which have been skeletonized and filled with white SuperLumiNova.

From a design perspective, several white accents reinforce the Ray of Light's purity, such as a ceramic cabochon on the crown and ceramic insets on both sides of the case. Inspired by the shape of the Brasilia bracelet, the Ray of Light offers a white rubber strap adorned with a playful butterfly buckle.

Ebel continues its focus on the Brasilia collection, launching its new Brasilia Fashion line with gem-set black and white models. Made for women who love the charming personality of jewelry watches, but also desire a larger watch, the Brasilia Fashion delivers a case that is 32.5mm in diameter, instead of the 28mm case of the standard Brasilia.

This new size will appeal to women who are wearing men's watches today because they can't find a ladies' model large enough to make the kind of bold fashion statement they want. The Brasilia Fashion satisfies their yearning for a generously proportioned case that still retains Ebel's signature *joie de vivre*.

Ebel's watch designers make good use of the larger size, adding an extra line of diamonds to the polished stainless steel case, which is paved with 106 brilliant-cut gems. Like the Ray of Light, the Brasilia Fashion uses 10 square diamonds as hour markers accompanied by the Roman numerals 12 and 6. The black and white versions of the Brasilia Fashion both offer matching rubber straps.

FACING PAGE
Ebel now offers the 1911 Discovery with a tachometric scale in orange, red or blue. These automatic chronographs are presented in a hexagonal stainless steel case and feature an ultra-precise COSC-certified movement.

THIS PAGE
TOP   The Brasilia Ray of Light's rectangular stainless steel case is set with 36 brilliant-cut diamonds arranged in a "halo of sunbeams."

BOTTOM   Larger than the standard Brasilia, Ebel's new Brasilia Fashion line is presented in a 32.5mm stainless steel case set with 106 diamonds. The watchmaker offers black and white models that utilize diamonds as hour markers, complemented by Roman numerals at 12 and 6.

EBEL 1911 TEKTON CHRONOGRAPH 137   REF. 1215886

Movement: Swiss Ebel automatic chronograph movement caliber 137; Ø 31mm, thickness: 6.40mm; 28,800 vph; COSC-certified movement; bi-directional rotor on ball bearing; 322 components; 48-hour power reserve.
Functions: 3 counters: 30 minutes at 3, 12 hours at 6, small seconds at 9; center seconds; tachometer scale on the flange; calendar aperture at 4.
Case: stainless steel case with rubber bezel and 6 oriented drill-through screws; double-sided antireflective sapphire crystal; sapphire crystal caseback; water resistant to 20atm.
Dial: black/gray; index markers with SuperLumi-Nova; inverted Clous de Paris motif.
Strap: black rubber; deployment clasp.
Suggested price: $8,950

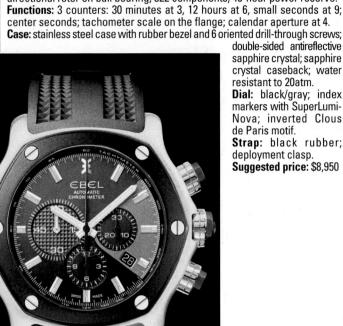

EBEL 1911 TEKTON CHRONOGRAPH 139   REF. 1215887

Movement: Swiss Ebel automatic chronograph movement caliber 139; Ø 31mm, thickness: 7.40mm; 28,800 vph; COSC-certified movement; bi-directional rotor on ball bearing; 322 components; 48-hour power reserve.
Functions: hours at 6, constant seconds at 9, minutes at 12; center seconds; minute track with divisions for 1/5 of a second; tachometer scale on the flange; semi-instantaneous action date disc at 3; fast date correction.
Case: stainless steel with 6 oriented drill-through screws on the bezel; double-sided antireflective sapphire crystal; sapphire crystal caseback; water resistant to 20atm.
Dial: black skeleton; 11 hand-applied hour-markers with SuperLumiNova.
Strap: black hand-sewn large-scale alligator leather; white stitching; deployment clasp.
Suggested price: $9,950

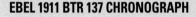

EBEL 1911 TEKTON CHRONOGRAPH 245   REF. 1215911

Movement: Swiss Ebel automatic chronograph movement caliber 245; Ø 31mm, thickness: 7.40mm; 28,800 vph; COSC-certified movement; bi-directional rotor on ball bearing; 349 components; 48-hour power reserve.
Functions: made to time soccer games with totalizer on a 45-minute graduated segment at 12, (soccer games have two halves of 45 minutes each), seconds counter in the center; calendar aperture at 4.
Case: black stainless steel; 6 oriented drill-through screws on the rubber bezel; double-sided antireflective sapphire crystal; sapphire crystal caseback; water resistant to 20atm.
Dial: black skeleton; 12 hand-applied hour-markers with SuperLumiNova.
Strap: black techno fiber; backed with leather; deployment clasp.
Suggested price: $12,900

EBEL 1911 BTR 137 CHRONOGRAPH   REF. 1215788

Movement: Swiss Ebel automatic chronograph movement caliber 137; Ø 31mm, thickness: 6.40mm; 28,800 vph; COSC-certified movement; bi-directional rotor on ball bearing; 322 components; 48-hour power reserve.
Functions: 3 counters: 30 minutes at 3, 12 hours at 6, small seconds at 9; center seconds; minute track with division for 1/5 of a second; tachometer scale on the flange; semi-instantaneous action date disc at 4; fast date correction.
Case: 44.5mm titanium; black rubber pushers and screw-down crown with "E" logo; black rubber bezel with 5 visible screws; scratch-resistant double-sided antireflective sapphire crystal; transparent sapphire crystal caseback; water resistant to 10atm.
Dial: black carbon fiber; applied markers; oversized seconds counter subdial.
Strap: black techno fiber; backed with leather; deployment clasp.
Suggested price: $7,900.

EBEL 1911 BTR CHRONOGRAPH   REF. 1215789

Movement: Swiss Ebel automatic chronograph movement caliber 137; Ø 31mm, thickness: 6.40mm; 28,800 vph; COSC-certified movement; bi-directional rotor on ball bearing; 322 components; 48-hour power reserve.
Functions: 3 counters: 12 hours at 6, 30 minutes at 3, small seconds at 9; center seconds; minute track with division for 1/5 of a second; tachometer scale on the flange; semi-instantaneous action date disc at 4; fast date correction.

Case: 44.5mm; brushed 18K rose gold; black rubber pushers and screw down crown with "E" logo, black rubber bezel with 5 visible screws; scratch-resistant double-sided antireflective sapphire crystal; transparent sapphire crystal case-back; water resistant to 10atm.
Dial: black carbon fiber; applied markers; over-sized seconds counter subdial.
Strap: black large-scale alligator; black hand-sewn stitching; deployment clasp.
Suggested price: $26,000

EBEL 1911 BTR CHRONOGRAPH   REF. 1215786

Movement: Swiss Ebel automatic chronograph movement caliber 139; Ø 31mm, thickness: 7.40mm; 28,800 vph; COSC-certified movement; bi-directional rotor on ball bearing; 322 components; 48-hour power reserve.
Functions: 3 counters: minutes at 12, hours at 6, constant seconds at 9; center seconds; minute track with divisions for 1/5 of a second; tachometer scale on the bezel; semi-instantaneous action date disc at 3; fast date correction.

Case: 44.5mm; brushed stainless steel; black rubber pushers and screw down crown with "E" logo; stainless steel bezel with tachometer scale and 5 visible screws; scratch-resistant double-sided anti-reflective sapphire crystal; transparent sapphire crystal caseback; water resistant to 10atm.
Dial: skeleton; Roman numerals.
Strap: black large-scale alligator; black hand-sewn stitching; deployment clasp.
Suggested price: $7,900.

EBEL 1911 DISCOVERY CHRONOGRAPH   REF. 1215889

Movement: Swiss automatic chronograph movement; COSC-certified.
Functions: 3 counters: 12 hours at 6, 30 minutes at 12, constant seconds at 9; center seconds; day-date at 3; minute track with division for 1/5 of a second; tachometer scale on the bezel.
Case: 43mm; brushed stainless steel with orange tachometer scale bezel and 5 visible screws; scratch-resistant antireflective sapphire crystal; water resistant to 10atm.
Dial: black; 12 applied hour-markers.
Strap: black techno fiber; backed with leather; orange stitching; deployment clasp.
Suggested price: $3,950

EBEL CLASSIC HEXAGON   REF. 1215872

Movement: Swiss automatic movement.
Functions: hours, minutes, seconds; day; big date calendar at 12; power reserve.
Case: stainless steel; scratch-resistant double-sided antireflective sapphire crystal.
Dial: black; 11-hand-applied hour-markers.
Strap: black large-scale alligator; deployment clasp.
Suggested price: $4,800

EBEL CLASSIC HEXAGON   REF. 1215833

Movement: Swiss automatic movement.
Functions: hours, minutes, seconds; day, date; power reserve.
Case: stainless steel; scratch-resistant double-sided antireflective sapphire crystal.
Dial: silver colored; full calendar; hand-applied gold hour-markers and hands.

Strap: brown large-scale alligator; deployment clasp.
Suggested price: $5,900

EBEL CLASSIC HEXAGON   REF. 1215873

Movement: Swiss automatic movement.
Functions: hours, minutes, seconds; day; second time-zone subdial at 6; big date calendar at 12.
Case: 18K rose gold; scratch-resistant double-sided antireflective sapphire crystal.
Dial: black dial; second time-zone subdial at 6; big date calendar at 12; 12 hand-applied hour-markers.
Strap: black large-scale alligator; deployment clasp.
Suggested price: $15,900

EBEL BELUGA LADY   REF. 1215855

Movement: Swiss quartz movement.
Functions: hour, minutes.
Case: stainless steel; set with 48 diamonds (0.619 total carat weight); scratch-resistant double-sided antireflective sapphire crystal; water resistant to 5atm.
Dial: mother-of-pearl; 12 diamond markers (0.104 total carat weight).
Bracelet: stainless steel.
Suggested price: $6,850

EBEL BELUGA MINI   REF. 1215871

Movement: Swiss quartz movement.
Functions: hour, minutes.
Case: polished 18K yellow gold; set with 46 diamonds (0.393 total carat weight); scratch-resistant double-sided antireflective sapphire crystal; water resistant to 5atm.
Dial: mother-of-pearl; 12 diamond markers (0.075 total carat weight).
Bracelet: 18K yellow gold.
Suggested price: $19,500

EBEL BRASILIA MINI   REF. 1215859

Movement: Swiss quartz movement.
Functions: hour, minutes.
Case: polished 18K rose gold; set with 34 diamonds (0.544 total carat weight); scratch-resistant double-sided antireflective sapphire crystal; water resistant to 5atm.
Dial: mother-of-pearl; 10 diamond markers (0.0620 total carat weight); Roman numerals 12 and 6.
Bracelet: polished 18K rose gold.
Suggested price: $21,500

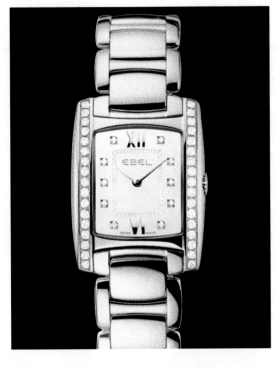

EBEL BRASILIA LADY   REF. 1215897

Movement: Swiss quartz movement.
Functions: hour, minutes.
Case: stainless steel; set with two rows of diamonds (102 diamonds, 0.663 total carat weight); scratch-resistant double-sided antireflective sapphire crystal; water resistant to 5atm.
Dial: mother-of-pearl; 10 diamond markers (0.0714 total carat weight); Roman numerals 12 and 6.
Bracelet: stainless steel.
Suggested price: $8,500

EBEL BRASILIA FASHION   REF. 1215900

Movement: Swiss quartz movement.
Functions: hour, minutes.
Case: stainless steel and black ceramic; set with two rows of diamonds (106 diamonds, 1.06 total carat weight); scratch-resistant double-sided antireflective sapphire crystal; water resistant to 5atm.
Dial: black; 10 diamond markers (0.16 total carat weight); Roman numerals 12 and 6.
Strap: black rubber; deployment clasp.
Suggested price: $10,900

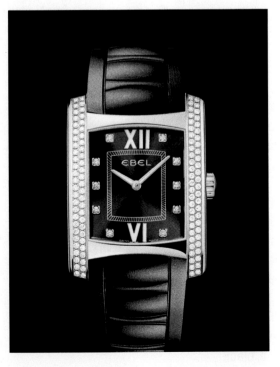

EBEL BRASILIA FASHION   REF. 1215910

Movement: Swiss quartz movement.
Functions: hour, minutes.
Case: stainless steel; white ceramic; set with 36 diamonds (0.219 total carat weight); scratch-resistant double-sided antireflective sapphire crystal; water resistant to 5atm.
Dial: white mother-of-pearl; 10 diamond markers (0.16 total carat weight); Roman numerals 12 and 6.
Strap: white rubber; deployment clasp.
Suggested price: $5,950

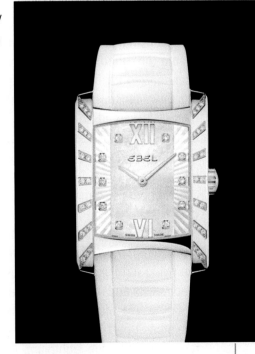

FRANC VILA
The Shape of Things to Come

Franc Vila's lifelong fascination with timepieces was inspired when he saw his father's unwound automatic watch spring to life, powered by the movement of his own arm. Vila's epiphany came full circle in 2005 when he brought his first watch design to life and introduced his eponymous brand at BaselWorld.

Since then, the Franc Vila collection of complicated, ultra-limited mechanical watches has grown in both size and stature with the addition of perpetual calendars, flyback chronographs and tourbillons paired with minute repeaters or chronographs. Each watch skillfully mixes creative designs, luxurious appointments and exclusivity; a philosophy that Vila describes as "esprit unique."

One visual constant that is featured throughout the collection is Franc Vila's instantly recognizable elliptical and round bezel, which contributes to the watch's clean-lined, architectural design. This original shape provides an elegant frame for the tourbillon mechanism positioned at 6:00 on the Tourbillon Planétaire Skeleton SuperLigero Concept (FVa6).

Balancing aesthetics and technical expertise to create an unconventional movement, the watch's skeletonized caliber is crafted from a state-of-the-art, aluminum/lithium-based alloy the company calls Lightnium. "I wanted to create a contemporary skeleton tourbillon that evokes the senses with clear influences of contemporary art, design and modern architecture," Vila says.

The hours and minutes are displayed on the watch's clear sapphire dial, along with an indicator at 9:00 that articulates the remainder of the five-day power reserve. The company's logo, rendered in Lightnium, decorates the flying tourbillon, which is equipped with an inertial control mechanism and wheel differential system.

Franc Vila offers two versions of the Tourbillon Planétaire Skeleton SuperLigero Concept—the first with red Lightnium and the other with blue Lightnium. Available exclusively in a black titanium case, the watchmaker will produce eight of each color.

Vila's "esprit unique" philosophy places high value on creativity, innovation, quality and exclusivity.

The Franc Vila collection includes other prestigious horological complications, such as the Chrono Flyback Perpétuel Auto (FVa11), which combines a flyback chronograph, perpetual calendar and moonphase. The watch's hand-finished automatic movement integrates the company's exclusive "gold concept rotor" design. Instead of the two parts used for most rotors, Franc Vila has created one with six parts—two in white gold, one in red gold, and the remaining in brass and the company's proprietary Die Hard Extreme Steel. This multi-part construction improves each rotor's balance, which results in improved winding.

Available in a variety of metal cases, Franc Vila also offers the Chrono Flyback Perpétuel Auto as part of its special El Bandido collection, which features all-black versions of popular models.

For this blackout version of the Chrono Flyback Perpétuel Auto, the watchmaker pairs a Die Hard Extreme Steel case with a carbon-fiber dial decorated with guilloché. Three subdials are used for the chronograph functions, which are indicated in red. The perpetual calendar functions are shown on the same subdials, but are displayed in photoluminescent black. A rotating disc at 3:00 is used to show the moon's waxing and waning.

Franc Vila will create El Bandido Chrono Flyback Perpétuel Auto in a limited edition of 48 pieces.

The watchmaker presents another special edition timepiece called the Cuatro Ferrero (FVa). Named for the Spanish tennis star Juan Carlos Ferrero, this groundbreaking tourbillon movement is the first to incorporate a chronograph mechanism on the dial side, including the column wheel, which is exposed at 12:00.

The watch's brushed and polished red-gold bezel frames an open-worked dial that features a flying tourbillon and two chronograph counters, as well as an indicator at 9:00 for the five-day power reserve. Franc Vila will create only eight pieces of the Cuatro Ferrero special edition. The brand does, however, offer a standard version of the Cuatro that is available in several different metal cases.

Collectors continue to revere the Franc Vila collection for its strong personality and Vila's "esprit unique" philosophy, which places a high value on creativity, innovation, quality and true exclusivity.

FACING PAGE
The bridge and plate of the Tourbillon Planétaire Skeleton Super-Ligero Concept (FVa6) is made of colored Lightnium, a lightweight yet strong alloy developed by Franc Vila. SuperLigero—meaning "super"—refers to the construction of the movement in Lightnium, an aluminum-lithium alloy more rigid and less dense than titanium.

THIS PAGE
TOP LEFT   This version of the Chrono Flyback Perpétuel Auto (FVa11) is part of Franc Vila's special El Bandido collection, which includes popular models created in all-black to hide their faces, like "bandits."

TOP RIGHT   Franc Vila will produce only eight of the Cuatro Ferrero (FVa) Special Edition in red gold.

LARGE DATE CHRONOGRAPH "DARK SIDE"   REF. FVa8ch 3.23

Movement: high-grade, mechanical self-winding, hand-finished complication caliber FVa8CH; FRANC VILA exclusive "gold concept rotor"; 42-hour power reserve.
Functions: hours at 6, minutes at 9, seconds at 3; large date in central window; chronograph seconds indication displayed by central hand.
Case: "Espirit Unique" shape in black DieHard Extreme Steel with elliptical and circular bezel.
Strap: comes with both crocodile and rubber straps.
Suggested price: $23,000
Also available: DieHard Extreme Steel (DHES); black DHES and red gold; 18K red gold or white gold; titanium and DHES or red or white gold. Price range $20,000 - $58,000
Note: limited edition of 88 pieces per metal version.

LARGE DATE CHRONOGRAPH   REF. FVa8ch 3.15

Movement: high-grade, mechanical self-winding, hand-finished complication caliber FVa8CH; FRANC VILA exclusive "gold concept rotor"; 42-hour power reserve.
Functions: hours at 6, minutes at 9, seconds at 3; chronograph seconds indication displayed by central hand; large date in central window.
Case: "Espirit Unique" shape in 18K white gold with elliptical and circular bezel.
Strap: comes with both crocodile and rubber straps.
Suggested price: $58,000
Other versions: $20,000 - $58,000
Note: limited edition of 88 pieces per metal version.

WORLD TIMER WITH CALENDAR   REF. FVa5 1.07

Movement: high-grade, mechanical self-winding, hand-finished complication caliber FVa5; FRANC VILA exclusive "gold concept rotor"; 42-hour power reserve.
Functions: hours, minutes, seconds; date; GMT (hour and city) and 24 time zones at 6 (each zone referenced by a city name).
Case: "Espirit Unique" shape in titanium and DieHard Extreme Steel with elliptical and circular bezel.
Strap: comes with both crocodile and rubber straps.
Suggested price: $23,000
Also available: DieHard Extreme Steel (DHES); black DHES; black DHES and red gold; 18K red or white gold; titanium and red or white gold. Price range: $23,000 - $59,000
Note: limited edition of 88 pieces per metal version.

ANNUAL CALENDAR WITH LARGE CALENDAR   REF. FVa8QA 4.09

Movement: high-grade, mechanical self-winding, hand-finished complication caliber FVa8QA; FRANC VILA exclusive "gold concept rotor"; 42-hour power reserve.
Functions: hours, minutes, seconds; large date via central windows; month window and seconds at 6.
Case: "Espirit Unique" shape in titanium and 18K red gold with elliptical and circular bezel.
Strap: comes with both crocodile and rubber straps.
Suggested price: $39,000
Also available: DieHard Extreme Steel (DHES); black DHES; black DHES and red gold; 18K red or white gold; titanium and DHES or white gold. Price range: $28,000 - $63,000
Note: limited edition of 88 pieces per metal version.

FIVE-DAY TOURBILLON CHRONOGRAPH   REF. FVa4 12.03

Movement: caliber FVa4; flying tourbillon with inertial moment control mechanism and wheel differential system; 262 components; chronograph monopushing function with dial-side column wheel directly coupled to tourbillon; 120-hour power reserve.
Functions: hours, minutes; chronograph monopusher; seconds at 2; minutes at 10; power-reserve indicator at 9.
Case: "Espirit Unique" shape in DieHard Extreme Steel with elliptical and circular bezel.
Strap: comes with both crocodile and rubber straps.
Suggested price: $265,000
Also available: black DHES; black DHES and red gold; 18K red or white gold; titanium and DHES or red or white gold. Price range: $265,000 - $355,000
Note: limited edition of 8 pieces per metal version.

SUPERLIGERO FIVE-DAY TOURBILLON   REF. FVa6 13.10

Movement: flying tourbillon with inertial moment control mechanism and advanced differential gear system; hand made and decorated; bridge and plate made in colored "Lightnium" a proprietary lithium-aluminum based alloy; 120-hour power reserve.
Functions: hours, minutes; power-reserve indicator at 9.
Case: "Espirit Unique" shape in black titanium with elliptical and circular bezel.
Dial: transparent sapphire crystal dial with hour and minute indicators.
Strap: comes with both crocodile and rubber straps.
Suggested price: $245,000
Note: limited edition of 8 pieces in red Lightnium and 8 in blue Lightnium.

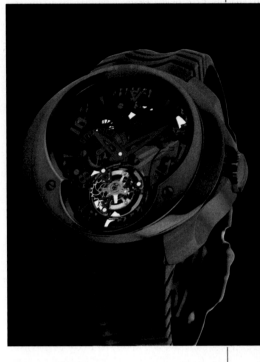

COMPLETE CALENDAR & MOON PHASE CHRONOGRAPH   REF. FVa9 5.13

Movement: high-grade, mechanical self-winding, hand-finished complication caliber FVa9; FRANC VILA exclusive "gold concept rotor"; 42-hour power reserve.
Functions: seconds and date at 12; moonphase at 3; minutes and day at 6; hours and month at 9; chronograph seconds displayed by central hand.
Case: "Espirit Unique" shape in titanium and 18K red gold with elliptical and circular bezel.
Strap: comes with both crocodile and rubber straps.
Suggested price: $38,000
Also available: DieHard Extreme Steel (DHES); black DHES; black DHES and red gold; 18K red or white gold; titanium and DHES or white gold. Price range: $27,000 - $62,000
Note: limited edition of 88 pieces per metal version.

COMPLETE CALENDAR WITH MOON PHASE   REF. FVa7 2.10

Movement: high-grade, mechanical self-winding, hand-finished complication caliber FVa7; FRANC VILA exclusive "gold concept rotor"; 42-hour power reserve.
Functions: hours, minutes, seconds; day of week and month via central windows; date and moonphase at 6.
Case: "Espirit Unique" shape in titanium and DieHard Extreme Steel with elliptical and circular bezel.
Strap: comes with both crocodile and rubber straps.
Suggested price: $22,000
Also available: DieHard Extreme Steel (DHES); black DHES; black DHES and red gold; 18K red or white gold; titanium and DHES or 18K red or white gold. Price range: $22,000 - $59,000
Note: limited edition of 88 pieces per metal version.

GÉRALD GENTA
Bucking Tradition

Blessed with a talent for evoking passionate responses from watch aficionados with its audacious designs, Gérald Genta is not shy about playing the artistic provocateur in the traditional world of Swiss watchmaking. Forty years after Gérald Genta was founded, the manufacture's dedication to individuality and creativity has given rise to a collection of technically advanced and boldly designed timepieces for both men and women.

For more than half its years, Gérald Genta has shared a playful line of quartz and mechanical timepieces with one of America's most endearing and enduring icons: Mickey Mouse. The watchmaker went all out to celebrate Mickey's 80th birthday in 2008 and unveiled the Octo Ultimate Fantasy, a distinctive model that combines the nobility of platinum with the exclusivity of a special tourbillon.

The Octo Ultimate Fantasy includes a tourbillon movement that is unusually thin—less than 6mm thick—and the tourbillon escapement appears to float on a clear sapphire bridge, bringing one's attention straight to the tourbillon's octagonal aperture.

The mechanism is created entirely in Gérald Genta's workshop, where skilled artisans finish the movement by hand with traditional decoration. One not-so-traditional adornment however, is the watch's 22-karat rotor, seen through the caseback. Shaped like Mickey's famous face and ears, the weight's oscillations fuel the watch's 64-hour power reserve.

In another flourish of watchmaking prowess, Gérald Genta uses a retrograde display—one of the brand's design signatures—to indicate the hours on the Octo Ultimate Fantasy. The design ensures that the hour hand never obscures the tourbillon.

Produced in a limited edition of 25 pieces, the watch is offered exclusively in a platinum case fitted with a tantalum bezel and paired with a red crocodile leather strap that's hard to miss.

Gérald Genta

THIS PAGE
Gérald Genta's proprietary movement in the Octo Ultimate Fantasy derives power from an oscillating weight that features the likeness of Mickey Mouse, who turned 80 in 2008.

FACING PAGE
Octo Ultimate Fantasy houses the watchmaker's acclaimed tourbillon movement. Suspended by a sapphire bridge, the escapement appears to float inside the dial's octagonal aperture.

In Gérald Genta's work-
shops, the Octo Ultimate
Fantasy's movement is
hand finished with tradi-
tional decoration.

With the Arena QP GMT, Gérald Genta offers a time-piece designed to appeal to forward-thinking watch enthusiasts who value cutting-edge style as much as the latest mechanical innovations.

The automatic movement combines a second time zone with a perpetual calendar, filling the multilayer dial with round subsidiary displays such as rotating discs that indicate the date and month. The round perforations covering the dial partially reveal the Gérald Genta movement below. It glows with a vintage patina courtesy of the old-gold "Potter" finish favored by the brand for many of its most prized movements. Despite the dial's dramatic design, it retains a timeless quality thanks to the black and red color combination, the watchmaker's preferred palette.

Another hallmark of Gérald Genta's pioneering watch design is the mixing of materials. For the Arena Perpetual Calendar GMT, Gérald Genta pairs the watch's fluted titanium case (45mm) with a polished platinum bezel.

Gérald Genta broke new ground in 2008 with the Arena Tourbillon Snow White, the brand's first watch for women to feature the prestigious spinning complication.

Crafted by passionately dedicated watchmakers working in Gérald Genta's workshops, the tourbillon with retrograde-hour movement operates for 64 hours between windings. The movement's golden Potter

finish is visible through slits on the circular-brushed gray dial. The clean composition serves to highlight the white-lacquer retrograde arc and rhodium-plated numerals as they stretch across much of the dial. To avoid blocking the view of the tourbillon and its small seconds display, the skeletonized hour hand never passes over the mechanism.

The beautiful touches continue to the Arena Tourbillon Snow White's 41mm case, which is decorated with fluting. Gérald Genta again indulges its love of mixing materials, pairing the platinum case with a palladium bezel. The watchmaker offers two versions of the bezel, one with a satin-finish and another set with 102 diamonds. The entire ensemble is brought together with a white crocodile strap.

With the Arena Tourbillon Snow White, Gérald Genta's daring mix of haute horlogerie and haute couture is evidence of the growing number of women captivated by complicated timepieces.

Gérald Genta again focuses on the elegance of white with another women's model, the Arena White Spice. The distinctive design takes visual inspiration from fashion designers André Courrèges and Paco Rabanne, as well as designs of the 1970s.

The luxurious design glitters with feminine charm thanks to a diamond-set bezel and mother-of-pearl dial. The dial's iridescent shimmer is home to the watch's retrograde minute arc and decorated with a number of graduated white circles. Spicing up the dial, the circle adjacent to the jump-hour window are perforated, allowing the colorful jump-hour wheel rotating beneath to peek through.

In a mix of materials familiar to fans of Gérald Genta, the Arena White Spice combines a 41mm stainless steel case with a rubber bezel encrusted with a row of white diamonds.

All four of these fine additions to the company's collection embody of the spirit of innovation driving Gérald Genta today: daring design, original materials, and top complications coming together in top style.

TOP The Arena QP GMT's subdials display the watch's perpetual calendar and indicate the second time zone. The perforated dial reveals sections of the movement, which is treated with a Potter finish, a hallmark of Gérald Genta's finest movements.

RIGHT A dash of color in the jump-hour window warms the stark elegance of the Arena White Spice. The watch's rubber bezel is studded with 60 white diamonds, a signature combination pioneered by Gérald Genta.

Arena Tourbillon Snow White combines a fluted platinum case with a palladium bezel adorned with 102 diamonds. The watch's tourbillon will never be blocked by the hour hand, which occupies only the traditional 8:00-4:00 surface area of the dial.

GEFICA BIRETRO   REF. GBS.Y.98.330.CB.BD

Movement: mechanical automatic-winding Gérald Genta GG 1004 caliber; 45-hour power reserve; 28,800 vph; 27 jewels; entirely decorated by hand with a circular-graining pattern and special old-gold galvanic color; 18K gold rotor. **Functions:** hour, minute, second; date.
Case: bronze and titanium four-piece case; Ø 46.5mm, thickness: 19.3mm; brushed finish; decorated with small spheres; antireflective curved sapphire crystal; screw-down crown decorated with small spheres; back fastened by 8 pentagon screws (to prevent tampering); displaying the movement through a sapphire crystal; water resistant to 10atm.

Dial: brass; silvered and grained, hollowed; minute track with numerals every 5 units and second scale with small lines and blind holes, with an opening on minute zone and bronze-color date with horizontal stripes delimited by pink bands with circular brushing and small-line scales; hours as red Arabic numerals; date frame in rhodium-plated steel; exclusive perforated hands in rhodium plated steel; red second hand.
Indications: jumping hour at 12; center retrograde minute and sweeping second (patented system); retrograde date at 6.
Strap: brown alligator leather; titanium fold-over clasp.
Suggested price: $17,400
Also available: with black/bronze dial and black leather strap.

GEFICA BIRETRO   REF. GBS.Y.98.331.CN.BD

Movement: mechanical automatic-winding Gérald Genta GG 1004 caliber; 45-hour power reserve; 28,800 vph; 27 jewels; entirely decorated by hand with a circular-graining pattern and special old-gold galvanic color; 18K gold rotor. **Functions:** hour, minute, second; date.
Case: bronze and titanium four-piece case; Ø 46.5mm, thickness: 19.3mm; brushed finish; decorated with small spheres; antireflective curved sapphire crystal; screw-down crown decorated with small spheres; back fastened by 8 pentagon screws (to prevent tampering); displaying the movement through a sapphire crystal; water resistant to 10atm.

Dial: brass; black, hollowed minute track with numerals every 5 units and second scale with small lines and blind holes, with an opening on minute zone and bronze-color date with horizontal stripes delimited by pink bands with circular brushing and small-line scales; hours as red Arabic numerals; date frame in rhodium-plated steel; exclusive perforated hands in rhodium-plated steel; red second hand.
Indications: jumping hour at 12; center retrograde minute and sweeping second (patented system); retrograde date at 6.
Strap: black alligator leather; titanium fold-over clasp.
Suggested price: $17,400
Also available: with argenté/bronze dial and brown leather strap.

ARENA CHRONO QUATTRO RETRO   REF. ABC.Y.55.395.CB.BD

Movement: mechanical automatic-winding Gérald Genta GG 7800 caliber; 45-hour power reserve; 21,600 vph; 37 jewels; decorated with circular-graining pattern and old-gold color; 18K gold rotor. **Functions:** jumping hours; retrograde minutes and date; central seconds; chronograph retrograde hours and minutes.
Case: red-gold three-piece case; 45mm, thickness: 16mm; fluted middle; tantalum bezel; Gérald Genta screw-down beaded crown; profiled chronograph push-pieces; open caseback with antireflective sapphire, secured with pentagon-shaped screws; water resistant to 10atm.

Dial: multilevel gray and pink satin-finish dial; applied Arabic numerals.
Indications: chronograph retrograde minute counter at 3; fan-shaped date display with retrograde hand at 6; retrograde chronograph hour counter at 9; jumping hour at 12; retrograde minute center counter (patented system); center seconds.
Strap: brown alligator leather; red-gold folding clasp.
Suggested price: $47,200
Also available: in white gold with tantalum bezel, gray dial, black alligator leather strap; in titanium with two-color ruthenium dial and black alligator leather strap.

ARENA CHRONO QUATTRO RETRO   REF. ABC.Y.66.295.CN.BD

Movement: mechanical automatic-winding Gérald Genta GG 7800 caliber; 45-hour power reserve; 21,600 vph; 37 jewels; decorated with circular-graining pattern and old-gold color; 18K gold rotor. **Functions:** jumping hours; retrograde minutes and date; central seconds; chronograph retrograde hours and minutes. **Case:** white-gold three-piece case; 45mm, thickness: 16mm; fluted middle; tantalum bezel; Gérald Genta screw-down beaded crown; profiled chronograph push-pieces; open caseback with antireflective sapphire, secured with pentagon-shaped screws; water resistant to 10atm.

Dial: multilevel gray satin-finish dial; applied Arabic numerals.
Indications: chronograph retrograde minute counter at 3; fan-shaped date display with retrograde hand at 6; retrograde chronograph hour counter at 9; jumping hour at 12; retrograde minute center counter (patented system); center seconds.
Suggested price: $47,200
Strap: black alligator strap; white-gold folding clasp.

ARENA BIRETRO REF. BSP.Y.55.279.CB.BD

Movement: mechanical automatic-winding Gérald Genta GG 7723 caliber; 45-hour power reserve; 28,800 vph; 27 jewels; decorated with circular-graining pattern and old-gold color; 18K gold rotor.
Functions: jumping hour at 12; center retrograde minute (patented system); central seconds; fan-shaped retrograde date at 6.
Case: red-gold three-piece case; 45mm, thickness: 12.8mm; fluted middle; tantalum bezel; Gérald Genta screw-down beaded crown; open caseback with antireflective sapphire secured with pentagon-shaped screws; water resistant to 10atm.
Dial: gray satin-finish dial; applied Arabic numerals; matte orange sapphire section.
Strap: brown alligator strap; red-gold folding clasp.
Suggested price: $30,800
Also available: in white gold with tantalum bezel, gray-green dial; in titanium with black bezel and dial and black rubber strap.

ARENA BIRETRO REF. BSP.Y.66.269.CN.BD

Movement: mechanical automatic-winding Gérald Genta GG 7723 caliber; 45-hour power reserve; 28,800 vph; 27 jewels; decorated with circular-graining pattern and old-gold color; 18K gold rotor.
Functions: jumping hour at 12; center retrograde minute (patented system); central seconds; fan-shaped retrograde date at 6.
Case: white-gold three-piece case; 45mm, thickness: 12.8mm; fluted middle; tantalum bezel; Gérald Genta screw-down beaded crown; open caseback with antireflective sapphire secured with pentagon-shaped screws; water resistant to 10atm.
Dial: gray satin-finish dial; applied Arabic numerals; matte green sapphire section.
Strap: black alligator strap; white-gold folding clasp.
Suggested price: $30,800

ARENA WHITE SPICE REF. RSP.X.10.156.RW.BD.SR1

Movement: mechanical automatic-winding GG 7510 caliber; 42-hour power reserve; 21 jewels; Gérald Genta circular finish.
Functions: automatic jumping hours; retrograde minutes.
Case: stainless steel; Ø 41mm; half-precious, half-casual bezel adorned with 60 diamonds (0.96 carats TW VS to VVS) and nestled within a rubber ring; water resistant to 3atm.
Dial: mother-of-pearl center; frosted sapphire windows; colorful rotating hour disc.
Strap: rubber.
Suggested price: $17,500

ARENA TOURBILLON SNOW WHITE REF. ATR.X.75.918.CD.BD.S02

Movement: mechanical automatic-winding GG 9053; Ø 29mm, 5.9mm thick; 64-hour power reserve; 21,600 vph; 54 jewels; 2-arm balance with screws; flat balance-spring; in-line lever tourbillon escapement; concentric perlage and special color finishing; 18K gold rotor.
Functions: tourbillon; retrograde hours.
Case: platinum 950; polished and fluted; Ø 41mm, thickness: 13.15mm; palladium 950 bezel with 102 diamonds (2.93 carats TW VS to VVS); water resistant to 10atm.
Dial: white lacquered; applied Arabic numerals; grid-like openings.
Strap: alligator leather.
Suggested price: $164,100
Also available: without diamonds on satin-brushed palladium 950 bezel.

ARENA TOURBILLON RETROGRADE HOURS — REF. ATR.Y.75.913.CN.BD

Movement: mechanical automatic-winding GG 9053; Ø 29mm, 5.9mm thick; 64-hour power reserve; 21,600 vph; 54 jewels; 2-arm balance with screws; flat balance-spring; in-line lever tourbillon escapement; concentric perlage and special color finishing; 18K gold rotor.
Functions: tourbillon; retrograde hours.
Case: platinum 950; polished and fluted; Ø 45mm, thickness: 13.15mm; satin-brushed palladium 950 bezel; water resistant to 10atm.
Dial: metallic anthracite; applied Arabic numerals; grid-like openings.'
Strap: alligator leather.
Suggested price: $159,000

ARENA PERPETUAL CALENDAR — REF. AQG.Y.87.916.CN.BD

Movement: mechanical automatic-winding GG7044 caliber; Ø 30mm, height: 4.98mm; 28,800 vph; 45-hour power reserve; 27 jewels; 3-arm Cupro-beryllium balance; flat balance-spring; 18K gold rotor.
Functions: perpetual calendar; GMT.
Case: titanium; polished and fluted; Ø 45mm, thickness: 13.90mm; platinum bezel; water resistant to 10atm.

Dial: black and satin-finish metallic; .net-like; red GMT display; applied Arabic numerals
Strap: alligator leather; titanium deployment buckle.
Suggested price: $71,900

OCTO BIRETRO — REF. OBR.Y.50.510.CN.BD

Movement: mechanical automatic-winding Gérald Genta GG 7722 caliber; 45-hour power reserve; 28,800 vph; 27 jewels; decorated with a circular-graining pattern and old-gold color; 18K gold rotor.
Functions: jumping hour at 12; center retrograde minute (patented system); fan-shaped retrograde date at 6.
Case: red-gold three-piece case; octagonal shape; 42.5mm, thickness: 11.9mm; Gérald Genta beaded crown with onyx cabochon; antireflective sapphire crystal; open caseback with antireflective sapphire secured with pentagon-shaped screws; water resistant to 10atm.

Dial: black and red lacquered dial.
Strap: black alligator strap; red-gold folding clasp.
Suggested price: $39,000
Also available: in white gold; red/ivory dial.

OCTO 48-MONTH PERPETUAL CALENDAR MOON PHASE — REF. OQM.Y.60.515.CN.BD

Movement: mechanical automatic-winding Gérald Genta GG 7080 caliber; 45-hour power reserve; 28,800 vph; 26 jewels; decorated with circular-graining pattern and old-gold color; 18K gold rotor.
Functions: 4-year cycle of months at 3; calendar at 6; 48-month perpetual calendar with day of the week at 9; moonphases in Northern and Southern hemispheres.

Case: white-gold three-piece case; octagonal shape; 42.5mm, thickness: 11.55mm; Gérald Genta beaded crown with falcon-eye cabochon; antireflective sapphire crystal; open caseback with antireflective sapphire secured with pentagon-shaped screws; water resistant to 10atm.
Dial: white-gold and cloisonné red and black lacquered dial.
Suggested price: $80,100
Strap: black alligator strap; white-gold folding clasp.
Also available: in red gold; black/red dial.

OCTO TOURBILLON RETROGRADE HOURS   REF. OTR.Y.50.930.CN.BD

Movement: mechanical automatic-winding tourbillon Gérald Genta GG 9051 caliber; 64-hour power reserve; 21,600 vph; 54 jewels; decorated with circular-graining pattern and old-gold color; 18K gold rotor.
Functions: tourbillon; retrograde hours.
Case: red-gold three-piece case; octagonal shape; 42.5mm, thickness: 11.95mm; Gérald Genta beaded crown with falcon-eye cabochon; open

caseback with antireflective sapphire secured with pentagon-shaped screws; water resistant to 10atm.
Dial: red-gold guilloché and cloisonné black and red ceramic dial; aperture on tourbillon carriage with sapphire crystal bridge.
Strap: exclusive Gérald Genta black, folded alligator strap; red-gold folding clasp.
Suggested price: $149,800
Also available: platinum case with tantalum bezel; red/ivory or red/black dial.

OCTO GRANDE SONNERIE   REF. OGS.Y.50.928.CN.BD

Movement: automatic tourbillon grande sonnerie; Ø 29mm, 7.2mm thick; 950 parts; 21,600 vph; 48-hour power reserve; 95 jewels; 2-arm balance with screws; 18K gold rotor; flat balance-spring; in-line lever tourbillon escapement; entirely hand decorated and hand engraved.
Functions: tourbillon; retrograde hours; minute repeater with grand and petite sonnerie and 4-hammer Westminster chime; double power-reserve indicators: 48 hours for movement, 18 hours for striking mechanism.
Notes played: first quarter: E-D-C-G; second quarter: D-G-E-C + E-D-C-G; third quarter: E-C-D-G + D-G-E-C + E-D-C-G.

Case: red gold; Gérald Genta beaded crown and pushpiece with falcon-eye cabochon; antireflective sapphire crystal
Dial: ceramic.
Strap: exclusive Gérald Genta pleated alligator leather strap with folding clasp.
Note: unique piece.
Suggested price: $810,200

OCTO PLACE DE L'ÉTOILE   REF. ORJ.X.50.999.ST.BD. S82

Movement: mechanical automatic-winding GG1002 caliber; Ø 26.20mm, height: 5.28mm; 28,800 vph; 45-hour power reserve; 26 jewels; 3-arm Cupro-beryllium balance; flat balance-spring.
Functions: jumping hour at 11; retrograde minutes.
Case: red gold; Ø 39mm, thickness: 11.70mm; red-gold bezel set with 22 diamonds (0.066 carat); water resistant to 10atm.
Dial: red gold set with 177 diamonds (0.533 carat); purple enamel.
Strap: mauve sea-snake leather.
Suggested price: $61,600

OCTO ULTIMATE FANTASY   REF. OTF.Y.76.340.CR.BD

Movement: mechanical automatic-winding tourbillon Gérald Genta GG9051 caliber; Ø 29mm, height: 5.90mm; 21,600 vph; 64-hour power reserve; 54 jewels; 22K gold Mickey Mouse face rotor; 2-arm balance with screws; flat balance-spring.
Functions: tourbillon; retrograde hours.
Case: platinum 950; polished; Ø 42.50mm, thickness: 11.95mm; Tantalus satin-brushed bezel; water resistant to 10atm.
Dial: white gold with Mickey Mouse sitting on the tourbillon.
Strap: exclusive Gérald Genta pleated red alligator leather strap; folding clasp.
Suggested price: $179,500

GREUBEL FORSEY
The Tourbillon Kings

One comes from Alsace, France, while the other grew up in St. Albans, England, and their passion for watchmaking has led them both to live in the Swiss Jura region. Self-styled Inventor Watchmakers Robert Greubel and Stephen Forsey decided to take a closer look at the tourbillon, the goal being to explore the limits of this complication. After years of fundamental research and experimentation, they are finally nearing their goal.

"It was a simple enough idea, but one that began a new chapter in the history of the tourbillon," is how Forsey modestly puts it. Expressing himself in fluent French, this English-born watchmaker is referring to the crucial Greubel Forsey discovery: inclining the escapement system in relation to the movement. "This specific arrangement paves the way for seventeen different and completely original variations."

We need to go back to the 18th century in order to grasp the full extent of the impact Greubel Forsey has had on the quest for horological precision. Invented by the famous watchmaker Abraham-Louis Breguet in 1795 and patented in 1801, the main purpose of the tourbillon was to alleviate the effects of gravity on the rate of a pocket watch movement. "Abraham-Louis Breguet had this brilliant idea of setting the escapement and balance into rotation on a given axis," says Forsey. "A closer look at the context of the era shows that he had reached the limits of what was possible at the time, given the available materials and lubricants. The principle was based on the fact that the escapement system pivots on its axis, and in doing so cancels out the possible variations in rate. Once installed in pocket watches, his invention fulfilled its regulating function since the movement was generally in a vertical position." But when positioned differently (such as in wristwatches), disruptive forces were exercised on the caliber and the tourbillon function, while not actually helping to stabilize the rate, could even become an aggravating factor conducive to the loss of precision.

Over the decades, watchmakers learned to reduce the size of the tourbillon before fitting it inside wristwatches in the 1930s and 1940s. However, the vast majority of them were content with merely using the mechanism as such, without attempting to find out if it was still effective. Due to its constant changes of position, a wristwatch has to face challenges different from those found in a pocket watch, and the research conducted by Forsey and Greubel proved that the tourbillon as devised by Abraham-Louis Breguet was not suited to wristwatches and required modification.

> The Quadruple Tourbillon à Différentiel Sphérique's two double cages necessitated updating testing instruments, so advanced was their technology.

THIS PAGE
The cages of the Double Tourbillon 30.°

FACING PAGE
TOP   All the individual parts of the Double Tourbillon 30° Vision are decorated meticulously.

CENTER   Double Tourbillon 30°.

BOTTOM LEFT   Sketch of the Double Tourbillon 30°.

Double Tourbillon 30°
Greubel Forsey Invention N°

...e only multi-axe
...urbillon designed
...cifically for the
...ristwatch

30°

...Minute
...otation.

4 Minute
Rotation.

ABOVE LEFT   Invention Piece 1.

ABOVE RIGHT   Close-up view of the Double Tourbillon 30° system on the semi-circular display of the hours and minutes in Invention Piece 1.

BELOW LEFT   Quadruple Tourbillon à Différentiel Sphérique.

BELOW CENTER   A window on the side of the case provides a view of one of the two double tourbillons in the Quadruple Tourbillon à Différentiel Sphérique.

BELOW RIGHT   The back of the Quadruple Tourbillon à Différentiel Sphérique.

BOTTOM   Illustration of the system of energy transmission between the four tourbillons.

"In 1999, around thirty-five brands were offering tourbillons; by 2004, the number had rocketed to one hundred and four," observes Forsey. "This explosion caught our attention and, since we are first and foremost watchmakers, we left aside the spectacular aspect of the tourbillon in order to analyze its technical efficiency, since—from our standpoint—enhanced mechanical precision is the real heart of the quest. We soon realized that the tourbillon reacts very badly, especially to the horizontal position, which is fairly commonplace in the usage of a wristwatch. Taking our research a step further, we also observed that a single rotation axis on a flat plane was not enough to properly solve the problem of gravity and balance amplitude variations. After studying various concepts, we reached the conclusion that maximum efficiency would require two carriages set at an angle to each other. Moreover, this arrangement also provided more space for the balance wheel. In their first invention, the Double Tourbillon 30°, for example, the balance wheel measures almost 11mm in diameter for a 9.65mm-thick caliber. By carefully avoiding both vertical and horizontal positions, this new architecture also afforded the advantage of reducing the amplitude variations of the balance by thirty percent. In the end, we therefore succeeded in creating a regular and accurate tourbillon system, since it displayed a maximum variation in rate of just four seconds per day."

Greubel and Forsey pursued their research in parallel with the activities of their small horological development company, CompliTime. "We didn't want to present anything that was not entirely complete. And since we had to self-finance our work, at the beginning we mostly only worked on this new tourbillon invention during our spare time." This development strategy was to bear fruit since in 2004, four and a half years after the start of research and development,

LEFT Tourbillon 24 Secondes Incliné.

ABOVE Close-up view of the cage of the Tourbillon 24 Secondes Incliné.

BOTTOM LEFT Sketch of the Double Tourbillon 30° Secret.

BOTTOM RIGHT Double Tourbillon 30° Secret.

the first Greubel Forsey watch made its first public appearance. A genuine founding model, the Double Tourbillon 30° Vision thus features a double tourbillon in which the outer cage performs a rotation in four minutes, while the second cage turns in just 60 seconds. This mechanism comprises a total of 128 parts and weighs 1.17 grams. And so as to reveal the mechanism in all its splendor, this latter has been placed on its own in the lower part of the watch where it displays its stunning complexity.

The second invention was unveiled as an initial working prototype in 2005: the Quadruple Tourbillon à Différentiel Sphérique. Equipped with four tourbillons (two double cages), this model even led to the development of new measuring instruments able to handle the significant technological breakthroughs it embodied. Thanks to the experience and know-how acquired, the third invention—the Tourbillon 24 Secondes Incliné—breaks from the multi-axis concept and features just one very special cage. Differences are compensated for by the high rotation speed of the inclined cage, which performs a complete turn in 24 seconds. Apparently simpler than the previous versions, the latter required the use of titanium for the cage and Avional for the pillars, in order to prove a match for the strong constraints implied by the cage's high speed of rotation.

Two very special models, the Invention Piece 1 and the Double Tourbillon 30° Secret, interpret the first invention, the Double Tourbillon 30°, in significantly different ways. A tribute to the original Greubel Forsey Double Tourbillon 30°, the Invention Piece 1 with the prominent position of the double tourbillon mechanism allowed a

completely original technical architecture of the movement. The semi-circular display of the hours and minutes is integrated into the surface of the movement and enhances the spectacular mechanism which one can almost touch. Meanwhile, the Double Tourbillon 30° Secret, issued in a limited edition of 11, opts for a resolutely discreet approach choosing to reveal the precious mechanism exclusively through the sapphire crystal caseback.

As a note, it is worth mentioning that Greubel Forsey systematically presents fully validated models that can be delivered within a few months, a token of top-rate professionalism.

GUY ELLIA
Don't Dream, Just Watch

Few contemporary elite watchmakers design both jewelry and timepieces. One notable exception is Guy Ellia. The avant-garde designer whose innovations create some of the most complicated watches in the industry considers horology his main passion. Yet his gem-filled background is evident in every watch design, right down to the beautiful mechanical movements that are as stunning as they are precise.

A s a diamond dealer and jewelry designer, Guy Ellia launched his first innovative line of timepieces in 1999, which immediately rocketed him into the realm of watchmaking royalty. Collaborating with such prestigious movement designers as Parmigiani, Piguet and, most recently, Christophe Claret, Guy Ellia's extraordinary creative vision continuously emerges in surprising ways through his watch designs. Ellia's Tourbillon Zephyr, introduced in Basel two years ago, is a marvel of form and function. The watch's transparency and extraordinarily high complications—yet ethereal and dreamlike visage—have made it an instant classic for men. This year's regal Queen, highlighted with two carats of diamonds with a mother-of-pearl dial and alligator strap, merges classical sophistication with forward-thinking fashion for women.

"Creation is a delicate thing," says Ellia. "Watch designs must be trendy, yet timeless. Each year, we must show something different; but luxury watches must be perfect. There is a constant need to create new and better technology. " Because of the level of complication in Ellia's designs, his watches can take five or six years to develop.

In his offices on the glamorous rue de la Paix in Paris, Guy Ellia's relaxed demeanor belies his opulent luxury businesses. Dressed in jeans, his striking white hair casually wind-tousled, Mr. Ellia exudes a mixture of understated elegance, bohemian charm and quintessential French intellectualism. It is this combination of characteristics that distinguishes Ellia and informs his designs.

> This year marks the integration of Ellia's three businesses: dealing priceless diamonds, creating haute joaillerie and, of course, luxury watches.

FACING PAGE
The Tourbillon Zephyr
is fitted with a GES
97 manual-winding
movement.

THIS PAGE
The Repetition Minute
Zephyr features an
exclusive manual-
winding Christophe
Claret caliber GEC 88,
visible through the
caseback.

"Guy Ellia is one of the best in the business for getting ideas and finding the techniques to make his complicated designs happen," says Carla Chalhoui, owner of the celebrated haute joaillerie and haute horlogerie boutiques, Arije, in Paris.

Infamously selective when it comes to choosing retailers, 2009 is a milestone year for Ellia and his businesses. With the opening of the first Guy Ellia boutique (on London's Sloan Street), this year marks the integration of Ellia's three businesses: dealing priceless diamonds, creating haute joaillerie and, of course, luxury watches. The London shop affords Ellia a perspective he believes will prove as invaluable to his creations as his fanciful imagination—customer feedback.

While Ellia declares that, "watches are one of the most difficult businesses in the luxury world," he also concedes that haute timepieces seem to be one of the few niches impervious to financial hardship. A watch is often the only accessory a man will allow himself; without a watch encircling her wrist, a woman still feels naked. In an era when watches are no longer necessities, the timepiece a person chooses to wear tells much more about that person than ever before. Men and women who favor Guy Ellia are hip, yet refined, savvy and individualistic—more likely to start their own trends than join in on someone else's.

Guy Ellia is enjoying ever-increasing attention around the globe. In the popular film L'Emmerdeur, which was released in December 2008, the lead character sports a Guy Ellia watch. Some of the biggest names in French cinema are said to own Ellia designs, including Jean Reno, Gerard Darmon and Gerard Lanvin. With his latest designs, Guy Ellia offers watches that transcend time.

REPETITION MINUTE ZEPHYR

Movement: mechanical manual-winding Christophe Claret caliber GEC 88; cage: 41.2x38.2mm, thickness: 9.41mm; 48-hour power reserve; gears wheels with different plating; 5-position adjustment; flat balance-spring: 18,000 vph; 720 pieces; 72 jewels.
Functions: hour, minute; power-reserve indicator; minute repetition function; 5-time zones with day/night indicators.

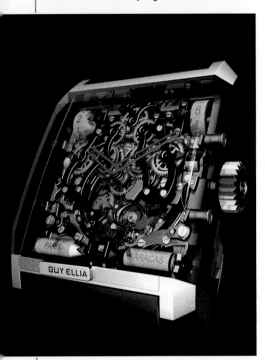

Case: 18K white-gold sides (70.76g); convex case; 53.6x43.7mm, thickness: 14.8mm; sapphire glass; sapphire 18K gold crown set with a Ø 2.2mm diamond; water resistant to 3atm.
Strap: alligator or rubber; width case/buckle: 33x24mm; 18K solid white-gold folding buckle (17.27g).
Note: limited edition of 20 numbered pieces.
Also available: pink gold and titanium.

TOURBILLON ZEPHYR

Movement: mechanical manual-winding Christophe Claret caliber GES 97; cage: 37x37mm, thickness: 6.21mm; 110-hour power reserve; winding ring set with 36 baguette-cut diamonds (1.04 carats) or engine turning; one minute tourbillon; entirely hand-chamfered cage; bottom plate and bridges in blue sapphire; 5-position adjustment; flat balance-spring: 21,600 vph; 233 pieces; 17 jewels.

Functions: hour, minute.
Case: 950 platinum sides (54.9g); convex case; 54x45.3mm, thickness: 15.4mm; white-sapphire glass with thermal counter-shock marking; transparent back cover, hearth engraving; crown set with a Ø 1mm diamond; water resistant to 3atm.
Strap: alligator; width case/buckle: 37x22mm; 18K solid white-gold folding buckle (15.64g).
Note: limited edition of 12 numbered pieces.
Also available: pink gold.

JUMBO HEURE UNIVERSELLE

Movement: mechanical automatic-winding Frédéric Piguet caliber PGE 1150; cage: Ø 36.2mm, thickness: 6.24mm; 72-hour power reserve; 5-position adjustment; blue sapphire disc; "Côtes de Genève" finished bridges with rhodium plating; "GUY ELLIA" engraved on rotor with rhodium-plating; 37 jewels.
Functions: hour, minute; 24 time zones indication; grand date; day/night indicator.

Case: 18K black gold (82.9g); Ø 50mm, thickness: 11mm; sapphire glass with thermal counter-shock marking; openwork caseback with sapphire glass; water resistant to 3atm.
Strap: alligator; width case/buckle: 26x20mm; 18K black-gold folding buckle (16g).
Also available: white gold; pink gold.

JUMBO CHRONO CARBONE

Movement: mechanical automatic-winding Frédéric Piguet caliber PGE 1185; cage: Ø 26.2mm, thickness: 5.5mm; chronograph with column wheel; 45-hour power reserve; 5-position adjustment; "Côtes de Genève" finished bridges with rhodium plating; "GUY ELLIA" engraved on rotor with rhodium-plating.
Functions: hour, minute at 12; date by coloration at 2; 30-minute counter at 3; subsidiary seconds at 6; 12-hour counter at 9; central chronograph sweep seconds.

Case: compressed carbon (5.98g) and 18K solid matte pink-gold case (42.35g); Ø 50mm, thickness: 11mm; sapphire glass with thermal counter-shock marking; water resistant to 3atm.
Strap: alligator; width case/buckle: 26x20mm; 18K pink-gold folding buckle (15.20g).
Also available: black gold; white gold.

TOURBILLON MAGISTERE

Movement: mechanical manual-winding Christophe Claret caliber PGE 97; cage: 37.4x29.9mm, thickness: 5.4mm; 110-hour power reserve; mysterious winding; one minute tourbillon; skeletonized barrel and ratchet-wheel; gears wheels with different plating; entirely hand-chamfered cage; set bridges in 18K gold; blued steel screws; flat balance-spring: 21,600 vph; 20 jewels.
Functions: hour, minute.
Case: 18K pink gold (70.95); set with 535 brilliants (8.25 carats); 43.5x36mm, thickness: 10.9mm; sapphire glass with thermal counter-shock marking; crown set with a Ø 1mm diamond; water resistant to 3atm.
Strap: alligator; width case/buckle: 24x20mm; 18K pink-gold folding buckle (14.61g).
Note: limited edition.
Also available: white gold; pink gold; platinum; full set white gold; full set platinum; bezel set white-gold with baguette-cut diamonds; full set white-gold with baguette-cut diamonds.

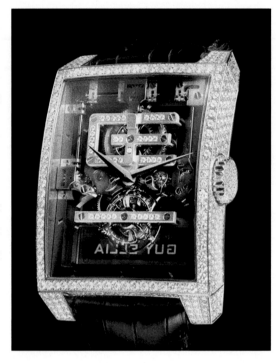

TOURBILLON MAGISTERE TITANIUM

Movement: mechanical manual-winding Christophe Claret caliber TGE 97; cage: 37.4x29.9mm, thickness: 5.4mm; 110-hour power reserve; mysterious winding; one minute tourbillon; skeletonized barrel and ratchet-wheel; entirely hand-chamfered cage; titanium bottom plate and bridges; flat balance-spring: 21,600 vph; 20 jewels.
Functions: hour, minute.
Case: titanium (18.20g); biconvex case; 43.5x36mm, thickness: 10.9mm; sapphire glass with thermal counter-shock marking; crown set with a Ø 1mm diamond; water resistant to 3atm.
Strap: alligator; width case/buckle: 24x20mm; 18K solid white-gold folding buckle (9.65g) and titanium hood.
Note: limited edition.

JUMBO CHRONO

Movement: mechanical automatic-winding Frédéric Piguet caliber PGE 1185; cage: Ø 26.2mm, thickness: 5.5mm; chronograph with column wheel; 45-hour power reserve; 5-position adjustment; "Côtes de Genève" finished bridges with rhodium plating; "GUY ELLIA" on rotor with rhodium-plating.
Functions: hour, minute at 12; day by coloration at 2; 30-minute counter at 3; subsidiary seconds at 6; 12-hour counter at 9; central chronograph sweep seconds.
Case: 18K black gold (87g); full set with 323 diamonds (7.86 carats); Ø 50mm, thickness: 11.9mm; sapphire glass with thermal counter-shock marking; water resistant to 3atm.
Strap: alligator; width case/buckle: 26x20mm; 18K black-gold folding buckle (16g) set with 35 diamonds (0.365 carat).
Also available: white gold; set bezel white gold; full set white gold; pink gold; set bezel pink gold; full set pink gold; black gold; set bezel black gold.

JUMBO CHRONO

Movement: mechanical automatic-winding Frédéric Piguet caliber PGE 1185; cage: Ø 26.2mm, thickness: 5.5mm; chronograph with column wheel; 45-hour power reserve; 5-position adjustment; "Côtes de Genève" finished bridges with rhodium plating; "GUY ELLIA" engraved on rotor with rhodium plating.
Functions: hour, minute at 12; day by coloration at 2; 30-minute counter at 3; subsidiary seconds at 6; 12-hour counter at 9; central chronograph sweep seconds.
Case: 18K black gold (87g); Ø 50mm, thickness: 11.5mm; sapphire glass with thermal counter-shock marking; water resistant to 3atm.
Strap: alligator; width case/buckle: 26x20mm; 18K black-gold folding buckle (16g).
Also available: white gold; set bezel white gold; full-set white gold; pink gold; set bezel pink gold; full set pink gold; set bezel black gold; full set black gold.

TIME SPACE QUANTIEME PERPETUEL

Movement: mechanical manual-winding Frédéric Piguet caliber PGE 5615 D; cage: Ø 35.64mm, thickness: 4.7mm; 43-hour power reserve; 5-position adjustment; "Côtes de Genève" finished bridges with black PVD treatment; "GE" engraved on stippled plate with black PVD treatment; 21,600 vph; watch box with a specific automatic winder integrated; 20 jewels.
Functions: hour, minute; day; date; month; moon phase; leap year.

Case: 18K black gold (32.87g); Ø 46.8mm, thickness: 7.75mm; white sapphire middle case ring; sapphire glass with thermal counter-shock marking; water resistant to 3atm.
Strap: alligator; width case/buckle: 26x18mm; 18K black-gold pin buckle (4.73g).
Also available: white gold; pink gold.

TIME SPACE 88

Movement: mechanical manual-winding Frédéric Piguet caliber PGE 15; cage: Ø 35.64mm, thickness: 1.9mm; 43-hour power reserve; 5-position adjustment; "Côtes de Genève" finished bridges with black PVD treatment; "GE" engraved on stippled plate with black PVD treatment; 21,600 vph; 20 jewels.
Functions: hour, minute.

Case: 18K white gold 33.5g; Ø 46.8mm, thickness: 4.9mm; sapphire glass with thermal counter-shock marking; water resistant to 3atm.
Strap: alligator; width case/buckle: 26x18mm; 18K white-gold pin buckle (4.73g).
Also available: set bezel white gold; full set white gold; pink gold; set bezel pink gold; full set pink gold; black gold; set bezel black gold; full set black gold.

CIRCLE

Movement: Frédéric Piguet caliber PGE 820; cage: Ø 18.8mm, thickness: 1.95mm.
Functions: hour, minute.
Case: 18K polished white gold (83.86g); bezel set with 124 diamonds (diamonds: Ø 1.5mm); cage: Ø 52mm, thickness: 7mm; sapphire glass with thermal counter-shock marking; crown set with one Ø 2.8mm diamond; mirror-polished

bottom cover set with a Ø 0.95mm diamond on the "I" of ELLIA; water resistant to 3atm.
Dial: 18K white-gold mirror; markers set with 168 brilliants (1 carat); dauphine shaped 18K white-gold hands.
Strap: alligator; 18K solid white-gold pin buckle set with 86 diamonds (0.384 carat); pin set with one Ø 0.9mm diamond; width case/buckle: 31.6x20mm.
Also available: case: bezel set matte white gold; full set white-gold; dial: matte black; shiny black; opaline; matte gold; markers: shiny black; mirror polished gold; outline gold; polished copper outlin.

CIRCLE

Movement: Fréderic Piguet caliber PGE 820; cage: Ø 18.8mm, thickness: 1.95mm
Functions: hour, minute.
Case: 18K polished yellow gold (80.72g); bezel set with 124 diamonds (diamonds: Ø 1.5mm); Ø 52mm, thickness: 7mm; sapphire glass with thermal counter-shock marking; crown set with one Ø 2.8mm diamond;

mirror-polished bottom cover set with a diamond of Ø 0.95mm on the "I" of ELLIA; water resistant to 3atm.
Dial: opaline; mirror polished yellow-gold markers; dauphine shaped 18K yellow-gold hands.
Strap: alligator; 18K solid yellow-gold pin buckle set with 86 diamonds (0.384 carat); pin set with one Ø 0.9mm diamond; width case/buckle: 31.6x20mm.
Also available: case: bezel set matte yellow gold; full set yellow-gold; dial: matte black; shiny black; mirror polished gold; matte gold; markers: shiny black; outline gold; set; polished copper outlin.

Z2 PETITE DATE

Movement: mechanical automatic-winding Fréderic Piguet caliber PGE 1150; cage: Ø 25.6mm, thickness: 4.6mm; 72-hour power reserve; 5-position adjustment; "Côtes de Genève" finished bridges with rhodium-plating; "GE" engraved on solid gold rotor.
Functions: hour, minute, second; date.
Case: 18K black gold (110.28g); width: 41mm, thickness: 10.3mm; sapphire glass with thermal counter-shock marking; water resistant to 3atm.
Strap: alligator, width case/buckle: 32x20mm; 18K black-gold folding buckle (15.48g).
Also available: white gold; pink gold.

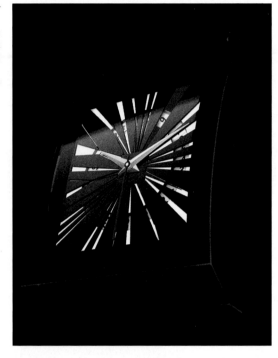

TIME SPACE 15

Movement: mechanical manual-winding Fréderic Piguet caliber PGE 15; cage: Ø 35.64mm, thickness: 1.9mm; 43-hour power reserve; 5-position adjustment; "Côtes de Genève" finished bridges with black PVD treatment; "GE" engraved on stippled plate with black PVD treatment; 21,600 vph; 20 jewels.
Functions: hour, minute.
Case: 18K black gold (44.34g); width: 43mm, thickness: 5.95mm; sapphire glass with thermal counter-shock marking; water resistant to 3atm.
Strap: alligator; width case/buckle: 25x20mm; 18K black-gold pin buckle (4.73g).
Also available: white gold; set bezel white gold; full set white gold; pink gold; set bezel pink gold; full set pink gold; set bezel black gold; full set black gold.

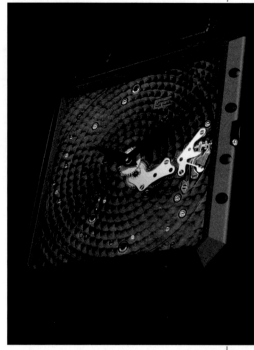

CIRCLE

Movement: Fréderic Piguet caliber PGE 820; cage: Ø 18.8mm, thickness: 1.95mm
Functions: hour, minute.
Case: 18K polished pink gold (80.72g); bezel set with 124 diamonds (diamonds: Ø 1.5mm); Ø 52mm, thickness: 7mm; sapphire glass with thermal counter-shock marking; crown set with one Ø 2.8mm diamond; mirror-polished bottom cover set with a diamond of Ø 0.95mm on the "I" of ELLIA; water resistant to 3atm.
Dial: shiny black; dauphine shaped 18K pink-gold hands; outline pink-gold markers
Strap: alligator; 18K solid pink-gold pin buckle set with 86 diamonds (0.384 carat); pin set with one Ø 0.9mm diamond; width case/buckle: 31.6x20mm.
Also available: case: bezel set matte pink gold; full set pink gold; dial: matte black; mirror polished gold; opaline; matte gold; copper; markers: shiny black; mirror polished gold; set; polished copper outline.

CONVEX SERTIE

Movement: Fréderic Piguet caliber PGE 820; cage: Ø 18.8mm, thickness: 1.95mm
Functions: hour, minute.
Case: 18K white gold; bezel set with 100 diamonds (diamonds: Ø 1.5mm); Ø 41x41 mm, thickness: 7.1mm; sapphire glass with thermal counter-shock marking; crown set with one Ø 2.3mm diamond; mirror polished bottom cover set with a Ø 0.95mm diamond on the "I" of ELLIA; water resistant to 3atm.
Dial: 18K solid white-gold dial (25.35g); full set with 558 diamonds (2.28 carats); 4 white-gold Arabic figures; dauphine shaped 18K white-gold hands.
Strap: alligator; width case/buckle: 32x26mm; 18K solid white-gold pin buckle set with 40 diamonds (0.49 carat); pin set with one Ø 0.9mm diamond.
Also available: pink gold; yellow gold.
Note: limited edition.

H. MOSER & CIE.

Ageless Appeal

H. Moser & Cie. is named for Heinrich Moser, who established his watch-making company more than 175 years ago. Moser's legacy was revived in 2002 with the re-launching of H. Moser & Cie. and, since then, the company has risen quickly, lifted by accolades for its novel solutions, attention to detail and timeless style.

The company's fine-tuned approach to the craft of horology reveals a heightened appreciation for the experiential aspects of owning a watch. The brand's patented "double pull crown" operates intuitively, making adjustments both quick and easy for the owner.

Another advancement sure to bring a smile to an aficionado's lips is an escapement that can be removed, improving accessibility to the module, which reduces the amount of time required for regular cleaning and service. In fact, the owner of an H. Moser & Cie. watch can take the timepiece into a dealer, who will replace the escapement module with a temporary module while the original is being serviced.

But the watchmaker's most revolutionary innovation to date is the Straumann double hairspring, first introduced in 2007. The invention was the result of watchmakers at H. Moser searching for a way to counteract the effects of gravity on the watch's precision. The solution was to equalize this gravitational error at its point of origin, using two balance springs—constructed identically—to offset one another's oscillations.

The patented mechanism was first installed in the Henry Double Hairspring, a tonneau-shaped watch that stands out alongside the mostly round timepieces presented.

The landmark double hairspring escapement is also featured in the Mayu Palladium. The module is the first in the world to incorporate an escape wheel and pallet fork made from hard, white gold.

Made of platinum or rose gold, Henry Double Hairspring's tonneau-shaped case houses a patented escapement module that compensates for the effects of gravity on a movement's rate using hairsprings tuned to offset one another.

The watchmaker's most revolutionary innovation to date is the Straumann double hairspring, first introduced in 2007.

This technological bounty is encased in solid palladium, giving the watch a distinguished look of ageless elegance. The brilliance of the exquisite case metal stands in contrast to the smoky patina of the watch's dial, which includes a pocket-watch seconds hand. H. Moser also offers the Mayu in rose gold paired with either a black lacquer or silver-colored dial.

Both the Mayu and the Monard were introduced in 2006, the year H. Moser debuted. The Monard maximizes sophistication with a minimalist approach that accentuates the case's sleek curves and the dial's clean design aesthetic, which favors markers over numerals.

A double spring barrel powers the Monard for seven days when fully wound. To monitor the spring's status, watchmakers have incorporated a power-reserve indicator that can be viewed through the clear crystal caseback.

The tradition founded by Heinrich Moser nearly two centuries ago thrives in the modern age as a new generation discovers the beauty and complexity of timepieces that bear the name H. Moser & Cie.

TOP A declaration of rakish understatement, Mayu pairs a sepia-toned dial with a palladium case, mixing classic taste with modern materials.

RIGHT Adorned simply with markers instead of numerals, Monard's visual appeal stems from the ageless combination of gold and black.

MAYU   REF. 321.503-005

Movement: HMC 321.503 caliber; 80-hour power reserve; interchangeable escapement module.
Functions: hours, minutes; large pocket-watch-style seconds hand.
Case: 18K rose gold; antireflective sapphire crystal caseback.
Dial: silver; applied indices; three-dimensional hands.
Strap: crocodile.

Price range: $12,000-$36,000
Also available: white gold, white lacquer dial; platinum, ardoise dial; rose gold, black lacquer dial; white gold, rhodié dial.
Limited edition: white gold, white enamel; Ladies': rose gold, black mother-of-pearl with diamond bezel and white gold, white mother-of-pearl with diamond bezel dial. Also a limited edition 18K rose gold, black lacquer dial with diamond bezel and Tsar Eagle engraved caseback.

MAYU   REF. 321.503-007

Movement: HMC 321.503 caliber; 80-hour power reserve; interchangeable escapement module.
Functions: hours, minutes; large pocket-watch-style seconds hand.
Case: 18K rose gold; antireflective sapphire crystal caseback.
Dial: black lacquer; applied indices; three-dimensional hands.
Strap: crocodile.

Price range: $12,000-$36,000
Also available: white gold, white lacquer dial; platinum, ardoise dial; rose gold, black lacquer dial; white gold, rhodium dial.
Limited edition: white gold, white enamel; Ladies': rose gold, black mother-of-pearl with diamond bezel and white gold, white mother-of-pearl with diamond bezel dial. Also a limited edition 18K rose gold, black lacquer dial with diamond bezel and Tsar Eagle engraved caseback.

MAYU   REF. 325.503-010

Movement: HMC 321.503 caliber; 80-hour power reserve; double hairspring oscillation system; interchangeable escapement module.
Functions: hours, minutes; large pocket-watch-style seconds hand.
Case: palladium; antireflective sapphire crystal caseback.
Dial: fumé; applied indices; three-dimensional hands.
Strap: crocodile.

Price range: $12,000-$36,000
Also available: white gold, white lacquer dial; platinum, ardoise dial; rose gold, black lacquer dial; white gold, rhodié dial.
Limited edition: white gold, white enamel; Ladies': rose gold, black mother-of-pearl with diamond bezel and white gold, white mother-of-pearl with diamond bezel dial. Also a limited edition 18K rose gold, black lacquer dial with diamond bezel and Tsar Eagle engraved caseback.

MONARD   REF. 343.505-017

Movement: manual-winding HMC 343.505 caliber; dual barrel; 7-day power reserve; interchangeable escapement module.
Functions: hours, minutes, center seconds; power-reserve indicator on movement side; seconds stop function.
Case: 18K rose gold; convex sapphire crystal caseback.
Dial: black lacquer dial.

Strap: crocodile.
Price range: $15,800-$21,800
Also available: white gold, rhodié dial; 18K rose gold, silver dial; platinum, ardoise dial.

MONARD   REF. 343.505-015

Movement: manual-winding HMC 343.505 caliber; dual barrel; 7-day power reserve; interchangeable escapement module.
Functions: hours, minutes, center seconds; power-reserve indicator on movement side; seconds stop function.
Case: platinum; convex sapphire crystal caseback.
Dial: ardoise dial.
Strap: crocodile.
Price range: $15,800-$21,800
Also available: white gold, rhodié dial; rose gold, silver dial; platinum, ardoise dial.

HENRY DOUBLE HAIRSPRING   REF. 324.607-004

Movement: manual-winding HMC 324.607 caliber; 4-day power reserve; double hairspring oscillating system; interchangeable escapement.
Functions: hours, minutes; pocket-watch-style seconds hand; power-reserve indicator on movement side.
Case: 18K rose gold; sapphire crystal caseback.
Dial: silver.
Strap: crocodile.
Price range: $18,900-$27,900
Also available: 18K rose gold, silver dial; 18K white gold, rhodié dial; platinum, ardoise dial.

HENRY DOUBLE HAIRSPRING   REF. 324.607-002

Movement: manual-winding HMC 324.607 caliber; 4-day power reserve; double hairspring oscillating system; interchangeable escapement.
Functions: hours, minutes; pocket-watch-style seconds hand; power-reserve indicator on movement side.
Case: white gold; sapphire crystal caseback.
Dial: rhodié dial.
Strap: crocodile.
Price range: $18,900-$27,900
Also available: 18K rose gold, silver dial; 18K white gold, rhodié dial; platinum, ardoise dial.

HENRY DOUBLE HAIRSPRING   REF. 342.607-006

Movement: HMC 324.607 caliber; 4-day power reserve; double hairspring oscillating system; nterchangeable escapement.
Functions: hours, minutes; pocket-watch-style seconds hand; power-reserve indicator on movement side.
Case: platinum; sapphire crystal caseback.
Dial: ardoise dial.
Strap: crocodile.
Price range: $18,900-$27,900
Also available: rose gold, silvered dial; platinum, ardoise dial.

HUBLOT
The Age of Reason

After a magnificent rebirth and recent acquisition by the LVMH Group, Hublot begins a new phase by concentrating on more traditional products. By doing so, CEO Jean-Claude Biver intends to offer a solid base for future development.

The Big Bang Red Devil Manchester United.

H ublot built its name on the Big Bang line which incarnates the concept of fusion between materials that are considered by most to be incompatible. But it is in a totally different domain that the Swiss brand provoked considerable shock waves last April: it announced its purchase by the French luxury group, **LVMH**.

2008: THE YEAR OF SOCCER

The element of surprise sets Hublot apart from all other companies. It was the first watchmaking company to be interested in the world of soccer and its star players. Entering boldly, Biver chose to sponsor the 2008 UEFA European Football Championship (Euro 2008). This is the elite tournament of European football in which all European national teams compete. He used this opportunity to introduce the Big Bang Euro 08 model, of which only 2,008 limited edition pieces were created. At 9:00, it has a micro-gauge showing the two 45-minute periods of the soccer match.

Hublot has always enjoyed extreme media publicity, therefore, it has chosen to invest heavily into extreme sports like that of Fusion Man, Yves Rossi, the first man to fly with wing micro-reactors. In nautical sports, this brand is the official partner of the Yacht Club of Monaco and the Real Club Nautico de Palma (Spain) represented by the PalmaVela model. On land, in addition to soccer, Hublot is fully invested in the sport of polo and chose as ambassador Miguel Novillo Astrada, one of the best players in the world. It also joined with the Gstaad Polo Club of Switzerland to create the Hublot Polo Gold Cup Gstaad honoring one of the finest matches of the World Polo Tour which was held last August. They unveiled a brand new, limited edition Big Bang model to celebrate this exceptional event

Hublot invests heavily into sports, including the activities of extreme athlete Fusion Man, yacht racing and polo.

THE GROWING PROCESS

Unlike previous years, Biver started wearing a suit and tie to present his innovations in 2008. "After the earlier period of total creativity where we implemented all of the ideas that came to mind, we begin a more selective process where we focus on quality instead of quantity," the CEO explains. This even reflects through his suit-and-tie attire demonstrating maturity and responsibility.

And Hublot is maturing in every aspect. Growing from a carefree adolescence into a more sophisticated and serious future, the brand is establishing a solid base. We definitely see this transformation through the construction of their new building, which is essential to Hublot's growth process.

TOP Available in All Black, this elegant Big Bang Classic model is the most popular watch in the collection.

BOTTOM LEFT The outrageous All Black King displays a powerful black ceramic bezel equipped with raised numerals.

BOTTOM RIGHT Hublot is the first brand to use cermet in a watch via the Bullet Bang model. Marrying ceramic and special metals, cermet is an extremely hard alloy.

TO THE EXTREME

Following the success of the Big Bang collection, Hublot redesigned this icon to create a model with three hands. Equipped with a glossed zirconium case, the Big Bang Classic illustrates perfectly the will to gain nobility. Classy with subdued elegance, it has a black ceramic crystal held in place with six polished, blocked screws. Inside, the carbon dial hides a mechanical movement with automatic rewind clearly displaying hours, minutes and seconds. It is also available in a completely black version, aptly named All Black.

The All Black King is endowed with a Ø 48mm ceramic case. Its dial bears raised numerals and contains a mechanical movement with automatic rewind displaying the hours, minutes, seconds and date. Limited to 500 watches, the model displays a sapphire caseback through which a tungsten movement treated in black PVD appears.

METAL AND CERAMICS FUSE

Inline with its tradition of exploring materials, Hublot pushes the envelope with the Bullet Bang model. This watch has no equivalent: its case is cut in microbille cermet, an extra-hard material combining ceramics and metals such as tungsten or bronze. This new 500-piece limited edition model displays the date and is equipped with a wheel movement, mechanical column and automatic rewind.

The Big Bang Aero Bang enables one to see the watch's heart through a skeleton dial. The mechanical movement with automatic rewind is seated in a glossed Ø 44.5mm tungsten case and boasts a chronograph in addition to the hours, minutes and seconds. To create a contrasting effect, the hands have a ruthenium sand color.

TUTTI FRUTTI

Women's watches burst with color in the Tutti Frutti collection. Displaying topaz, amethysts or sapphires on top of the bezel, these vibrant watches have a dominant color assigned to their lateral inserts or rubber bracelet. Displaying a chronograph with date in addition to the usual functions, the mechanical movement is rewound automatically. For chocolate lovers, the Day Dream Cappuccino Gold has an obviously smaller diameter than the 38mm Big Bang, but preserves the same lines. With a brilliant bezel set with 126 diamonds, the watch has a pink-gold case sheltering a quartz movement.

TOP The women's Tutti Frutti collection incorporates a festival of colors. Here, the Big Bang Purple Carat model displays a bezel encrusted with amethyst baguettes.

BOTTOM Smaller than the Ø 38mm Big Bang models, but keeping the same proportions, the Day Dream Cappuccino Gold presents a bezel covered with two rows of diamonds.

EURO 2008   REF. 318.PM.1123.RX.EUR08

Movement: HUB 45 self-winding chronograph 45-minutes movement.
Case: 18K red gold; black ceramic bezel.
Dial: black.
Strap: black rubber.
Note: limited edition of 250 pieces.
Suggested price: $23,900

EURO 2008   REF. 318.CM.1123.RX.EUR08

Movement: HUB 45 self-winding chronograph 45-minute movement.
Case: black ceramic; black ceramic bezel.
Dial: black.
Strap: black rubber.
Note: limited edition 2008.
Suggested price: $14,900

POLO CLUB GSTAAD   REF. 301.CM.1140.RX.PCG08

Movement: HUB 44 self-winding chronograph movement.
Case: black ceramic; black ceramic bezel.
Dial: black.
Strap: black rubber.
Note: limited edition of 250 pieces.
Suggested price: $14,900

BULLET BANG   REF. 303.BI.1190.RX

Movement: HUB 44 RAC self-winding chronograph movement with column-wheel.
Case: cermet; cermet bezel.
Dial: black.
Strap: black rubber.
Note: limited edition of 500 pieces.

Suggested price: $24,900

ALL CHOCOLATE   REF. 301.CC.3190.RC

Movement: HUB 44 self-winding chronograph movement.
Case: chocolate ceramic; chocolate ceramic bezel.
Dial: chocolate.
Strap: chocolate rubber.
Note: limited edition of 500 pieces.
Suggested price: $14,900

AERO BANG GOLD/CERAMIC   REF. 301.PM.1180.RX

Movement: skeleton HUB 44 self-winding chronograph movement.
Case: 18K red gold; black ceramic bezel.
Dial: black.
Strap: black rubber.
Note: limited edition of 500 pieces.
Suggested price: $25,900

AERO BANG ALL BLACK   REF. 310.CM.1110.RX

Movement: skeleton HUB 44 self-winding chronograph movement.
Case: black ceramic; black ceramic bezel.
Dial: black.
Strap: black rubber.
Note: limited edition of 500 pieces.
Suggested price: $18,900

BIG BANG KING ALL BLACK   REF. 322.CM.1110.RX

Movement: HUB 21 self-winding movement.
Case: black ceramic; black ceramic rotating bezel with black index.
Dial: black.
Strap: black rubber.
Note: limited edition of 500 pieces.
Suggested price: $15,900

BIG BANG KING RED GOLD/WHITE CERAMIC   REF. 322.PH.230.RW

Movement: HUB 21 self-winding movement.
Case: 18K red gold; white ceramic rotating bezel.
Dial: white.
Strap: white rubber.
Suggested price: $29,500

BIG BANG BLUE CARAT   REF. 341.PL.2010.RB.1907

Movement: HUB 41 self-winding chronograph movement.
Case: 18K red gold; 18K red-gold bezel set with 48 topaz baguettes.
Dial: white.
Strap: blue rubber.
Suggested price: $29,900

BIG BANG ORANGE CARAT   REF. 341. PO.2010.RO.1906

Movement: HUB 41 self-winding chronograph movement.
Case: 18K red gold; 18K red-gold bezel set with 48 orange sapphire baguettes.
Dial: white.
Strap: orange rubber.
Suggested price: $29,900

BIG BANG PURPLE CARAT   REF. 341.PV.2010.RV.1905

Movement: HUB 41 self-winding chronograph movement.
Case: 18K red gold; 18K red-gold bezel set with 48 amethyste baguettes.
Dial: white.
Strap: purple rubber.
Suggested price: $29,900

BIG BANG CLASSIC GOLD/CERAMIC REF. 501.PM.1680.RX

Movement: self-winding.
Case: 18K red gold; black ceramic bezel.
Dial: carbon.
Strap: black rubber.
Suggested price: $17,900

BIG BANG CLASSIC GOLD REF. 501.PX.1180.RX

Movement: self-winding.
Case: 18K red gold; 18K red-gold bezel.
Dial: black.
Strap: black rubber.
Suggested price: $19,900

BIG BANG CLASSIC ZIRCONIUM REF. 501.ZX.1170.RX

Movement: self-winding.
Case: zirconium; zirconium bezel.
Dial: black.
Strap: black rubber.
Suggested price: $6,500

BIG BANG 38 GOLD REF. 361.PX.1280.RX.1704

Movement: quartz.
Case: 18K red gold set with 135 diamonds (0.82 carat); 18K red-gold bezel set with 126 diamonds (0.87 carat).
Dial: black.
Strap: black rubber.
Suggested price: $21,900

INVICTA
Uncharted Territories

In the infinite world of time, this past year was all about everything Invicta! And with demand only on the rise, this next year is sure to be another year of remarkable growth for this privately owned, powerhouse company.

L imitless. This concept is the driving idealism behind the crafting of each and every watch. The Invicta Watch Group has followed this core belief while revolutionizing the term "affordable luxury." High price points do not always define luxury and quality along with innovation is always in style, which is why Invicta successfully embraces consumers and collectors at any spending tier.

Armed with three generations of horological know-how, Invicta continues to blaze a path all its own. And, with its trademark free spirit as the signifying element running through all of the brand's diverse collections, it continues to claim new and unchartered industry territories. Invicta remains free from outside influences, free from economic trends—free to move consumers and collectors into a dimension in time that is all Invicta!

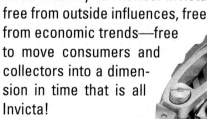

INVICTA
RESERVE
FOR THE FEW WHO KNOW BEST

The Invicta Specialty Reserve Chronograph: The "metal" behind pure mastery.

The Invicta Akula Reserve:
Your attention, dominated.

Invicta successfully embraces consumers and collectors at any spending tier.

INVICTA
AKULA
RESERVE
FOR THE FEW WHO KNOW BEST

LEFT The Invicta Speedway Vasuki: Time to square up and fly right.

BOTTOM LEFT The Invicta Quinotaur Russian Diver: Braving the spectrum of forward motion.

BELOW The Invicta S1 Touring Edition: Systems of an elegant persuasion.

INVICTA
S
SPEEDWAY
COLLECTION
GAINED MOMENTUM

GOING THE DISTANCE

INVICTA
RUSSIAN
SINCE 1959 DIVER
BETWEEN THE DEVIL AND THE DEEP BLUE SEA
COME HELL OR HIGH WATER

The Invicta Sea Spider: Mechanisms
perfectly integrated for adventure.

INVICTA
SEASPIDER
COLLECTION

IWC
Vintage Spirit

To honor its remarkable history, IWC gave six of its classic timepieces refreshing new beginnings. The Portuguese, Ingenieur, Pilot's Watch, Da Vinci, Aquatimer, and Portofino are the true original timepieces that established the brand and they re-emerge today under a crisp new light.

When the American gentleman Florentine Ariosto Jones founded IWC and settled in Schaffhausen in 1868, he could have no idea that his company would become one of the most prestigious companies in the mechanical clock industry of the 21st century. One hundred and forty years later, CEO Georges Kern and his team pay tribute to IWC's beginnings by recreating the six trademark timepieces that started it all.

"To invent the present by rediscovering the past" could have been the motto that IWC explored when creating the Vintage Collection—Jubilee Edition 1868-2008. These timekeepers are inventive new interpretations, not remakes or re-releases of old models. One may feel a touch of nostalgia by looking at these timepieces but IWC has fully integrated all of today's cutting-edge modern technology into them. From the style of their large boxes to their ultra-precise movements, these high-quality masterpieces meet today's standards without a doubt.

The revived models will be released in 140 complete sets of all six watches in platinum. An additional 360 platinum pieces of each model will be sold individually.

These six revived models are new interpretations—not simply re-releases—of old models.

To secure the vintage spirit of these new watches, three models (the Pilot's Watch, Portuguese, and Portofino), have a manual pocket-watch movement. For the others (the Ingenieur, Da Vinci and Aquatimer), IWC used the 80110 or the 80111 caliber, the successors of the original automatic movement 8531 with the Pellaton winder of 1955. All of these timepieces are available in stainless steel with black dials.

Platinum versions of each model were created for IWC's special Vintage Collection—Jubilee Edition 1868-2008 in which all six models are presented together in exclusive handcrafted leather boxes. Just 140 of these complete sets will be available.

IWC GOES OUT TO SEA

IWC has always been immensely supportive of the luxury yachting industry. The brand recently signed a partnership with the prestigious Swiss shipyard, Boesch, located on the banks of Lake Zurich. The exclusive Boesch—known for the irreproachable quality of its mahogany boats and their flawless lines—builds fewer than forty boats per year, each unit requiring more than 2,000 hours of workmanship. IWC honors this exceptional naval manufacturer with the 300-piece limited-edition Aquatimer Chronographe Edition Boesch. One may admire the mahogany wood inlay in the shape of a propeller that pays tribute to the fine woodwork of the Boesch boats.

IWC has also expanded its sphere of ambassadors. Among other personalities, retired French soccer star Zinédine Zidane represents the people who carry high the colors of the company. To celebrate the partnership with Zidane, IWC has developed a 1,000-piece limited series of the Ingenieur Automatic.

TOP RIGHT Celebrating IWC's 140th anniversary, the Portofino, Pilot's Watch, Portuguese, Da Vinci, Ingenieur, and Aquatimer return with contemporary, radiant looks while retaining their original styles.

TOP RIGHT Boesch boats are handcrafted in mahogany and IWC kept the dark amber color to dress the special 300-piece Aquatimer Chronographe Edition Boesch series.

ABOVE The Aquatimer Chronographe Edition Boesch's caseack bears a propeller surrounded by inserts in mahogany with the model number engraved around it.

LEFT The Ingenieur Automatic Edition Zinédine Zidane takes on the colors of the French soccer team and features a red numeral 10 to honor the soccer icon.

IWC DA VINCI CHRONOGRAPH EDITION LAUREUS   REF. IW376404

Movement: mechanical automatic-winding IWC manufacture 89360 caliber with a double-pin winding device and seconds-stopping system; column wheel; 28,800 vph; 68-hour power reserve; 40 jewels.
Functions: hours, minutes, small seconds at 6; date at 6; chronograph with 3 counters.
Case: stainless steel three-piece case in tonneau shape; 44x43mm, thickness: 14.4mm; polished and brushed finish; domed sapphire crystal, antireflective on both sides; screw-down crown; rocking pushers; back fastened by 6 screws, displaying the movement through a sapphire crystal; water resistant to 3atm.

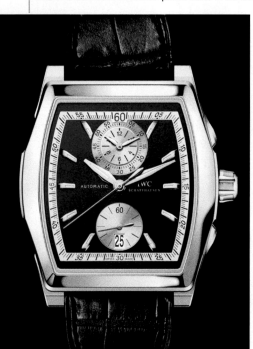

Dial: blue; recessed subdials decorated with circular beads; silvered minute ring with circular brushing; applied luminescent rhodium-plated markers; luminescent rhodium-plated Alpha hands; custom engraving on the back done by a 15-year-old girl from Mumbai.
Strap: blue crocodile leather; steel fold-over clasp.
Suggested price: $14,200
Note: limited to 1,000 pieces worldwide.

IWC DA VINCI PERPETUAL CALENDAR EDITION KURT KLAUS   REF. IW376204

Movement: mechanical automatic-winding IWC 79261 caliber (integrated chronograph on thoroughly modified Valjoux base + calendar module); with seconds-stopping system; 28,800 vph; 44-hour power reserve; 39 jewels. **Functions:** hours, minutes, small seconds; perpetual calendar; date at 3; month and hour counter at 6; 4-digit year between 7 and 8; day of the week and small seconds at 9; perpetual moonphase and minute counter at 12; center second counter; minute track with divisions for 1/4 second and numerals at every 5 units.

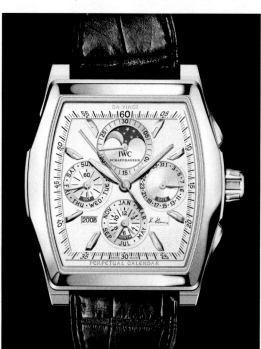

Case: stainless steel three-piece case in tonneau shape; 44x43mm, thickness: 15.5mm; polished and brushed finish; domed sapphire crystal, antireflective on both sides; white-gold screw-down crown for the correction of the whole calendar; rocking white-gold pushers; back fastened by 6 screws with engraved Kurt Klaus portrait; water resistant to 3atm.
Dial: silvered, guilloche with a vertical-line pattern; subdials decorated with circular beads, rings with circular brushing with Kurt Klaus's signature; applied luminescent rose-gold markers; luminescent rose-gold Alpha hands. **Strap:** black crocodile leather; stainless steel fold-over clasp.
Suggested price: $24,000

IWC DA VINCI AUTOMATIC: VINTAGE COLLECTION   REF. IW546101

Movement: Pellaton automatic-winding mechanical movement featuring caliber 80111; 28,800 vph / 4 Hz; 44-hour power reserve; 28 jewels.
Functions: hours, minutes, seconds; date at 3.
Case: stainless steel; ø 41mm, thickness: 13.5mm; antireflective sapphire crystal; sapphire crystal back; screw-down crown; water resistant to 3atm.

Dial: black dial with extra-long markers and simple bâton hands.
Strap: black crocodile strap; stainless steel clasp.
Suggested price: $7,300-$38,000
Also available: platinum (limited to 500 pieces).

IWC BIG INGENIEUR   REF. IW500503

Movement: Pellaton automatic-winding mechanical movement with caliber 51113; 21,600 vph / 3 Hz; 7-day power reserve when fully wound; 42 jewels.
Functions: hours, minutes, seconds; power-reserve display at 3; date at 6.
Case: rose gold; Ø 45.5mm, thickness: 15mm; convex, antireflective sapphire crystal; sapphire crystal back; screw-down crown; water resistant to 12atm.

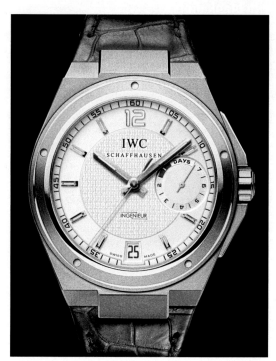

Dial: silvered, rhodium-plated dial with gold indexes.
Strap: brown crocodile strap.
Suggested price: $11,800-$42,000
Also available: in stainless steel and in platinum (limited to 500 pieces).

INGENIEUR AUTOMATIC EDITION CLIMATE ACTION REF. IW323402

Movement: Pellaton automatic-winding mechanical movement with integrated shock-absorption system housing caliber 80111; 28,800 vph / 4 Hz; 44-hour power reserve; 28 jewels.
Functions: hours, minutes, seconds; date at 3.
Case: stainless steel case with two ceramic rings; Ø 44mm, thickness: 14mm; antireflective sapphire crystal; screw-down crown; water resistant to 12atm.
Dial: white; decorated with a weft pattern; applied luminescent rhodium-plated bâton markers; Arabic 6 and 12; smooth, raised printed minute-track ring with 2 brushed platelets at poles showing black printed marks and red numerals; luminescent rhodium-plated skeletonized bâton hands.
Strap: soft black strap; polished steel clasp.
Suggested price: $8,900
Note: limited to 1,000 pieces.

INGENIEUR AUTOMATIC REF. IW322701

Movement: mechanical automatic-winding IWC 80110 caliber; 28,800 vph; 44-hour power reserve; 28 jewels; shockproof and antimagnetic complying with The NICHS 91 standard.
Functions: hours, minutes, seconds; date at 3.
Case: stainless steel three-piece case; 47x41.8mm, thickness: 14.9mm; polished and brushed finish; additional inside case in soft iron for protection against magnetic fields; bezel with 5 holes; antireflective flat sapphire crystal, resistant against depressurization; screw-down crown; screw-on back; water resistant to 12atm.
Dial: black, guilloché; luminescent, applied, faceted rhodium-plated bâton markers; Arabic 6 and 12; white printed minute track with 5-minute graduation; luminescent, rhodium-plated faceted bâton hands.
Bracelet: stainless steel; polished and brushed; steel fold-over safety clasp.
Suggested price: $5,600-$6,600
Also available: in titanium; AMG version; on soft and multilayer strap or bracelet.

IWC INGENIEUR AUTOMATIC: VINTAGE COLLECTION REF. IW323301

Movement: Pellaton automatic-winding mechanical movement featuring caliber 80111; 28,800 vph / 4 Hz; 44-hour power reserve; 28 jewels.
Functions: hours, minutes, seconds; date at 3.
Case: stainless steel; Ø 42.5mm, thickness: 14.5mm; crossed out, antireflective sapphire crystal; sapphire crystal back; screw-down crown; water resistant to 12atm.
Dial: rhodium-plated black dial; dot-and-line markers (the dots are luminescent); dauphine hands.
Strap: black crocodile strap; stainless steel clasp.
Suggested price: $7,300-$38,000
Also available: platinum (limited to 500 pieces).

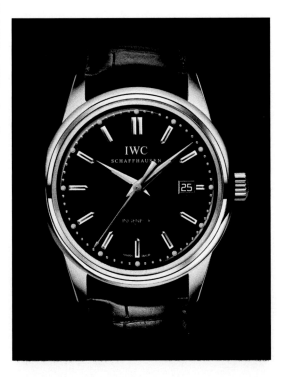

IWC PORTOFINO HAND-WOUND: VINTAGE COLLECTION REF. IW544801

Movement: hand-wound mechanical movement with caliber 98800; 18,800 vph / 2.5 Hz; 46-hour power reserve; 18 jewels; Breguet spring.
Functions: hours, minutes, small seconds at 6; moonphase at 12.
Case: stainless steel; Ø 46mm, thickness: 11mm; crossed out, antireflective sapphire crystal; sapphire crystal back; water resistant to 3atm.
Dial: black dial with elongated Roman-style numerals.
Strap: black crocodile strap; stainless steel clasp.
Suggested price: $12,500-$44,000
Also available: platinum (limited to 500 pieces).

IWC PILOT'S WATCH HAND-WOUND: VINTAGE COLLECTION   REF. IW325401

Movement: hand-wound mechanical movement with caliber 98300; 18,000 vph / 2.5 Hz; 46-hour power reserve; 18 jewels.
Functions: hours, minutes, small seconds at 6.
Case: stainless steel; Ø 44mm, thickness: 12mm; antireflective sapphire crystal; sapphire crystal back; rotating bezel with pointer; water resistant to 6atm.

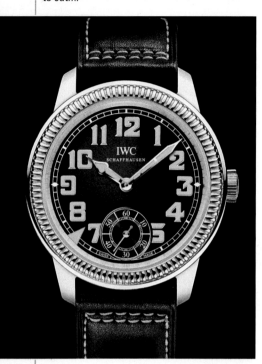

Dial: black dial with the classical IWC cockpit-style design; luminescent hands and numerals.
Strap: brown buffalo strap; stainless steel clasp.
Suggested price: $10,800-$41,600
Also available: platinum (limited to 500 pieces).

PILOT'S WATCH UTC EDITION ANTOINE DE SAINT EXUPERY   REF. IW326103

Movement: automatic-winding mechanical movement with caliber 30710; 28,800 vph / 4 Hz; 42-hour power reserve; 23 jewels.
Functions: hours, minutes, seconds; date at 4; 24-hour Universal Time Coordinated (UTC) display at 6.
Case: rose gold; Ø 44mm, thickness: 12.9mm; screw-down crown and soft iron inner case for protection against magnetic fields; sapphire crystal, coated on both sides and secured against displacement by drop in air pressure; water resistant to 6atm.

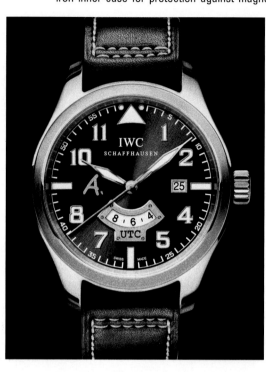

Dial: brown; Arabic numerals; rose-gold gilded hands.
Strap: brown buffalo strap.
Suggested price: $5,200-$19,200
Also available: platinum (1 piece), white gold (250 pieces), and stainless steel (1,188 pieces).

IWC PILOT'S WATCH CHRONO-AUTOMATIC   REF. IW371701

Movement: mechanical automatic-winding IWC 79320 caliber; 28,800 vph; 44-hour power reserve; 25 jewels.
Functions: hours, minutes; small seconds hand with stop function; day and date indicator, stopwatch at 6, 9 and 12.
Case: stainless steel three-piece case; Ø 42mm, thickness: 14.7mm; soft iron for protection against magnetic fields; sapphire, convex antireflective crystal resistant against pressure drop.

Dial: black; applied Arabic numerals; chapter ring; propeller-like hands.
Strap: black hand-stitched crocodile leather strap with a stainless steel fold-over clasp.
Suggested price: $4,400-$14,500
Also available: on a stainless steel bracelet equipped with a folding clasp and the special IWC bracelet system that allows for quick adjustment; in rose gold on a brown hand-stitched crocodile leather strap with a rose-gold fold-over clasp.

PILOT'S WATCH MARK XVI   REF. IW325501

Movement: automatic-winding mechanical IWC 30110 caliber; 28,800 vph; 42-hour power reserve; 21 jewels.
Functions: hours, minutes, seconds; date at 3.
Case: stainless steel three-piece case; Ø 39mm, thickness: 11.5mm; soft iron for protection against magnetic fields; convex sapphire antireflective crystal; resistant against pressure drop.

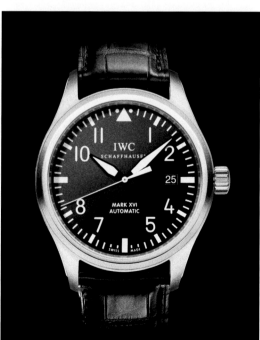

Dial: black; Arabic numerals; propeller-like hands.
Strap: black hand-stitched crocodile leather; stainless steel fold-over clasp.
Suggested price: $3,500-$4,900
Also available: on stainless steel bracelet with the special IWC bracelet system enabling quick adjustment.

IWC BIG PILOT'S WATCH   REF. IW500401

Movement: mechanical automatic-winding IWC 51110 caliber; 21,600 vph; 7-day power reserve; 44 jewels; balance with Breguet spring.
Functions: hours, minutes; date at 6; power-reserve display at 3; central seconds hand with stop function.
Case: stainless steel three-piece case; Ø 46.2mm, thickness: 15.8mm; soft iron for protection against magnetic fields; sapphire, convex antireflective crystal resistant against pressure drop.
Dial: black; applied Arabic numerals; propeller-like hands.
Strap: black hand-stitched crocodile leather strap; stainless steel fold-over clasp
Suggested price: $13,500-$26,500
Also available: 18K gold on a dark brown hand-stitched crocodile leather strap.

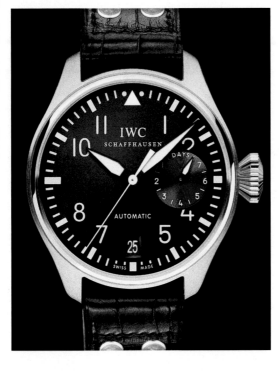

IWC PILOT'S WATCH CHRONO-AUTOMATIC EDITION TOP GUN   REF. IW378901

Movement: automatic-winding mechanical chronograph movement with caliber 79320; 28,800 vph / 4 Hz; 44-hour power reserve; 25 jewels.
Functions: hours, minutes, small seconds at 6; hacking seconds at 9; chronograph at 12; date and date display at 3.
Case: soft iron inner case for protection against magnetic fields; Ø 44mm, thickness: 15.9mm; convex sapphire crystal, antireflective on both sides and secured against displacement by drop in air pressure; caseback with TOP GUN insignia; screw-down crown; water resistant to 6atm.
Dial: black dial with distinctive cockpit-style design; white, luminescent hands and numerals; one of the TOP GUN Edition's most conspicuous features—the bright red counterweight on the central hand, which resembles the silhouette of a jet.
Strap: soft nylon strap.
Suggested price: $7,000

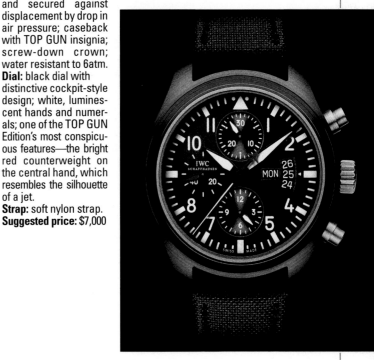

PILOT'S WATCH DOUBLE CHRONOGRAPH EDITION TOP GUN   REF. IW379901

Movement: mechanical automatic-winding IWC 79230 caliber (integral chronograph modified for the split-second feature) with a seconds-stopping system; 28,800 vph; 44-hour power reserve; 29 jewels. **Functions:** hours, minutes, center seconds; day and oversized date at 3; split-second chronograph with 3 counters: hour at 6, small second at 9, minute at 12. **Case:** black ceramics and natural titanium; two-piece case; Ø 46mm, thickness: 17.8mm; matte finish; additional ductile iron inside case for the deviation of magnetic fields; very thick, curved sapphire crystal, antireflective on both sides, strongly depressurization-resistant; screw-down crown and pushers with case protections (the one for the split-second chronograph at 10 in titanium); screw-on back in titanium with Top Gun logo; water resistant to 6atm. **Dial:** matte black; chronograph subdials decorated with circular beads; white Arabic numerals; triangular and bâton markers, luminescent at quarters; luminescent matte-black lozenge hands; split-second counter with white hands and red counter-weights; minute track.
Strap: black fabric; brushed titanium clasp.
Suggested price: $10,900

IWC AQUATIMER AUTOMATIC: VINTAGE COLLECTION   REF. IW323101

Movement: Pellaton automatic-winding mechanical with caliber 80111; 28,800 vph / 4 Hz; 44-hour power reserve; 28 jewels.
Functions: hours, minutes, seconds; date at 3.
Case: stainless steel; Ø 44mm, thickness: 14.5mm; screw-down, self-sealing main crown; mechanical rotating inner bezel; antireflective sapphire crystal and sapphire crystal back; water resistant to 12atm.
Dial: rhodium-plated black dial; luminescent elements on hands, dial and rotating inner bezel.
Strap: black rubber strap.
Suggested price: $7,300-$38,000
Also available: platinum (limited to 500 pieces).

IWC AQUATIMER CHRONOGRAPH EDITION COUSTEAU DIVERS   REF. IW378203

Movement: automatic-winding mechanical movement with caliber 79320; 28,800 vph / 4 Hz; 44-hour power reserve; 25 jewels.
Functions: chronograph; hours at 9, minutes at 12, small seconds at 6; day and date display at 3.
Case: stainless steel; 44mm, thickness: 15mm; mechanical rotating inner bezel; sapphire crystal, antireflective on both sides; screw-down crown; water resistant to 12atm.

Dial: black, blue and yellow rhodium-plated dial; white indexes and luminescent elements on hands, dial and rotating inner bezel.
Strap: black rubber strap.
Suggested price: $5,800
Note: limited edition of 2,500 pieces.

AQUATIMER SPLIT MINUTE CHRONOGRAPH   REF. IW372301

Movement: mechanical IWC 79470 caliber.
Functions: chronograph; hours, minutes, small seconds with stop function; split-minute; date.
Case: titanium; Ø 44mm, thickness: 16.3mm, weight: 153g; mechanical rotating inner bezel.
Dial: black; recessed subdial displays; white indexes; applied numerals

on rotating inner bezel; yellow highlights on numerals and rotating inner bezel to enhance readability.
Bracelet: titanium; IWC bracelet system with pushbutton safety release clasp.
Suggested price: $8,800-$9,800
Also available: titanium on black rubber strap.

IWC PORTUGUESE TOURBILLON MYSTERE   REF. IW504207

Movement: mechanical automatic-winding IWC 50900 caliber with tourbillon volant device; 7-day power reserve; 44 jewels; 19,900 vph; balance with Breguet spring; yellow-gold rotor with the Probus Scafusia seal; finished by hand.
Functions: hours, minutes, small seconds at 9; power reserve between 4 and 5.

Case: 18K white-gold three-piece case; Ø 44.2mm, thickness: 15.45mm; polished and brushed finish; back fastened by 6 screws, displaying the movement through a sapphire crystal; water resistant to 3atm.
Dial: ardoise; subdial decorated with circular beads; aperture on the tourbillon inside a sector decorated with a Côtes de Genève pattern; applied gilded Arabic numerals and hollowed minute track; gilded leaf-style hands.
Strap: hand-stitched crocodile leather; white-gold fold-over clasp.
Note: limited edition of 250 pieces.
Also available: in 5N rose gold (50 pieces).
Suggested price: $94,000-$104,000

IWC PORTUGUESE PERPETUAL CALENDAR   REF. IW502213

Movement: Pellaton mechanical automatic-winding movement with IWC 51612 caliber; 21,600 vph; 7-day power reserve, 64 jewels; balance with Breguet spring; rotor with 18K yellow-gold weight.
Functions: perpetual calendar; perpetual moonphase display with four-digit year display at 12; double phase of the moon for the northern and southern hemispheres, countdown indicator until the next full moon;

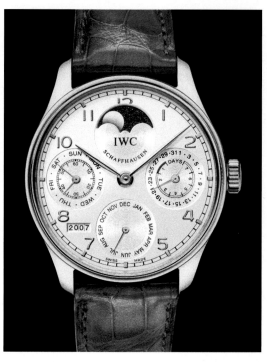

power-reserve display at 3; monthly calendar display at 6; weekly calendar display at 9; small seconds hand with stop function.
Case: 18K rose-gold three-piece case; Ø 44.2mm; thickness 15.5mm; polished and brushed finish; see-through sapphire crystal.
Dial: silver; subdial decorated with circular beads; applied gilded Arabic numerals.
Strap: hand-stitched crocodile leather; rose-gold fold-over clasp.
Suggested price: $30,500-$35,000
Also available: in white gold on brown crocodile strap.

IWC PORTUGUESE CHRONO-AUTOMATIC   REF. IW371402

Movement: mechanical automatic-winding IWC 79350 caliber; 28,800 vph; 44-hour power reserve; 31 jewels.
Functions: hours, minutes; chronograph with two counters: minutes at 12, small seconds at 6.
Case: 18K white-gold three-piece case; Ø 40.9mm, thickness: 12.3mm; polished and brushed finish; convex, antireflective sapphire crystal; water resistant to 3atm.
Dial: ardoise; railway-style minute chapter ring; applied gilded Arabic numerals; recessed sub-dials for the minutes and seconds counters; rhodium plated.
Strap: dark brown hand-stitched crocodile leather strap; white-gold fold-over clasp.
Suggested price: $6,800-$15,800
Also available: with all-silvered or black dial; in yellow gold with silvered dial; in stainless steel with white dial; in rose gold with black or silvered dial.

IWC PORTUGUESE AUTOMATIC   REF. IW500106

Movement: Pellaton mechanical automatic-winding IWC 51010 caliber; 21,600 vph; 7-day power reserve; 44 jewels; balance with Breguet spring; rotor with 18K yellow-gold weight.
Functions: power-reserve display at 3; date display at 6; small seconds hand with stop function at 9.
Case: 18K white-gold three-piece case; Ø 42.3mm, thickness: 13.9mm; convex, antireflective sapphire crystal.
Dial: ardoise; railway-style minute style minute chapter ring; applied gilded Arabic numerals; recessed subdials for the minutes and seconds counters; rhodium plated.
Strap: dark brown hand-stitched crocodile leather strap; white-gold fold-over clasp.
Suggested price: $10,900-$20,500
Also available: in rose gold on a brown hand-stitched crocodile leather strap; in stainless steel on a blue or black hand-stitched crocodile strap.

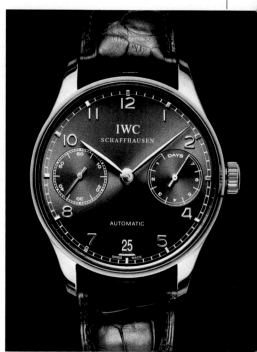

PORTUGUESE REGULATOR   REF. IW544404

Movement: mechanical manual-winding IWC98245 caliber; 18,000 vph; 46-hour power reserve; 22 jewels.
Functions: off-center hour at 12; center minute; small second at 6.
Case: 18K white-gold three-piece case; Ø 43.1mm, thickness: 11.8mm; polished and brushed finish; domed sapphire crystal, antireflective on both sides; white-gold crown; back fastened by 6 screws, displaying the movement through a sapphire crystal; water resistant to 3atm.
Dial: slate-gray brushed with a sun pattern; sub-dials decorated with circular beads; applied rhodium-plated Arabic numerals; white printed railway minute track with numerals every 5 units; rhodium-plated leaf-style hands.
Strap: brown crocodile leather; white-gold clasp.
Note: limited edition of 1,000 numbered pieces to celebrate the first pocket-watch made by the watchmaker F. A. Jones in 1868.
Suggested price: $11,000-$34,500
Also available: in pink gold with silvered dial and black leather strap; in stainless steel with silvered dial and brown leather strap; in platinum with silvered dial and black leather strap (500 pieces).

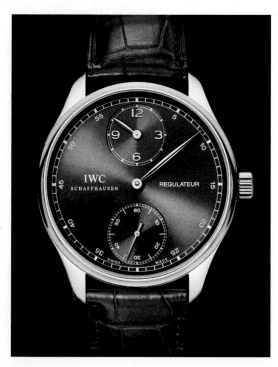

IWC PORTUGUESE HAND-WOUND: VINTAGE COLLECTION   REF. IW544501

Movement: hand-wound mechanical movement with caliber 98295; 18,000 vph / 2.5 Hz; 46-hour power reserve; 18 jewels; Breguet spring.
Functions: hours, minutes, small seconds at 6.
Case: stainless steel; Ø 44mm, thickness: 10mm; antireflective, crossed out sapphire crystal and sapphire crystal back; water resistant to 3atm.
Dial: black rhodium-plated dial; silvered indexes; railway-style minute chapter ring; applied gilded Arabic numerals.
Strap: black leather strap.
Suggested price: $11,700-$41,500
Also available: platinum (limited to 500 pieces).

JACOB & CO.
Heart of a Goldsmith

Jacob Arabo's timepieces are impossible to ignore. His expressive designs began pushing the boundaries of Swiss watchmaking in 2002 with audacious haute joaillerie for the rich and fabulous. His firm, Jacob & Co., turned its attention to complicated watchmaking a few years later, creating a stir with its flair for imaginative complications and attention to luxurious detail.

Among his latest inspirations, Epic is a line of automatic chronographs offered in both square (Epic I) and round (Epic II) cases, each with its own distinct personality.

Epic I channels a Cubist sensibility through its dial design, juxtaposing angular shapes around the dial, including a triangular small seconds hand. For Epic II, the layout of the subdials is skewed, creating a funhouse effect that is whimsical without sacrificing legibility. The small seconds display at 9:00 is split into two 30-second arcs couched inside one another. The clever design uses the short end of the hand to indicate 0 to 30 on the inside arc and the long end to point from 30 to 60 on the outside arc.

In both models, a pusher at 2:00 starts and stops the chronograph while a second pusher at 4:00 resets the timer. The 51x47mm Epic I and the Ø 47mm Epic II are both offered in rose gold, stainless steel and black PVD.

RIGHT The multilayer dial of the rose-gold Epic II includes round chronograph subdials controlled by pushers at 2:00 and 4:00. Black rubber is used for both the strap and chronograph pushers.

FAR RIGHT Black PVD is used for the Epic I case, which is curved subtly for an ergonomic fit on the wrist.

The new Epic II's subdials are skewed, creating a funhouse effect that is whimsical without sacrificing legibility.

With its Napoleon collection, Jacob & Co. offers two outrageous tourbillon watches—both aesthetically and technically speaking.

The Napoleon Quadra is the world's first timepiece whose four time zones are each paired with a dedicated tourbillon. Despite the large number of elements at play on the dial, it remains well proportioned and balanced. The four time zones are indicated with blue hour and minute hands that rotate around indexes featured on clear crystal. The transparency of the time zones allows full view of the tourbillon escapements.

Comprised of 60 parts, the Napoleon Quadra's round 46mm case includes four crowns—one for each time zone—positioned at 2:00, 4:00, 8:00 and 10:00 on the caseband.

The second timepiece in the Napoleon collection is titled simply Napoleon. Its skeletonized dial uncovers portions of the manual-wind movement, including the watch's mainspring providing 72 hours of reserve power. The dial includes centrally fixed blued steel hour and minute hands as well as a 60-second tourbillon cage anchored by a diamond-studded bridge. The sparkling accents continue onto the large Jacob & Co. logo that dominates the dial's upper half.

Designed by Arabo, Napoleon's round 46mm case is offered in rose or white gold and fitted with a clear caseback, providing a view of the hand-finished movement, which includes detailed etching and engraving, as well as sophisticated sapphire bridges.

Jacob & Co. will limit production of this innovative model to 36 pieces.

ABOVE   Napoleon's 46mm case is fitted with a sapphire disc, providing a view of the skeletonzied tourbillon movement and the Jacob & Co. logo.

TOP RIGHT   Jacob & Co. will produce Napoleon Quadra in a limited edition of 36 pieces. The watch's transparent caseback exposes the manual-wind movement, which provides 72 hours of reserve power.

Jacob & Co. keeps the focus on tourbillons with a pair of exceptional timekeepers from recent years.

The first is Rainbow Tourbillon, a limited edition that uses a trio of subdials to simultaneous indicate the time in 24 different time zones. Each subdial includes its own 24-hour index, which wraps around a rotating disc featuring eight different destination cities from around the world. Each city points to its hour using a red line.

Visible through an aperture at 6:00 and the exhibition caseback, the tourbillon mechanism rotates once every 60 seconds and is decorated with the Jacob & Co. logo.

The second model, named Crystal Tourbillon, features a transparent dial and caseback that emphasizes the watch's movement, which has been skeletonized down to the bare basics. The daring 47mm round case is adorned with white baguette diamonds totaling more than 17 carats. Using an audacious "invisible" setting that highlights Arabo's legendary skill as a jeweler, the gemstones cover the entire case without betraying how they are attached.

Jacob & Co. focuses its attention on sophisticated watchmaking with Quenttin, a vertical mechanical timepiece that features the first-ever 31-day power reserve.

Introduced in 2006, Quenttin's movement is similar to a car's transmission, using wheels positioned around several axles that are lined up horizontally instead of around a central axis. Seven barrels house multiple mainsprings, giving this remarkable movement a full month of power from a single winding.

Quenttin's unusual configuration requires the hours, minutes and power reserve all to be displayed using vertical rollers. The arrangement also provides a clear view of the watch's movement, which is also revealed through the crystal caseback. Looking at the side of the case, the watch's tourbillon mechanism can be seen. In a complex twist, it is suspended without roller bearings and positioned vertically.

In just a short time, Jacob & Co. has secured its place in high horology with complicated watches that are compelling both visually and mechanically. Its past successes have set the bar high, a challenge the company clearly relishes.

FAR LEFT In addition to the reference time, the Rainbow Tourbillon displays 24 separate times zones simultaneously. This limited edition timepiece includes the Jacob & Co. logo on top of the tourbillon mechanism.

CENTER More than 17 carats of white diamonds cover Crystal Tourbillon's white-gold case. The dial is transparant, revealing the hand-finished details of the skeletonized movement.

ABOVE Quenttin's rose-gold case (56x47x21.5mm) houses a complex vertical movement that uses vertical rollers to display the hours and minutes, as well as the status of its 31-day power reserve.

In the wake of its 20th anniversary two years ago, Kriëger continues to ride a wave of change. The introduction of the Tidal Wave Chronoscope in 2007 was a nod to the Swiss watchmaker's past achievements, but it is a new generation of timepieces that is charting a course to the company's future.

The journey began in 1987 with Ira Krieger, the accidental watchmaker who founded the company and added the umlaut to its name for effect. An avid boater, Krieger was frustrated to find that no watch that could forecast the tide's rise and fall, a useful function for any serious mariner. His solution: invent one that did.

Two decades later, not only has Krieger's creation—aptly named the Tidal Chronometer—become an icon amongst weekend and professional seafarers, but the Kriëger brand itself has grown to become one of the world's most prestigious.

One important factor behind the company's longevity is its ability to create watches that are both innovative and beautiful. Company president Lance Burstyn has overseen the incredible expansion of the Kriëger collection in recent years, introducing a flurry of particularly memorable timepieces.

The latest wave of new arrivals began to appear in 2004, when the company introduced the Gigantium, an oversized watch powered by a vintage pocket-watch movement. Its bold design, which includes a large "king's" crown with a sapphire tip, has become a popular choice among aficionados, celebrities and business moguls.

Since its introduction, the Gigantium line has expanded to include models for ladies, as well as specialized watches that deliver practical functions.

With its large size and chic style, the Elite appeals to women with personalities to match, like actress Jessica Biel, one of the watch's biggest admirers. The Elite offers a wide range of options—from dials and straps to metals and diamonds—resulting in a perfectly personalized expression of taste.

The case's bold design works equally well when paired with complicated movements, including the COSC-certified Gigantium Chronograph. It has subdials for minutes, hours and running seconds, plus a central seconds hand that can be engaged as a stopwatch. Another example is the Power Reserve, which displays the status of the 42-hour power reserve with a retrograde subdial positioned at 6:00.

In 2005, Kriëger followed the original Gigantium with one of the watchmaker's most revolutionary designs, the Mysterium. Demanding four years to research and develop, the watch's transparent aluminum case defies logic. A time-consuming manufacturing process is needed to create the Mysterium's 51mm case, greatly limiting production; Kriëger will create only 1,000.

The brand's momentum continues to gain speed, thanks to several fresh designs that uphold the company's reputation for function, design and performance.

> Kriëger's momentum gains speed with several fresh designs that uphold the company's reputation for function, design and performance.

Perhaps the most recognizable is the Gigantium Skeleton, which features a movement sculpted by Kriëgers' skilled artisans. The brand adds a macabre twist to its popular skeleton design with the Skeleton Skeleton. The movement of this limited edition timepiece is hand-carved to reveal bones that form a K—and a skull with eyes of rubies or diamonds.

With another new model, the Sea Stallion, Kriëger builds on its reputation for creating watches designed to perform under water. First there was the Kriëger Hammerhead, the only watch with an exhibition caseback able to withstand water pressure of 1,000 feet. The new Sea Stallion goes deeper—offering water resistance up to a half mile (2,640 feet) under water. The diver bezel's oversized relief markings make it easy for divers to monitor their times, even in murky waters.

Together, Sea Stallion and Skeleton Skeleton represent the spirit filling Kriëger's sails these days: a respect for tradition and a willingness to test uncharted waters.

ABOVE LEFT   The case of the limited edition Mysterium is made from transparent aluminum, the technology for which took more than four years to develop.

ABOVE RIGHT   The Skeleton Skeleton's movement is hand-carved into a skull and bones.

FAR RIGHT   Perfect for land or sea, the Sea Stallion is a stylish dive watch that is water resistant up to a half mile (2,640 feet) under water.

GIGANTIUM   REF. K5005R.6.C

Movement: mechanical manual-winding Kriëger Caliber K46.06/02 skeletonized movement (Unitas 6498 skeleton base); 17 jewels; 42-hour power reserve.
Functions: hours, minutes, small seconds hand at 6.
Case: 18K rose gold; 43mm; double dome antireflective sapphire crystal; exhibition back with sapphire crystal; oversized king's crown, sapphire tip; water resistant to 5atm. **Dial:** skeletonized engraved movement.

Strap: 20mm chestnut alligator strap; rose-gold Kriëger buckle.
Also available: in 18K rose gold (shown; 500 pcs), 18K yellow gold (500 pcs), 18K white gold (250pcs), PVD processing (250 pcs) and stainless steel (2,000 pcs) with or without diamonds and a variety of natural mother-of-pearl and enamel dial colors. Diamond bezel features 86 SI1G color, 1-carat stones or large diamonds upon request. Available in a variety of interchangeable strap colors and skins or bracelets.
Note: limited edition.

GIGANTIUM CHRONO   REF. K9009R.6.178R

Movement: self-winding automatic, COSC-certified Kriëger Caliber K70.01/01(ETA AO7.211 Base); 16 ½ lignes; specialized Kriëger engraved logo on the rotor; 25 jewels; 42-hour power reserve. **Functions:** date display; hours, minutes, seconds; chronograph with 3 counters: small seconds, 12-hour, 30-minute. **Case:** 18K rose gold; 43mm; double dome antireflective sapphire crystal; exhibition back with sapphire crystal; oversized king's crown, sapphire tip; water resistant to 5atm. **Dial:** chocolate brown enamel with white mother-of-pearl subdials, large rose-gold Roman numerals.

Strap: 20mm chocolate brown alligator strap; rose-gold Kriëger buckle.
Also available: in 18K rose gold (shown; 50 pcs), 18K yellow gold (50 pcs), PVD processing (500 pcs) and stainless steel (2,500 pcs) with or without diamonds and a variety of natural mother-of-pearl or enamel dial colors. Diamond bezel features 86 SI1G color 1-carat stones or large diamonds upon request. Available in a variety of interchangeable strap colors and skins or bracelets.
Note: limited edition.

GIGANTIUM POWER RESERVE   REF. K8008.1.5R

Movement: self-winding automatic, COSC-certified Kriëger Caliber K70.02/01 (ETA AO7.161 Base); 16 ½ lignes; specialized Kriëger engraved logo on rotor; 25 jewels; 42-hour power reserve.
Functions: date display; power-reserve indicator.
Case: stainless steel; 43mm; double dome antireflective sapphire crystal; exhibition back with sapphire crystal; oversized king's crown, sapphire tip; water resistant to 5atm.

Dial: white enamel dial with white mother-of-pearl subdial, large black Roman numerals.
Strap: 20mm black alligator strap; stainless steel Kriëger buckle.
Also available: in 18K rose gold (50 pcs), 18K yellow gold (50 pcs), PVD processing (500 pcs) processing and stainless steel (shown; 2,500 pcs) with or without diamonds and a variety of natural mother-of-pearl or enamel dial colors. Diamond bezel features 86 SI1G color 1-carat stones or large diamonds upon request. Available in a variety of interchangeable strap colors and skins or bracelets.
Note: limited edition.

MYSTERIUM   REF. G5100.1.C

Movement: mechanical manual-winding Kriëger Caliber K46.06/01 skeletonized movement (Unitas 6498 skeleton base); 17 jewels; 42-hour power reserve.
Functions: hours, minutes, small seconds hand at 6.
Case: clear aluminum case with stainless steel skeleton case; 51mm; double dome antireflective sapphire crystal; exhibition back with sapphire crystal; oversized king's crown, sapphire tip; water resistant to 5atm.

Dial: skeletonized engraved movement.
Strap: 20mm black alligator strap; stainless steel Kriëger buckle.
Also available: in 18K rose-gold movement with or without diamonds and a variety of natural mother-of-pearl or enamel dial colors; diamond bezel features SI1G color. Available in a variety of interchangeable strap colors and skins.
Note: limited edition of 1,000 stainless steel pcs.
Special features: comes in a luxurious alligator skin and wood briefcase with combination lock.

ELITE REF. K4004WD.6.C

Movement: self-winding automatic, COSC-certified Kriëger Caliber K82.06/01 skeletonized movement (ETA 2892 skeleton base); 21 jewels; 42-hour power reserve. **Functions:** hours, minutes, seconds. **Case:** 18K white gold; 38mm; diamond bezel; double dome antireflective sapphire crystal; exhibition back with sapphire crystal; oversized king's crown, sapphire tip; water resistant to 10atm. **Dial:** skeletonized movement with small Roman numerals in inner ring.

Strap: 20mm white alligator strap; white-gold Kriëger buckle.

Also available: in 18K yellow gold, 18K rose gold, PVD processing and stainless steel with or without diamonds and a variety of natural mother-of-pearl or enamel dial colors. Diamond bezel features 75 SI1G color 3/4-carat stones or large diamonds upon request. Available in a variety of interchangeable strap colors and skins or bracelets.

Note: skeleton movement: limited edition of 25 white-gold pcs, 100 stainless steel pcs, 25 yellow-gold pcs. Natural mother-of-pearl or enamel dials: limited edition of 3,000 stainless steel pcs, 500 rose-gold pcs, 500 yellow-gold pcs, 100 white-gold pcs, 300 PVD pcs.

MARINE CHRONOMETER REF. K6006.2.6

Movement: specialized digital thermal compensation quartz movement; COSC-certified Kriëger Caliber K89.01/01.
Functions: alarm; dual time zone; stopwatch function; day/date/month display.
Case: stainless steel; 43mm; double dome antireflective sapphire crystal; large relief caseback; oversized king's crown, sapphire tip; water resistant to 3atm.

Dial: blue enamel dial; two digital window displays; steel Arabic numerals.
Bracelet: stainless steel bracelet.
Also available: in 18K rose gold with or without diamonds and a variety of enamel dial colors. Diamond bezel features 86 SI1G color 1-carat stones or large diamonds upon request. Available in a variety of interchangeable strap colors and skins or bracelets.
Note: limited edition of 500 stainless steel pcs; 50 rose-gold pcs.

SEA STALLION REF. K1001S.1R.20

Movement: self-winding automatic, COSC-certified Kriëger Caliber K82.01/01(ETA 2892 Base); 21 jewels; 42-hour power reserve.
Functions: hours, minutes, seconds; date display.
Case: stainless steel; 44mm; double dome antireflective sapphire crystal; indestructible special construction stainless steel matte and high polished; diver bezel; back engraved relief of Sea Stallion; screwed down crown; water resistant to 80atm.
Dial: orange enamel dial.
Strap: black rubber strap with Kriëger engraving.
Also available: in a variety of enamel dial colors and luxurious rubber strap colors or stainless steel bracelets in matte or polished finish.
Note: limited edition of 2,500 pcs.

TIDE WAVE REF. K1001T.2.56

Movement: specialized quartz movement, Kriëger Caliber K11.01/01.
Functions: date display; subdial indicates moonphase; tide hand indicates high and low tide ranges.
Case: stainless steel; 44mm; double dome antireflective sapphire crystal; indestructible special construction stainless steel matte and high polished; solar compass bezel; back engraved relief of Compass Rose; screwed down pushbuttons; water resistant to 80atm.
Dial: white and blue enamel dial.
Bracelet: high-polished stainless steel bracelet.
Also available: in 18K yellow gold and PVD processing; available in a variety of enamel dial colors and luxurious rubber strap colors or stainless steel bracelets in matte or polished finish.
Note: limited edition of 2,000 stainless steel pcs, 200 PVD pcs.

LEVIEV
Catering to the Elite of the Elites

Lev Leviev was born in Uzbekistan in 1956. When he immigrated to Israel as a boy, he discovered the art of cutting diamonds in the workshops of a neighbor. Leviev, who had known since a very young age that he would someday become a captain of industry, was hooked. Tenacious, industrious and endowed with an exceptional business sense, he succeeded in beating the De Beers monopoly on the world diamond trade. Holding 30% of the world's diamond production, Leviev has created his own brand of watches for his pleasure and that of his customers.

When you walk down **Old Bond Street in London**, home to many jewelers, you might stop in front of the Leviev shop window and realize that this store shelters more carats than all the other stores on the street combined—four thousand carats, worth more than 200 million pounds sterling at its opening in 2006! This is also the case for Leviev's other boutiques in New York, Moscow and Dubai. You have just met one of the rare and truly colossal men of the diamond world.

Leviev is the direct competitor of De Beers, another giant in the world's production of commercial diamonds. The South African company had reigned as the master of the sector, but since his arrival, Leviev has broken the negotiating monopoly of a billion-dollar industry.

ABOVE Leviev's Moscow boutique.

BOTTOM RIGHT Interior of the Madison Avenue boutique in New York City.

Known as hardworking, intelligent, and tenacious, Leviev had a talent for cutting diamonds that spoke for itself.

THE BIRTH OF AN ÜBER-LUXURY BRAND

Controlling the entire chain of diamond production, Leviev has become over the years the world's largest cutter and polisher of diamonds. He is the supplier to many luxury jewelry brands who do not own their diamonds, but rather purchase their regular assortments, whether it is to sell engagement rings or set small diamonds on watches in industrial quantities. However, when it comes to diamonds larger than five carats, the industry-wide practice has been to rely on consignments. Indeed, no luxury brand can afford to immobilize in one window alone millions of dollars worth of large, rare diamonds, as it makes no economic sense for them. When they do occasionally display one or two such exceptional diamonds, chances are that they are on loan from a diamond producer, such as Leviev. Lev Leviev thus decided in 2005 to launch his own brand under none other than the Leviev name, a name that is synonymous with extraordinary diamonds. By doing so he is able to sell directly to diamond collectors and connoisseurs alike, and he chose resolutely to position it in the "uber-luxury" market—not the mass luxury market. But that was not all. A great admirer of the watch industry, he asked Thierry Chaunu, President and COO of Leviev, and a widely respected executive who worked previously at Cartier and Chopard, to also create a line of exclusive Swiss timepieces that would cater to the same clientele, available only in the Leviev boutiques. Thierry Chaunu began this exciting project in 2006 and immediately contracted renowned Swiss watchmaker Christophe Claret to work on an exceptional Leviev Double Eagle Platinum and Diamond Tourbillon, a COSC-certified chronometer that is one of the only watches in the world equipped with a power reserve of more than 100 hours.

THIS PAGE
LEFT   Created by Swiss watchmaker Christophe Claret, the Leviev Double Eagle Platinum and Diamond Tourbillon boasts an exceptional power reserve exceeding 100 hours.

BELOW   The GMT Alarm in 18-karat pink gold.

FACING PAGE
TOP   The Double Elle models are equipped with the Swiss manufacturer ETA quartz movements.

CENTER   Each series of the Double Elle collection has 8 to 12 numbered pieces.

BOTTOM   The Double Barillet model has a maximum power reserve of 120 hours and its automatic-winding mechanical movement is a COSC-certified chronometer.

A TIMEPIECE COLLECTION ON PAR
WITH SUPERLATIVE DIAMONDS

Exclusive, rare, precious, and all stamped with two inverted Ls—the brand's symbol representing the initials of the proprietor—the pieces are produced in very limited editions. "To mark the fact that they are from a master of gems," says Chaunu, "all have at least one diamond on the crown or in the case. Luxury market analysts have placed the Leviev brand in the über-luxury category, which is the top of the pyramid. Our brand caters to the elite of the elites." When it comes to timepieces, the prices of the first women's day-time models range from $16,000 to $200,000, and the tourbillon model is currently the most complex in the catalog.

"So far, the men's collection has included the GMT Alarm with a specially decorated movement, the GMT Chrono, and the GMT Chrono Mega Yacht, whose success has been resounding," explains Chaunu. "This is why we created a second version called the GMT Chrono Mega Yacht 2. As in the others, the latter is equipped with a movement, A. Schild 5008, to which we added an additional module from the Lajoux-Perret workshops to obtain the hours, minutes, seconds, chronograph, second time-zone and date functions. The most recent introduction, the Double Barillet, houses an automatic-winding Muller-Laville mechanical movement. As its name indicates, it draws its energy from a pair of barrels offering a total reserve of 120 hours, displayed at 1:30. Equipped with the hours, minutes, seconds, and retrograde date functions, the Double Barillet boasts a partially diamond-set dial and a diamond on the crown. Carefully skeletonized, it reveals the escapement and features a delicately guilloché sun whose center is at 9:00. The symbol of Lev Leviev serves as a counterweight on the second hand. For women, Leviev invented a uniquely shaped case framed by the two symmetrically placed Ls. Named the Double Elle, the collection offers models whose bezels are set with one or two rows of diamonds, and whose dials are often decorated with mother-of-pearl.

These initial first steps in the world of horology are carefully controlled. Maybe, in the future, will these fine watches be available to the best retailers worldwide? Judging from the meteoric rise of the Leviev business empire, one may expect the brand to extend its reach to all five continents before too long…

Longines can look back on more than 175 years of watchmaking anchored in tradition, elegance and high quality. The brand's timepieces are inspired by a history rich in technical daring and avant-garde designs. Longines' fundamental virtue—elegance—has always been the principle that governs the entire scope of its worldwide activities.

Longines' timeless elegance rests on a rich, constantly updated design heritage, expressed in a subtle mix of classic spirit and inventive refinement. Its timepieces represent the best of a corporate history marked by many a proprietary technical and styling first, conceived in its own design and manufacturing facilities, where a close eye was kept on the profile of its creations. The Art Deco movement and its refinements have for instance often inspired the company, not least in building tonneau-shaped, oval or rectangular movements tailored to watches displaying the essential styles of that fabulous period.

The care and sophistication the company always invests in its model lines guarantee the smooth, thoroughbred styling that sets them apart so distinctively, fostering a reputation for elegance that has rewarded Longines with a number of styling prizes for the excellence of its designs. Ceaseless technical innovation and aesthetic objectives open to the world's art and fashion trends thus come together in Longines timepieces.

THIS PAGE
Top to bottom: Longines DolceVita; La Grande Classique de Longines; and The Longines Master Collection Moonphases Ladies.

FACING PAGE
Longines ambassadress of elegance Aishwarya Rai.

...elegance

LONGINES

...tradition

320

Whether they are aesthetic or technical, Longines' innovative ideas have elevated the winged hourglass to a true emblem of know-how and elegance. Since the birth of Longines in 1832, the original aims of its founders, Auguste Agassiz and Ernest Francillon, have remained unchanged: to seize the spirit of the moment, to dare to adopt technically and aesthetically avant-garde designs without giving in to giddy round of fashion, and to achieve excellence without abandoning sobriety. As the oldest brand name patented with the WIPO still in existence, Longines has acquired an enviable reputation of quality and precision. The brand has accompanied many pioneers of the air, land and sea and this expertise stands behind the Longines timepieces.

Today, Longines is taking into consideration both the original aesthetic of the brand's milestones and modern watchmaking techniques. Its traditional watches are genuine tributes to the pioneering spirit that has inspired Longines' watchmakers and designers since the brand's earliest days. They are perfect examples of the continuity of the brand's spirit as well as its ability to continually spotlight history through art and elegance.

The Longines Sport Collection expresses its essence in those exceptional men and women who—with a record, an exploit, a demonstration of courage—have left their marks in history.

Over land, underwater, in the air, Longines has always been profoundly attached to sport in every dimension. It also takes form in the close bond between the winged hourglass brand and sporting pioneers and their legends. The Longines Sport Collection expresses its essence in those exceptional men and women who—with a record, an exploit, a demonstration of courage—have left their marks in history and inspire new generations of sportsmen and -women.

The Longines Sport Collection pays homage to the transcending of self, a form of emulation by which performance is transcended by elegance. However remarkable they be, the value of sporting exploits is increased by the attitude adopted to attain them. Coupled with a ceaselessly renewed innovative spirit, this touch of elegance has always typified Longines' watches, and more than ever constitutes the linchpin of The Longines Sport Collection.

...performance

LOUIS MOINET
The Royal Treatment

The French-born watchmaker Louis Moinet dedicated his life to the advancement of horology. Considered one of the greatest innovators of his time, Moinet created a number of groundbreaking improvements, collaborated with Abraham-Louis Breguet and manufactured sophisticated clocks for presidents, royalty and an emperor.

In addition to his technical background in watchmaking, Moinet also studied drawing and painting as a young boy, moving to Rome when he was 20 years old to study architecture and sculpting. When he returned to Paris in 1795, Moinet was made professor of Fine Arts at the Louvre. It was during his tenure, that he renewed his study of watchmaking, a passion that would soon overtake his life.

Serving as president of the Chronometry Society in 1800, Moinet was an acknowledged authority on watchmaking. He invented a counter, regulator and astronomical watch that was considered groundbreaking in the 19th century and whose designs remain vital today. Moinet's clever inventions caught the attention of Breguet, the father of modern watchmaking. Moinet accepted Breguet's invitation to become his personal adviser, living in Breguet's home until Breguet died in 1823.

While Moinet's technical achievements were impressive, it's important to remember that he was also an in-demand clockmaker whose creations were coveted by King George IV as well as U.S. Presidents Thomas Jefferson and James Monroe. Today, Moinet's work is displayed at the Louvre, Versailles and the White House.

Napoleon received this Louis Moinet-designed clock in 1806, two years after he was crowned Emperor of France. More than 200 years later, the clock is restored and on display

Fittingly, Moinet's most extravagant clock was presented to Napoleon in 1806, two years after he and wife Joséphine were crowned Emperor and Empress of France. The masterpiece includes an opening below the dial where mechanically animated angels lower crowns onto heads representing Napoleon and Joséphine every hour. More than 200 years after Moinet unveiled the clock, it has been restored to its original glory and is on display in Europe.

Before his death in 1853, Moinet shared his vast wealth of knowledge, writing a seminal treatise about timekeeping that has influenced generations of watchmakers.

Jean-Marie Schaller and Micaela Bartolucci founded the Louis Moinet brand five years ago in Switzerland and opened a watch atelier near the Jura Mountains in the heart of the watchmaking universe. To ensure quality, Louis Moinet limits production of its watches to a maximum of 1,000 per year.

In a few short years, Schaller and Bartolucci have assembled a collection of limited edition and one-of-a-kind timepieces that embody Moinet's technical and design sensibilities. In fact, the watchmaker based the Twintech's movement on drawings Moinet made of a double-barrel pocket watch.

The company highlights Moinet's fine arts background with its newly introduced Côtes du Jura dial decoration. Created using a proprietary process, the deep grooves of the Côtes du Jura can be found adorning the watchmaker's round designs—Spiroscope, Datascope, Tempograph and Vertalis Tourbillon—and the Twintech, the only rectangular case offered by Louis Moinet.

More than half of the Louis Moinet collection features tonneau-shaped cases. Along with distinguished design, many offer precision functionality, including the Variograph world timer and two chronographs—Olympia and Artemis. Vintage move-

Louis Moinet limits production to just 1,000 pieces per year.

ments steal the show in both the Montecristo and Chronovintage. Each houses a rare movement that has been restored by master craftsmen.

Coupled with that attention to detail, Louis Moinet demonstrates a dedication to exclusivity with two exquisite designs. The first is the rose- and white-gold Vertalis Tourbillon, available in a limited edition of 12 pieces. Upon request, the watchmaker will also produce a one-of-a-kind personalized version of this watch.

The second rarity represents a pinnacle of haute horlogerie that would make Moinet proud. The rose-gold Magistralis is a pièce unique that employs a century-old movement, an actual piece of the moon for its moonphase indication, is delivered in a beautiful wooden display box that amplifies the watch's minute repeater, and includes a copy of Moinet's treatise.

Many things have changed since Moinet published his great dissertation on watchmaking, but one thing has not: the Moinet name still stands for mechanical works of art worthy of royalty.

TOP The black dial of the limited edition Vertalis Tourbillon includes an opening that reveals the watch's barrel spring, allowing the wearer to see the state of the power reserve.

BOTTOM A century-old movement designed in Geneva powers the one-of-a-kind Magistralis, which features a single-button column-wheel chronograph, repeater and perpetual calendar. A world's first, the Magistralis' moonphase incorporates real pieces of the moon, an obviously rare and expensive material!

MONTECRISTO - LIMITED EDITION

Movement: manually wound, very rare vintage movement (1950s) with screw-balance.
Functions: hours, minutes, sweep seconds.
Case: 35x45.8mm; stainless steel; two sapphire crystals with an exhibition caseback.
Dial: brown.

Strap: hand-sewn Louisiana alligator leather; folding clasp.
Also available: old rose, copper, ivory and burgundy dials.
Approximate price: $7,500

SPIROSCOPE - LIMITED EDITION

Movement: mechanical automatic; semi-openworked balance.
Functions: hours, minutes, sweep seconds; power reserve.
Case: 45mm; stainless steel; two sapphire crystals with an exhibition caseback.
Dial: burgundy.
Strap: hand-sewn Louisiana alligator leather; folding clasp.

Also available: silver and black dials.
Approximate price: $7,800

TEMPOGRAPH - LIMITED EDITION

Movement: exclusive; mechanical self-winding; comprised of 125 parts.
Functions: hours, minutes, 10-second retrograde mechanism.
Case: 47mm; two sapphire crystals with an exhibition caseback.
Dial: black.
Strap: hand-sewn Louisiana alligator leather; folding clasp.
Also available: grade-5 titanium & 316L steel with black PVD-coated bezel and black or silver dial (approx. $28,000); 18K rose-gold 5N & grade-5 titanium & 316L steel with black or silver dial (approx. $36,000); 18K rose-gold 5N & grade-5 titanium & 316L steel with silver dial (approx. $36,000); 18K gold (deep rose 5N & medium rose 3N) with black dial (approx. $59,000).

TWINTECH - LIMITED EDITION

Movement: manually wound LM01 Calibre.
Functions: hours, minutes, sweep seconds; power reserve; date.
Case: 40x54mm; stainless steel; two sapphire crystals with an exhibition caseback.
Dial: black.
Strap: hand-sewn Louisiana alligator leather; folding clasp.

Also available: old rose, charcoal, silver and chocolate dials.
Approximate price: $17,900

VARIOGRAPH - LIMITED EDITION

Movement: automatic LM02 Calibre; chronograph with full-moon indicator and 24-hour world map.
Functions: hours, minutes, sweep seconds; chronograph; world time; date; day; month; moonphase.
Case: 40x52.33mm; stainless steel; two sapphire crystals with an exhibition caseback.
Dial: old rose.
Strap: hand-sewn Louisiana alligator leather; folding clasp.
Also available: black and silver dials.
Approximate price: $13,100

VERTALIS TOURBILLON - LIMITED EDITION

Movement: manually wound LM06 Calibre.
Functions: hours, minutes.
Case: Ø 47mm; 18K white gold and 18K rose gold 5N; two sapphire crystals with an exhibition caseback.
Dial: black.
Strap: hand-sewn Louisiana alligator leather; folding clasp.
Approximate price: $215,000

CHRONOVINTAGE - LIMITED EDITION

Movement: extremely rare vintage chronograph.
Functions: hours, minutes, small seconds positioned at 9; 60-minute chronograph.
Case: polished 316L stainless steel; two sapphire crystals with an exhibition caseback.
Dial: silver.
Strap: hand-sewn Louisiana alligator leather; folding clasp.
Also available: charcoal dial.
Approximate price: $9,900

DATOSCOPE - LIMITED EDITION

Movement: mechanical automatic LM03 Calibre with date.
Functions: hours, minutes, central seconds; calendar.
Case: polished 316L stainless steel; two sapphire crystals with an exhibition caseback.
Dial: silver.
Strap: hand-sewn Louisiana alligator leather; folding clasp.
Also available: black and burgundy dials.
Approximate price: $7,200

MANUFACTURE CONTEMPORAINE DU TEMPS
Shifting Perspective

Driven by a desire to explore new and unique ways to display time, Denis Giguet formed a watch atelier in Geneva three years ago. His company, Manufacture Contemporaine du Temps (MCT), debuted last year with Sequential One, an unconventional timepiece that incorporates rotating prisms and a jumping sapphire dial.

A t 40 years of age, Giguet is already a veteran of the Swiss watch industry. His career has taken him from engineering at Rolex to head of development and production at Harry Winston, where he was responsible for the famous Opus range of timepieces, to launching his own brand.

Giguet began assembling his own pieces in 2006, creating an atelier where he could be free to cultivate his own creations. In 2007, Giguet assembled the MCT team of more than 20 specialists dedicated to producing Sequential One. To help Giguet achieve the design of his dreams, he approached leading architectural watch designer Eric Giroud, known for his avant-garde watch designs and his cutting-edge work with Maximillian Busser of MB&F, as well as others. Sequential One has come to life thanks to the hard work of the entire MCT team.

MCT's expert level of craftsmanship naturally requires a great investment of time to achieve, which limits the brand's production output but ensures that ownership of an MCT creation will be a pleasure enjoyed exclusively by a privileged few.

Bespoke, handcrafted MCT timepieces are made only to order. In 2008, Westime in Los Angeles was the first U.S. boutique to acquaint watch collectors with MCT's exceedingly rare timepiece. Even today, Sequential One is available only through a coterie of the world's finest watch retailers.

Sequential One uses a groundbreaking system of rotating triangular prisms to display the hour and a rotating sapphire disc to show the minutes. This limited edition timepiece is offered in 45mm case made from rose gold or white gold.

Sequential One's hours are read from four sections positioned on the dial like the points on a compass.

Sequential One is groundbreaking because it displays time in a unique, unconventional and highly legible way. With this timepiece, the hour is read at one of 4 positions situated at the 4 points of a compass.

Each position has a prism assembly consisting of five triangular prisms that rotate in unison, coming together to form the hour. Every 60 minutes the hour is displayed in a different position, shifting around the dial counterclockwise. In other words, the numeral 12, located at 12, gives way to the numeral 1 located at 9, and so on, around the dial.

Form meets function with the minute indicator, a sapphire crystal disc fixed at the center of the dial. The opaque 60-minute disc, covers three-fourths of the dial, leaving one quarter section entirely clear for unobstructed readabliity of the hour. The minutes are equally easy to read, courtesy of a bright red hand.

What makes the minute mechanism even more remarkable is the action that occurs at the conclusion of each hour. Instead of the minute hand snapping back to zero as in a retrograde display, it remains at a standstill at 60 as the sapphire dial sweeps 90 degrees counterclockwise, revealing the next hour, thereby ensuring the minute hand is in position again, at zero minutes.

If the dial reflects the influence of modern technology and taste, it's only logical that the flipside would bear the stamp of tradition. The clear caseback provides a vision of the time-honored decoration used to finish the movement, including Côtes de Genève on the bridges, as well as the beautiful escapment. Beyond its mechanical beauty, the mechanism represents a triumph for MCT, which developed and builds the movement in-house, a rarity for such a young brand.

Moving to a view of Sequential One's exterior, one sees a 45mm square case whose edges have been blunted by subtle curves that confer a fair measure of individuality on the design.

MCT will produce Sequential One in a limited edition: 99 pieces in rose gold and 99 pieces in white gold.

The complex movement that powers Sequential One was developed in-house by MCT. It is finished with Côtes de Genève decoration and includes a rose-gold rotor equipped with a double balance-spring.

MONTBLANC
The Write Time

Synonymous with luxury writing instruments for more than a century, Montblanc has made a new name for itself over the past decade with a collection of timepieces that has captured the imaginations of serious collectors. With the company's recent acquisition of Minerva—a renowned Swiss manufacture—things are about to get even more interesting.

I t's only fitting that the first caliber that Montblanc produced in-house would have ink-stained roots. The proprietary movement (MB R100) debuted in 2008 in the Montblanc Star Nicolas Rieussec Monopusher Chronograph, a timepiece named for the French horologist who patented the first chronograph in 1821. True to the chronograph's entomological roots—stemming from the Greek "chronos" (time) and "graphos" (writing)—Rieussec's chronograph deposited dots of ink on a pair of rotating indexes to measure elapsed time.

Those rotating indexes are reborn nearly two centuries later on the dial of the Montblanc Star Nicolas Rieussec Monopusher Chronograph. For this modern reincarnation, stationary, blued steel hands replace the ink-filled styli of the past and 60-second and 30-minute counters showcased against a Côtes de Genève pattern take the place of Rieussec's rotating porcelain dials.

THIS PAGE An enlarged view of the movement driving the Montblanc Le Locle MB R100 caliber.

FACING PAGE This fascinating chronograph masterpiece can be admired in detail through its sapphire crystal caseback. The Star Nicolas Rieussec Monopusher is strictly limited: 25 chronographs in 950 platinum, 75 in 18-karat white or yellow gold, and 125 in 18-karat red gold.

A column wheel governs the watch's chronograph mechanism, which uses an advanced clutch system that enables the watch to maintain a steady rate while the chronograph is engaged for extended periods. Not only does the chronograph represent technical achievement, but its well-planned design also considers first the owner's comfort. The designers make the chronograph easier to operate by moving its pusher from the typical 3:00 position on the caseband to the more intuitive location of 8:00.

The movement draws power from a pair of mainsprings that, when fully wound, allows the watch to run for 72 hours. A power-reserve indicator is visible through the clear caseback, as is the chronograph's column wheel and the traditional decoration that adorns the movement.

It's worth noting that the chronograph is the first complication of the modern horologic era not created by Abraham-Louis Breguet, the influential Swiss-born watchmaker responsible for inventing a number of watch complications, including the tourbillon.

Today, the revolution Rieussec launched with his chronograph has blossomed. In fact, the chronograph has become one of the most popular complications in the world of watchmaking.

The combination of the horologic expertise that resides at Montblanc's watchmaking atelier and the company's tradition of creating beautiful *objets d'art* is proving to be a winner among the world's top collectors.

The rotating indexes are reborn nearly two centuries later on the dial of the Montblanc Star Nicolas Rieussec Monopusher Chronograph.

STAR NICOLAS RIEUSSEC MONOPUSHER LIMITED REF. 102334

Movement: mechanical manual-winding MB R 100 caliber; Ø 31mm, thickness: 7.60mm; 13'''3/4; 286 components; column wheel; 72-hour power reserve; 28,800 vph; 33 jewels; rhodium-plated pillar-plate and bridges; decorated with circular-graining and Côtes de Genève patterns. **Functions:** hours, minutes; date with hand at 12; single-pusher chronograph with 2 counters: hour at 4, minute at 8 with turning discs and fixed pointers in blued steel and red-gold bridges. **Case:** 18K red-gold three-piece case; Ø 43mm, thickness: 14.8mm; polished finish; curved sapphire crystal, antireflective on both sides; red-gold crown with a black lacquer and mother-of-pearl insertion; red-gold, shaped pusher at 8; back fastened by 6 screws, displaying the movement through a sapphire crystal; water resistant to 3 BAR (30 meters). **Dial:** matte beige; decorated with a Côtes de Genève pattern on the lower part; applied brushed hour ring; applied guilloché subdials; black Arabic numerals and minute track; blued-steel leaf-style hands. **Indications:** power-reserve indicator on the caseback. **Strap:** hand-stitched brown alligator leather; red-gold double folding clasp. **Note:** limited edition of 125 pieces. **Suggested price:** $30,600
Also available: yellow gold with beige dial and brown alligator strap, $30,600, limited to 75 pieces (REF. 102335); white gold with anthracite dial and black alligator strap, $32,100, limited to 75 pieces (REF. 102333); platinum with rhutenium dial and black alligator strap, $52,700, limited to 25 pieces (REF. 102332).

STAR NICOLAS RIEUSSEC MONOPUSHER AUTOMATIC REF. 102337

Movement: mechanical automatic-winding MB R 200 caliber; Ø 31mm, thickness: 8.46mm; 13'''3/4; 300 components; column wheel; 2 barrels; 72-hour power reserve; 28,800 vph; 40 jewels; rhodium-plated pillar-plate and bridges; decorated with circular-graining and Côtes de Genève patterns; personalized skeleton rotor with logo. **Functions:** hours, minutes; date with hand at 12; single-pusher chronograph with 2 counters: hour at 4, minute at 8 with turning discs and fixed pointers in blued steel and steel bridge; dual time; day-night indication at 9. **Case:** stainless steel three-piece case; Ø 43mm, thickness: 14.8mm; polished and brushed finish; curved sapphire crystal, anti-reflective on both sides; steel crown with a black lacquer and mother-of-pearl insertion; shaped pusher at 8; back fastened by 6 screws, displaying the movement through a sapphire crystal; water resistant to 3 BAR (30 meters). **Dial:** matte anthracite; decorated with a Côtes de Genève pattern on the lower part; applied hour ring; guilloché subdials; black Arabic numerals and minute track; rhodium-plated leaf-style hands (blued chronograph and dual-time hands). **Strap:** hand-stitched black alligator leather; steel double-folding clasp. **Suggested price:** $9,700
Also available: with anthracite dial and stainless steel bracelet, $10,000 (REF. 102336).

STAR 4810 AUTOMATIC REF. 102339

Movement: mechanical automatic-winding Montblanc 4810/401 caliber; approx. 42-hour power reserve; 28,800 vph; 21 jewels; COSC-certified chronometer.
Functions: hours, minutes, seconds; oversized date at 6 with applied red-gold red-enameled pointer.
Case: 18K red-gold three-piece case; Ø 41.5mm, thickness: 11.5mm; polished finish; curved, antireflective sapphire crystal; red-gold crown with a black lacquer and mother-of-pearl insertion; back fastened by 6 screws, displaying the movement through a sapphire crystal; water resistant to 3 BAR (30 meters). **Dial:** silver; guilloché; applied red-gold bâton markers and Roman numerals; black minute track with luminescent dots and black-red numerals every 10 units on the flange; luminescent red-gold Dauphine hands (seconds hand with logo on the counterweight). **Strap:** brown alligator leather; hypoallergenic and water repellent; red-gold triple-folding clasp with 2 safety pushers. **Suggested price:** $12,800

STAR 4810 AUTOMATIC REF. 102340

Movement: mechanical automatic-winding Montblanc 4810/401 caliber; approx. 42-hour power reserve; 28,800 vph; 21 jewels.
Functions: hours, minutes, seconds; oversized date at 6 with applied rhodium-plated red-enameled pointer. **Case:** stainless steel three-piece case; Ø 41.5mm, thickness: 11.5mm; polished and brushed finish; curved, anti-reflective sapphire crystal; steel crown with a white-black lacquer insertion; back fastened by 6 screws, displaying the movement through a sapphire crystal; water resistant to 3 BAR (30 meters). **Dial:** anthracite; guilloché; applied rhodium-plated bâton markers and Roman numerals; white minute track with luminescent dots and white-red numerals every 10 units on the flange; luminescent rhodium-plated Dauphine hands (seconds hand with logo on the counterweight). **Bracelet:** polished and brushed stainless steel; steel triple-folding clasp with 2 safety pushers. **Suggested price:** $2,500
Also available: with black guilloché dial and black alligator strap, $2,265 (REF. 102341); with silver guilloché dial and brown alligator strap, $2,265 (REF. 102342).

SPORT CHRONOGRAPH TANTALUM AUTOMATIC   REF. 103113

Movement: mechanical automatic-winding Montblanc 4810/501 caliber (Valjoux 7750 base); 2 barrels; approx. 46-hour power reserve; 28,800 vph; 25 jewels; COSC-certified chronometer. **Functions:** hours, minutes, seconds; date at 3; chronograph with 3 counters: hour at 6, small second at 9, minute at 12. **Case:** tantalum and 18K red-gold three-piece case; Ø 44mm, thickness: 15.9mm; polished and brushed finish; antireflective flat sapphire crystal with a magnifying lens on the date display;

counterclockwise turning brushed red-gold ring with a luminescent pointer, polished round markers and an engraved scale for the calculation of diving times; red-gold screw-down crown with case protection and a white-black lacquer insertion; red-gold screw-down pushers with case protections; back fastened by 8 screws, with engraved logo; water resistant to 30 BAR (300 meters). **Dial:** matte black; subdials decorated with circular beads with red-gold-plated crowns; luminescent, applied red-gold-plated markers; luminescent red-gold-plated sword-style hands; minute track with divisions of 1/5 second. **Strap:** black rubber strap with diving strap extension; pin buckle in 18K red gold.
Suggested price: $23,500

TIMEWALKER LARGE RETROGRADE AUTOMATIC   REF. 103095

Movement: mechanical automatic-winding Montblanc 4810/909 caliber; approx. 42-hour power reserve; 28,800 vph; 30 jewels.
Functions: hours, minutes, seconds; retrograde date at 3; power-reserve indicator at 6; day of the week at 9.
Case: stainless steel three-piece case; Ø 42mm, thickness: 12mm; polished finish; domed, antireflective sapphire crystal; perforated lugs with logo engraved

on the attachment; crown with antiskid profile and a white-black lacquer insertion; back fastened by 6 screws, displaying the movement through a sapphire crystal; water resistant to 3 BAR (30 meters).
Dial: black; brushed with a sun pattern; day subdial crown; power-reserve and date sectors decorated with circular beads; applied rhodium-plated Arabic numerals and bâton markers; white minute track with luminescent dots; luminescent rhodium-plated trapezoid hands.
Bracelet: polished stainless steel; triple-folding steel clasp with 2 safety pushers.
Suggested price: $4,900
Also available: with silver dial and brown alligator leather strap, $4,600 (REF. 102367).

TIMEWALKER XL CHRONO AUTOMATIC   REF. 103094

Movement: mechanical automatic-winding Montblanc 4810/502 caliber (ETA 7753 base); 28,800 vph; 27 jewels.
Functions: hours, minutes, seconds; date between 4 and 5; chronograph with 3 counters: minute at 3, hour at 6, small seconds at 9.
Case: stainless steel and black ceramic three-piece case; Ø 43mm, thickness: 14.5mm; polished finish; domed, antireflective sapphire crystal; black

ceramic bezel; perforated lugs with logo engraved on the attachment; black ceramic crown with anti-skid profile and a white-black lacquer insertion; pushers with case protections; back fastened by 6 screws, displaying the movement through a sapphire crystal; water resistant to 3 BAR (30 meters).
Dial: semi-glossy black; rhodium-plated subdial crowns; applied rhodium-plated Arabic numerals and bâton markers; luminescent rhodium-plated trapezoid hands; minute track with divisions of 1/4 and luminescent dots.
Bracelet: stainless steel and polished black ceramic; triple-folding steel clasp with 2 safety pushers.
Suggested price: $6,300

STAR CHRONO GMT AUTOMATIC   REF. 103092

Movement: automatic-winding Montblanc 4810/503 caliber; 28,800 vph; 25 jewels; chronometer.
Functions: hour, minute, small second; date; chronograph with 3 counters.
Case: 18K yellow gold; Ø 42mm; thickness: 14.7mm; fixed bezel; antireflective domed sapphire crystal; glass caseback; non-screw crown; 1 O-ring; 22/20mm between horns and clasp; water resistant to 3 BAR (30 meters).
Dial: black guilloché dial; yellow-gold colored feuille and baton hands.
Indications: date at 3; hour counter at 6; small second at 9; minute counter at 12; center second; minute track with divisions for 1/5 second.
Strap: black alligator; triple-folding clasp.
Suggested price: $14,200
Also available: 18K yellow gold with beige guilloché dial on brown alligator strap (REF. 102345).

SPORT WHITE GOLD LADY — REF. 103118

Movement: quartz; Montblanc 4810/101 caliber; 7 jewels.
Functions: hour, minute, second; end-of-life indicator for battery.
Case: 18K white gold; Ø 38mm, thickness: 11.5mm; fixed bezel set with 48 Top Wesselton VVS baguette diamonds (2.6 cts) and 12 baguette black sapphires (0.72 ct); scratch-resistant flat sapphire crystal with antireflective coating; screwed white-gold caseback; screw-down 18K white-gold crown with mother-of-pearl star signet; 2 O-rings; 19/17mm between horns and clasp; water resistant to 20 BAR (200 meters).

Dial: white mother-of-pearl dial set with 63 Top Wesselton VVS baguette diamonds (0.88 ct), 4 baguette black sapphires (0.77 ct), and the Montblanc patented diamond (0.1088 ct); rhodium-plated Luminova hands.
Indications: minute track with division for 1 second.
Strap: white rubber with 18K white-gold triple-folding clasp.
Suggested price: $114,000

SPORT WHITE GOLD LADY — REF. 103815

Movement: quartz; Montblanc 4810/101 caliber; 7 jewels.
Functions: hour, minute, second; end-of-life indicator for battery.
Case: 18K white gold; Ø 38mm, thickness: 11.5mm; fixed bezel set with 48 baguette black sapphires (2.88 cts) and 12 Top Wesselton VVS baguette diamonds (0.65 ct); scratch-resistant flat sapphire crystal with antireflective coating; screwed white-gold caseback; screw-down 18K white-gold crown with mother-of-pearl star signet; 2 O-rings; 19/17mm between horns and clasp; water resistant to 20 BAR (200 meters).

Dial: black mother-of-pearl dial set 43 Top Wesselton VVS baguette diamonds (0.508 ct), 24 baguette black sapphires (0.461 ct) and the Montblanc patented diamond (0.1088 ct); rhodium-plated Luminova hands.
Indications: minute track with division for 1 second.
Strap: white rubber with 18K white-gold triple-folding clasp.
Suggested price: $99,800

PROFILE STAR LADY GOLD — REF. 103892

Movement: automatic movement with moonphase display; Montblanc 4810/908 caliber; 28,800 vph; 26 jewels.
Functions: hour, minute, second; power-saving function.
Case: 18K red-gold case; Ø 36mm; thickness: 12mm; fixed bezel and horns set with 104 Top Wesselton VVS baguette diamonds (1.80 cts); scratch-resistant domed sapphire crystal with antireflective coating; 18K red-gold caseback with sapphire crystal aperture in the shape of the Montblanc signet; 18K red-gold non-screw crown with mother-of-pearl Montblanc signet; 1 O-ring; 19/17mm between horns and clasp; water resistant to 3 BAR (30 meters).

Dial: brown mother-of-pearl dial set with the Montblanc patented diamond (0.055 ct), 24 brilliant-cut diamonds around the date counter (0.072 ct), and 80 diamonds set on flange (0.17 ct).
Strap: brown satin strap with 18K red-gold pin buckle.
Suggested price: $64,100
Also available: 18K white gold with white mother-of-pearl dial and beige satin strap (REF. 103685).

SPORT LADY DIAMONDS — REF. 102362

Movement: quartz; Montblanc 4810/101 caliber; 7 jewels.
Functions: hour, minute, second; end-of-life indicator for battery.
Case: stainless steel; Ø 34.5mm; thickness: 11mm; fixed bezel set with diamonds and Montblanc patented diamond (0.055 ct); antireflective flat sapphire crystal; screwed stainless steel caseback; screw-down crown; 2 O-rings; 17/17mm between horns and clasp; water resistant to 20 BAR (200 meters).

Dial: white mother-of-pearl with 11 diamonds; rhodium-plated Luminova hands.
Indications: date at 3; center second; minute track with divisions for 1 second.
Bracelet: polished stainless steel bracelet; triple-folding clasp.
Suggested price: $3,705
Also available: with black shiny dial and stainless steel bracelet, $3,705 (REF. 102363); with black shiny dial without diamonds on stainless steel bracelet, $2,500 (REF. 102364); with white mother-of-pearl dial without diamonds on white rubber strap, $2,280 (REF. 103893).

GARDE TEMPS "RETOUR À ZÉRO" REF. 103836

Movement: Minverva 16-18 caliber; realized on an exclusivity basis for Montblanc; manually wound movement with Retour-à-Zéro function activated by pulling out crown and horizontal clutch; Ø 38.4mm; height 6.3mm; 209 parts (complete movement); 21 jewels; (hemispherical, cambered, olive-cut); 55-hour power reserve; 18,000 vph (2.5 Hz); screw balance (Ø 14.5mm, 59 mgcm²); balance spring with Phillips curve; rhodium-plated German silver plate, circular-grained on both sides, hand-chamfered edges; rhodium-plated German silver bridges with Côtes de Genève, recesses circular-grained on both sides, hand-chamfered edges; going train: wheels are 2N gold-plated with circular-grained, chamfered, diamond hubs on both sides and pinions have polished faces and toothing, burnished pivots. **Functions:** hours, minutes and large center seconds. **Case:** limited edition 18K white gold; Ø 47mm, thickness: 13.65mm; horns with patented cuvette release mechanism; crown with mother-of-pearl Montblanc signet; convex, anti-reflective, chevé sapphire glass and screw-in sapphire glass back under hinged cuvette; water resistant to 3 BAR (30 meters) **Dial:** solid gold enameled with "Champs levé Grand Feu" technique; hand-guilloché decoration; 18K gold hands; large seconds hand in Pfinodal. **Strap:** black, hand-stitched alligator leather; pin buckle in 18K white gold. **Note:** limited edition of 8 pieces. **Suggested price:** $59,900 **Also available:** 950 platinum with 18K gold dial, mother-of-pearl inlays, black alligator strap, $110,400, unique piece (REF. 103835); 18K red gold with 18K gold dial and brown strap, $54,500, limited to 58 pieces (REF. 103837).

GRAND CHRONOGRAPH "EMAIL GRAND FEU" REF. 103845

Movement: Minerva 16-29 caliber; manually wound movement with chronograph (monopusher mechanism, chronograph with column wheel, horizontal clutch and semi-instantaneous minute counter); Ø 38.4mm; height 6.3mm; 252 parts (complete movement); 22 jewels (hemispherical, cambered, olive-cut); 55-hour power reserve; 18,000 vph (2.5 Hz); screw balance (Ø 14.5mm, 59 mgcm²); balance spring with Phillips curve; rhodium-plated German silver plate, circular-grained on both sides, hand-chamfered edges; rhodium-plated German silver bridges with Côtes de Genève, recesses circular-grained on both sides, hand-chamfered edges; going train: wheels are 2N gold-plated with circular-grained, chamfered, diamond hubs on both sides and pinions have polished faces and toothing, burnished pivots. **Functions:** center hours and minutes, small seconds at 9:00; chronograph: center seconds, 30-minute counter at 3:00. **Case:** 18K white gold; Ø 47mm, thickness: 13.65mm; horns with patented cuvette release mechanism; crown/ chronograph button with integrated button in the crown at 3:00 and the Montblanc signet in mother-of-pearl; convex, antireflective, chevé sapphire glass and screw-in sapphire glass back under a hinged cuvette; water resistant to 3 BAR (30 meters). **Dial:** solid gold with Grand Feu champlevé enamel; 18K gold hands; chronograph hands in Pfinodal. **Strap:** black, hand-stitched alligator leather; pin buckle in 18K white gold. **Note:** limited edition of 8 pieces. **Suggested price:** $79,800 **Also available:** 950 platinum with 18K gold dial, mother-of-pearl inlays and black alligator strap, $126,400, unique piece (REF. 103844); in 18K red gold with 18K gold dial and brown strap, $69,200, limited to 58 pieces (REF. 103846).

GRAND TOURBILLON "HEURES MYSTERIEUXES" REF. 103843

Movement: Minerva 65.50 caliber, realized on an exclusivity basis for Montblanc; manually wound movement with Tourbillon at 12:00, hours and minutes indicated on mysterious sapphire crystal discs; Ø 38.4mm; height 9.70mm; 286 parts (complete movement); 26 jewels (hemispherical, cambered, olive-cut); 50-hour power reserve; 18,000 vph (2.5 Hz); screw balance (Ø 14.5mm, 59 mgcm²); balance spring with Phillips curve; rhodium-plated (4N) German silver plate with circular-grained on both sides, hand-chamfered edges; rhodium-plated (4N) German silver bridges with Côtes de Genève, recesses circular-grained on both sides, hand-chamfered edges; going train: wheels are 2N gold-plated with circular-grained, chamfered, diamond hubs on both sides and pinions have pulled faces and toothing, burnished pivots. **Functions:** "mysterious" hours and minutes at 6:00; rotation of the tourbillon cage 1 turn/minute; chronograph: center seconds, 30-minute counter at 3:00. **Case:** 18K red gold; Ø 47m, thickness: 14.4mm; horns with patented cuvette release mechanism; crown with mother-of-pearl Montblanc signet; convex, antireflective chevé sapphire glass; water resistant to 3 BAR (30 meters). **Dial:** solid gold with hand-guilloché decoration; black metallic hands on sapphire discs. **Strap:** brown, hand-stitched alligator leather; pin buckle in 18K red gold. **Note:** limited edition of 8 pieces. **Suggested price:** $252,700 **Also available:** in 18K white gold on black alligator strap, limited to 8 pieces, $266,000 (REF. 103842).

GARDE TEMPS "RETOUR À ZÉRO" REF. 103840

Movement: Minverva 13-18 caliber, realized on an exclusivity basis for Montblanc; manually wound movement with Retour-à-Zéro function activated by pulling out crown and horizontal clutch; Ø 29.5mm, thickness: 6.4mm; 196 parts (complete movement); 21 jewels (hemispherical, cambered, olive-cut); 60-hour power reserve; 18,000 vph (2.5 Hz); screw balance (Ø 11.40mm, 26 mgcm²); balance spring with Phillips curve; rhodium-plated German silver plate with circular-grained on both sides, hand-chamfered edges; rhodium-plated German silver bridges with Côtes de Genève, recesses circular-grained on both sides, hand-chamfered edges; going train: wheels are in 2N gold-plated with circular-grained, chamfered, diamond hubs on both sides and pinions have polished faces and toothing, burnished pivots. **Functions:** hours, minutes and large center seconds. **Case:** limited edition 18K red gold; Ø 41mm, thickness: 13.65mm; horns with patented cuvette release mechanism; crown with mother-of-pearl Montblanc signet; convex, antireflective, chevé sapphire glass and screw-in sapphire glass back under hinged cuvette; water resistant to 3 BAR (30 meters). **Dial:** solid gold enameled with "Champs levé Grand Feu" Technique, hand-guilloché decoration; 18K gold hands; large seconds hand in Pfinodal. **Strap:** black, hand-stitched alligator leather; pin buckle in 18K red gold. **Note:** limited edition of 58 pieces. **Suggested price:** $49,200 **Also available:** 950 platinum with 18K gold dial, mother-of-pearl inlays and black alligator strap, $97,100, unique piece (REF. 103838); 18K white gold with 18K gold dial and black alligator strap, $53,200, limited to 8 pieces (REF. 103839).

The extensive Movado collection spans a range of styles—from complicated to casual and sport to jewelry. Yet despite that diversity, every watch is connected by the brand's devotion to the timeless balance of form and function, a quality found in the very best examples of modern design.

To mark the debut of its Red Label mechanical collection, Movado unveiled a pair of one-of-a-kind timepieces that epitomize elegance and complication, two of the collection's hallmarks. Both watches include Movado's legendary Museum dial—a revered icon of modern design for more than 60 years. The dial also features the watchmaker's name, which is rendered in a daring crimson hue unique to the Red Label collection.

The Red Label Museum Tourbillon is the first to combine the Museum dial with a reversed tourbillon movement, which is visible only through the exhibition caseback. This unexpected twist on the classic watchmaking complication allows the black Museum dial, created by Nathan George Horwitt in 1947, to maintain the integrity of its clean design.

Housed in a 42mm platinum case, the Red Label Museum Tourbillon's hand-wound movement is generously decorated. A mirror-polished "M" chevron logo is positioned atop the circular-finished gear train, while the movement's bridge and mainplate are both embellished with a classic bird's eye finish. A pair of polished plates are screwed to the bridge, one engraved with the "Tourbillon 1/1" (designating the watch's unique status) and the other with the company's name.

Another pièce unique from the Red Label mechanical collection is the Museum Tourbillon Retrograde. It shares some elements with the Museum Tourbillon, such as a platinum case, minimalist dial and "M" chevron logo, but adds a pair of retrograde indicators to the reversed tourbillon movement. The first is a date display positioned at 8:00 with a 24-hour display at 4:00 and both feature blue retrograde hands with red tips. The tourbillon mechanism, located between the two indicators, includes a small seconds.

Beyond these exclusive examples, the Red Label mechanical collection features an ever-expanding range of models for men and women.

An unexpected twist on a classic complication allows the black Museum dial to maintain the integrity of its clean design.

The company enhances its exceptional Movado Series 800 with four limited and special edition chronographs developed in cooperation with Derek Jeter, one of the watchmaker's best-known brand ambassadors.

"Movado is very proud of our association with Derek Jeter," says Jeff Cohen, President of Movado Worldwide. "He is one of the most renowned baseball players in Major League Baseball, and he embodies everything that Movado Series 800 stands for—timing, innovation and a commitment to excellence."

The most exclusive of the four models is the rose-gold Series 800 Derek Jeter Automatic Chronograph, offered in a limited edition of 10 pieces. Certified to chronometer accuracy by the Swiss COSC, the movement powers a trio of counters: 30 minute, 12 hour and small seconds. The 47mm case is equipped with a sapphire crystal caseback through which the rose-gold rotor is visible. Both the rotor and the caseback's outer ring are engraved with a 2, Jeter's number.

The second limited edition is the Series 800 Derek Jeter Automatic Chronograph in rose gold and black PVD-finished Performance Steel. Movado will create 100 pieces of this rugged model, which is outfitted with the same movement as the previously mentioned chronograph. This timepiece is decorated with a stripe-textured black dial that elegantly complements its black strap, which is made from Movado's trademark KEVLAR®-reinforced XTremeResin.

Movado offers two models in the Special Edition Series 800 Derek Jeter Chronograph collection, one with a blue dial and the other with a black dial. Both feature an ETA Swiss quartz chronograph movement with 30-minute and 12-hour counters, plus small seconds. The cases and bracelets are made of Movado's signature Performance Steel, as is the caseback, which is engraved with Jeter's name and number.

FACING PAGE

BOTTOM LEFT   A COSC-certified chronometer, the Series 800 Derek Jeter Automatic Chronograph includes 30-minute and 12-hour counters in addition to seconds. The caseback ring is engraved with Jeter's name and his number 2. Movado will produce this model in an edition of just 10 pieces.

BOTTOM RIGHT   The Series 800 Derek Jeter Chronograph is shown here in a black PVD case with 18-karat rose-gold bezel. This version is produced in a limited edition of 100 pieces.

THIS PAGE

BELOW   This Series 800 Women's Chronograph in Performance Steel features a diamond bezel, diamond markers and is fitted on a supple white ThermoResilient strap.

RIGHT   The Special Edition Series 800 Derek Jeter Chronograph is crafted from Movado's Performance Steel. This model is also available with a black dial.

The watchmaker recently re-visited its Vizio collection of sport luxury timepieces, integrating carbon fiber to the watch's design; a first for the brand. Movado returns to this fashionable collection, adding the stainless steel Vizio Chronograph.

The black carbon-fiber dial features a trio of round chronograph counters—1/10th second, seconds, and 30-minute—complemented by a round date aperture. The carbon-fiber accents continue onto the bracelet, which uses the dark material for its center links, creating an attractive counterpoint to the stainless steel, bullet-shaped hinges.

The Vizio Chronograph's 44.5mm case is fitted with a bezel made of tungsten carbide, an alloy that is practically impossible to scratch. The round bezel frames the dial's white minute index, triangular hour markers, and luminescent hour and minute hands.

This impressive addition to the Vizio line deftly balances bold design with Swiss-engineered precision to create a memorable timekeeper.

Among Movado's most popular contributions to the world of fashion watches is the Esperanza, one of the company's best-selling designs.

The watchmaker introduced a redesigned version of the Esperanza last year, enhancing the gracefulness of its characteristic openworked vertical-link bracelet with recessed satin-finished details. Esperanza's bracelets connect seamlessly to the low-profile cases bearing Movado's iconic Museum dials.

Movado also creates an Esperanza for men, using the classic combination of a stainless steel bracelet and a black Museum dial, and choices abound for women in this newly updated line. One model creates visual drama with a bracelet that alternates between polished and satin-finished stainless steel; one version is gold-plated with a diamond bezel and mother-of-pearl Museum dial; and, finally, a breathtaking stainless steel model combines a diamond bezel with a bracelet that features links that alternate between diamond-pavé and white ceramic.

Not only does Movado have a reputation for being one of the world's most sought-after luxury watchmakers, it is also recognized for its prestigious jewelry designs. The Museum dial's circle-in-a-circle theme provides the inspiration for Movado's signature Ono collection—which encompasses everything from rings and necklaces to fine crystal and tabletop designs.

Along with the jewelry, the Ono collection also features several chic timepieces. The watchmaker gives these fashion watches a new look, adding a bracelet design that features two rows of interconnected dots instead of open circles.

These new stainless steel models feature the Museum dial in either black or white, which is accompanied by a bracelet whose circles are filled with matching ceramic. Movado also offers a version with a diamond-set bezel.

The Ono's newly introduced double-circle bracelet shows that two truly are better than one.

Epitomizing refined style and feminine charm, Movado's Bela collection contains watches that double as jewelry pieces.

Bela features a Museum dial available in a sensual shade of pink that mirrors the rose quartz Movado uses in its Pebble line of jewelry. A black-dialed version is also available, providing the perfect companion to the classic black evening dress. An extraordinary example of how less can be more, Bela features a Swiss quartz movement balanced atop a thin stainless steel bangle. For a touch of scintillating sparkle, the bracelet can be adorned with eight brilliant diamonds.

Renowned for its Museum dial and the rugged appeal of its Series 800, Movado continues to create unique timepieces designed for the modern world.

FACING PAGE
Movado crafted the Vizio Chronograph's dial out of carbon fiber. The dark material is also used on the stainless steel bracelet, which includes bullet-shaped hinges.

THIS PAGE
TOP The newly redesigned Esperanza bears the line's openwork details on its vertical-link bracelet. The model shown here includes a bracelet with links that alternate from diamond-pave to white ceramic.

CENTER The stainless steel Ono boasts a new bracelet design made with two rows of dots filled with ceramic to match the iconic Museum dial.

BOTTOM A Swiss quartz movement powers Bela. The stainless steel bracelet is set with diamonds where it connects to the round case.

PANERAI
Seas of Time

Panerai sailed to national recognition in 1936 when the brand was commissioned to create precision instruments for the Royal Italian Navy. Over the next 80 years, Panerai continued to create groundbreaking timepieces such as the Radiomir and Luminor, propelling the brand onto the international stage, gaining cult-like status among enthusiasts.

Panerai launched its first proprietary caliber in 2005 and kept the momentum going by adding three new movements just two years later. Two of these new calibers now power the 44mm Luminor 1950 8 Days Chrono Monopulsante and Luminor 1950 Titanium Tourbillon GMT models.

The Luminor 1950 8 Days Chrono houses the P.2004 movement with eight days of power reserve and a GMT function.

Luminor 1950 Titanium Tourbillon GMT contains the P.2005 caliber displaying a second time zone and 30-second tourbillon movement. A power-reserve indicator is featured on the back.

Always innovative in design, Panerai uses titanium, known for its light weight and extreme strength, for these two styles. Built with the "sandwich" technique, the dials display Arabic numerals treated with luminescent paint.

LEFT The titanium Luminor 1950 8 Days Chrono Monopulsante has a chronograph with two counters in addition to a second time zone.

RIGHT The 47mm Luminor 1950 Titanium Tourbillon GMT model bears the P.2005 caliber, which was entirely developed and manufactured by Panerai. Its power reserve is visible through the reverse side of the watch.

Panerai unveiled eleven new creations in 2008.

In honor of the 2008 Panerai Classic Yachts Challenge, Panerai unveiled the special edition (500 pieces) Luminor Regatta Chronograph equipped with a five-minute countdown to the signal of departure. The Radiomir Titanium, in 150 pieces—50 with brown dials and 100 with black dials—and with the Minerva 16-17 movement, offers small seconds at 9:00.

Panerai has also introduced the 40mm Luminor Chronograph, the 44mm Luminor GMT, and the Luminor Marina Automatic. The latter two are available on updated steel bracelets.

Out of the water, Panerai's partnership with Ferrari began in 2006 and resulted in several exceptional pieces. To celebrate the union of these two iconic Italian brands, Panerai created four autographed models: the 45mm Ferrari 8 Days Chrono Monopulsante GMT, the 45mm Ferrari 10 Days GMT, the 45mm Ferrari 1/8 of a second, and the 45mm pink-gold Ferrari Chronograph with the Minerva 13-20 movement.

TOP LEFT From the Panerai Special Editions 2008 collection, the 47mm Radiomir Titanium model houses a hand-crafted Minerva 16-17 movement.

TOP RIGHT In honor of the 2008 Panerai Classic Yachts Challenge, Panerai created 500 numbered, limited edition Luminor Regatta Chronograph watches. Its COSC-certified movement passed 15 days of precision testing in various positions and temperatures.

ABOVE A member of Panerai's Contemporary Collection, the 44mm Luminor Marina Automatic is updated with a steel bracelet.

LEFT The Ferrari 8 Days Chrono Monopulsante GMT is equipped with the manual-winding mechanical P.2004/6 movement.

RADIOMIR PLATINUM TOURBILLON GMT   REF. PAM00316

Movement: mechanical manual-winding Panerai P.2005 caliber executed entirely by Panerai; tourbillon device; 16 ¼"; 31 jewels; Glucydur® balance with 28,800 alternations/hour; KIF Parechoc® anti-shock device; 3 barrels; 239 components; 6-day power reserve. **Functions:** hours, minutes, small seconds and tourbillon indicator at 9; 24-hour hand and AM/PM indicator at 3; power-reserve indicator on caseback; dual time with center 12-hour hand, tourbillon. **Case:** platinum three-piece cushion-shaped case; 48mm, thickness: 17.15mm; polished and brushed finish; curved, anti-

reflective sapphire crystal made from corundum (1.9mm thick); OP personalized screw-down platinum winding crown; patented removable wire loop strap attachments fastened to the back by four screws; dodecagonal screw-on exhibition caseback with sapphire crystal displaying the movement; water resistant to 100 meters. **Dial:** matte black sandwich dial with knurled pink-gold outer ring; perforated, luminescent baton markers and 2 Arabic numerals with SuperLumiNova on a lower support; luminescent pink-gold baton hands; leaf-style subdial hands and arrow-tip dual-time hand. **Strap:** PANERAI personalized hand-stitched black alligator strap with double fold-over 18K white-gold adjustable buckle with 2 safety pushers.
Suggested price: $139,900
Also available: in titanium with brown dial and brown alligator strap.

LUMINOR '1950' TITANIUM TOURBILLON GMT   REF. PAM00306

Movement: mechanical manual-winding Panerai P.2005 caliber executed entirely by Panerai; tourbillon device; 16 ¼"; thickness: 9.1mm; 31 jewels; Glucydur® balance with 28,800 alternations/hour; KIF Parechoc® anti-shock device; 3 barrels; 239 components; 6-day power reserve. **Functions:** hours, minutes, small seconds and tourbillon indicator at 9; 24-hour hand and AM/PM indicator at 3; power-reserve indicator on caseback; dual time with center 12-hour hand, tourbillon. **Case:** brushed grade-2 titanium three-piece 1950-style case with polished

grade-5 titanium bezel; 47mm; domed, antireflective sapphire crystal made from corundum (1.9mm thick); crown waterproofed by brushed titanium patented crown-protecting device; bridge fastened to the middle by two screws with a screw level pressing the crown against the water-resistance gasket; screw-on exhibition caseback with sapphire crystal displaying the movement; water resistant to 100 meters. **Dial:** brown sandwich dial; perforated, luminescent baton markers and 2 Arabic numerals with SuperLumiNova on a lower support; luminescent baton hands; leaf-style subdial hands; arrow-tip dual-time hand. **Strap:** PANERAI personalized hand-stitched brown alligator strap with large-size brushed titanium buckle.
Suggested price: $122,000
Also available: in brushed and polished steel with black dial and black alligator strap.

LUMINOR '1950' 8 DAYS CHRONO MONOPULSANTE GMT   REF. PAM00317

Movement: mechanical manual-winding Panerai P.2004/B caliber executed entirely by Panerai; 13 ¾"; 29 jewels, monometallic Glucydur® balance with 28,800 alternations/hour; KIF Parechoc® anti-shock device; 3 barrels; 8-day power reserve; 321 components. **Functions:** hours, minutes, seconds; seconds reset; single-button chronograph with 2 counters, minutes at 3, small seconds and 24-hour hand and AM/PM indicator at 9; dual time with center 12-hour hand; linear power reserve at 6. **Case:** matte black ceramic three-piece 1950-style case and bezel; 44mm, thickness: 19mm; domed, antireflective sapphire crystal made from corundum (2mm thick); black ceramic

pushbutton at 8 for chronograph function; crown waterproofed by matte black ceramic patented crown-protecting device; bridge fastened to the middle via 2 screws with a screw level pressing the crown against the water-resistance gasket; screw-on caseback with sapphire crystal displaying the movement; water resistant to 100 meters. **Dial:** matte black sandwich dial; perforated, luminescent baton markers and 2 Arabic numerals with SuperLumiNova on a lower support; luminescent, black enameled baton hands; leaf-style subdial hands; arrow-tip dual time hands. **Strap:** PANERAI personalized leather strap; large-size titanium buckle with special hard black coating.
Suggested price: $25,600
Also available: in stainless steel (P.2004/1 caliber) with black dial and black alligator strap; in pink gold (P.2004/1 caliber) with blue dial and brown alligator strap; in brushed titanium (P.2004 caliber) with brown dial and brown alligator strap.

LUMINOR '1950' 8 DAYS CHRONO MONOPULSANTE GMT REF. PAM00311

Movement: mechanical manual-winding Panerai P.2004 caliber executed entirely by Panerai; 13 ¾"; 29 jewels; monometallic Glucydur® balance with 28,800 alternations/hour; KIF Parechoc® anti-shock device; 3 barrels; 8-day power reserve; 321 components. **Functions:** hours, minutes, seconds; seconds reset; linear power-reserve at 6; AM/PM indicator at 9; single-button chronograph with two counters: minutes at 3; small seconds and 24-hour hand at 9; dual time with center 12-hour hand; linear power reserve. **Case:** brushed grade-2 titanium three-piece 1950-style case with polished grade-5 titanium bezel; 44mm, thickness: 19mm; domed, antireflective sapphire crystal made from corundum

(2mm thick); brushed titanium pushbutton at 8 for chronograph function; crown waterproofed by brushed titanium patented crown-protecting device; bridge fastened to the middle via two screws with a screw level pressing the crown against the water-resistance gasket; screw-on caseback with sapphire crystal displaying the movement; water resistant to 100 meters. **Dial:** matte brown sandwich dial; perforated, luminescent baton markers and 2 Arabic numerals with SuperLumiNova on a lower support; luminescent brown enameled baton hands; leaf-style subdial hands; arrow-tip dual time hands. **Strap:** PANERAI personalized alligator strap with large-size brushed titanium buckle; supplied with second interchangeable strap.
Suggested price: $21,100
Also available: in stainless steel (P.2004/1 caliber) with black dial and black alligator strap; in pink gold (P.2004/1 caliber) with blue dial and brown alligator strap; in black ceramic (P.2004/B caliber) with black dial and black alligator strap.

LUMINOR '1950' 10 DAYS GMT   REF. PAM00270

Movement: mechanical automatic-winding Panerai P.2003 caliber executed entirely by Panerai; 13 ¾"; thickness: 8mm; 25 jewels; Glucydur® balance with 28,800 alternations/hour; KIF Parechoc® anti-shock device; 3 barrels; 296 components; 10-day power reserve. **Functions:** hours, minutes, small seconds and 24-hour hand at 9; date at 3; dual time with center 12-hour hand; linear power-reserve indicator at 6; AM/PM indicator at 9; second reset. **Case:** stainless steel three-piece 1950-style case; 44mm; brushed and polished finish; domed, antireflective sapphire crys-

tal made from corundum (2mm thick); stainless steel crown waterproofed by a patented crown-protecting device; bridge fastened to the middle via two screws with a screw lever pressing the crown against the water-resistance gasket; screw-on polished steel caseback with sapphire crystal displaying the movement; water resistant to 100 meters. **Dial:** matte black sandwich dial; perforated, luminescent baton markers and 3 Arabic numerals with SuperLumi-Nova on a lower support; luminescent stainless steel baton hands and leaf-style subdial hand; luminescent black enameled arrow-tip dual time and 24-hour hands. **Strap:** antique brown, PANERAI personalized, hand-stitched alligator strap with large-size brushed steel buckle.
Suggested price: $17,300

LUMINOR '1950' 8 DAYS GMT PINK GOLD   REF. PAM00289

Movement: mechanical manual-winding Panerai P.2002/1 caliber executed entirely by Panerai; 13 ¾"; thickness: 6.6mm; 21 jewels; monometallic Glucydur® balance; 28,800 alternations/hour; KIF Parechoc® anti-shock device; 3 barrels; 247 components; 8-day power reserve. **Functions:** hours, minutes, small seconds and 24-hour hand at 9; date at 3; dual time with center 12-hour hand; linear power reserve indicator at 6; AM/PM indicator at 9; second reset. **Case:** brushed 18K pink-gold three-piece 1950-style case; 44mm; brushed and polished finish; domed, antireflective

sapphire crystal made from corundum (2mm thick); water-proofed by a patented crown-protecting device; bridge fastened to the middle via two screws with a screw lever pressing the crown against the water-resistance gasket; screw-on polished 18K pink-gold caseback with sapphire crystal displaying the move-ment; water resistant to 100 meters. **Dial:** brown sandwich dial; perforated, luminescent baton markers and 2 Arabic numerals with SuperLumiNova on a lower support; lumine-scent 18K pink-gold hands; leaf-style subdial hand; arrow-tip dual time hand. **Strap:** PANERAI personalized hand-stitched alligator strap with brushed 18K pink-gold buckle.
Suggested price: $30,200
Also available: in stainless steel with black dial and black vintage calf strap with large-size historic brushed steel buckle.

RADIOMIR 8 DAYS   REF. PAM00268

Movement: mechanical manual-winding Panerai P.2002/3 caliber executed entirely by Panerai; 13 ¾"; thickness: 6.6mm; 21 jewels; monometallic Glucydur® balance with 28,800 alternations/hour; KIF Parechoc anti-shock device; 3 barrels; 247 components; 8-day power reserve. **Functions:** hours, minutes, small seconds at 9; date at 3; linear power reserve indicator at 6. **Case:** polished stainless steel cushion-shaped case; 45mm; OP personalized screw-down stainless steel winding crown and

patented removable wire loop strap attachments fixed to the case by small screws; curved, antireflective sap-phire crystal made from corundum (1.9mm thick) with magnifying lens on date display; screw-on pol-ished steel caseback with sapphire crystal display-ing the movement; water resistant to 100 meters. **Dial:** matte black sandwich dial; perforated, lumine-scent baton markers and 2 Arabic numerals with SuperLumiNova on a lower support; small seconds at 9; date at 3; luminescent; stainless steel baton hands and leaf-style subdial hand. **Strap:** black, PANERAI personalized, hand-stitched alligator strap and large-sized polished steel buckle.
Suggested price: $11,900

RADIOMIR TITANIUM 47MM   REF. PAM00309

Movement: mechanical manual-winding Panerai OP XXVII caliber (Minerva 16-17 base); 16 ¾"; 18 jewels; monometallic Glucydur® balance with 18,000 alternations/hour; balance spring with Phillips curves; KIF Parechoc® anti-shock device; bridges in Mallechort; 55-hour power reserve. **Functions:** hours, minutes, small seconds at 9. **Case:** titanium three-piece cushion-shaped case; 47mm; thickness: 14.15mm; polished and brushed finish; curved, antireflective sapphire crystal made from corundum (1.9mm thick); OP

personalized screw-down titanium winding crown patented removable wire loop attachments fastened to the back by four screws; dodecagonal screw-on exhibition caseback with sapphire crystal display-ing the movement; water resistant to 100 meters. **Dial:** matte black sandwich dial with knurled pink-gold outer ring; perforated, luminescent baton mark-ers and 3 Arabic numerals with SuperLumiNova on a lower support; luminescent pink-gold baton hands; leaf-style subdial hand. **Strap:** PANERAI personal-ized hand-stitched black alligator strap with large-size brushed titanium buckle.
Suggested price: $27,300
Also available: 50 pieces with brown dial and brown alligator strap.

LUMINOR MARINA LEFT HANDED   REF. PAM00026

Movement: mechanical manual-winding exclusive Panerai OPII caliber; 16 ½"; 17 jewels; monometallic Glucydur® balance with 21,600 alternations/hour; Incabloc® anti-shock device; personalized bridges and rotor; COSC-certified chronograph; 56-hour power reserve. **Functions:** hours, minutes, small seconds at 3. **Case:** stainless steel three-piece case covered with special hard black coating; 44mm, thickness: 14.4mm; antireflective sapphire crystal made from corundum (3.5mm thick); coated steel crown and patented crown-protecting device; bridge fastened to the middle via 2 screws with a screw lever pressing the crown against the water-resistance gasket; located on left side of the case; brushed steel screw-on back with sapphire crystal displaying the movement; water resistant to 100 meters. **Dial:** matte black sandwich dial; perforated, luminescent baton markers and 3 Arabic numerals with SuperLumiNova on a lower support; luminescent black enameled hands; leaf-style seconds hand. **Strap:** PANERAI personalized black hand-stitched leather strap and brushed steel buckle with special hard black coating.
Note: limited edition of 1000 pieces.
Suggested price: $8,900

LUMINOR REGATTA CHRONOGRAPH SPECIAL EDITION   REF. PAM00308

Movement: mechanical manual-winding exclusive Panerai OP XXVI caliber; 13 ¼"; 24 jewels; monometallic Glucydur® balance with 28,800 alternations/hour; Incabloc® anti-shock device; PANERAI personalized bridges engraved by hand; COSC-certified chronograph; 46-hour power reserve. **Functions:** hours, minutes; chronograph with 2 counters; small seconds at 9; minute counter and regatta countdown at 3; tachymeter scale. **Case:** stainless steel three-piece case; 44mm, thickness: 16.7mm; brushed and polished finish; stainless steel crown waterproofed by a patented crown-protecting device; bridge fastened to the middle via 2 screws with a screw lever pressing the crown against the water-resistance gasket; brushed steel pushbuttons for chronograph functions integral with crown-protecting device at 2 and 4; screw-on polished steel caseback engraved with "Classic Yachts Challenge 2008"; antireflective sapphire crystal made from corundum (2.55mm thick); water resistant to 100 meters. **Dial:** black; decorated with Paris hobnails pattern; matte black subdial; applied luminescent round hour-markers and 2 Arabic numerals; luminescent black enameled baton markers; leaf-style subdial hands; blue enameled chronograph hand.
Strap: PANERAI personalized rubber accordion strap with large-size brushed steel buckle.
Suggested price: $8,900
Note: limited edition of 500 numbered pieces.

LUMINOR '1950' PANGAEA SUBMERSIBLE DEPTH GAUGE   REF. PAM00307

Movement: mechanical automatic-winding exclusive Panerai OP XV caliber; 13 ¼"; second stop device; 21 jewels; monometallic Glucydur® balance with 28,800 alternations/hour; Incabloc® anti-shock device; hand finished with Côtes de Genève decoration on the bridges; PANERAI personalized oscillating weight; COSC-certified chronograph; electronic depth-gauge module with individual certificate issued by METAS (the Swiss Federal Office of Metrology based in Berne, Switzerland); 42-hour power reserve. **Functions:** hours, minutes, small seconds at 9; calculates immersion times; depth-gauge functions include indication of maximum depth from most recent dive, remaining battery power and current dive depth. **Case:** titanium three-piece case with brushed stainless steel pushbutton at 10 for depth-gauge functions; 47mm, thickness: 22.35mm; brushed finish; antireflective sapphire crystal (3mm thick); brushed steel counterclockwise unidirectional rotating bezel with graduated scale case and anti-skid profile, luminescent pointer, engraved 15-minute scale with applied polished markers for the calculation of diving times; brushed stainless steel crown waterproofed by a patented crown-protecting device; bridge fastened to the middle via 2 screws with a screw lever pressing the crown against the water-resistance gasket; titanium screw-on caseback with 6 grooves and silicone membrane for the depth measure and engraved with logo of Mike Horn's Pangaea expedition; water resistant to 120 meters. **Dial:** matte dark blue; luminescent baton markers and 2 Arabic numerals; luminescent steel skeleton hands; leaf-style subdial hand, yellow enameled depth-gauge hand. **Strap:** PANERAI personalized rubber accordion strap with large-size brushed steel buckle; supplied with second interchangeable strap for diving.
Suggested price: $17,600
Note: limited edition of 500 numbered pieces commemorating Mike Horn's PANGAEA Expedition.

LUMINOR CHRONOGRAPH 40MM   REF. PAM00310

Movement: mechanical automatic-winding Panerai OP XII caliber; 13 ¼"; 27 jewels; monometallic Glucydur® balance with 28,800 alternations/hour; Incabloc® anti-shock device; Côtes de Genève decoration and blued screws; PANERAI personalized oscillating weight; COSC-certified chronograph; 46-hour power reserve. **Functions:** hours, minutes, small seconds; chronograph with two counters: minutes at 3, small seconds at 9; central chronograph hand. **Case:** brushed stainless steel three-piece case; 40mm; polished stainless steel bezel; antireflective sapphire crystal made from corundum (1.9mm thick); brushed stainless steel crown waterproofed by patented crown-protecting device; bridge fastened to the middle via two screws with a screw lever pressing against the water-resistance gasket; brushed stainless steel pushbuttons for chronograph functions at 2 and 4 integral with crown-protecting device; screw-on caseback; water resistant to 100 meters. **Dial:** matte black; applied luminous markers and 2 Arabic numerals; luminescent black enameled hands. **Strap:** PANERAI personalized black alligator strap with brushed stainless steel adjustable buckle.
Suggested price: $8,600

LUMINOR MARINA AUTOMATIC 44MM   REF. PAM00299

Movement: mechanical automatic-winding exclusive Panerai OP III caliber; 13 ¼''; 21 jewels; monometallic Glucydur® balance, 28,800 alternations/hour; Incabloc® anti-shock device; Côtes de Genève decoration on bridges; PANERAI personalized oscillating weight; COSC-certified chronograph; 42-hour power reserve. **Functions:** hours, minutes, small seconds at 9; date at 3. **Case:** brushed stainless steel three-piece case; 44mm, thickness: 15.7mm; polished stainless steel bezel; antireflective sapphire crystal made from corundum (3.5mm thick) with a magnifying lens on the date display; crown waterproofed by brushed stainless steel patented crown-protecting device; bridge fastened to the middle by two screws and a screw lever pressing against the water-resistance gasket; brushed steel screw-on caseback; water resistant to 300 meters. **Dial:** matte black; applied luminescent markers and 2 Arabic numerals; luminescent steel batonhands;leaf-styleseconds hand. **Bracelet:** PANERAI personalized stainless steel bracelet with vertical brushed finish and polished finish on surface between the links; brushed steel, double fold-over buckle with 2 safety pushers. **Suggested price:** $7,400 **Also available:** in polished steel with black dial and black alligator strap; in titanium with brown dial and brown alligator strap; in titanium with brown dial and titanium bracelet.

RADIOMIR BLACK SEAL AUTOMATIC   REF. PAM00287

Movement: mechanical automatic-winding exclusive Panerai OP III caliber; 13 ¼''; 21 jewels; monometallic Glucydur® balance; 28,800 alternations/hour; Incabloc® anti-shock device; Côtes de Genève decoration on the bridges; PANERAI personalized oscillating weight; COSC-certified chronograph; 42-hour power reserve. **Functions:** hours, minutes, small seconds; date. **Case:** polished stainless steel cushion-shaped case; 45mm; curved, antireflective sapphire crystal made from corundum (1.9mm thick) with magnifying lens on date display; OP personalized screw-down winding crown and patented removable wire loop strap attachments fixed to the case by small screws; screw-on caseback in steel; water resistant to 100 meters. **Dial:** matte black sandwich dial; perforated, luminescent baton markers and 2 Arabic numerals with Super-Lumi-Nova on a lower support; small seconds at 9; date at 3; luminescent, black enameled baton hands and leaf-style subdial hand. **Strap:** black, PANERAI personalized, hand-stitched alligator strap with polished stainless steel adjustable buckle. **Suggested price:** $6,200

RADIOMIR BLACK SEAL CERAMIC   REF. PAM00292

Movement: mechanical manual-winding exclusive Panerai OP XI caliber; 16 ½''; 17 jewels; monometallic Glucydur® balance with Nivarox® spring; 21,600 alternations/hour; Incabloc® anti-shock device; COSC-certified chronograph; 56-hour power reserve. **Functions:** hours, minutes, small seconds. **Case:** matte black ceramic cushion-shaped case; 45mm; curved, antireflective sapphire crystal made from corundum (2.2mm thick); OP personalized screw-down ceramic winding crown and patented removable wire loop strap attachments in steel with special hard black coating fixed to the case by small screws; screw-on caseback in steel with special hard black coating; water resistant to 100 meters. **Dial:** matte black sandwich dial; perforated; luminescent baton markers and 3 Arabic numerals with SuperLumiNova on a lower support; small seconds at 9; luminescent; black enameled baton hands and leaf-style subdial hand. **Strap:** black, PANERAI personalized, hand-stitched calf strap with large-size brushed steel buckle with special hard black coating. **Suggested price:** $8,000 **Also available:** in polished stainless steel with black dial and Calf gold vintage strap.

RADIOMIR BASE PINK GOLD   REF. PAM00231

Movement: mechanical manual-winding exclusive Panerai OP X caliber; 16 ½''; 17 jewels; monometallic Glucydur® balance; 21,600 alternations/hour; Incabloc® anti-shock device; "swan neck" index with micrometer screw adjustment; Côtes de Genève decoration and polished blued screws; 56-hour power reserve. **Functions:** hours, minutes. **Case:** 18K pink-gold polished three-piece cushion-shaped case; 45mm; curved, antireflective sapphire crystal made from corundum (1.9mm thick); OP personalized screw-down; winding crown; patented removable wire loop strap attachments fixed to the case by small screws; dodecagonal screw-on caseback with sapphire crystal displaying the movement; water resistant to 100 meters. **Dial:** matte black sandwich dial; perforated, luminescent baton markers and 4 Arabic numerals with SuperLumiNova on a lower support; luminescent pink-gold baton hands. **Strap:** antique brown, PANERAI personalized, hand-stitched alligator strap with PANERAI personalized 18K pink-gold buckle. **Suggested price:** $14,900 **Also available:** in polished steel with black dial and black calf strap.

PARMIGIANI FLEURIER
Divine Details

Before opening his manufacture workshop in Fleurier, Switzerland, more than a decade ago, Michel Parmigiani restored timekeeping treasures for others—an experience that heightened his passion for craftsmanship. Today, that obsession with fine detail is one of the reasons collectors around the world prize the watches that bear his name.

Emblematic of that meticulous approach is the watchmaker's new Kalpa Hemispheres collection. Inspired by the around-the-world adventures of Swiss sailor Bernard Stamm, this elegant line of travel watches includes an easily adjustable second time-zone display.

Parmigiani engineers developed the innovative PF337 automatic caliber in-house to power the Kalpa Hemispheres. The watch includes a second crown that enables the destination time zone to be set independently from the local time. This allows the second time zone to be set to the minute—an extraordinary feat rarely seen in horology. Using an intricate system of clutches, the crown sets the time for destinations like Nepal, which deviates from GMT by 45 minutes rather than the typical 60-minute variation. Day/night indicators for each time zone are also included, further enhancing the Kalpa Hemispheres's functionality.

The dial's clean design is both aesthetically pleasing and practical. The display's logical arrangement guarantees legibility, even for the weary-eyed intercontinental traveler. The Kalpa Hemispheres is offered in stainless steel with a silver, graphite or blue dial. A rose-gold version is also available, paired exclusively with a Havana-brown dial.

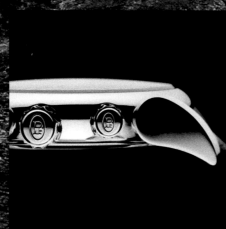

Available in rose gold or stainless steel, the watches of the Kalpa Hemispheres collection include two crowns allowing the second time-zone indicator to be set independently from the reference time.

Parmigiani again finds inspiration upon the crashing waves and launches a new partnership with Pershing, the famed Italian yacht maker. These prestigious luxury brands bring their shared passion for craftsmanship to bear on this new collection of aquatic sport watches.

The Pershing Collection encompasses two lines: the standard production Pershing Chronograph and the limited edition Pershing One-One-Five Chronograph. Both models integrate stylistic flourishes from the watchmaker and boat builder. The round case is a sportier version of Parmigiani's Kalpa, while the numerals on the dial and rotating bezel echo the typeface used for Pershing's logo. The delta-shaped hour and minute hands are typical Parmigiani while the case's tight curves reference a ship's hull.

Beyond the visual parallels, the Pershing Chronograph and Pershing One-One-Five Chronograph share technical similarities. Both are water resistant to 660 feet and offer a central chronograph

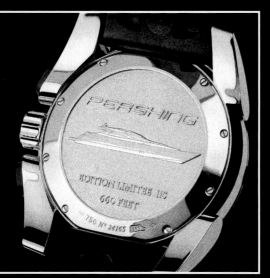

seconds with 12-hour and 30-minute counters, which are controlled with ovoid-shaped rubber pushers integrated into the lugs.

The Pershing Chronograph is available exclusively in stainless steel with a Côtes de Genève-decorated dial that is offered in four colors: graphite, blue, red and silver. The caseback is engraved with an illustration of a Pershing yacht.

The Pershing One-One-Five Chronograph takes its name from Pershing's largest vessel, which measures 115 feet. A rendering of this impressive ship is engraved on this model's caseback. Parmigiani will produce 115 pieces each of the Pershing One-One-Five in rose gold with Havana-brown dial and palladium with silver dial.

"These two models are just the beginning of a long-term partnership," Parmigiani says. "In the future, the Pershing collection may incorporate more complicated movements that reflect our clients' desires for watches designed for an active lifestyle that also feature traditional complications."

Parmigiani presents a wide range of timepieces in its Grand Complication collection, including the Toric Corrector QPR Minute Repeater. In addition to the hours and minutes, this mechanical marvel displays the phases of the moon along with a perpetual calendar that features a leap-year indicator; day and month subdials at 12:00 and 6:00 respectively; and a centrally fixed retrograde hand that points to the date along the dial's edge.

On the crown side of the Toric Corrector QPR Minute Repeater's round 42mm case, Parmigiani adds a corrector button, allowing for quick date adjustments. Opposite the crown, a slide activates the watch's two-gong repeater, which sounds the hours, quarter hours and minutes.

Two rings of knurling on the bezel distinguish the attractive Toric case that is available in rose gold or platinum. The decoration provides an attractive frame for the watch's dial, which is offered in various colors and skeletonized to reveal the movement's intricacies.

The Kalpa XL Tourbillon is another highlight from Parmigiani's Grand Complication collection. The watchmaker presents a handsome version with a slate dial that is offered in a limited edition of 30 pieces. Its rose-gold tonneau case (53x37.2mm) is ergonomically curved, conforming to the wrist comfortably.

Not only is the dial decorated with the Côtes de Genève design, but its center has also been removed to expose the hand-wound movement beneath it. The opening extends to reveal the tourbillon mechanism positioned at 6:00, which rotates once every 30 seconds. At the other end of the dial, an indicator shows the level of the watch's one-week power reserve.

The new Hemispheres and Pershing collections, coupled with an exciting selection of Grand Complications, all serve to elevate Parmigiani's status as one of today's elite independent Swiss watchmakers.

FACING PAGE

TOP The Pershing One-One-Five Chronograph's caseback is engraved with an illustration of the 115-foot Pershing yacht that lends this limited edition watch its name.

BOTTOM The lugs of the stainless steel Pershing Chronograph include egg-shaped rubber pushers that control the watch's chronograph counters.

THIS PAGE

TOP LEFT The Toric Corrector QPR Minute Repeater's skeletonized dial offers a view of the complex movement, which combines a perpetual calendar, moonphase and minute repeater.

TOP RIGHT Parmigiani will produce only 30 pieces of the Kalpa XL Tourbillon with slate dial. The 30-second tourbillon is positioned at 6:00 and the display at 12:00 tracks how much of the watch's seven-day power reserve remains.

TORIC RETROGRADE PERPETUAL CALENDAR — REF. PF002622.01

Movement: automatic-winding Parmigiani manufactured PF333.01; caliber: 12'''– 27mm; 55-hour power reserve; 28,800 vph; 32 jewels; double barrel; "Côtes de Genève" decoration; hand-chamfered bridges; steel stoned lengthwise; 22K gold oscillating weight.
Functions: hours, minutes, center seconds; precision moonphases; perpetual calendar with apertures (day, retrograde date, month and leap year).

Case: 18K rose gold; Ø 40.5mm, thickness: 11.4mm; 4.5mm genuine sapphire cabochon crown; bezel with knurling, anti-reflective sapphire crystal; water resistant to 30 meters.
Dial: black and silver colored; snailed center; applied sector with circular satin-finish sectors, javelin-shaped hands.
Strap: Hermès alligator with polished ardillon buckle.
Suggested price: $57,100
Also available: in white gold with silver colored dial.

KALPA XL HEBDOMADAIRE SQ — REF. PF600377.01

Movement: manual-winding Parmigiani manufactured PF118.02 18K solid gold skeleton movement; caliber: 13x10½'''– 29.3x23.6mm; 8-day power reserve; 21,600 vph; 28 jewels; double barrel; swan-neck regulator; hand-engraved "feuille de laurier" decoration; hand-chamfered bridges.
Functions: hours, minutes, small seconds at 6; power-reserve indicator.
Case: 18K rose-gold tonneau case; 53x37.2mm, thickness: 11.2mm; anti-reflective sapphire crystal; individual number and Special Edition x/30 engraved "feuille de laurier" on the caseback; water resistant to 30 meters.

Dial: white-gold exterior with hand-engraved "bay leaf" decoration; transparent sapphire interior with transfer; delta-shaped hands.
Strap: Hermès alligator with polished ardillon buckle.
Note: special edition of 30 pieces.
Suggested price: $109,600

KALPA TONDA 42 TOURBILLON — REF. PF600695.01

Movement: manual-winding Parmigiani manufactured PF510.01 tourbillon movement with 1-week power reserve.
Functions: hours, minutes, center seconds; power-reserve indicator.
Case: 18K rose gold; polished finish; Ø 42mm, thickness: 11.5mm; antireflective sapphire crystal; sapphire crystal caseback engraved with individual number; water resistant to 30 meters.

Dial: "Côtes de Genève" exterior; veloute center; applied trapezoid indexes with luminescent coating; delta-shaped hands.
Strap: Hermès alligator with folding buckle, polished finish.
Note: limited edition of 100 pieces.
Suggested price: $191,800
Also available: in platinum with slate dial, $210,500

KALPA HEMISPHERES — REF. PF600217

Movement: automatic-winding Parmigiani manufactured PF337; caliber made fully in-house; Ø 15 ¼'''; 48-hour power reserve; 28,800 vph; 38 jewels; gold oscillating weight for the 18K rose-gold version; "Côtes de Genève" decoration.
Functions: hours, minutes, small seconds at 6; day/night indicator linked to local time at 6; 2nd time-zone hour and minute display at 12; 2nd time-zone day/night indicator at 1; large calendar window.

Case: 18K rose gold; polished finish; 42mm, thickness: 10.7mm; anti-reflective sapphire crystal; caseback with sapphire crystal; individual number engraved on caseback.
Dial: Havana-brown; counter in azur finish; center in velvet finish; "Côtes de Genève" exterior; applied rhodium-plated pointed markers and Arabic numerals; delta-shaped hands with luminescent coating.
Strap: Hermès alligator with rose-gold ardillon buckle.
Suggested price: $27,000
Also available: in steel.

PERSHING 115 CHRONOGRAPH — REF. PF600094.06

Movement: automatic-winding Parmigiani manufactured PF190.01 chronograph movement; caliber: 13'''– 29.8mm; 50-hour power reserve; 36,000 vph; 31 jewels; column-wheel chronograph; "Côtes de Genève" decoration; hand-chamfered bridges; steel stoned lengthwise; 22K gold oscillating weight.
Functions: hours, minutes, small seconds at 9; date window; 1/5 second chronograph (large second hand, 30-minute counter, 12-hour counter).

Case: polished and satin-finished palladium; Ø 45mm, thickness: 14.2mm; unidirectional turning bezel; 8mm screwed down crown; rubber pushpieces; antireflective sapphire crystal; caseback engraved with Pershing boat and individual number; water resistant to 200 meters.
Dial: "Côtes de Genève" with ring overlaid on counter; applied indexes; delta-shaped hands with luminescent coating.
Strap: natural rubber; polished and satin-finished adjustable safety folding buckle.
Note: limited edition of 115 pieces.
Suggested price: $49,500
Also available: on bracelet; rose-gold/Havana-brown dial.

KALPA GRANDE — REF. PF011327.02

Movement: automatic-winding Parmigiani manufactured PF331.01; caliber: 11½'''– 25.6 mm; 55-hour power reserve; 28,800 vph; 32 jewels; double barrel; "Côtes de Genève" decoration; chamfered bridges; 22K gold oscillating weight on gold models.
Functions: hours, minutes, seconds.
Case: steel tonneau case; 46.6x34mm, thickness: 9.25mm; 5.5mm crown; 2 outer rows set with brilliant-cut diamonds (1.19 ct); antireflective sapphire crystal; sapphire crystal caseback engraved with individual number; water resistant to 30 meters.

Dial: sunburst guilloche; indexes at 6 and 12 set with brilliant-cut diamonds (.11 ct); delta-shaped hands with luminescent coating.
Bracelet: polished finish; folding buckle.
Suggested price: $12,300
Also available: with black dial; in rose gold.

KALPA TONDA 42 SKELETON — REF. PF601395.01

Movement: automatic-winding Parmigiani manufactured PF338.01 skeleton movement; caliber: 11½'''– 25.6mm; 55-hour power reserve; 28,800 vph; 32 jewels; double barrel; hand-finished bridges and mainplate; 22K gold oscillating weight.
Functions: hours, minutes, center seconds; peripheral date indicator.
Case: 18K white gold; polished finish; Ø 42mm, thickness: 8.6mm; 5.5mm crown; antireflective sapphire crystal; sapphire crystal caseback engraved with individual number; water resistant to 30 meters.

Dial: transparent sapphire interior; metal exterior with print and translucent lacquer; delta-shaped hands with luminescent coating; central second hand with "PF" logo counterweight.
Strap: Hermès alligator with polished ardillon buckle.
Note: special edition of 10 pieces.
Suggested price: $44,700
Also available: with black dial (100 pieces); in rose gold with Havana-brown dial (100 pieces); in 39mm.

KALPAGRAPH — REF. PF003741

Movement: automatic-winding Parmigiani manufactured PF 334; caliber: 13 1/4'''– 30.3mm, thickness: 6.8mm; 55-hour power reserve; 28,800 vph; 68 jewels; mounted, decorated and finished by hand with a "Côtes de Genève" pattern and beveled.
Functions: hours, minutes, center seconds; large-sized date at 12; 3-counter chronograph: small seconds at 3, hours at 6, minutes at 9.
Case: steel tonneau-shaped case; 53.4x39.2mm, thickness: 12.8mm; polished finish; anti-reflective sapphire crystal; caseback displays movement through a sapphire crystal; water resistant to 30 meters.

Dial: black; chronograph subdials decorated with circular beads and red enameled frame; applied rhodium-plated pointed markers and Arabic numerals; luminescent rhodium-plated delta-shaped Parmigiani hands.
Strap: Hermès calf with steel deployment buckle.
Suggested price: $15,600
Also available: on steel bracelet or black natural rubber strap; in 18K rose gold or palladium.

PATEK PHILIPPE
Spirit of Independence

One of the core values that's driven Patek Philippe's global success for 170 years is the company's independence. It enjoys a rare level of freedom from outside influence, putting the celebrated watch brand in the much-envied position of dictating its own path and making only the watches it wants to make.

Another value essential to Patek Philippe's winning formula is its uncompromising commitment to traditional craftsmanship. To emphasize this point, all of the movements produced by the manufacture are emblazoned with the coveted Geneva Seal (Poinçon de Genève).

Starting in 1886, this official hallmark has been awarded to movements that are crafted in Geneva and also meet or exceed the city's traditional watchmaking standards. To be considered for this prestigious seal, a movement must fulfill a dozen exacting criteria that are among the most rigorous rules established for any manufactured product. To meet these demanding benchmarks, Patek Philippe is supported by a cadre of experienced artisans, skilled at everything from micromechanical engineering to meticulous finishing.

To highlight the company's historic commitment to handcrafted beauty and mechanical precision, it opened the Patek Museum in Geneva in 2001. Housed in a glorious example of Art Deco architecture, the exhibit encapsulates more than 400 years of watchmaking, including antique watches from the 16th century as well as the entire Patek Philippe collection; from its 1839 debut to today.

World Time watch, one of the latest models from Patek Philippe, provides a prime example of the work performed by the company's master craftsmen. Decorated by hand, the watch's cloisonné enamel dial is prized for its beauty by aficionados. In fact, the World Time watches made by the company in the '40s and '50s are highly prized today by collectors.

The World Time watch, unveiled last year, features a stationary ring of 24 cities that encircles the enamel depiction of the world at the center of the dial. A rotating ring couched between the cities and the map displays the current hour for each city and indicates if it's night or day. This clean arrangement achieves a level of at-a-glance legibility rare in other world time watches.

Another impressive model introduced by Patek Philippe last year is the platinum Quantième Perpétuel (Ref. 5207), a grand complication that boasts a minute repeater, instantaneous perpetual calendar, moon-phase, and tourbillon.

The watch's unassuming exterior reflects an appreciation for timeless watch design, while at the same time concealing the movement's tremendous complexity. A crystal caseback (interchangeable with a solid caseback) provides a view of the minute-repeater mechanism and the tourbillon escapement.

Perhaps the most elaborate portion of the movement is the complication that switches all the calendar displays (day, date, month, and leap year) instantaneously. Five years to develop, the mechanism includes more than 200 pieces and is currently being considered for two patents. This special function makes Quantième Perpétuel one of the most complicated ever produced by Patek Philippe.

To highlight the company's historic commitment to handcrafted beauty and mechanical precision, it opened the Patek Philippe Museum in Geneva in 2001.

FACING PAGE
TOP   Patek Philippe's skilled artisans craft the cloisonné enamel dial at the center of the World Time watch. The watchmaker will produce only a few examples of this watch each year.

BOTTOM   Highly legible, the yellow-gold World Time watch employs a rotating hour ring to simultaneously show the hour in 24 different cities, and to indicate if it is night or day.

FACING PAGE
The crystal caseback is a window into the soul of the Quantième Perpétuel, revealing its repeater mechanism and whirling tourbillon. Patek Philippe's logo, the Calatrava Cross, can also be seen adorning the top of the movement.

WORLD TIME REF. 5131J

Movement: mechanical automatic-winding Patek Philippe 240 HU manufacture caliber; decorated with a Côtes de Genève pattern and beveled; 22K gold off-center micro-rotor; hallmarked with the Geneva Seal. **Functions:** hour, minute; world time by a 24 hour turning ring and town disc. **Case:** 18K yellow-gold three-piece case; Ø 39.5mm, thickness: 10mm; polished and brushed finish; bezel with engraved brand name; curved sapphire crystal; crown in yellow gold with case protection; yellow-gold world-time pusher for

basic adjustment and dual-time updating (makes the hours hand advance by one hour at a time clockwise and the 24-hour and reference-town time-zone discs counter-clockwise); screwed-on back displaying the movement through a sapphire crystal; water resistant to 3atm. **Dial:** solid gold; center disc with gold-bordered hand-enameled Cloisonné world map; silvered 24-hour ring; blue and brushed with a sun pattern; reference-town disc brushed with a sun pattern; 4-applied cabochon markers in yellow gold; hands in yellow gold: hour hands with tip in circle shape, dauphine minute hands. **Strap:** brown alligator leather; hand-stitched; yellow-gold fold-over clasp. **Also available:** platinum with blue guilloché dial (Ref. 5130); white or pink gold with silvered guilloché dial.

CALATRAVA SQUELETTE REF. 5180/1G

Movement: mechanical automatic-winding extra-flat Patek Philippe 240 SQU manufacture caliber; 27 jewels; skeletonized; chased; rhodium-plated; decorated by hand and beveled; balance bridge in the shape of the Calatrava cross; engraved; 22K gold off-center micro-rotor; hallmarked with the Geneva Seal.
Functions: hour, minute.

Case: 18K white-gold two-piece case; Ø 39mm, thickness: 6.85mm; polished finish; with an aperture on the movement; curved sapphire crystal; crown in white gold; screwed-on back displaying the movement through a sapphire crystal with blue fumé border; water resistant to 3atm. **Dial:** baton hands on the aperture; blued gold leaf-style hands. **Bracelet:** white gold; invisible white-gold double fold-over clasp.

CHRONOGRAPH PERPETUAL CALENDAR REF. 5970J

Movement: mechanical manual-winding Patek Philippe CHR 27-70 Q manufacture caliber; decorated with a Côtes de Genève pattern and beveled; hallmarked with the Geneva Seal.
Functions: hour, minute, small second; perpetual calendar; chronograph with 2 counters; minute counter and four-year cycle at 3; date and moonphase at 6; small second and 24 hour at 9; day of the week and month at 12;

center second; minute track; tachometer scale. **Case:** 18K yellow-gold three-piece case; Ø 40mm, thickness: 13mm; polished and brushed finish; curved sapphire crystal; 4 correctors on the middle; crown and pushers in yellow gold; dodecagon screwed-on back displaying the movement through a sapphire crystal; water resistant to 3atm. **Dial:** gold; opaline silvered; subdials decorated with circular beads; applied yellow-gold baton markers; yellow-gold leaf-style hands. **Strap:** brown alligator leather; hand-stitched; yellow-gold fold-over clasp.

CHRONOGRAPH REF. 5070P

Movement: mechanical manual-winding Patek Philippe CH 27-70 Q manufacture caliber; decorated with a Côtes de Genève pattern and beveled; hallmarked with the Geneva Seal.
Functions: hour, minute, small second; minute counter at 4; small second at 9; center second; minute track with divisions for 1/6 second; tachometer scale chronograph with 2 counters.

Case: platinum two-piece case; Ø 42mm, thickness: 11.8mm; polished finish; curved sapphire crystal; stepped bezel; crown and rectangular pushers in white gold; dodecagon screwed-on back displaying the movement through a sapphire crystal; water resistant to 3atm. **Dial:** blue; brushed with a sun pattern; subdials decorated with circular beads; applied white-gold Arabic numerals; white-gold leaf-style hands. **Strap:** navy blue alligator leather; hand-stitched with silver thread; white-gold fold-over clasp.

ANNUAL CALENDAR
REF. 5146R

Movement: mechanical automatic-winding Patek Philippe 315 S IRM QA LU manufacture caliber; decorated with a Côtes de Genève pattern and beveled; 21K gold rotor; hallmarked with the Geneva Seal. **Functions:** hour, minute, second; power reserve; annual calendar; month at 3; moonphase and date at 6; day of the week at 9; power reserve at 12; takes the days of the months into account over an entire year. **Case:** 18K pink-gold three-piece case Ø 39mm, thickness: 11.6mm; polished finish; curved

sapphire crystal; 4 correctors on the middle; crown in pink gold; screwed-on back; displaying the movement through a sapphire crystal; water resistant to 3atm. **Dial:** cream-color lacquered; subdials decorated with circular beads; applied pink-gold baton markers and Arabic numerals; luminescent dots on the black painted railway minute track; luminescent pink-gold leaf-style hands. **Strap:** brown alligator skin; hand-stitched; pink-gold clasp.

Also available: with slate-gray dial with a sun pattern; in white or yellow gold with cream-color lacquered dial or slate-gray dial with a sun pattern; alligator leather strap or bracelet; in platinum with slate-gray dial with a sun pattern and alligator leather strap.

LADIES' ANNUAL CALENDAR
REF. 4937R

Movement: mechanical automatic-winding Patek Philippe 315 S QA LU manufacture caliber; decorated with a Côtes de Genève pattern and beveled; 21K gold rotor; hallmarked with the Geneva Seal. **Functions:** hour, minute, second; annual calendar; month at 3; moonphase and date at 6; day of the week at 9; takes the days of a month into account over an entire year. **Case:** 18K pink-gold three-piece case; with a pavé of 431 brilliant-cut diamonds (2.79 carats); Ø 37mm, thickness: 11.5mm; curved sapphire crystal; 4 correctors on the middle; crown in pink gold and brilliants (1 row—0.07 carat); screwed-on back displaying the movement through a sapphire crystal; water resistant to 3atm. **Dial:** white mother-of-pearl; Calatrava cross-engraved at 6; applied pink-gold Breguet markers; black painted minute track with 11 applied pink-gold cabochons; luminescent pink-gold leaf-style hands. **Strap:** white alligator leather; hand-stitched; pink-gold clasp with 27 brilliants (0.20 carat).

Also available: in white gold.

NAUTILUS POWER RESERVE MOONPHASE
REF. 5722G

Movement: mechanical automatic-winding Patek Philippe 240 PS IRM C LU manufacture caliber; decorated with a Côtes de Genève pattern and beveled; 22K gold off-center micro-rotor; hallmarked with the Geneva Seal. **Functions:** hour, minute, small second; small second at 4; date and moonphase at 7; power reserve between 10 and 11. **Case:** 18K white-gold three-piece case in tonneau shape (height, width incl. shoulders 38x43mm, thickness 9.2mm); polished and brushed finish; set with diamonds (36 baguettes on the octagonal bezel for 5.7 carats) flat sapphire crystal; 2 correctors on the middle; screw-down crown with a shoulder case protection; screwed-on back displaying the movement through a sapphire crystal; water resistant to 6atm. **Dial:** from black (perimeter) to blue (center); with horizontal linear embossed decoration; luminescent applied white-gold baton markers; luminescent white-gold baton hands; secondary hands in white enameled gold. **Strap:** navy blue alligator leather; hand-stitched; integral with the case; pink-gold double-fold-over safety clasp.

CALATRAVA ANNUAL CALENDAR
REF. 5396G

Movement: mechanical automatic-winding Patek Philippe 324 S QA LU 24H manufacture caliber; decorated with a Côtes de Genève pattern and beveled; 21K gold rotor; hallmarked with the Geneva Seal. **Functions:** hour, minute, second; 24 hour; annual calendar; moonphase and date at 6; day of the week and month beneath 12; takes the days of the months into account over an entire year. **Case:** 18K white-gold three-piece case; Ø 38mm, thickness: 11.4mm; polished; curved sapphire crystal; 4 correctors on the middle; crown in white gold; snap-on back displaying the movement through a sapphire crystal; water resistant to 3atm. **Dial:** silvered; grained; two-toned; with transfer-printed dark-blue concentric frames; baton markers and minute track on the inner ring; railway minute track and numerals every 5 units on the outer ring; blued steel leaf-style hands. **Strap:** brown alligator leather; hand-stitched; white-gold fold-over clasp. **Also available:** in pink gold.

PIAGET
The Art of Watchmaking with a Capital *A*

For the past ten years, Piaget has been very busy designing 17 proprietary mechanical movements in its workshops. In 2008, Piaget's dynamic team developed new complication calibers and continued to demonstrate its astounding expertise in enameling and gem setting.

The year 2008 was one of remarkable success for Piaget. After some large investments in developing its two manufacturing sites, Plan-les-Ouates and La Côte-aux-Fées, Piaget clearly demonstrated the degree of its commitment to satisfying the aficionado of the elite watch industry.

After the tourbillon, the relative tourbillon, and the chronograph, Piaget launched the manufacture of its new 855P caliber, which brings to life the heart of the Piaget Emperador Coussin Quantième Perpetuel. With the ability to manage all of the irregularities of the calendar up to the year 2100, the perpetual calendar is one of the most intricate complications to implement. Piaget brilliantly meets the challenge by creating this complication with a 5.6mm-thick self-winding movement offering: month and leap year at 12:00; retrograde date at 3:00; hours, minutes, and small seconds; second time zone at 8:00; and retrograde days of the week at 9:00. The Piaget Emperador Coussin Quantième Perpetuel is extremely complex and exceptional talent was required to marry the art and craftsmanship of this caliber into one stunning package. Inspired by the historical model revived in 2006, the 46mm case mirrors perfectly today's aesthetic trends. The polished and brushed surfaces alternate subtly on the outline of the dial and it is available in 18-karat pink gold or 18-karat white gold. The sapphire caseback reveals Piaget's circular Côtes de Genève emblem. The attachments are hand finished with a circular-grained mainplate, circular Côtes de Genève, beveled and hand-drawn bridges, blued screws and pearl-lined angles.

Piaget's craftsmen used their exceptional knowledge and experience to design their 2008 interpretation of the Altiplano collection. Uniquely recognized for its perfect mastery of the extra-thin movement, Piaget launched the 40mm Altiplano Squelette. For the first time, this 18-karat white-gold case has the generous dimensions to accommodate a skeleton movement. Top craftsmen created the light and airy cases and designed the manual-winding mechanical Piaget 838P caliber with exquisite transparency. A hand-crafted sun radiates from the center of the small seconds at 10:00, and illuminates the face with 60 rays of light.

FACING PAGE
The Piaget Emperador Coussin Quantième Perpetuel is powered by the new Piaget 855P.

THIS PAGE
At last, the premier Altiplano collection offers not only new dimensions with it 40mm diameter case, but also a manual-winding, skeleton Piaget 838P.

The Piaget Emperador Coussin Quantième Perpetual manages all irregularities of the calendar up to the year 2100 and includes a dual time-zone function.

A PASSIONATE KNOWLEDGE

Whether in the watchmaking field or luxury jewelry design, Piaget passionately applies its knowledge and experience to all it creates. Last year, Piaget demonstrated its mastery of enameling with incredibly intricate detail. The artisans used their mastery of "high fire" enameling to create exceptional products such as the Piaget Protocole XXL Paris-New York collection. These exquisite works of art are encased in 18-karat white or yellow gold and host miniature enamel scenes of New York or Paris, which attest to the master enamelers' patience and creativity. We also can see this dedication in the four unique Altiplano models decorated with miniature orchids.

Piaget is a glamorous brand for women and 2008's unveilings further enhanced this reputation. Piaget's art of stone setting is as impressive as its enameling, to which the jewelry-watch Limelight Paris-New York collection is its most dazzling testimony. Positively captivating is the white-gold line of sensuous reinterpretations of laces and corsets, which are delightfully interwoven under a setting of 1,576 brilliant diamonds and 83 diamond baguettes.

Precious treasures them all, Piaget's creations scintillate with their unique glows, drawing upon its craftsmen's skills and creativity that are endlessly renewed and passionately maintained.

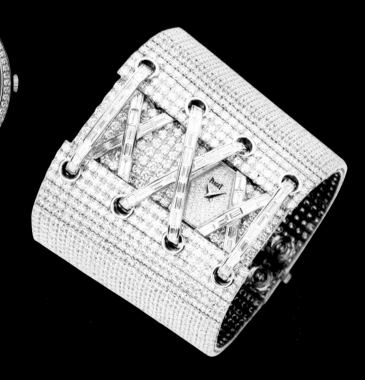

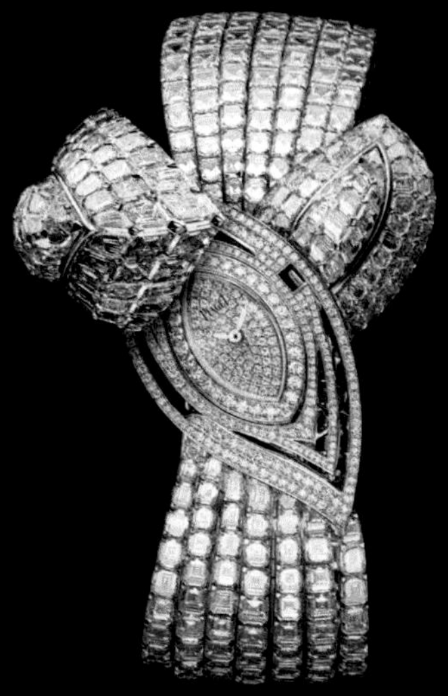

FACING PAGE

TOP
Piaget Polo Tourbillon Relatif, dedicated to New York.

LEFT
This Piaget Protocole XXL is inspired by Paris and just three pieces have been created. An alternate version features a New York scene and is also limited to three pieces.

BOTTOM CENTER
The technique of miniature enamel requires the most patience and artistic skill by the enameller. Piaget masters this process for the four unique timepieces representing the sensuous beauty of orchids.

BOTTOM RIGHT
Piaget dares to be sexy with voluptuous, stylish watches inspired by hot Parisian nights. This watch is laced with 18-karat white gold crimped with 1,576 brilliant diamonds and 83 diamond baguettes.

THIS PAGE
Piaget Limelight Exceptional Piece.

363

PIAGET EMPERADOR COUSSIN PERPETUAL CALENDAR   REF. G0A33018

Movement: mechanical automatic-winding perpetual calendar movement; Piaget 855P; Ø 28.4mm, thickness: 5.6mm; 38 jewels; 21,600 vph; approx. 72-hour power reserve; circular Côtes de Genève; circular-grained plate; bridges beveled and drawn with a file; blued screws; oscillating weight engraved with the Piaget coat of arms.
Functions: hour, minute, small seconds at 4; retrograde date indicator at 3; dual time at 8; retrograde day indicator at 9; month/leap year at 12.
Case: 18K white gold; sapphire crystal caseback revealing the movement.
Dial: silvered; satin-finished counters; applied 18K white-gold hour-markers.
Strap: black alligator leather; 18K white-gold pin buckle.

PIAGET EMPERADOR   REF. G0A33070

Movement: mechanical automatic-winding Piaget 551P; Ø 20.5mm, thickness: 4.95mm; 27 jewels; 21,600 vph; approx. 40-hour power reserve; circular Côtes de Genève; beveled hand-drawn bridges; blued screws.
Functions: hour, minute, small second at 10; power-reserve indicator at 6.
Case: 18K pink gold.
Dial: silvered sunburst dial; applied 18K pink-gold hour-markers and the Piaget coat of arms.
Strap: brown alligator leather; 18K pink-gold pin buckle.

PIAGET ALTIPLANO DOUBLE JEU   REF. G0A32152

XL model; two superimposed cases on black alligator leather strap with 18K white-gold folding clasp.

UPPER CASE: 18K white gold; caseback fitted with sapphire crystal revealing the movement. **Movement:** mechanical manual-winding, ultra-thin Piaget 838P; Ø 26.8mm, thickness: 2.5mm; 19 jewels; 21,600 vph; approx. 65-hour power reserve; circular Côtes de Genève finishing; circular-grained mainplate; bridges beveled and drawn out; blued screws. **Functions:** hour, minute, small seconds at 10. **Dial:** silver-color; black bâton hour-markers; bâton hands; caseback fitted with sapphire crystal revealing the movement.

LOWER CASE: 18K white gold; caseback engraved with the Piaget coat of arms. **Movement:** mechanical hand-wound, ultra-thin Piaget 830P; Ø 26.8mm, thickness: 2.5mm; 19 jewels; 21,600 vph; approx. 65-hour power reserve; circular Côtes de Genève finishing; circular-grained mainplate; bridges beveled and drawn out; blued screws. **Functions:** hour, minute. **Dial:** slate-gray; black and silver hour-markers; bâton hands caseback engraved with the Piaget coat of arms.

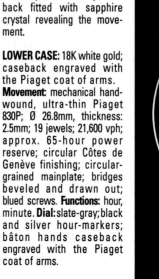

PIAGET ALTIPLANO   REF. G0A33112

Movement: mechanical manual-winding, ultra-thin Piaget 838P; ø 26.8mm, thickness: 2.5mm; 19 jewels; 21,600 vph; approx. 65-hour power reserve; circular Côtes de Genève; circular-grained plate; bridges beveled and drawn with a file; blued screws.
Functions: hour, minute, small seconds at 10.
Case: large model; 18K white gold.
Dial: silver colored; black bâton hour-markers; bâton hands.
Strap: black alligator leather; 18K white-gold pin buckle.

PIAGET POLO CHRONO — REF. GOA32039

Movement: mechanical self-winding Piaget 880P chronograph movement; Ø 26.8mm, thickness: 5.6mm; 25 jewels; 28,800 vph (balance with screws); 52-hour power reserve (double barrel); circular Côtes de Genève finishing, circular-grained mainplate; bridges beveled and drawn out; blued screws.
Functions: hour, minute, small seconds at 6; double time zone (24-hour indication) at 9; flyback chronograph function (30-minute counter) at 3.
Case: large model; 18K pink gold; 18K pink-gold bezel with alternating polished and satin-brushed surfaces; sapphire crystal caseback.
Dial: silver color; applied 18K pink-gold hour-markers.
Strap: brown alligator leather strap; 18K pink-gold folding clasp.

PIAGET POLO TOURBILLON RELATIF — REF. GOA31123

Movement: manual-winding Piaget 608P tourbillon; thickness: 3.28mm; thickness including hand fitting: 9.14mm; caging: 11 1/2''' (Ø 25.6mm); 27 jewels; 21,600 vph; approx. 70-hour power reserve; oscillating organ—balance: Ø 7.75mm; mainplate, bridges and carriage beveled and drawn out by hand with a file; circular Côtes de Genève finishing; blued screws.
Note: flying tourbillon: the minute hand, which has its center of rotation at the center of the watch, performs one complete rotation per hour; the 0.2g tourbillon carriage with 3 titanium bridges, suspended on the minute hand, spins once per minute on its own axis.
Functions: hour, minute, second.
Case: 18K white gold.
Dial: silvered dial; white-gold applied Arabic numerals and hour markers.
Strap: black alligator leather; 18K white-gold folding clasp.
Also available: diamond-set version.

PIAGET LIMELIGHT MAGIC HOUR — REF. G0A32096

Movement: Piaget 56P quartz.
Case: 18K pink gold; set with 36 brilliant-cut diamonds (approx 1.1 carats). For the very first time, thanks to an invisible mechanism developed in house, a timepiece is endowed with the unique power to be three watches in one. When positioned horizontally, the ellipse provides a generous dial opening with a free-spirited yet timeless style. With a gentle touch, the oval swivels to take an impish slant. With another 45° turn, the watch reveals its diamond-set golden numerals.
Strap: white satin; 18K pink-gold pin buckle.
Also available: in white gold.

PIAGET ALTIPLANO — REF. GOA31107

Movement: mechanical ultra-thin Piaget 450P; thickness: 2.1mm; 18 jewels; 21,600 vph; approx. 40-hour power reserve; circular Côtes de Genève finishing; rhodium-plated beveled bridges.
Functions: hour, minute, second.
Case: medium model; 18K pink gold; set with 72 brilliant-cut diamonds (approx. 0.5 carat).
Dial: white mother-of-pearl dial; stylized gilded Arabic numerals; small seconds at 10, ringed with 28 brilliant-cut diamonds (approx. 0.1 carat).
Strap: white satin; 18K pink-gold pin buckle.
Also available: in white gold.

RAYMOND WEIL
Independence is a State of Mind

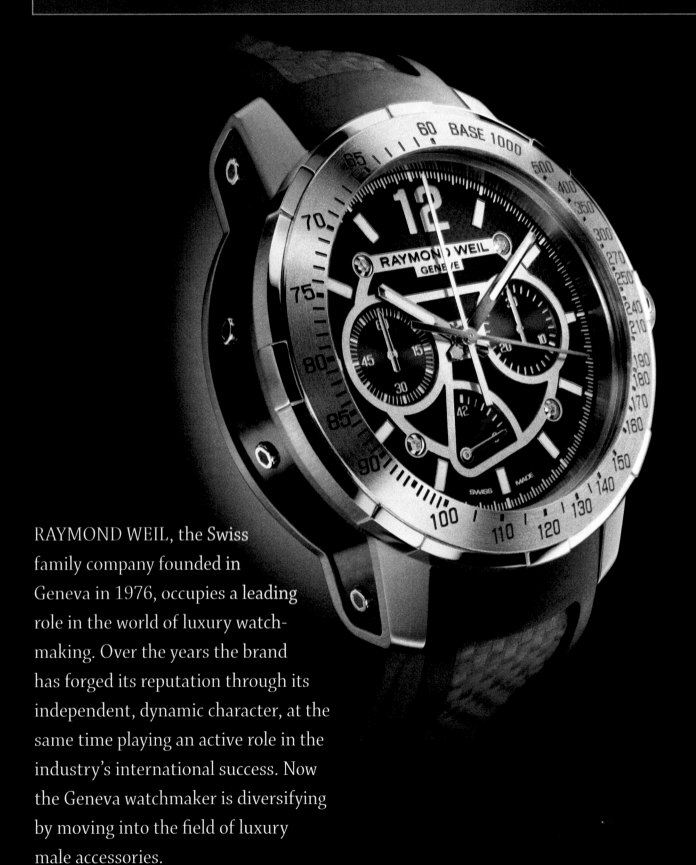

RAYMOND WEIL, the Swiss
family company founded in
Geneva in 1976, occupies a leading
role in the world of luxury watchmaking. Over the years the brand
has forged its reputation through its
independent, dynamic character, at the
same time playing an active role in the
industry's international success. Now
the Geneva watchmaker is diversifying
by moving into the field of luxury
male accessories.

RAYMOND WEIL has always enjoyed rapid growth in each of the markets where it is present around the world. Under President and CEO Olivier Bernheim, supported by his two sons Elie (Marketing Director) and Pierre (Sales Director), grandsons of M. Raymond Weil, the company continues to grow and innovate in the fields of research and product development, marketing, and communication. This expansion, and its impact on the world of prestige watchmaking, are underpinned by the strategic initiatives adopted in recent years.

Today, the brand's global offer concentrates mainly on men's mechanical watches (*nabucco*, *freelancer*, *don giovanni così grande*, *parsifal*), although ladies' designs such as the jewelry watch named *shine*, and the mechanical *freelancer* ladies' watch also play a significant role. Deluxe materials like diamonds, gold, alligator leather and precious stones are all essential components.

As a dynamic and innovative brand, RAYMOND WEIL has always successfully adapted to watchmaking developments, introducing all the innovations required to remain in the vanguard of progress. The launch of an internal Research & Development Department in 1999—one of Olivier Bernheim's signal achievements—has enabled the family company to exercise full, perfect control over the watchmaking process, from the initial concept through to production. R&D is at the cutting-edge of technology and behind numerous innovations unique to RAYMOND WEIL—such as the GMT function for the men's mechanical *don giovanni così grande* two time zones, or the patented, quick and easy interchangeable bracelet system for the ladies' *shine* collection. The department is also responsible for developing RAYMOND WEIL's latest timepiece, the *nabucco cuore caldo* split-second chronograph with power-reserve indicator, manufactured in a special limited edition of 500 pieces and unveiled at BaseWorld 2008: a first in the history of the company.

Shine, the iconic ladies' timepiece from the Swiss watchmaker, exudes style, character and femininity. The rectangular steel case is set with 48 diamonds. The glamour and elegance of the silky-toned dial in anthracite or pearl gray—soft, mysterious, bold, and profound—catches the eye beneath its sapphire crystal. To sublimate feminine charm in all its diversity, *shine* watches have a gift for metamorphosis: the strap, in black satin or finely polished steel, is easy to change thanks to the patented RAYMOND WEIL interchangeable bracelet system.

Although a leading name in Swiss watch-making, RAYMOND WEIL is also now keen to diversify, and is investing in the sector of luxury accessories for men. The first successful venture—a range of cufflinks launched at the same time as the limited *nabucco cuore caldo* edition—was presented at BaselWorld 2008 and warmly received by clients. The launch was accompanied by a collection of fluted, ballpoint pens made from steel and carbon fiber—the same high-tech materials used for the *nabucco* collection.

The enthusiastic response has prompted RAYMOND WEIL to pursue the initiative. The brand has recently introduced a range of accessories in an unlimited series in all its markets. The new collection respects the aesthetic codes of the emblematic, carbon-fiber *nabucco* chrono model, and reinforces the firm's desire to appeal to a young, confident, elegantly self-aware clientele.

ABOVE The first date chronograph from the mechanical *freelancer* collection by RAYMOND WEIL is full of character and urban personality: an audacious blend of technique and modernity. With its matte black dial, refined style and contemporary colors, *freelancer*'s new date chronograph adopts a daringly minimalist feel, in perfect keeping with the collection's original spirit. Space is shared ingeniously by the various functions—hours, minutes, seconds, chronograph and date—to give this timepiece a sophisticated look.

RIGHT The new ladies' *freelancer* with natural mother-of-pearl and diamonds.

RICHARD MILLE
The Maverick Who Made it Happen

RICHARD MILLE

With minimalistic production numbers relative to any other well-known watch brand in the market today, Richard Mille never stops shocking and delighting—often simultaneously—everyone in the watch world from collectors to industry insiders and experts. He takes positive glee in following nothing except his own instincts—translated, this means that one can never precisely predict where he is heading with his collection or which surprise the future will hold. Always looking forward and never looking back, you never know which way he will cut through the next turn on the track. But one thing is very clear for watch collectors: Mille's unfailing intuition is so remarkable that the best thing to do is just go with the flow—because he is always spot on with his inimitable sense of direction and timing.

TOP Richard Mille has been a major and extremely active supporter of motor sports such as the Le Mans Classic for many years in addition to regularly racing himself in one of the several original restored racing cars that he owns.

This year is, of course, no exception and the new 2009 additions have already shocked the industry just by the sheer number of new models being released: seven in total, something virtually unheard of for a brand that produces only some 2,000 watches per year. Even more remarkable are the extreme differences between them, which cover a whole palette of ranges and tastes, visually as well as technically.

The first new release is one that many collectors have awaited a very long time: the RM 025 Tourbillon Chronograph Diver's model. The first questions everyone immediately asks are: Why does it have a round case, (the first in the entire Richard Mille collection), and does this mean that Mille has joined the ranks of the conventional? "This watch is a total water animal, a beast of a watch," exclaims Richard Mille while handling the first prototype case of the RM 025. "You know, I have been working on this idea, almost since the RM 001 was introduced nine years ago. The main problem to overcome was the water resistance. Whatever I tried, no shape would hold up to the pressure of these depths except a round shape, and this took me time to accept. The breakthrough came for me when I got the curvature of the caseback and the lug placement exactly right. This restored the ergonomic feeling that I find absolutely essential, also for a round case design. After all, this is a watch that is first and foremost a tool, albeit a very expensive one, that has to work reliably under very extreme conditions."

"Technological developments—especially those of a mechanical nature—are one of the greatest sources of fascination and passion for me, a driving force behind everything I do. It is at the center of nearly everything that represents motion: racing cars, watches, jets, satellites, even travel in outer space. But the bottom line is that is has to be useful and bring something to further a particular application—even more so when it concerns horology."

The unique tripartite case design uses miniature torque screws that can be tensioned individually and precisely with high accuracy around the exterior circumference of the case, thus guaranteeing a waterproof closure of evenly distributed pressure along the case edge, essential for a long term seal. The bezel is also unlike any other. It is constructed with three layers, connected with 24 screws, turning unidirectionally following ISO 6425 norms in order to avoid timing miscalculations. In addition, the entire bezel system is screwed to the watchcase making it absolutely stable as well as impossible to inadvertently dislocate or loosen. This unique use of screws allows for perfect adjustment since the bezel is not tensioned into position. For clearer visibility under murky conditions, starting at 12:00, the five-minute markers of the first quarter are highlighted red. All this attention to detail is just the icing on the cake however; within ticks the caliber RM 025, a carbon nanofiber tourbillon chronograph based upon the famed caliber RM 008, one of the major and uniquely new chronograph designs of the 21st century. The caliber RM 025 unites 2 extremes: the complication of a tourbillon with the notorious complexities of a chronograph movement, within a water resistant case able to withstand serious use in actual underwater situations.

Despite the round shape of this case (a technical necessity for diving watches), the new RM 025 is unmistakably Richard Mille in the realization of every part and the close attention to every detail.

With specially designed watertight pushers and a screwed down crown, the RM 025 is a tourbillon chronograph that is ready for action under extreme conditions. All models have 18-karat red-gold lugs with a titanium central casing and turning bezel, with a choice of the secondary front bezel and back bezel in 18-karat red or white gold and titanium.

Following the tremendous popularity of the women's automatic RM 007, this year sees the introduction of the first ladies' manual-winding tourbillon to the Richard Mille lineup. In comparison to the other watches in the collection, this watch is poles apart from the new diver's watch. The RM 025 is all business, while the RM 019 Celtic Knot tourbillon is a totally feminine expression of the poetic and mysterious. With its unlimited and returning pathway, the Celtic knot symbolizes an uninterrupted life; it is both an emblem of longevity and the never-ending cycle of our existence.

Brought into the domain of technical haute horlogerie, this eternal symbol takes on a new relationship with the timelessness of time itself, winding through the movement's structure. The baseplate of Black Onyx is a gemstone able to deflect and channel harmful energy towards Earth, thus providing stability. Due to this ability, Black Onyx is considered a stone of protection against negative thoughts, as well being the stone of equilibrium and inspiration. Adding a refined visible touch, the tourbillon endstone bridge on the back of the watch is also engraved with a Celtic triquetra knot.

Keeping with the technical nature of all watches created by the brand, the RM 019 Celtic Knot utilizes a newly developed power-reserve indicator that makes use of a differential gearing system, directly connected to the winding barrel. Via a red line etched on its surface, the direct turning of the power-reserve barrel allows the wearer to easily note if the watch requires winding.

Giving existing materials a new impulse by applying them in a new manner, as well as the implementation of new materials to watchmaking, is completely second nature to Richard Mille Watches' philosophy. Mille shocked everyone in 2000 by creating tourbillons with titanium cases and movements. Who would ever have thought that "lowly" titanium, a primarily industrial and aerospace material, would find its way into such high-end watchmaking creations such as tourbillons and split-seconds chronographs? Today, 2009, nearly everyone is offering high-end watches with cases and parts of titanium as well as a dozen other metals, a great compliment as well as the tangible proof that a barrier has definitely been broken down and new frontiers opened. That first step was quickly followed by the use of carbon nanofiber for movement baseplates, marking the premier use of this material in watchmaking. This is a composite composed of carbon fibers many times thinner than a human hair, which takes on an isotropic structure possessing mechanical, physical and chemical stability when molded under high pressure (750 bars) and temperature (2,000° C). The reason why this material is so well suited for use in watchmaking is that it is amorphous, chemically neutral and dimensionally stable within a wide range of temperatures. In this way it provides the ideal basis for any kind of complicated horological creation, whether tourbillon or split-seconds chronograph.

The combination of titanium and carbon nanofiber have set a high challenge for watchmaking today, and have been proven more useful, more interesting and more beautiful than others might have dared imagine.

New for 2009, in celebration of those new impulses started with experiments in 21st century watchmaking, Richard Mille Watches has created the All Grey series: the RM 002-V2 All Grey, RM 003-V2 All Grey, RM 004-V2 All Grey, and RM 008-V2 All Grey. Each watch in the series has a specially manufactured carbon nanofiber baseplate made with gray PVD-treated carbon nanofibers, combined with a case of microblasted titanium. If you think "gray" means dull, boring and uninteresting—you had better think again!

RICHARD MILLE

The elegant exterior of the skeletonized RM 023 automatic with its smaller dimensions (45x37.80x11.45mm), houses the winding rotor with variable geometry, and weight segment along the outer edge milled from a special tungsten/cobalt alloy with ball bearings created from synthetic ceramics. The special double barrel system lowers wear and tear on the movement, also evening out any variations in the flow of power to the movement.

The story behind yet another creation, the new RM 023, builds upon the success of two earlier models that Richard Mille created. Not just another variation on a theme, this new automatic adds an extra dimension to the entire Richard Mille collection, at the same time acknowledging the ongoing and continuous dialogue between the brand and the watch lovers who cherish it. The original and hugely popular automatic RM 005 with hours, minutes, central seconds and date was a moderately sized watch that later made way for its slightly larger, transparent cousin, the RM 010, which was outfitted with the skeletonized 005-S movement.

For 2009, the skeletonized RM 023, which makes its appearance in 2009, has been given new dimensions (45x37.80x11.45 mm) and its size is midway between that of the RM 007 and RM 010. It has a new and elegant dial design, using an asymmetrical layout with Roman numerals in appliqué on sapphire with an unusually sculpted, Alcryn collared crown. Designed for both men and women, this new model unites everything essential in Richard Mille's philosophy with a sophisticated appearance, convincing as well as comfortable under all imaginable conditions from the racetrack to the concert hall.

Whilst the case size of the RM 023 combined with the new dial and crown brings an air of elegance to the exterior, the interior—as can be expected from any Richard Mille creation—is focused solely on timekeeping and nothing else. Great attention to everydetail is insured, in this case starting with the winding rotor and its white-gold V-shaped ribs and variable geometry, which can be personally adjusted to each wearer's activity level before leaving the workshop. The weight segment along the outer edge is milled from a special tungsten/cobalt alloy with the rotor's ball bearings created from synthetic ceramics. The PVD-treated titanium baseplate, bridges and balance-cock with many skeletonized parts have been developed to guarantee excellent rigidity and accurate surface flatness, which in the case

of skeletonized movements requires additional considerations. The special double-barrel system lowers wear and tear on the movement, also evening out any variations in the flow of power to the movement. This extreme care and attention to the rotor and winding aspects of the watch's going train are directly connected with the necessity of an even energy supply as the essential basis for ensuring excellent chronometric results. The creation of such a movement, in titanium having such minimalist dimensions, represents yet another highpoint of the watchmaker's skill and patience, embodied in the RM 023.

Back to the fundamentals, back to the roots....or is it back to the future?

The RM 001 and RM 002 proved beyond a doubt that innovative ideas and technology could be integrated simultaneously with all that was rare, exceptional and traditional in the world haute horology.

Now, eight years after that watershed moment, in a moment of simultaneous recollection and foresight, the RM 021 Aerodyne is introduced: a watch that takes its place at the center of everything 21st century watchmaking is all about. The numeric composition of this model number is not just a coincidence—it is a statement. The model number reflects those first two landmark models, as well as the number of our present century. It also marks the entrance of the theme of air, space and supersonic speed to the brand's imagery and inspiration.

Continuing the expansion and application of truly unique materials to watchmaking, the RM 021 Aerodyne is the first watch created with a composite baseplate utilizing a titanium exterior framework in combination with honeycombed orthorhombic titanium alumide and carbon nanofiber. Orthorhombic titanium aluminides are new group of alloys, developed from the main class of titanium aluminides, which possess a specific crystalline molecular structure ordered on the orthorhombic phase of Ti2AlNb. Its use within a honeycombed geometrical pattern was originally the subject of research by NASA for application as a core material of supersonic aircraft wings, where resistance to extremely high temperatures and torsion is paramount. The alloy in this honeycombed form has unparalleled stiffness, a low thermal expansion coefficient and exceptional torsion resistance. The actual shape of the baseplate itself as seen from the dial side resembles the trench-like V-shaped profile of a flying wing aircraft where the wing tips are positioned higher than the central body of the aircraft itself. The winding barrel and the tourbillon are both placed in the central depth of this aerodynamic structure, balancing on light and airy bridges with four arms on two sides. The RM 021 Aerodyne represents the extraordinary union of all the aspects that comprise the Richard Mille philosophy of watchmaking—now and in the future.

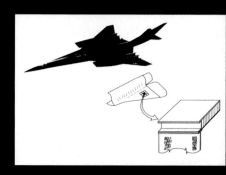

The alloy used in the RM 021 Aerodyne's baseplate construction uses a honeycombed structure with unparalleled stiffness, a low thermal expansion coefficient and exceptional torsion resistance. The actual shape of the baseplate itself as seen from the dial side resembles the trench-like V-shaped profile of a flying wing aircraft where the wing tips are positioned higher than the central body of the aircraft itself. The winding barrel and the tourbillon are both placed in the central depth of this aerodynamic structure, balancing on light and airy bridges with four arms on two sides.

TOURBILLON · RM 002-V2

Movement: mechanical manual-winding tourbillon caliber RM 002-V2; carbon nanofiber baseplate; approx. 70-hour power reserve; variable inertia balance with overcoil hairspring; fast rotating barrel; function selector gearbox with indicator; ceramic tourbillon endstone; central bridge in rigidified ARCAP; spline screws in grade-5 titanium for the bridges and case; winding barrel and third pinion teeth with central involute profile; jewels set in white-gold chatons.

Functions: hours, minutes; power-reserve indicator; torque indicator; function indicator.

Case: 18K red-gold anatomically curved tripartite case; 45x38.9x11.85mm; assembled with 12 spline screws in grade-5 titanium; sapphire crystal front and back with double-sided antiglare coating; water resistant to 50 meters.

Dial: sapphire with double-sided antiglare treatment; protected with 8 silicon braces in grooved edges.

Strap: leather or crocodile attached via titanium screws to the case; with matching buckle individually engraved with model number.

Also available: in titanium, 18K white gold or platinum.

TOURBILLON · RM 002-V2 ALL GREY

Movement: mechanical manual-winding "gray" tourbillon caliber RM 002-V2; gray PVD-coated carbon nanofiber baseplate; approx. 70-hour power reserve; variable inertia balance with overcoil; fast rotating barrel; function selector gearbox with indicator; ceramic tourbillon endstone; central bridge in rigidified ARCAP; spline screws in grade-5 titanium for the bridges and case; winding barrel and third pinion teeth with central involute profile; jewels set in white gold chatons.

Functions: hours, minutes, power reserve indicator, torque indicator, function indicator.

Case: microblasted titanium, anatomically curved tripartite case 45x38.9x11.85mm; assembled with 12 spline screws in grade-5 titanium; sapphire crystal front and back with double-sided antiglare coating; water resistant to 50 meters.

Dial: in sapphire with doubled sided antiglare treatment; protected with 8 silicon braces in grooved edges.

Strap: special composite strap; attached via titanium screws to the case; matching buckle individually engraved with model number.

TOURBILLON · RM 003-V2

Movement: mechanical manual-winding tourbillon caliber RM 003-V2; carbon nanofiber baseplate; approx. 70-hour power reserve; variable inertia balance with overcoil hairspring; fast rotating barrel; function selector gearbox with indicator; ceramic tourbillon endstone; central bridge in rigidified ARCAP; spline screws in grade-5 titanium for the bridges and case; winding barrel and third pinion teeth with central involute profile; jewels set in white-gold chatons.

Functions: hours, minutes, second time zone; power-reserve indicator; torque indicator; function indicator.

Case: 18K white-gold, anatomically curved tripartite case; 48x39.3x13.84mm; tripartite case assembled with 12 spline screws in grade-5 titanium; sapphire crystal front and back with double-sided antiglare coating; water resistant to 50 meters.

Dial: sapphire with double-sided antiglare treatment; protected with 8 silicon braces in grooved edges.

Strap: leather or crocodile attached via titanium screws to the case; with matching buckle individually engraved with model number.

Also available: in titanium, 18K red gold or platinum.

TOURBILLON · RM 003-V2 ALL GREY

Movement: mechanical manual-winding "gray" tourbillon caliber RM 003-V2; gray PVD-coated carbon nanofiber baseplate; approx. 70-hour power reserve; variable inertia balance with overcoil; fast rotating barrel; function selector gearbox with indicator; sapphire glass disc for second time zone; ceramic tourbillon endstone; central bridge in rigidified ARCAP; spline screws in grade-5 titanium for the bridges and case; winding barrel and third pinion teeth with central involute profile; jewels set in white gold chatons.

Functions: hours, minutes, second time zone, power reserve indicator, torque indicator, function indicator.

Case: microblasted titanium, anatomically curved tripartite case 48x39.3x13.84mm; assembled with 12 spline screws in grade-5 titanium; sapphire crystal front and back with double-sided antiglare coating; water resistant to 50 meters.

Dial: in sapphire with doubled sided antiglare treatment; protected with 8 silicon braces in grooved edges.

Strap: special composite strap; attached via titanium screws to the case; matching buckle individually engraved with model number.

SPLIT SECONDS CHRONOGRAPH   RM 004-V2

Movement: mechanical manual-winding caliber RM 004-V2; carbon nanofiber baseplate; approx. 60-hour power reserve; titanium column wheel, gear wheels and lever; split seconds mechanism with improved and patented functions; fast rotating barrel; function indicator; variable inertia balance with overcoil hairspring; newly designed 3-tiered titanium bridge with inline lever escapement; spline screws in grade-5 titanium for the bridges and case; winding barrel and third pinion teeth with central involute profile.

Functions: hours, minutes, seconds, split seconds; chronograph minute counter; power-reserve indicator; torque indicator; function indicator.

Case: 18K red-gold anatomically curved tripartite case; 48x39x15.05mm; tripartite case assembled with 20 spline screws in grade-5 titanium; sapphire crystal front and back with double-sided antiglare coating; water resistant to 50 meters.

Dial: sapphire with double-sided antiglare treatment; protected with 8 silicon braces in grooved edges.

Strap: leather or crocodile; attached via titanium screws to the case; with matching buckle individually engraved with model number.

Also available: in titanium, 18K white gold or platinum.

SPLIT SECONDS CHRONOGRAPH   RM 004-V2 ALL GREY

Movement: mechanical manual-winding movement; RM 004-V2 "gray" caliber with gray PVD-coated carbon nanofiber baseplate; approx. 60-hour power reserve; titanium column wheel, gear wheels and lever; split seconds mechanism with improved and patented functions; fast rotating barrel; function indicator; variable inertia balance with overcoil; newly designed three tired titanium bridge with inline lever escapement; spline screws in grade-5 titanium for the bridges and case; winding barrel and third pinion teeth with central involute profile.

Functions: hours, minutes, seconds, split seconds, chronograph minute counter, power reserve indicator, torque indicator, function indicator.

Case: microblasted titanium anatomically curved tripartite case 48x39x15.05mm; assembled with 20 spline screws in grade-5 titanium; sapphire crystal front and back with double-sided antiglare coating; water resistant to 50 meters.

Dial: in sapphire with doubled-sided antiglare treatment; protected with 8 silicon braces in grooved edges.

Strap: special composite strap; attached via titanium screws to the case; matching buckle individually engraved with model number.

AUTOMATIC (TITANIUM VERSION)   RM 007

Movement: mechanical self-winding caliber RM 007; approx. 38-hour power reserve; rotor fitted with a patented auto-reverse system integrated into the rotor ball bearing; rotor segment in sandblasted 18K gold with weight comprising more than 100 18K gold micro-balls within a transparent, PVD-coated container; grade-5 titanium screws; date aperture at 6 with sapphire crystal calendar disc treated with double-sided antiglare coating; crown with double-seal O-ring and collar in Alcryn; teeth with central involute profile.

Functions: hours, minutes; date.

Case: titanium tripartite case anatomically curved; 45x31x10.09mm; assembled with 12 spline screws in grade-5 titanium; sapphire crystal front and back with double-sided antiglare coating; water resistant to 50 meters.

Strap: leather, crocodile and various fabrics; attached via titanium screws to the case; with matching buckle individually engraved with model number.

AUTOMATIC (W/DIAMOND MARKERS)   RM 007

Movement: mechanical self-winding caliber RM 007; approx. 38-hour power reserve; rotor fitted with a patented auto-reverse system integrated into the rotor ball bearing; rotor segment in 18K sandblasted gold with weight comprising more than 100 18K gold micro-balls within a transparent, PVD-coated container; grade-5 titanium screws; date aperture at 6 with sapphire crystal calendar disk treated with double-sided antiglare coating; crown with double-seal O-ring and collar in Alcryn; teeth with central involute profile.

Functions: hours, minutes; date.

Case: 18K red-gold tripartite case; anatomically curved; 45x31x10.09mm; assembled with 12 spline screws in grade-5 titanium; sapphire crystal front and back with double-sided antiglare coating; water resistant to 50 meters.

Strap: leather, crocodile or various fabrics; attached via titanium screws to the case; with matching buckle individually engraved with model number.

AUTOMATIC (DIAMOND VERSION) RM 007

Movement: mechanical self-winding caliber RM 007; approx. 38-hour power reserve; rotor fitted with a patented auto-reverse system integrated into the rotor ball bearing; rotor segment in 18K sandblasted gold with weight comprising more than 100 18K gold micro-balls within a transparent, PVD-coated container; grade-5 titanium screws; date aperture at 6 with sapphire crystal calendar disc treated with double-sided antiglare coating; crown with double-seal O-ring and collar in Alcryn; teeth with central involute profile.

Functions: hours, minutes; date.

Case: 18K white-gold, anatomically curved tripartite case; 45x31x10.09mm; set with white diamonds on bezel and sides with black diamonds on the case columns; assembled with 12 spline screws in grade-5 titanium; sapphire crystal front and back with double-sided antiglare coating; water resistant to 50 meters.

Strap: crocodile or various fabrics; attached via titanium screws to the case; with matching buckle individually engraved with model number or with deployant.

TOURBILLON SPLIT SECONDS CHRONOGRAPH RM 008

Movement: mechanical manual-winding tourbillon caliber RM 008; titanium baseplate; approx. 60-hour power reserve; titanium column wheel, gear wheels and lever; split seconds mechanism with improved and patented functions; fast rotating barrel; function indicator; variable inertia balance with overcoil hairspring; newly designed inline lever escapement; spline screws in grade-5 titanium for the bridges and case; winding barrel and third pinion teeth with central involute profile.

Functions: hours, minutes, seconds, split seconds; chronograph minute counter; power-reserve indicator; torque indicator; function indicator.

Case: 18K red-gold anatomically curved tripartite case; 48x39x15.05mm; tripartite case assembled with 20 spline screws in grade-5 titanium; sapphire crystal front and back with double-sided antiglare coating; water resistant to 50 meters.

Dial: sapphire with double-sided antiglare treatment; protected with 8 silicon braces in grooved edges.

Strap: leather or crocodile; attached via titanium screws to case; with matching buckle individually engraved with model number.

Also available: in titanium, 18K white gold or platinum.

TOURBILLON SPLIT SECONDS CHRONOGRAPH RM 008-V2 ALL GREY

Movement: mechanical manual-winding "gray" tourbillon caliber RM 008; gray PVD-coated carbon nanofiber baseplate; approx. 60-hour power reserve; titanium column wheel, gear wheels and lever; split seconds mechanism with improved and patented functions; fast rotating barrel; function indicator; variable inertia balance with overcoil; inline lever escapement; spline screws in grade-5 titanium for the bridges and case; winding barrel and third pinion teeth with central involute profile.

Functions: hours, minutes, seconds, split seconds, chronograph minute counter, power reserve indicator, torque indicator, function indicator.

Case: microblasted titanium anatomically curved tripartite case 48x39x15.05mm; assembled with 20 spline screws in grade-5 titanium; sapphire crystal front and back with double-sided antiglare coating; water resistant to 50 meters.

Dial: in sapphire with doubled sided antiglare treatment; protected with 8 silicon braces in grooved edges.

Strap: special composite strap; attached via titanium screws to the case; matching buckle individually engraved with model number.

AUTOMATIC RM 010

Movement: mechanical self-winding skeletonized caliber RM 005-S; approx. 55-hour power reserve; rotor with variable geometry via white-gold wings adjustable to 6 positions; ceramic rotor ball bearings; titanium PVD-coated baseplate, bridges and balance cock; crown in grade-5 sandblasted titanium with double-seal O-ring and collar in Alcryn; double-winding barrel; grade-5 titanium spline screws for movement and case.

Functions: hours, minutes, seconds; date.

Case: 18K red-gold anatomically curved tripartite case; 48x39.3x13.84mm; assembled with 12 spline screws in grade-5 titanium; sapphire crystal front and back with double-sided antiglare coating; water resistant to 100 meters.

Dial: sapphire with double-sided antiglare treatment; protected with 8 silicon braces in grooved edges.

Strap: leather or crocodile; attached via titanium screws to the case; with matching buckle in titanium, 18K red or white gold or platinum; individually engraved with model number.

Also available: in titanium, 18K white gold or platinum.

AUTOMATIC FLYBACK CHRONOGRAPH   RM 011 FELIPE MASSA

Movement: mechanical with skeletonized self-winding chronograph caliber RM 011; approx. 55-hour power reserve; rotor with variable geometry via white-gold wings adjustable to 6 positions; ceramic rotor ball bearings; titanium PVD-coated baseplate, bridges and balance cock; large date; double-winding barrel; titanium column wheel, gear wheels and lever; split seconds mechanism with improved and patented functions; crown in grade-5 sandblasted titanium with double-seal O-ring and collar in Alcryn; grade-5 titanium spline screws for movement and case.

Functions: hours, minutes, seconds; flyback chronograph; 60-minute countdown timer; 12-hour totalizer; large date; month.

Case: titanium central case ring, anatomically curved tripartite case; 50x42.5x15.85mm; 18K white-gold bezel; assembled with 12 spline screws in grade-5 titanium; sapphire crystal front and back with double-sided antiglare coating; water resistant to 100 meters.

Dial: sapphire with double-sided antiglare treatment; protected with 8 silicon braces in grooved edges.

Strap: leather or crocodile; attached via titanium screws to the case; with matching buckle individually engraved with model number.

Also available: with 18K red-gold front and back bezel or full titanium.

AUTOMATIC FLYBACK CHRONOGRAPH   RM 011 LE MANS CLASSIC

Movement: mechanical with skeletonized self-winding chronograph caliber RM 011; approx. 55-hour power reserve; rotor with variable geometry via white-gold wings adjustable to 6 positions; ceramic rotor ball bearings; titanium PVD-coated baseplate, bridges and balance cock; large date; double-winding barrel; titanium column wheel, gear wheels and lever; split seconds mechanism with improved and patented functions; crown in grade-5 sandblasted titanium with double-seal O-ring and collar in Alcryn; grade-5 titanium spline screws for movement and case.

Functions: hours, minutes, seconds; flyback chronograph; 60-minute countdown timer; 12-hour totalizer; large date; month.

Case: 18K red-gold central case ring, anatomically curved tripartite case; 50x42.5x15.85mm; green interior bezel; assembled with 12 spline screws in grade-5 titanium; sapphire crystal front and back with double-sided antiglare coating; water resistant to 100 meters.

Dial: sapphire with double-sided antiglare treatment; protected with 8 silicon braces in grooved edges.

Strap: leather or crocodile; attached via titanium screws to the case; with matching buckle individually engraved with model number.

Note: limited to 150 pieces in 18K red gold.

AUTOMATIC FLYBACK CHRONOGRAPH   RM 011 LE MANS CLASSIC

Movement: mechanical with skeletonized self-winding chronograph caliber RM 011; approx. 55-hour power reserve; rotor with variable geometry via white-gold wings adjustable to 6 positions; ceramic rotor ball bearings; titanium PVD-coated baseplate, bridges and balance cock; large date; double-winding barrel; titanium column wheel, gear wheels and lever; split seconds mechanism with improved and patented functions; crown in grade-5 sandblasted titanium with double-seal O-ring and collar in Alcryn; grade-5 titanium spline screws for movement and case.

Functions: hours, minutes, seconds; flyback chronograph; 60-minute countdown timer; 12-hour totalizer; large date; month.

Case: titanium central case ring, anatomically curved tripartite case; 50x42.5x15.85mm; green interior bezel; assembled with 12 spline screws in grade-5 titanium; sapphire crystal front and back with double-sided antiglare coating; water resistant to 100 meters.

Dial: sapphire with double-sided antiglare treatment; protected with 8 silicon braces in grooved edges.

Strap: leather or crocodile; attached via titanium screws to the case; with matching buckle individually engraved with model number.

Note: limited to 150 pieces in titanium.

TOURBILLON   RM 014 PERINI NAVI CUP

Movement: mechanical manual-winding marine tourbillon caliber RM 014; carbon nanofiber baseplate; nautical pattern-finished case, screws and crown; approx. 70-hour power reserve; variable inertia balance with Breguet-Phillips spiral; fast rotating barrel; function selector gearbox with indicator; ceramic tourbillon endstone; central bridge in rigidified INOX; spline screws in grade-5 titanium for the bridges and case; winding barrel and third pinion teeth with central involute profile; jewels set in white-gold chatons.

Functions: hours, minutes; power-reserve indicator; torque indicator; function indicator.

Case: platinum, anatomically curved tripartite case; 45x38.9x11.85mm; assembled with 12 spline screws in grade-5 titanium; sapphire crystal front and back with double-sided antiglare coating; water resistant to 50 meters.

Dial: sapphire with double-sided antiglare treatment; protected with 8 silicon braces in grooved edges.

Strap: leather or crocodile; attached via titanium screws to the case; with matching buckle in titanium, 18K red or white gold or platinum; individually engraved with model number.

Also available: 18K red or white gold.

TOURBILLON   RM 015 PERINI NAVI CUP

Movement: mechanical manual-winding marine tourbillon caliber RM 015; carbon nanofiber baseplate; nautical pattern-finished case, screws and crown; approx. 70-hour power reserve; variable inertia balance with overcoil hairspring; fast rotating barrel; function selector gearbox with indicator; ceramic tourbillon endstone; central bridge in rigidified INOX; spline screws in grade-5 titanium for the bridges and case; winding barrel and third pinion teeth with central involute profile; jewels set in white-gold chatons.

Functions: hours, minutes; power-reserve indicator; torque indicator; second time zone; function indicator.
Case: platinum, anatomically curved tripartite case; 45x38.9x11.85mm; assembled with 12 spline screws in grade-5 titanium; sapphire crystal front and back with double-sided antiglare coating; water resistant to 50 meters.
Dial: sapphire with double-sided antiglare treatment; protected with 8 silicon braces in grooved edges.
Strap: leather or crocodile; attached via titanium screws to the case; with matching buckle in titanium, 18K red or white gold or platinum; individually engraved with model number.
Also available: 18K red or white gold.

AUTOMATIC   RM 016

Movement: mechanical self-winding skeletonized RM 005-S caliber; approx. 55-hour power reserve; rotor with variable geometry via white-gold wings adjustable to 6 positions; ceramic rotor ball bearings; titanium PVD-coated baseplate, bridges and balance cock; crown in grade-5 sandblasted titanium with double-seal O-ring and collar in Alcryn; double-winding barrel; grade-5 titanium spline screws for movement and case.

Functions: hours, minutes, seconds; date.
Case: 18K red-gold anatomically curved tripartite case; 49.8x38x8.25mm; assembled with 12 spline screws in grade-5 titanium; sapphire crystal front and back with double-sided antiglare coating; water resistant to 50 meters.
Dial: sapphire with double-sided antiglare treatment; protected with 8 silicon braces in grooved edges.
Strap: leather or crocodile; attached via titanium screws to the case; with matching buckle in 18K red gold; individually engraved with model number.
Also available: in titanium, 18K white gold or platinum with matching buckle.

TOURBILLON   RM 018 HOMMAGE A BOUCHERON

Movement: mechanical manual-winding tourbillon RM 018 caliber; two-layered synthetic sapphire Al$_2$O$_3$ baseplate construction; wheels created from precious and semi-precious stones; approx. 48-hour power reserve; variable inertia balance with overcoil hairspring; fast rotating barrel; ceramic tourbillon endstone; spline screws in grade-5 titanium for the bridges and case; winding barrel and third pinion teeth with central involute profile; jewels set in white-gold chatons.

Functions: hours, minutes.
Case: 18K white gold; 48x39.30x13.84mm; assembled with 12 spline screws in grade-5 titanium; sapphire crystal front and back with double-sided antiglare coating; water resistant to 50 meters.
Dial: sapphire with double-sided antiglare treatment; protected with 8 silicon braces in grooved edges.
Strap: crocodile; attached via titanium screws to the case; matching buckle individually engraved with model number.
Note: limited to 30 pieces worldwide in 18K white gold.

TOURBILLON LADIES' WATCH   RM 019 CELTIC KNOT

Movement: mechanical manual-winding tourbillon RM 019 caliber; black onyx baseplate; approx. 48-hour power reserve; variable inertia balance with overcoil hairspring; fast rotating barrel; ceramic tourbillon endstone; spline screws in grade-5 titanium for the bridges and case; winding barrel and third pinion teeth with central involute profile; je wels set in white-gold chatons.

Functions: hours, minutes; power-reserve indicator.
Case: 18K white gold; 45x38.30x12.15mm; assembled with 12 spline screws in grade-5 titanium; sapphire crystal front and back with double-sided antiglare coating; water resistant to 50 meters.
Dial: sapphire with double-sided antiglare treatment; protected with 8 silicon braces in grooved edges.
Strap: leather or crocodile; attached via titanium screws to the case; matching buckle individually engraved with model number.
Also available: in 18K red gold.

TOURBILLON POCKET WATCH   RM 020

Movement: mechanical manual-winding tourbillon RM 020 caliber; carbon nanofiber baseplate; approx. 10-day power reserve via two winding barrels; variable inertia balance with overcoil hairspring; fast rotating barrel; function selector gearbox with indicator; ceramic tourbillon endstone; central bridge in rigidified ARCAP; spline screws in grade-5 titanium for the bridges and case; winding barrel and third pinion teeth with central involute profile; jewels set in white-gold chatons.

Functions: hours, minutes; power-reserve indicator; torque indicator; function indicator.

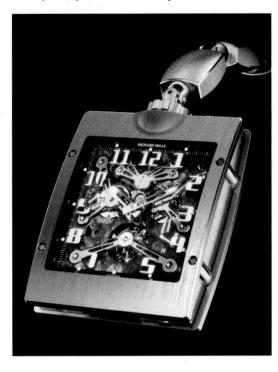

Case: titanium central case ring with both front and back bezels in titanium; 62x52x15.60mm; assembled with 12 spline screws in grade-5 titanium; sapphire crystal front and back with double-sided antiglare coating; water resistant to 50 meters.

Dial: sapphire with double-sided antiglare treatment; protected with 8 silicon braces in grooved edges.

Note: supplied with specially designed titanium chain with quick release mechanism.

Also available: with front and back bezels in either 18K red or white gold, or platinum.

TOURBILLON   RM 021 AERODYNE

Movement: mechanical manual-winding tourbillon RM 021 caliber; movement baseplate of titanium and honeycombed orthorhombic titanium aluminide with carbon nanofiber; approx. 70-hour power reserve; variable inertia balance with overcoil hairspring; fast rotating barrel; function selector gearbox with indicator; ceramic tourbillon endstone; central bridge in rigidified ARCAP; spline screws in grade-5 titanium for the bridges and case; winding barrel and third pinion teeth with central involute profile; jewels set in white-gold chatons.

Functions: hours, minutes; power-reserve indicator; torque indicator; function indicator.

Case: 18K white-gold tripartite case; anatomically curved; 48x39.3x13.84mm; assembled with 12 spline screws in grade-5 titanium; sapphire crystal front and back with double-sided antiglare coating; water resistant to 50 meters.

Dial: sapphire with double-sided antiglare treatment; protected with 8 silicon braces in grooved edges.

Strap: leather or crocodile attached via titanium screws to the case; with matching buckle individually engraved with model number.

Also available: in titanium and 18K red gold.

AUTOMATIC   RM 023

Movement: mechanical automatic RM 021 caliber; movement baseplate of titanium and honeycombed orthorhombic titanium aluminide with carbon nanofiber; approx. 55-hour power reserve; variable inertia balance with overcoil hairspring; fast rotating barrel; function selector gearbox with indicator; ceramic tourbillon endstone; central bridge in rigidified ARCAP; spline screws in grade-5 titanium for the bridges and case; winding barrel and third pinion teeth with central involute profile; jewels set in white-gold chatons.

Functions: hours, minutes; power-reserve indicator; torque indicator; function indicator.

Case: 18K white-gold anatomically curved tripartite case; 48x39.3x13.84mm; assembled with 12 spline screws in grade-5 titanium; sapphire crystal front and back with double-sided antiglare coating; water resistant to 50 meters.

Dial: sapphire with double-sided antiglare treatment; protected with 8 silicon braces in grooved edges.

Strap: leather or crocodile; attached via titanium screws to the case; with matching buckle individually engraved with model number.

Also available: in titanium and 18K red gold.

TOURBILLON CHRONOGRAPH   RM 025 DIVER'S WATCH

Movement: mechanical manual-winding RM 025 caliber; carbon nanofiber baseplate; approx. 70-hour power reserve; titanium column wheel; gear wheels and lever; chronograph mechanism with improved and patented functions; fast rotating barrel; variable inertia balance with overcoil hairspring; newly designed inline lever escapement; spline screws in grade-5 titanium for the bridges and case; screwed crown; winding barrel and third pinion teeth central involute profile.

Functions: hours, minutes, seconds; chronograph minute counter; power-reserve indicator; torque indicator; function indicator.

Case: full titanium, anatomically curved tripartite case; 18K red-gold lugs; 50.70x19.20mm; assembled with 20 torque screws in grade-5 titanium; unidirectionally turning timing bezel; screwed crown; sapphire crystal front and back with double-sided antiglare coating; water resistant to 300 meters according to ISO 6425.

Dial: sapphire with double-sided antiglare treatment protected with silicon braces in grooved edges.

Strap: RICHARD MILLE designed rubber strap; fastened to lugs with screws; matching buckle.

Also available: secondary front bezel and back bezel in 18K red or white gold.

AUTOMATIC (ARCHIVE)   REF. RM 005

Movement: mechanical self-winding caliber RM 005; approx. 55-hour power reserve; rotor with variable geometry via white-gold wings adjustable to 6 positions; ceramic rotor ball bearings; titanium PVD-coated baseplate, bridges and balance cock; crown in grade-5 sandblasted titanium with double-seal O-ring and collar in Alcryn; double winding barrel; grade-5 titanium spline screws for movement and case.

Functions: hours, minutes, seconds; date.
Case: titanium, anatomically curved three-piece case; 45x37.8mm, thickness: 11.45mm; assembled with 12 spline screws in grade-5 titanium; sapphire crystal front and back with double-sided antiglare coating; water resistant to 100 meters.
Dial: sapphire with double-sided antiglare treatment; protected with 8 silicon braces in grooved edges.
Strap: crocodile leather; attached via titanium screws to the case; matching buckle individually engraved with model number.
Note: no longer in collection.

AUTOMATIC (ARCHIVE)   RM 005-FM (TITANIUM)

Movement: mechanical self-winding caliber RM 005; yellow interior flange with green luminous area on hour and minute hands; approx. 55-hour power reserve; rotor with variable geometry by means of 18K white-gold wings adjustable to 6 positions; rotor with ceramic ball bearings; ribbed, titanium PVD-coated baseplate, bridges and balance cock; crown in grade-5 sandblasted titanium with double-seal O-ring and collar in Alcryn; double-winding barrel; grade-5 titanium spline screws for movement and case.

Functions: hours, minutes, seconds; date.
Case: titanium, anatomically curved tripartite case; 45x37.8x11.45mm; assembled with 12 spline screws in grade-5 titanium; sapphire crystal front and back with double-sided antiglare coating; water resistant to 100 meters.
Dial: sapphire with double-sided antiglare treatment; protected with 8 silicon braces in grooved edges.
Strap: special strap; buckle individually engraved with model number.
Note: sold out limited edition of 300 pieces in microblasted titanium.

AUTOMATIC (ARCHIVE)   RM 005-FM (PLATINUM)

Movement: mechanical caliber self-winding caliber RM 005; approx. 55-hour power reserve; rotor with variable geometry by means of 18K white-gold wings adjustable to 6 positions; rotor with ceramic ball bearings; ribbed, titanium PVD-coated baseplate, bridges and balance cock; crown in grade-5 sandblasted titanium with double-seal O-ring and collar in Alcryn; double-winding barrel; grade-5 titanium spline screws for movement and case.

Functions: hours, minutes, seconds; date.
Case: platinum, anatomically curved tripartite case; 45x37.8x11.45mm; assembled with 12 spline screws in grade-5 titanium; sapphire crystal front and back with double-sided antiglare coating; water resistant to 100 meters.
Dial: sapphire with double-sided antiglare treatment; protected with 8 silicon braces in grooved edges; yellow minute ring with blue interior flange.
Strap: special strap; buckle individually engraved with model number.
Note: sold out limited edition of 50 pieces.

TOURBILLON (ARCHIVE)   REF. RM 006

Movement: mechanical manual-winding tourbillon caliber RM 006; approx. 48-hour power reserve; baseplate made of carbon nanofiber; barrel and third wheel pinion with corrected involute tooth profile; spline screws in grade-5 titanium for the bridges and case; hand-polished anglage; lapped and polished ends, burnished pivots; 19 jewels set in beryllium copper alloy chatons; entire movement is mounted entirely on the dial side of the carbon nanofiber baseplate.

Functions: hours and minutes.
Case: titanium; anatomically curved three-piece case; 45x37.8mm, thickness: 12.05mm; assembled with 12 spline screws in grade-5 titanium; sapphire crystal front and back with double-sided antiglare treatment; water resistant to 50 meters.
Dial: sapphire with double-sided antiglare treatment; protected with 8 silicon braces in grooved edges inserted in the upper and lower grooves.
Strap: special composite strap; buckle engraved with model number.
Note: sold out limited edition of 20 pieces.

TOURBILLON (ARCHIVE) — RM 009

Movement: mechanical manual-winding skeletonized tourbillon caliber RM 009; baseplate of aluminum-lithium alloy; approx. 48-hour power reserve; variable inertia balance with overcoil hairspring; fast rotating barrel; ceramic tourbillon endstone; spline screws in grade-5 titanium for the bridges and case; winding barrel and third pinion teeth with central involute profile; jewels set in white-gold chatons; lightest tourbillon wristwatch ever made (under 30 grams without strap).
Functions: hours, minutes.
Case: ALUSIC, anatomically curved tripartite case; 45x37.8x12.65mm; tripartite case made of ALUSIC (Aluminum AS7G0Silicium-Carbon); assembled with 12 spline screws in grade-5 titanium; sapphire crystal front and back with double-sided antiglare coating; water resistant to 50 meters.
Dial: sapphire with double-sided antiglare treatment; protected with 8 silicon braces in grooved edges.
Strap: special composite, black satin finish strap; engraved with model number.
Note: sold out limited edition of 25 pieces in ALUSIC.

TOURBILLON (ARCHIVE) — RM 012

Movement: mechanical manual-winding tourbillon RM 012 caliber; world's first tubular network construction functioning as a baseplate; floating bridges; approx. 48-hour power reserve; variable inertia balance with overcoil; fast rotating barrel; ceramic tourbillon endstone; spline screws in grade-5 titanium for the bridges and case; winding barrel and third pinion teeth with central involute profile; jewels set in white-gold chatons.
Functions: hours, minutes.
Case: platinum, anatomically curved tripartite case; 45x37.8x12.65mm; assembled with 12 spline screws in grade-5 titanium; sapphire crystal front and back with double-sided antiglare coating; water resistant to 50 meters.
Dial: sapphire with double-sided antiglare treatment; protected with 8 silicon braces in grooved edges.
Strap: special composite strap; model number engraved on buckle.
Note: sold out limited edition of 30 pieces in platinum.

MILLE-STARCK ONLY WATCH 2005 (ARCHIVE)

Movement: mechanical self-winding caliber RM 005; approx. 55-hour power reserve; rotor with variable geometry via white-gold wings adjustable to 6 positions; ceramic rotor ball bearings; titanium PVD-coated baseplate, bridges and balance cock; crown in grade-5 sandblasted titanium with double-seal O-ring and collar in Alcryn; double-winding barrel; grade-5 titanium spline screws for movement and case.
Functions: hours, minutes, seconds; date.
Case: microblasted titanium; 53.85x35mm (without crown), thickness: 11.4mm; assemble with 16 "headless" spline screws; sapphire crystal front and back with double-sided antiglare coating; water resistant to 50 meters.
Baseplate/movement cover: smoked sapphire crystal.
Strap: leather; attached via an integrated case attachment system.
Note: edition of 1, sold at auction.

MILLE-STARCK ONLY WATCH 2007 (ARCHIVE)

Movement: mechanical with skeletonized self-winding flyback chronograph caliber RM 011; approx. 55-hour power reserve; rotor with variable geometry via white gold wings adjustable to six positions; ceramic rotor ball bearings; titanium PVD-coated baseplate, bridges and balance cock; oversized date; double winding barrel; titanium column wheel, gear wheels and lever; split seconds mechanism with improved and patented functions; crown in grade-5 sandblasted titanium with double-seal O-ring and collar in Alcryn; grade-5 titanium spline screws for movement, case and intregral bracelet.
Functions: hours, minutes, seconds, chronograph (countdown) minute counter, flyback chronograph, oversize date, month.
Case: fully integrated anatomically curved titanium case and bracelet; water resistant to 50 meters.
Dial: sapphire with double-sided antiglare treatment; protected with 8 silicon braces in grooved edges.
Note: edition of 1, sold at auction.

ROLEX
Passion Meets Compassion

Founded in 1905 by Hans Wilsdorf, Rolex experienced a meteoric rise on its way to becoming the most recognized name in luxury watchmaking. A true icon of horology, the company's list of innovations encompasses the first waterproof case; the first wrist-watch with a date on the dial; and the first wristwatch to meet the rigid requirements for chronometer certification.

Beyond the Geneva-based company's myriad technical achievements, Rolex counts philanthropy among its foremost pursuits outside the sphere of watchmaking. The legacy of giving back dates to 1944 when Wilsdorf created the Hans Wilsdorf Foundation to fund charitable endeavors.

In more recent times, Rolex launched Awards for Enterprise, a prestigious grant program that funds projects to improve the human condition. Since its launch in 1976, the program has supported efforts in the areas of science and medicine; technology and innovation; exploration and discovery; the environment; and cultural heritage. To date, Rolex has honored more than 100 projects, ranging from the protection of rare and endangered species, to the introduction of useful technology in isolated areas.

A second program—Rolex Mentor and Protégé Arts Initiative—followed in 2002. The company called upon its unique relationships with many of the world's greatest living artists to create a mentoring program like no other. Through the program, the company fosters artistic excellence across generations by pairing emerging artists with masters for yearlong collaborations.

The Rolex Awards and Rolex Arts Initiative mesh like the brand's watch gears, promoting Rolex's vision of ingenuity and excellence by supporting it in others.

THIS PAGE
LEFT (*from left*) The 2008 Rolex Awards for Enterprise Laureates: Tim Bauer, Elsa Zaldívar, Talal Akasheh, Andrew McGonigle and Andrew Muir.

CENTER Talal Akasheh of Jordan was named a 2008 Laureate for creating a geo-archaeological information system (GIS) to ensure and manage the conservation of the endangered rock-carved monuments located in Petra, Jordan.

RIGHT Andrew McGonigle of the United Kingdom, pictured here on Vulcano Island Italy, was selected as one of the 2008 Laureates for developing a small-scale, remote-controlled helicopter that measures volcanic gas emissions and helps predict eruptions.

FACING PAGE
Waterproof to 3,900 meters, Oyster Perpetual Sea-Dweller DEEPSEA is outfitted with a helium valve that allows the watch to adjust to the pressure experienced at extreme depths.

© ROLEX AWARDS/MARC LATZEL
© ROLEX AWARDS/MARC LATZEL

The Rolex Awards
and Rolex Arts
Initiative mesh
like the brand's
watch gears,
promoting Rolex's
vision of ingenuity
and excellence
by supporting it
in others.

Rolex's reputation as a pioneer in waterproof watchcases began in 1926 when Wilsdorf unveiled the company's revolutionary Oyster case. Over the years, the company has earned a reputation for durability and reliability at great depths with diving tools such as the Submariner and Sea-Dweller.

In 1960, Rolex went deeper than any other watch with Deep Sea Special, a prototype that accompanied the U.S. Navy bathyscaphe Trieste 10,916 meters underwater to the bottom of the Mariana Trench; the deepest location on the Earth's surface.

To honor the success of Deep Sea Special's extreme expedition Rolex now offers Oyster Perpetual Sea-Dweller DEEPSEA, a diver's watch waterproof to 3,900 meters. The case design features Rolex's patented "Ringlock" system, which allows the case to withstand the depth's intense pressure.

The company leaves the sea behind for terra firma with a newly released version of Rolex's flagship Day-Date model. Introduced in 1956, the original was the first watch to display the day of the week spelled out in full. Day-Date II, the watch's sequel, was unveiled last year. In keeping with contemporary tastes, the new model uses a 41mm diameter case, which is 5mm larger that the diameter of the original.

Day-Date II is brought to life by a caliber developed and manufactured exclusively by Rolex. The company's watchmakers equip the movement with patented technology—Paraflex shock absorbers and a Parachrom hairspring—that contributes to the watch's chronometer-certified precision.

After more than a century of acclaim for its philanthropy and groundbreaking timepieces, Rolex remains firmly ensconced in the pantheon of watchmakers thanks to its unyielding pursuit of perfection.

Contemporary savoir-faire personified, Rolex's new Day-Date II features a larger case than the original model along with new dial options. Chronometer-certified, the watch's movement is truly a precision timekeeping instrument

ROMAIN JEROME
Going Deep

A few years after Romain Jerome made its debut at BaselWorld, the avant-garde firm is quickly redefining the boundaries of extreme watchmaking with a growing collection of imaginative timepieces made with steel salvaged from the Titanic wreckage and the shipyard where it was built.

A close-up view spotlights the intricacies of the extraordinary transverse tourbillon movement in Romain Jerome's Cabestan.

The latest additions to Romain Jerome's Made with Parts of the Titanic collection—the Cabestan—is the result of a collaboration between the brand's CEO Yvan Arpa and visionary watch designer Jean-François Ruchonnet.

Ruchonnet is responsible for creating the unusual architecture of the watch's movement, a transverse tourbillon with a chain fusee that displays the hours, minutes, seconds and 72-hour power reserve. Instead of using the crown to wind the watch, the Cabestan uses a removable hand-crank that is stored in the folding buckle. Three thermoformed sapphire crystals protect the watch, which measures 46mm long, 36mm wide, and 15mm thick.

The collection includes six unique pieces, one named for each for the Earth's five oceans and the other for the coordinates of where the Titanic was discovered—41°43' 55'' N and 49°56' 45'' W. Each watch offers a different color scheme: Indian Ocean, copper; Antarctic Ocean, vermeil; Pacific Ocean, bronze; Atlantic Ocean, silver; Arctic Ocean, charcoal gray; and 41°43' 55'' N and 49°56' 45'' W, black.

All six of these one-of-a-kind watches contain authentic steel from the shipwreck and are covered with a coat of rust, the signature design flourish of Romain Jerome's Made with Parts of the Titanic collection.

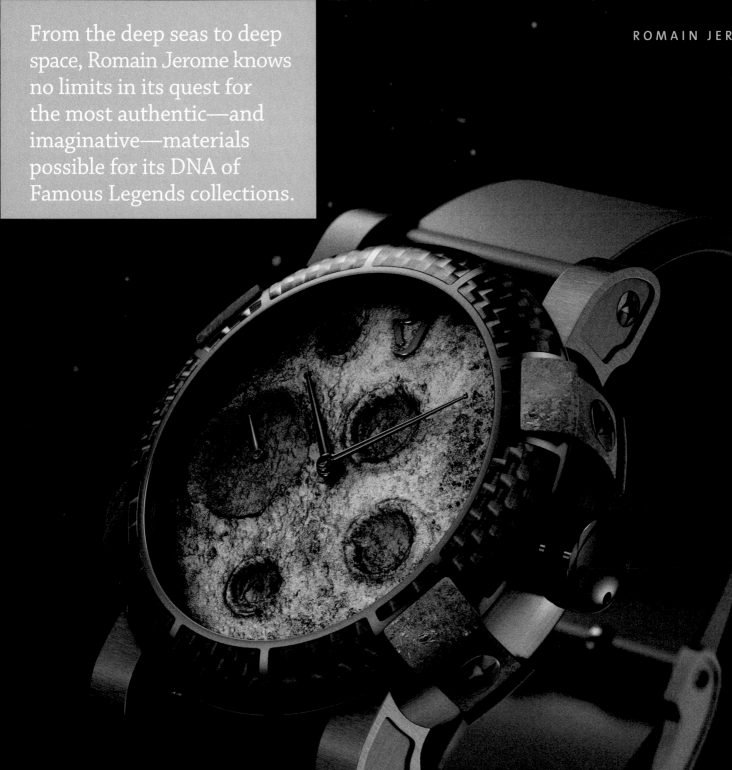

From the deep seas to deep space, Romain Jerome knows no limits in its quest for the most authentic—and imaginative—materials possible for its DNA of Famous Legends collections.

Romain Jerome gives the phrase "timeless design" a whole new meaning with the world premiere of Day & Night, a timepiece that, incredibly, does not display the time at all. Instead, this most unusual watch indicates the movement from day to night with the clever use of two tourbillon mechanisms. The "day" tourbillon operates for 12 hours, before stopping and giving way to the "night" tourbillion, which runs for the remaining 12 hours. According to the watchmaker, the effect is meant to symbolize the opposing worlds in which we live—public and private, work and play.

"The Day & Night has a strong emotional value. History is, quite literally, part of its composition," Arpa says. "It's presented to those of privilege as a trophy of history. A true testimony that life is ongoing and that it should be celebrated."

The Day & Night contains the first Romain Jerome movement, which was created by the innovative caliber maker, BNB Concept. The design represents a world-first in watchmaking thanks to the pioneering differential used to transfer power from one tourbillon to the other.

The technology behind this anti-watch adds to the visual mystique that defines the Day & Night. The stainless steel and titanium case is fitted with a bezel made from stabilized oxidized steel from the Titanic. The dial is coated with black carbon created from coal recovered from the shipwrecked luxury liner, giving it an unforgettable dark patina. Romain Jerome will produce Day & Night in a limited edition of nine pieces.

Splitting the day in half, the Day & Night's sun-shaped tourbillon runs for 12 hours during the day, before stopping and switching to the moon-shaped mechanism for 12 hours of night.

TOP LEFT The dial of the T-oxy Concept is coated with coal dust recovered from the wreckage of the ill-fated luxury liner.

BOTTOM LEFT T-oxy III Chronograph is made in a limited edition of 2012, a number that represents the year that will mark the 100th anniversary of the Titanic's maiden voyage.

TOP RIGHT Romain Jerome will limit production of the Ultimate Rust T-oxy IV Tourbillon to nine pieces.

From a watch that does not tell time to a watch that cannot be worn, the T-oxy Concept is a wild new addition to Romain Jerome's DNA of Famous Legends collection. The watch features a case made of steel that has not been stabilized and will continue to oxidize and deteriorate if it is removed from the argon-gas filled jar in which it is sold.

The T-oxy Concept's RJ Caliber C22RJ51 Concepto by Jacquet is housed in a 46mm case comprised of a mixture of steel recovered from the Titanic—located more than 12,500 feet under the sea—and steel supplied by the Harland & Wolff shipyard in Belfast, where the Titanic was built nearly a century ago.

Romain Jerome adds the Ultimate Rust T-oxy IV Tourbillon to its Made with Parts of the Titanic collection. Like the other wristwatches in the collection, it features an oxidized steel bezel. For this version, the watchmaker allowed the bezel to decay until its structural integrity was nearly compromised; this natural process of decomposition imbues each bezel with a truly individual mien.

Its multi-level dial features raised Roman numerals on top of a carbon fiber plate as well as hour and minute hands that resemble anchors. The tourbillon mechanism at 6:00 is slightly raised, adding another layer of dimension to the watch's impressive design.

A new movement developed by Concepto for Romain Jerome powers the T-oxy III Chronograph. Push buttons on the side of the 50mm case control the chronograph counters, which are made to look like gauges used for steam engines. The crystal caseback offers a view of the movement's anchor-shaped oscillating weight.

Having witnessed five years of amazing watch after amazing watch from Romain Jerome, one question remains: just how will this extreme watchmaker top itself in 2010?

SALVATORE FERRAGAMO
High-Tech Fashion

Salvatore Ferragamo, the revered Florence-based fashion house, wins praise around the world for bringing together luxury and creativity with its visionary designs. To celebrate its 80th anniversary last year, the company unveiled several new additions to its burgeoning line of classic and contemporary timepieces.

Launched in 2007, Salvatore Ferragamo's partnership with Timex Group Luxury Watches has already generated three collections for men and three more for women. Each is defined by the same principles that inspire the company's fine fashions—use of superior materials, traditional craftsmanship, detailed finishing, exclusivity, and comfort.

The F-80 GMT, named in honor of Salvatore Ferragamo's recent milestone, is a handsome dual time-zone watch that will adorn the wrist of elegant travelers. The linear style reflects the influence of Italian architecture's well-proportioned design, while the 44mm brushed titanium case and ceramic accents embody Ferragamo's tradition of experimenting with different materials. The bezel and the bracelet's inserts are made of scratch-resistant ceramic, and the screw-down crown and chronograph pushers feature a combination of ceramic and titanium.

Ferragamo adds a splash of color with the red center seconds, which is decorated with the brand's double-gancino symbol. The horizontal texture of the black dial gives the watch a dynamic look to match its impeccable mechanics.

The Soprod automatic movement controls the F-80's chronograph counters as well as its GMT function. For readability, a blue-tipped hand indicates the hour in the second time zone on a 24-hour flange colored black and white to denote night and day.

In the same collection, Ferragamo offers a limited edition tourbillon model that epitomizes exclusivity. The F-80 Automatic Tourbillon was featured last spring in Salvatore Ferragamo's retrospective at Shanghai's modern art museum.

Finished by hand, the exquisite detailing includes a black textured dial that spotlights the tourbillon mechanism through a round opening at 6:00. Opposite the tourbillon, a subdial indicates the date with a red hand.

When flipped over, the F-80 Tourbillon's SF 8 movement and gold rotor are visible through the sapphire crystal caseback. This precision caliber provides power for 110 hours between windings. Much like the F-80 GMT, the F-80 Tourbillon's 44mm brushed titanium case features a black ceramic bezel and bracelet inserts. Adding flourish to the design, the screw-down crown is engraved with the script "F" from Ferragamo's logo.

Along with the tourbillon and GMT models, the F-80 collection also contains an automatic chronograph in a 44mm titanium and ceramic case. For those who prefer smaller timepieces, Ferragamo offers a range of 38mm automatics and 33mm quartz pieces, all available with or without gems.

An F-80 Automatic Tourbillon was also featured in Ferragamo's retrospective at Shanghai's modern art museum.

GANCINO

The "gancino" has become an instantly recognizable symbol of the Salvatore Ferragamo brand. Used to close handbags or as decoration on other accessories, this shapely symbol is the inspiration behind the trendy Gancino watch. Its curvy form is reflected in the 30mm case, which is available in rose gold or stainless steel.

For all Gancino models, Ferragamo adds diamond indexes to the dials. Options are also available for diamond-set bezels, plus a special stainless steel model upon which the case and clasp are set entirely with white brilliants.

The straps that accompany these stylish timekeepers bear the unmistakable Salvatore Ferragamo panache. The company uses the same luxurious materials found in its other products, including lizard skin, patent leather and silk satin in black, white or fuchsia.

Each watch is equipped with an ETA quartz movement and is water resistant to 30 meters.

VARA

Coveted around the world for their comfort and style, Salvatore Ferragamo shoes are truly iconic, from the metal-reinforced stiletto heels made famous by Marilyn Monroe to the "invisible" sandals with uppers made from nylon thread. In 1947, the latter design earned Salvatore Ferragamo the prestigious Neiman Marcus Award (the Oscar of the fashion world), an award his eldest daughter, Fiamma, would earn two decades later.

Among Fiamma Ferragamo's most acclaimed footwear designs is the Vara shoe with its distinctive grosgrain bow. The shoe's buckle is re-imagined for the Vara watch collection, using the shape to create a stylish case. Rose-gold and stainless steel models are available, either unadorned or set with 44 white or black brilliants. Ferragamo offers the options of mother-of-pearl and diamond-pavé dials.

In tribute to the fashion house's creative use of colors and materials, each Vara watch includes a trio of interchangeable straps that give a woman the freedom to change her mind and the look of her watch at any time. Materials include grosgrain, crocodile and lizard leather in white, black, red, silver and orange.

With these new collections of men and women's timepieces, Ferragamo brings its tradition of fashion excellence to the wrist, creating a superbly tailored look that personifies classic Italian style.

STÜHRLING ORIGINAL
Time for Everyone

Stührling Original has come to embody the concept of "aristocracy for all" that Max Stührling espoused in the 19th century as an elite watchmaker in Switzerland. From the beginning, the company has honored Stührling's vision, producing luxury timepieces that meet the highest standards of Swiss craftsmanship while maintaining sensitivity to price. Stührling Original's popularity has grown on the strength of its collection's mix of sophisticated watchmaking and timeless style. As the American market clamors for larger and even more technical timepieces, Stührling Original has stepped up to the plate. Broadening its horizons and appealing to new fans, Stührling Original is embracing its unique manufacturing formula of Swiss engineering and artisanship to create bold new designs in the ever-expanding category of sports timepieces.

A mong the brand's newer designs is the Apocalypse Skeleton. Boasting one of the most fashionable looks in the watch industry, the Apocalypse Skeleton features a self-winding mechanical movement that reveals its inner workings. On closer examination, one can see that the skeletonized dial has been blanketed with carbon fiber, and all the steel indices have been individually applied to the dial and treated with SuperLumi-Nova™ for ease of nighttime reading. However, the dial's primary attraction is the "propeller-style" ring-plate covering the exposed mainspring. Apocalypse Skeleton's strong masculine character is also emphasized by its large case (47x51mm).

Equally daring in its design is the Expedition from Stührling Original's Safari Series. The machine that powers this lion is a world-class quartz chronograph movement, starring a 1/20th-of-a-second indication and featuring a 60-minute counter, small seconds, 24-hour subdial and a quick-set date complication. With a first-rate engine in tow, Stührling Original's designers have engineered a spectacular case befitting such a movement. Blanked from solid 316L surgical-grade stainless steel, the case features scissor-cut faceting and is treated to a high-polish finish on its topside and a brushed satin finish on its sides.

While the main body of the case and its bezel are certainly remarkable, it is the eye-catching bridge protecting the crown that best symbolizes the Expedition's fierceness. Such an impressive case and movement warrant a brilliant dial to match—and the Expedition does not disappoint. The five-piece dial is anchored by the embossed main dial, which provides texture and depth. With an applied subdial for the 24-hour indicator at 3:00, and a color-coordinated tinted transparent dial-plate for the chronograph-function subdials and date aperture, the primary charm of the dial is the kidney-shaped dial-plate stretching from 5:00 to 10:00.

FACING PAGE
LEFT Expedition's five-piece dial includes an applied 24-hour subdial with a kidney-shaped faceplate featuring 1/20th-of-a-second indication and minute counters on tinted dial-plates, small seconds, and a quick-set date complication.

RIGHT A propeller-style plate partially reveals Apocalypse Skeleton's mainspring, while its open-worked carbon fiber dial exposes the engravings that decorate the skeletonized movement.

Stührling Original is a player on the modern watch scene with its popular new collection of masculine and daring sports watches.

Another new model from Stührling's Sportsman's Collection is the Falcon—a contemporary mix of stainless steel, carbon fiber and rubber. The Falcon is a force on your wrist in its impressive tonneau-shaped case measuring 48.5mm from East to West and 15mm thick. Inside the aggressive case beats the extraordinary Swiss Ronda Startech 5030-D quartz movement, which has been customized specifically for Stührling Original. Featuring an add-and-split-function chronograph with small seconds, a 12-hour counter, and quick-set date complication, this world-class movement incorporates six jewels.

Of course, displaying such an elaborate mechanism in an urbane manner calls for intricate detailing. The four-piece dial is highlighted by a stylized dial-plate that frames the chronograph subdials and the date aperture while presenting a minute-track around the circumference of the carbon-fiber-covered main dial. Adding to the look of the Falcon is the hand for the small-seconds subdial: the stylized Falcon-head insignia is blued and the "beak" is treated with luminescence serving as the pointer for the seconds. No falcon is complete without spectacular wings, and this Falcon boasts wings of steel on the right side of the case that serve as pushers for the chronograph.

Stührling Original has built a reputation for classic timepieces of elegance, and the legacy continues

with two of its latest designs from its Boardroom Collection: the Saturnalia and Brumalia. Both models reveal skilled finishing techniques that speak to Stührling Original's attention to detail, such as their distinctive and spectacular Ø 45mm case with its intricate double-milled bezel.

Named for the Roman festival celebrating the Temple of Saturn, the Saturnalia presents a feast of elegance and grace. Its Stührling caliber ST-92504, 33-jewel mechanical self-winding movement features retrograde day and date complications while boasting a "faux-tourbillon" open heart at 6:00. The opening in the dial reveals a clear view of the balance wheel while just beneath, a rotating propeller-style flywheel provides one complete revolution every minute.

On the triumphant heels of Saturnalia, Stührling Original wastes no time in presenting Brumalia, a skeletonized mechanical timepiece. Marked by the same spectacular case as Saturnalia, Brumalia offers a poignant expression of the art and tradition of horological fascination. The skeletonized dial and Krysterna™ crystal reveal the inner workings of the colossal 17-jewel "pure" mechanical engine (caliber ST-90911). With its extra-large mainspring clearly visible at 5:00, and the oversized balance wheel beating for all to see, the mesmerizing aura of Brumalia is accentuated by hand-engraved scrollwork on the engine plates. Underscoring its appeal is the striking bridge on the left side of its face arching across the small-seconds subdial. The real star of Brumalia, its oversized mechanical movement, is laced with hand-engraved scrollwork, dotted with blued steel screws and ruby jewels, and can be truly cherished through the Krysterna™ crystal exhibition caseback.

Collectors of assertive timepieces will fall for Stührling Original's new Centurion, a skeleton mechanical self-winding timepiece. Named for a British tank that was designed during World War II (later becoming the most successful and widely used military tank of all time), the Centurion timepiece lives up to its inspiration in its massive 38x44mm case. The well-conceived wrist adornment is blanked from the solid 316L surgical-grade stainless steel. The impressive 15mm-thick, sandwich-style case with its vertically striped side motif brings to mind the six-wheel design of its famous namesake, as does the unique ridged rubber belt wrapped tightly around the steel crown.

The Centurion is as attractive to look at as it is rugged and masculine to wear. The skeletonized 20-jewel self-winding engine that drives this timepiece not only delivers a precision three-hand mechanical movement, but also doubles as its own dial. With hand-engraved scrollwork on what remains of the front-plates as a backdrop, the individually applied electro-plated, high-tech Arabic numerals appear to be floating as there is no visible dial to hold the distinctive markers.

The underbelly of this tank is impressive as well. With six screws total to secure the custom silicon strap alone and another four screws holding the case together, the bottom view of the Centurion reaffirms the tank-like build. Under the Krysterna™ crystal in the stainless steel caseback, the steadfast Stührling caliber ST-90089 movement beats at 21,600 vibrations per hour. Featuring blued steel screws and a skeletonized and hand-engraved rotor, this tank is just as attractive under the hood as it is from afar.

Content in the workshop, Max Stührling preferred the joy of discovery to the spotlight's glow. In fact, his penchant for keeping to himself earned him the nickname, the "ghost watchmaker." The company honors Stührling's legacy with King's Court Tourbillon, a limited edition timepiece that includes a complication many consider to be the ultimate expression of watchmaking skill. Handmade in Switzerland, the company produced only 14 pieces in the edition with executions in yellow gold, rose gold, or stainless steel. Twin barrels provide steady power for 72 hours, driving the tourbillon as well as the elegant leaf-style minute and hour hands as they make their way around the hand-guilloché dial.

Stührling Original employed the same time-honored Swiss techniques on the King's Court Tourbillon to decorate the movement, embellishing the caliber with Côtes Circulaire and blued steel screws; all of which can be seen through the round crystal caseback.

Stührling Original turns to matters of the heart with Venus, a diamond-set ladies' model from the watchmaker's aptly titled Love Series.

A heart-shaped opening frames Venus's mechanical heart, a hand-decorated 20-jewel movement. Nearly one full carat of diamonds adorns the watch's Ø 35mm case, transforming the bezel into a dazzling ring of 60 sparkling minute markers. With its chic mechanical timepiece invoking the Goddess of Love, Stührling Original creates a watch that has both beauty and brains.

More than a century after Max Stührling first dreamt of adorning the wrists of the world with Swiss-quality timepieces, Stührling Original reaches a global audience through non-traditional electronic retailing.

FACING PAGE The limited edition King's Court Tourbillon includes the highly prized regulating mechanism at 6:00. The 40mm round solid 18K gold case houses a fully decorated movement, which is on view through the sapphire crystal caseback.

THIS PAGE Part of the watchmaker's Love Series, Venus's bezel is channel-set with 60 white diamonds. The jeweled circle frames the dial's heart-shaped opening, exposing the watch's skeletonized automatic movement.

TAG HEUER
Swiss Avant-Garde Since 1860

After its scene-stealing debut on Steve McQueen's wrist in Le Mans, the TAG Heuer Monaco, the square-cased icon of sporting glamour that captured the spirit of an era and changed forever the face of luxury Swiss watchmaking, remains as cool and cutting edge as ever.

L aunched simultaneously in Geneva and New York on March 3rd, 1969, the Monaco caught the watchmaking world by storm. The provocative look of the timepiece—with its fire-red chronograph hand, metallic blue dial, domed crystal, and big, squared-off case—represented a complete break from the conventional codes of watch design aesthetics. Equally radical was the engineering required to ensure the chronograph's perfect water resistance—a world first for a square-shaped timepiece. But what was ticking inside was even more revolutionary: the famous self-winding Chronomatic "Calibre 11," the first self-winding automatic chronograph movement with micro-rotor so precise that, to this day, it rivals the exacting standards of professional chronometer instruments.

THE TAG HEUER MONACO 1969 ORIGINAL RE-EDITION

1969-2009: To commemorate this historic anniversary, TAG Heuer has proudly republished the iconic blue-dialed timepiece in a limited series of 1,000 pieces with an exclusive caseback signed by Jack Heuer and engraved in honor of its lengendary ambassador, Steve McQueen. Outfitted with the Calibre 11, its other classic features include pushbuttons at 2:00 and 4:00, crown at 9:00, counters at 9:00 and 3:00, hand-applied date window at 6:00, and diamond-tipped horizontal hour-indexes.

TAG Heuer celebrates Monaco's 40th anniversary with a new, 1,000-piece limited edition.

For *Le Mans*, Steve McQueen's source of inspiration was his friend, Jo Siffert, the Swiss racecar legend who, in 1969, became the first-ever driver sponsored by a watch brand, Heuer. The Heuer Monaco had just been launched and so impressed McQueen that he insisted on wearing it in the film. The Monaco became the preferred chronograph of the racing and fashion world—another world first. Its unique, uncompromising geometry started a trend toward "shaped" watches. Instantly recognizable, often copied, never equaled, the "McQueen Monaco" (Model 1133B) is one of the most highly prized pieces in the international vintage markets. Demand far exceeds supply—only a hand-

ful is known to still exist, all in the hands of well-informedcollectors.

Ever since, the Monaco's emblematic square-shaped dial has been synonymous with TAG Heuer's innovative aesthetic. Reissued in 1998 in a limited edition of 5,000 pieces, it was entirely redesigned in 2003, refitted with a 7-row steel bracelet of square links echoing the daring aesthetics of the case. The watch became a must-have among racing purists and collectors, but it also surprised the industry by becoming the huge breakout fashion hit of the year, adored by haute couture and Hollywood.

The re-interpretations that followed were even more revolutionary.

THE MONACO CLASSIC CHRONOGRAPH

To celebrate the Monaco's 40th anniversary, TAG Heuer is proud to present a new Classic Chronograph collection fitted with a TAG Heuer "Calibre 12" automatic movement. Directly inspired by the original design, these chronographs are fitted with a sapphire crystal glass and case-back, revealing the beat of the Calibre 12.

Standout features include a dark blue alligator strap and a stylish silver and blue dial with red hands. The new, fashion-forward animation on the chronograph dial is completely in line with the line's iconic heritage.

FACING PAGE
Monaco Calibre 12 Gulf
limited edition chronograph.

THIS PAGE
Side view of the new Monaco Classic Chronograph.

GRAND CARRERA CALIBRE 17 RS2 CHRONOGRAPH TI2

It's a High Tech GT speed machine ready to tear up the tarmac: sophisticated, powerful, unmistakably virile and technical, the Grand Carrera Caliber 17 RS2 is clearly cut out for race tracks. Streamlined to order to win the race for precision, the chassis is made from grade-2 titanium (Ti2), a pure metal ultra-resistant and bio-compatible. The matte black alligator strap with a "soft touch" coating, together with the smoothly dipping lugs, ensures optimal user-friendliness: this mechanical chronograph will cling to the wrist as surely as a GT coupé hugs the road. This competition-style bodywork has been given a black titanium carbide treatment further protecting the Ti2 case. The red color of the seconds hand, echoed on the crown, the stitching and the inside of the strap, sets the finishing touch to a design obviously heading for ultimate performance.

The engine is on a par with the exterior: a COSC-certified chronograph movement, equipped with the famous Rotating Systems that are the hallmark of the Grand Carrera collection. This revolutionary display mode enables intuitive reading of elapsed time, since the index remains fixed while the time indications rotate: small seconds at 3:00 and chronograph minute counter at 9:00. From the Geneva stripes motif to the polished, beveled finish of the Rotating Systems; and from the black-gold hand-applied hands, logo and hour-markers to the double sapphire crystal caseback revealing a "turbine" obviously powering this model towards the future, an impressive wealth of details further enhances the exclusive nature of this series.

GRAND CARRERA CALIBRE 36
RS CALIPER CHRONOGRAPH

TAG Heuer has pulled off yet another world first: powered by a column wheel movement, the Grand Carrera Calibre 36 RS Caliper Concept Chronograph is the only automatic chronograph capable of measuring and displaying 1/10th of a second via the central hands. Visible through a tinted double sapphire crystal, the COSC-certified movement oscillates at an astonishing 36,000 vibrations per hour. This enables the central seconds hand to tick off 1/10th second intervals, giving at-a-glance readings of an unparalleled exactitude—an engineering feat of the highest level. The breathtaking new creation has a stylish 43mm, black titanium carbide-coated case, and a Calibre 36 RS movement with power reserve of about 50 hours and two "Black Gold" Rotating Systems indicating the chronograph minutes at 3:00 and the chronograph hours at 6:00. It also features a linear second at 9:00. Another principal design innovation is the way in which it displays this information. TAG Heuer has developed an exclusive Rotating Scale that permits a precise reading of 1/10th of a second magnified by 10! The new titanium carbide-coated and rubber bracelet with folding buckle is another stunning innovation.

FACING PAGE
Grand Carrera Calibre 17 RS 2
Chronograph Ti2.

THIS PAGE
Grand Carrera Calibre 36 RS
Caliper Concept Chronograph.

**Grand Prix d'Horlogerie
de Genève**

TAG Heuer proudly announces the launch of the 360 Virtual Museum on www.tagheuer.com. This is a unique chance to discover the brand's private museum based in La Chaux-de-Fonds, Switzerland, and to travel deep inside the TAG Heuer history.

All of the elements are present to make visitors' experiences seem as though they were taking place on the ground floor of TAG Heuer headquarters: vistiors can navigate around the 200-square-meter museum, go through the windows and the brand's historical timepieces, and look up and view the outstanding conical 360° panoramic film displaying more than 1 million images per hour!

The complete History section of the website has been updated: read Jean-Christophe Babin's edito,

experience the TAG Heuer 360 Museum through the eyes of TAG Heuer collectors and access the virtual museum.

It is a museum unlike any other. Built on ingenious design, the TAG Heuer 360 Museum is where time officially stops, thanks to the brand's rich culture and fascinating showcasing of a rare 300-piece collection spanning the company's 150-year history. The vitrines, designed to resemble the subdials of a wristwatch, chart the history of TAG Heuer—from its founding in 1860 to the present day—and are enhanced by 50 magnifying lenses of varying sizes.

The TAG Heuer 360 Museum is the mirror of the brand's motto "Swiss Avant-Garde since 1860" and its tradition of innovation.

TAG Heuer 360 Museum.

CHRONOLOGY

1860

The TAG Heuer watchmaking company is founded in Saint-Imier, Switzerland, by Edouard Heuer.

1886

TAG Heuer invented the famous "oscillating pinion" for mechanical chronographs.

1911

TAG Heuer presents the first watch for automotive instrument panels, featuring a trip-duration indicator.

1916

TAG Heuer tests the Micrograph, the first stopwatch measuring time with an accuracy of 1/100th of a second.

1933

The Autavia: the first chronograph dashboard for both automobiles and aviation.

1964

First Carrera automatic chronograph with a hand-winding movement.

1971-1979

TAG Heuer becomes the official timekeeper of the Scuderia Ferrari.

1985

TAG Heuer becomes McLaren partner, one of the longest successful partnerships ever.

1986

Launch of the TAG Heuer Formula 1 in stainless steel and fiberglass. Driver Alain Prost emphasizes the house's return in Formula 1 racing by winning the World Championship.

1987

TAG Heuer link collection is created, which will become an icon thanks to Ayrton Senna.

1992-2003

TAG Heuer is appointed official timekeeper of the Formula 1 World Championship.

1998

TAG Heuer collection is enriched with a new edition of the Monaco, the square chronograph worn by actor Steve McQueen in the 1971 movie *Le Mans*.

2004-2006

TAG Heuer becomes official timekeeper and chronograph of the Indy Racing League (IRL).

2006

TAG Heuer Carrera Calibre 360 chronograph: the first-ever mechanical chronograph accurate to 1/100th of a second, wins the Grand Prix d'Horlogerie de Genève in the Sport's category.

2007

TAG Heuer launches the Grand Carrera: the premium avant-garde TAG Heuer collection inspired by unrivalled motor racing heritage.

2008

In the Sport category, TAG Heuer wins the Grand Prix de Genève with its Grand Carrera Calibre 36 RS Caliper Chronograph.

GRAND CARRERA CALIBRE 6 RS   REF. WAV511C.FC6230

Movement: mechanical automatic-winding TAG Heuer Calibre 6 RS; COSC-certified; Rotating System (RS) indicating the small second at 6; oscillating weight decorated with "Côtes de Genève". **Functions:** hours, minutes, seconds; date at 3. **Case:** fine-brushed steel case with curved faceted polished horns; Ø 40.2mm, thickness: 11.8mm; double antireflective curved sapphire crystal; oversized screw-in crown; double sapphire caseback sealed by 6-screws; water resistant to 100

meters. **Dial:** brown; opaline central area and external spiral effect area; Rotating small second System decorated with "Côtes de Genève" and diamond-polished facets; hand-applied curved faceted indexes with double finishing; hand-applied TAG Heuer logo; polished hands with polished facets; luminescent hands. **Strap:** brown alligator strap; solid steel folding clasp with safety push-buttons and applied TAG Heuer logo. **Also available:** in black or silver dial; on black alligator strap or a 3-row multi-faceted steel bracelet with solid steel folding clasp with safety pushbuttons and applied TAG Heuer logo.

GRAND CARRERA CALIBRE 8 RS GRANDE DATE GMT STEEL & ROSE GOLD   REF. WAV5153.FC6231

Movement: mechanical automatic-winding TAG Heuer Calibre 8 RS; COSC-certified; Rotating System (RS) displaying the second time zone at 6; oscillating weight decorated with "Côtes de Genève". **Functions:** hours, minutes, seconds; grand date at 12; second time zone. **Case:** fine-brushed steel case with curved faceted polished horns; Ø 42.5mm, thickness: 13.0mm; fine-brushed and polished bezel in massive rose gold (18K 5N); double antireflective curved sapphire crystal; oversized screw-in crown in

massive rose gold (18K 5N); double sapphire caseback sealed by 6-screws; water resistant to 100 meters. **Dial:** brown dial with opaline central area and external spiral effect area; Rotating GMT System (2nd Time Zone) in massive rose gold (18K 5N) decorated with "Côtes de Genève" and diamond-polished facets; hand-applied grande date window in massive rose gold (18K 5N); hand-applied curved faceted indexes with double finishing in massive rose gold (18K 5N); monochrome TAG Heuer logo; polished hands with polished facets in massive rose gold (18K 5N); luminescent hands. **Strap:** brown alligator strap; solid steel folding clasp with safety pushbuttons and applied in massive rose gold (18K 5N) TAG Heuer logo. **Also available:** in silver dial.

GRAND CARRERA CALIBRE 8 RS GRANDE DATE GMT   REF. WAV5112.BA0901

Movement: mechanical automatic-winding TAG Heuer Calibre 8 RS; COSC-certified; Rotating System (RS) displaying the second time zone at 6; oscillating weight decorated with "Côtes de Genève". **Functions:** hours, minutes, seconds; grand date at 12; second time zone. **Case:** fine-brushed steel case with curved faceted polished horns; Ø 42.5mm, thickness: 13mm; fine-brushed and polished bezel; double antireflective curved sapphire crystal; oversized screw-in crown, double sapphire caseback

sealed by 6-screws; water resistant to 100 meters. **Dial:** silver dial with opaline central area and external spiral effect area; Rotating GMT System (2nd Time Zone) decorated with "Côtes de Genève" and diamond-polished facets; hand-applied grande date window; hand-applied curved faceted indexes with double finishing; hand-applied TAG Heuer logo; polished hands with polished facets; luminescent hands. **Bracelet:** 3-row multi-faceted steel bracelet; alternated polished and fine-brushed central row and fine-brushed lateral rows with polished edges; solid steel folding clasp with safety pushbuttons and applied TAG Heuer logo. **Also available:** in black or brown dial; on a black or brown alligator strap.

GRAND CARRERA CALIBRE 17 RS2 CHRONOGRAPH TI2   REF. CAV518B.FC6237

Movement: mechanical automatic-winding TAG Heuer Calibre 17 RS; COSC-certified; Rotating Systems (RS) indicating the small second and the chronograph minute; oscillating weight decorated with "Côtes de Genève". **Functions:** hours, minutes, seconds; chronograph; date; 2 Rotating Systems displaying the small second at 3 and the chronograph minute at 9. **Case:** sandblasted titanium grade-2 case with curved horns; Ø 43mm, thickness: 14.85mm; Titanium Grade 2 bezel with tachymeter scale; date window at 6; scratch-resistant

black titanium coated case and bezel; screw-in massive pushbuttons; antireflective curved sapphire crystal; oversized screw-in crown; black titanium caseback sealed by 6-screws; smoked double sapphire caseback; water resistant to 100 meters. **Dial:** black dial with opaline central area and external spiral effect area; 2 Rotating Systems in black gold decorated with "Côtes de Genève" and diamond-polished facets; hand-applied black gold curved faceted indexes with double finishing; hand-applied black gold TAG Heuer logo; polished black gold hands with polished facets; luminescent hands; hand-applied black gold date window. **Strap:** "soft touch" black alligator strap with red stitching and lining; solid titanium folding clasp with safety pushbuttons and applied TAG Heuer logo. **Also Available:** on rubber strap.

GRAND CARRERA CALIBRE 17 RS CHRONOGRAPH   REF. CAV511A.BA0902

Movement: mechanical automatic-winding TAG Heuer Calibre 17 RS; COSC-certified, Rotating Systems (RS) indicating the small second and the chronograph minute; oscillating weight decorated with "Côtes de Genève". **Functions:** hours, minutes, seconds; chronograph; date; 2 Rotating Systems displaying the small second at 3; chronograph minute counter at 9; date window at 6. **Case:** fine-brushed steel case with curved faceted polished horns; Ø 43mm, thickness: 14.85mm; screw-in pushbuttons; fine-brushed and polished bezel with

tachymeter scale; double antireflective curved sapphire crystal; oversized screw-in crown; double sapphire caseback sealed by 6-screws; water resistant to 100 meters. **Dial:** black dial with opaline central area and external spiral effect area; 2 Rotating Systems decorated with "Côtes de Genève" and diamond-polished facets; hand-applied curved faceted indexes with double finishing; hand-applied TAG Heuer logo; polished hands with polished facets; luminescent hands; hand-applied date window. **Bracelet:** 3-row multi-faceted steel bracelet; alternated polished and fine-brushed central row and fine-brushed lateral rows with polished edges; solid steel folding clasp with safety pushbuttons and applied TAG Heuer logo. **Also available:** in silver dial with black or brown alligator strap.

TAG HEUER FORMULA 1 GRANDE DATE CHRONOGRAPH   REF. CAH1012.BT0717

Movement: quartz chronograph. **Functions:** hours, minutes, seconds; chronograph; grand date; small second at 3; "Twin hand" semi-circular chronograph minutes counter at 9; 1/10th of a second counter at 6 during the 30 first minutes then hour counter; grand date window at 12. **Case:** black titanium carbide coated steel case; Ø 44mm, thickness: 12.5mm; scratch-resistant titanium carbide coated unidirectional turning bezel with raised fine-brushed figures; scratch-resistant sapphire crystal; scratch-resistant

titanium carbide coated "Easy Grip" screw-in crown with raised fine-brushed TAG Heuer logo; scratch-resistant titanium carbide coated steel safety crown and pushbuttons; circular steel fine-brushed screwed caseback with special checked decoration; TAG Heuer engraving on the side of the case; water resistant to 200 meters. **Dial:** black dial; hand-applied indexes; faceted hour and minute hands; colored TAG Heuer logo; second hands; luminescent markers on hands and indexes. **Strap:** rubber strap with pin buckle. **Also available:** steel case with silver or black dial; 3-row fine-brushed stainless steel bracelet, double safety clasp with diving extension system or rubber strap.

TAG HEUER FORMULA 1 CHRONOGRAPH DIAMONDS   REF. CAC1310.FC6219

Movement: quartz chronograph. **Functions:** hours, minutes, seconds; chronograph; date; 1/10th of a second at 2; small second at 6; chronograph minute counter at 10; date window at 4:30. **Case:** polished stainless steel; Ø 37mm, thickness: 10.95mm; polished fixed stainless steel bezel with 120 Wesselton diamonds (total 0.75 carats); sapphire crystal; polished stainless steel safety crown and pushbuttons; polished stainless steel bumpers with "TAG Heuer" branding engraved; polished screw-in crown; polished screw fitting caseback with "TAG Heuer" logo engraved; water resistant to 200 meters. **Dial:** white mother-of-pearl; 11 Wesselton diamonds (total 0.081 carat); luminescent markers on faceted minute and hourhands; monochrome TAG Heuer logo. **Strap:** white nizza fabrics strap with folding clasp. **Also available:** pink mother-of-pearl dial with steel bracelet or pink nizza strap.

TAG HEUER FORMULA 1 GRANDE DATE CHRONOGRAPH   REF. CAH101B.BA0854

Movement: quartz chronograph. **Functions:** hours, minutes, seconds; chronograph; grand date; small second at 3; "Twin hand" semi-circular chronograph minutes counter at 9; 1/10th of a second counter at 6 during the 30 first minutes then hour counter; grand date window at 12. **Case:** stainless steel case; Ø 44mm, thickness: 12.3mm; polished steel fixed bezel with tachymeter scale and INDY 500 writennig; scratch-resistant sapphire crystal; polished steel "Easy Grip" screw-in crown with raised fine-brushed TAG Heuer logo; polished stainless steel safety crown and pushbuttons; circular fine-brushed screwed caseback with special checked decoration; red INDY 500 engraving on the side of the case; water resistant to 200 meters. **Dial:** silver dial with perlage; hand-applied indexes; polished finished hands with polished facets; luminescent markers on hands and indexes; colored INDY 500 logo; colored TAG Heuer logo. **Bracelet:** 3-row fine-brushed steel bracelet with double safety clasp and diving extension system. **Also available:** in "black gold" dial with perlage.

AQUARACER 500M CALIBRE 5   REF. WAJ2110.FT6015

Movement: mechanical automatic-winding TAG Heuer Calibre 5.
Functions: hours, minutes, seconds; date.
Case: fine-brushed steel case with fine brushed edges; Ø 43mm; 13.4mm thickness; unidirectional turning bezel in fine brushed steel with a colored rubber-like coating, fine brushed steel numerals and luminescent dot at 12; fine brushed steel crown with colored rubber-like coating on the

face; sapphire crystal and sapphire caseback; automatic helium valve at 10; water resistant to 500 meters.
Dial: black with vertical streak effect; hand-applied indexes; polished finished hands; second hands with orange at the extremity; luminescent markers on hands and indexes; date window at 9 with a magnifying glass; hand applied TAG Heuer logo
Strap: black rubber strap with solid steel clasp, diving extension system and safety pushbuttons
Also available: black OR blue dial and with 3-row fine-brushed steel bracelet with solid steel clasp, diving extension system and safety push-buttons.

AQUARACER CHRONOTIMER   REF. CAF1010.BA0821

Movement: 1/100th second quartz chronograph. **Functions:** hours, minutes, seconds, perpetual calendar, countdown, daily and diary alarm, second time zone.
Case: fine-brushed steel with polished edges; Ø 43mm, 14.5mm thickness; unique dual bezel composed of fixed colored aluminum ring and unidirectional turning bezel in fine-brushed steel with polished studs and minutes scale : engraved numerals with black varnish on the turning base and luminescent dot at 12; scratch-resistant sapphire crystal

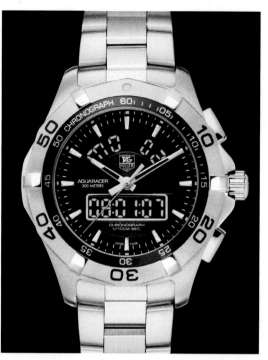

with antireflective treatment; polished pushbuttons and pushbutton crown for dial lighting; screw-in caseback with stamped diver decoration; water resistant to 300 meters.
Dial: black dial with spiral effect in central zone; 3 dial openings for multi-functional displays; hand-applied indexes; polished finished hands; luminescent markers on hands and indexes; hand-applied monochrome TAG Heuer logo.
Indications: analog time display with central hour, minute and second hands; digital time display with backlit dial.
Bracelet: 3-row alternate fine-brushed and polished steel bracelet with solid steel clasp, diving extension system and safety pushbuttons.
Also available: black rubber strap with protruded TAG Heuer logo & inscription and steel pin buckle.

AQUARACER CALIBRE S 1/100TH CHRONOGRAPH   REF. CAF7010.BA0815

Movement: TAG Heuer Calibre S - Electro-mechanical Chronograph, invented, patented, developed and manufactured by TAG Heuer. **Functions:** hours, minutes, seconds; Perpetual Retrograde Calendar; time & chronograph display using central hour, minute, second hands; Chronograph, 1/100th of a second, simple & additional timing, split time. **Case:** fine-brushed steel with polished edges; Ø 43mm; 13.2mm thickness; unique dual bezel composed of fixed aluminium ring and unidirectional turning bezel in fine-brushed steel with polished studs and minutes scale, engraved numerals with black varnish on the turning base and luminescent dot at 12; scratch-resistant

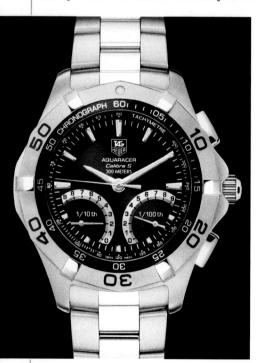

sapphire crystal with antireflective treatment; polished screw-in crown; screw-in caseback with stamped diver decoration; water resistant to 300 meters. **Dial:** black dial with spiral effect in the interior zone; 2 hand-applied semi-circular counters (in the watch mode, perpetual date indicated through hands of both sub counters; in the chrono mode, indication of the 1/100th of a second through both sub counters); hands with orange at the extremity; hand-applied indexes; polished finished hands; central second hand with orange in the extremity; luminescent markers on hands and indexes. **Indications:** 1/10th second at 7:30; 1/100th second at 4:30. **Bracelet:** 3-row alternate fine-brushed and polished steel bracelet with solid steel clasp, diving extension system and safety pushbuttons. **Also available:** black rubber strap with protruded TAG Heuer logo & inscriptions and steel pin buckle; blue dial with steel bracelet, silver dial with steel bracelet or rubber strap.

AQUARACER CALIBRE 16 CHRONOGRAPH   REF. CAF2110.BA0809

Movement: mechanical automatic-winding TAG Heuer Calibre 16.
Functions: hours, minutes, seconds; date; chronograph with 3 counters.
Case: fine-brushed steel with polished edges; Ø 41mm, 14.9mm thickness; unique dual bezel composed of fixed colored aluminum/steel ring and unidirectional turning bezel in fine-brushed steel with polished studs and minutes scale, engraved numerals with black varnish on the turning base, luminescent dot at 12; scratch-

resistant sapphire crystal with antireflective treatment; polished screw-in crown and polished shaped pushbuttons; screw-in caseback with stamped diver decoration; water resistant to 300 meters.
Dial: black dial with sun-ray effect; hand-applied indexes; polished hands; luminescent markers on hands and indexes; polished rings on counters at 6 and 12; monochrome TAG Heuer logo.
Indications: hours at 6, seconds at 9, minutes at 12, date window at 3.
Bracelet: 3-row alternate polished and fine-brushed steel bracelet with double safety clasp, diving extension system and safety pushbuttons.
Also available: blue dial OR silver dial in steel and gold version.

AQUARACER CALIBRE 16 DAY DATE CHRONOGRAPH   REF. CAF5011.BA0815

Movement: mechanical automatic-winding TAG Heuer Calibre 16 Day Date; COSC-certified.
Functions: hours, minutes, small seconds; date, day; chronographs with 3 counters.
Case: fine-brushed steel with polished edges; Ø 43mm, 15.15mm thickness; Unique dual bezel composed of fixed aluminium ring and unidirectional turning bezel in fine-brushed steel with polished studs and minutes scale, (engraved numerals with black varnish on the turning base, white luminescent dot at 12); scratch-resistant sapphire crystal with an-

tireflective treatment; polished screw-in crown and push buttons; screw-in caseback with stamped diver decoration; water resistant to 300 meters.
Dial: Anthracite dial with spiral effect; tachymeter scale on the dial; hand-applied polished rings on counters at 12 and 6; silver ring on running second counter at 9; hand-applied indexes; polished finished hands; luminescent markers on hands and indexes; hand-applied monochrome TAG Heuer logo; hand-applied polished day-date frame (only available in English).
Indications: hour counter at 6; running second counter at 9; minute counter at 12; day and date at 3.
Bracelet: 3-row alternate polished and fine-brushed steel bracelet with solid steel clasp, diving extension system and safety pushbuttons.
Also available: black dial.

AQUARACER GRANDE DATE CHRONOGRAPH   REF. CAF101C.BA0821

Movement: quartz chronograph 1/10th second. **Functions:** hours, minutes, seconds; grande date.
Case: fine-brushed steel with polished edges; Ø 43mm; 12.5mm thickness; unique dual bezel composed of fixed aluminium ring and unidirectional turning bezel in fine-brushed steel with fine-brushed studs and minutes scale (engraved numerals with black varnish on the turning base, luminescent dot at 12); scratch-resistant sapphire crystal with antireflective treatment; polished screw-in crown; screw-in caseback with stamped diver decoration; water resistance to 300 meters.

Dial: blue dial with spiral effect; "Twin-hand" semi-circular counter at 6 with spiral effect: 1/10th of a second counter during 30 minutes and then changes to hour counter, red side indicating from 00 to 05, polished finished side indicating from 05 to 10; hand-applied polished indexes and TAG Heuer logo; polished finished hands; luminescent markers on hands and indexes; large date window at 12.
Indications: grande date at 3, minute counter at 9, small second counter at 3.
Bracelet: 3-row fine-brushed steel bracelet with solid steel clasp, diving extension system and safety pushbuttons.
Also available: Black, silver dials with steel bracelet or black rubber strap with protruded TAG Heuer logo & inscription and steel pin buckle.

AQUARACER LADY DIAMOND DIAL   REF. WAF1415.BA0824

Movement: quartz.
Functions: hours, minutes, seconds; date.
Case: polished steel with polished edges; Ø 27mm, 9.0mm thickness; unidirectional turning bezel with engraved numerals on the base of the bezel; polished screw-in crown; screw-in caseback with stamped diver decoration; water resistant to 300 meters.

Dial: white mother-of-pearl diamond dial; hand-applied numeral; 10 Top Wesselton diamonds (Ø 1.2mm, total 0.07 carats); polished finished hands with polished facets and luminescent markers; monochrome TAG Heuer logo.
Indications: date at 3.
Bracelet: 3-row steel bracelet with solid steel clasp, diving extension system and safety pushbuttons; completely polished.
Also available: pink or blue mother-of-pearl diamond dial.

AQUARACER LADY DIAMOND DIAL & DIAMOND BEZEL   REF. WAF1313.BA0819

Movement: quartz.
Functions: hours, minutes, seconds; date.
Case: fine-brushed steel with polished edges; Ø 32mm, 9.55mm thickness; unidirectional turning bezel with polished steel base set with 42 Top Wesselton diamonds, 35 diamonds with Ø 1.5mm, 7 diamonds with Ø 1.4mm (total 0.567 carats); polished screw-in crown; scratch-resistant sapphire crystal; screw-in caseback with stamped diver decoration; water resistant to 300 meters.

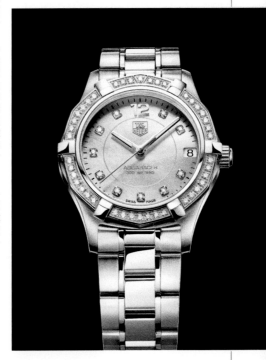

Dial: white mother-of-pearl; diamond dial; hand-applied curved numeral at 12; 10 Top Wesselton diamonds (Ø 1.3mm, total 0.098 carats); polished finished hands and luminescent markers; polished & protruded TAG Heuer logo.
Indications: date at 3.
Bracelet: 5-row alternate fine-brushed and polished steel bracelet with solid steel folding clasp and safety pushbuttons.

CARRERA LADY CALIBRE 4 DIAMOND DIAL & DIAMOND BEZEL   REF: WV2413.BA0793

Movement: mechanical automatic-winding TAG Heuer Calibre 4.
Functions: hours, minutes, seconds; date.
Case: polished steel case; Ø 27mm, 10.5mm thickness; polished steel fixed bezel set with 54 Top Wesselton diamonds (Ø 1.30mm, total 0.51 ct); polished crown; scratch-resistant sapphire crystal; scratch-resistant sapphire caseback; water resistant to 50 meters.

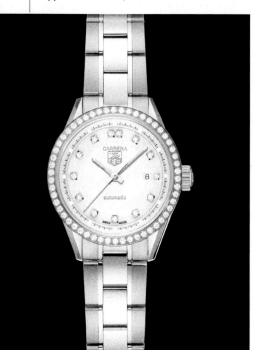

Dial: white mother-of-pearl; diamond dial with spiral effect in exterior zone; 13 Top Wesselton diamonds (12 diamonds with Ø 1.2mm, 1 diamond with Ø 1.1mm, total 0.0981 carats); polished finished hands with luminescent markers; polished & protruded TAG Heuer logo.
Indications: date indicated at 3.
Bracelet: 5-row alternate fine-brushed and polished steel bracelet with solid steel folding clasp and safety pushbuttons; fine-brushed steel for rows 1 and 5; polished steel for rows 2, 3 and 4.
Also available: black diamond dial.

CARRERA LADY DIAMOND DIAL   REF. WV1417.BA0793

Movement: quartz.
Functions: hours, minutes, seconds; date.
Case: polished steel case; Ø 27mm, 9.07mm thickness, polished steel fixed bezel; polished crown; scratch-resistant sapphire crystal; polished steel caseback, water resistant to 50 meters.
Dial: pink mother-of-pearl; diamond dial with spiral effect in exterior zone; 13

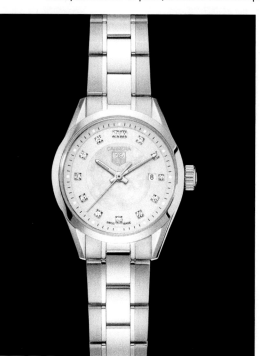

Top Wesselton diamonds (12 diamonds with Ø 1.20mm, 1 diamond with Ø 1.1mm, total 0.0981 ct); polished finished hands with luminescent markers; polished & protruded TAG Heuer logo.
Indications: date indicated at 3.
Bracelet: 5-row alternate fine-brushed and polished steel bracelet with solid steel folding clasp and safety pushbuttons.
Also available: white mother-of-pearl diamond dial and black diamond dial.

CARRERA CALIBRE 16 DAY-DATE CHRONOGRAPH   REF: CV2A11.FC6235

Movement: mechanical automatic-winding TAG Heuer Calibre 16 Day-Date.
Functions: hours, minutes, seconds; date; chronograph with 3 counters.
Case: polished stainless steel case; Ø 43mm, 16.3mm thickness; polished steel fixed bezel with tachymeter scale; polished enlarged crown and pushbuttons; scratch-resistant domed sapphire crystal with double-sided antireflective treatment; scratch-resistant sapphire caseback; water resistant to 100 meters.

Dial: silver; hand-applied numerals; polished finished hour and minute hands with luminescent markers; polished finished second hand and hour and minute counters' hands with red at the extremity; silver-ringed hour and minute counters; monochrome TAG Heuer logo.
Indications: date at 3; chronograph hour at 6, small second at 9, minute counter at 12, center seconds.
Strap: black alligator strap with polished steel folding clasp with safety pushbuttons.
Also available: 5-row alternate fine-brushed and polished steel bracelet and solid steel folding clasp with safety pushbuttons, black and brown dial.

CARRERA CALIBRE 16 RACING CHRONOGRAPH   REF. CV2014.FT6014

Movement: mechanical automatic-winding TAG Heuer Calibre 16.
Functions: hours, minutes, seconds; date; chronograph with 3 counters.
Case: polished steel; Ø 41mm, 15.3mm thickness; black tachymeter scale on an aluminum fixed bezel; scratch-resistant sapphire crystal; scratch-resistant sapphire caseback; water resistant to 50 meters.
Dial: black; sunray-effect center; spiral-effect outer band; hand-applied

faceted indexes; luminescent hour and minute hands; red central chronograph hand; monochrome TAG Heuer logo.
Indications: date at 3; chronograph hour at 6 with red hand, small second at 9, minute counter at 12, center seconds.
Strap: black perforated rubber strap with embossed "TAG Heuer" and polished steel folding clasp with safety pushbuttons.
Also available: on a 5-row alternate fine-brushed and polished steel bracelet and solid steel folding clasp with safety pushbuttons.

CARRERA CALIBRE S LAPTIMER — REF. CV7A10.FT6012

Movement: TAG Heuer Calibre S - Electro-mechanical Chronograph, invented, patented, developed and manufactured by TAG Heuer. **Functions:** hours, minutes, seconds; Perpetual Retrograde Calendar; time & chronograph display using central hour, minute, second hands: flyback chronograph, 1/100th of a second, laptimer function with direct access to best lap time. **Case:** polished steel case; Ø 43mm,13.55mm thickness; polished pushbutton crown with black varnish on the face and side; fixed black aluminium bezel with tachymeter scale; scratch-resis-

tant sapphire crystal; screw-in caseback; water resistant to 100 meters. **Dial:** black; spiral effect; 3 hand-applied semi-circular counters, hand applied indexes; polished finished hour, minute and semi-circular counters' hands (Hour and semi-circular counters' hands with red at the extremity) luminescent markers on hands and indexes; red second hand; hand applied TAG Heuer logo.
Indications: at 12 lap counter with Chrono mode indicator at 9:30 and Best Lap mode indicator at 2:30, at 4:30 1/10th of a second retrograde counter, at 7:30 1/100th of a second retrograde counter. **Strap:** black perforated rubber strap with embossed "TAG Heuer" and polished steel folding clasp with safety pushbuttons.
Also available: 5-row fine-brushed and polished steel bracelet and polished steel folding clasp with safety pushbuttons; silver dial.

LINK CALIBRE 6 SMALL SECOND — REF. WJF211C.BA0570

Movement: mechanical automatic-winding TAG Heuer Calibre 6.
Functions: hours, minutes, small second; date.
Case: fine-brushed stainless steel; Ø 39mm, 11.5mm thickness; antireflective double-sided treatment on the curved glass to ensure readability; polished stainless steel fixed bezel; sapphire crystal caseback; screw-in polished steel crown; water resistant to 200 meters.
Dial: brown; vertical line texturing; silver-ringed brown small second counter, luminescent markers on polished rhodium-plated faceted hands; hand-applied faceted and curved indexes; hand-applied monochrome TAG Heuer logo.

Bracelet: fine brushed stainless steel; solid steel folding clasp with safety pushbuttons.
Indications: small second at 6; date at 6.
Also available: black or silver dial.

LINK CALIBRE S CHRONOGRAPH — REF. CJF7110.BA0587

Movement: TAG Heuer Calibre S – patented electro-mechanical movement chronograph, invented, developed and manufactured by TAG Heuer.
Functions: hours, minutes, seconds; time & chronograph indications by central hands; chronograph 1/100 th of a second: simple, additional timing, slip time; perpetual "retrograde" calendar. **Case:** fine brushed stainless steel; Ø 42mm, 13.0mm thickness; curved scratch sapphire crystal with antireflective double-sided treatment; caseback with set-up instruction for hour and date initialization; polished fixed bezel with black tachymeter scale; polished steel pushbuttons; polished pushbutton crown; water resistant to 200 meters.
Dial: hand-applied curved and faceted indexes; faceted polished rhodium-plated minute and hour hands; luminescent markers on minute and hour hands; flange with 05 to 60 minute indication.
Indications: 2 semi-circular counters diplay either a perpetual "retrograde" calendar in the watch mode or an exclusive 1/100th of a second accuracy in chronograph mode.
Bracelet: solid steel folding clasp with folding buckle, fine brushed stainless steel.
Also available: silver dial, with 2 bluish hands in the 2 subcounters.

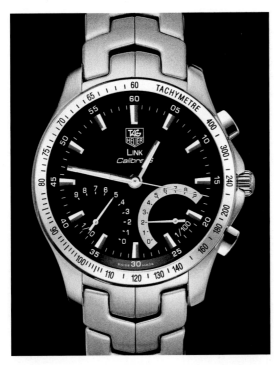

LINK CALIBRE 16 CHRONOGRAPH DAY DATE — REF. CJF211A.BA0594

Movement: mechanical automatic-winding chronograph TAG Heuer Calibre 16.
Functions: hours, minutes, seconds; date; day; chronograph.
Case: fine brushed stainless steel; polished fixed bezel with black tachymeter scale; Ø 42mm, 15.13mm thickness; screw-in polished steel crown; curved scratch resistant sapphire crystal with antireflective double-sided treatment; screw fitting caseback in sapphire crystal; water resistant to 200 meters.
Dial: black, with two zones: the central zone is decorated with vertical and horizontal streaks; hand-applied curved and faceted indexes; luminescent markers on minute and hour hands and on the flange; faceted polished rhodium-plated minute and hour hands; rhodium circles on the 3 counters; monochrome TAG Heuer logo.
Indications: 3 counters, hour at 6, 30-minute at 12, oversized small second at 9; date at 3.
Bracelet: fine brushed stainless steel, solid steel folding clasp with safety pushbuttons.
Also available: silver dial.

LINK CALIBRE 5 DAY DATE   REF. WJF2050.BB0593

Movement: mechanical automatic-winding TAG Heuer Calibre 5.
Functions: hours, minutes, seconds; Day Date.
Case: fine-brushed stainless steel; Ø 42mm, 13.05mm thickness; massive gold 18K (3N) fixed bezel; curved scratch resistant sapphire crystal with antireflective double-sided treatment; water resistant to 200 meters.
Dial: silver; hand-applied curved and faceted indexes; faceted polished minute and hour hands; luminescent markers on faceted minute and hour hands; hand-applied TAG Heuer logo.
Indications: date window at 6; day window at 12 both angled.
Bracelet: fine-brushed stainless steel and 18K massive gold capped, solid steel folding clasp with safety pushbuttons.

LINK CHRONOGRAPH LADY - JEWELLERY   REF. CJF1314.BA0580

Movement: quartz.
Functions: hours, minutes, seconds; date; chronograph with 3 counters.
Case: polished stainless steel; Ø 33mm, 13.05mm thickness; polished steel fixed bezel set with 56 Top Wesselton diamonds (Ø 1.5mm, 0.8 carat), screw-in polished steel crown; curved scratch-resistant sapphire crystal; water resistant to 200 meters.
Dial: white mother-of-pearl dial set with 12 Top Wesselton diamonds (Ø 1.3mm, 0.114 carat); polished rhodium-plated faceted minute and hour hands; minute circle on the flange; monochrome TAG Heuer logo.
Indications: 3 counters at 2, 6 and 10; date at 4:30.
Bracelet: polished stainless steel, double safety clasp with folding buckle.

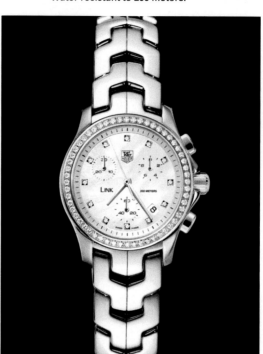

LINK LADY DIAMOND DIAL & DIAMOND BEZEL   REF. WJF1319.BA0572

Movement: quartz.
Functions: hours, minutes, seconds; date.
Case: polished stainless steel, Ø 27mm, 13.05mm thickness; polished steel fixed bezel set with 52 Top Wesselton diamonds (Ø 1.2mm, 0.385 carat); screw-in polished steel crown; curved scratch-resistant sapphire crystal; water resistant to 200 meters.
Dial: white mother-of-pearl dial set with 11 Top Wesselton diamonds (Ø 1.1mm, 0.081 carat); polished rhodium-plated faceted minute and hour hands; timer on the flange; monochrome TAG Heuer logo.
Indications: date at 3.
Bracelet: polished stainless steel, double safety clasp with folding buckle.

MONACO CLASSIC CHRONOGRAPH   REF. CAW2111.FC6183

Movement: mechanical automatic-winding TAG Heuer Calibre 12.
Functions: hours, minutes, seconds; date; chronograph with 2 counters.
Case: fine-brushed and polished stainless steel; 39mm, 13.05mm thickness; curved scratch resistant sapphire crystal with antireflective double-sided treatment; polished crown; polished steel pushbuttons; sapphire caseback fixed with 4 screws; water resistant to 100 meters.
Dial: metallic blue; sunray effect; hand-applied faceted indexes with luminescent markers; faceted polished rhodium-plated minute and hour hands, with luminescent markers; silver square small second and minute counters with red hands; red seconds hand; monochrome TAG Heuer logo.
Indications: small second counter at 3; date at 6; minute counter at 9.
Strap: blue alligator; folding buckle with safety pushbuttons.

MONACO CLASSIC CHRONOGRAPH   REF. CAW2110.FC6177

Movement: mechanical automatic-winding TAG Heuer Calibre 12.
Functions: hours, minutes, seconds; date; chronograph with 2 counters.
Case: fine-brushed and polished stainless steel; 39mm, 13.05mm thickness; curved scratch resistant sapphire crystal with antireflective double-sided treatment; polished crown; polished steel pushbuttons; sapphire caseback fixed with 4 screws; water resistant to 100 meters.
Dial: black; hand-applied faceted indexes with luminescent markers; faceted polished rhodium plated minute and hour hands, with luminescent markers; black square small second and minute counters with silver hands; seconds hand; monochrome TAG Heuer logo.
Indications: small second counter at 3; date at 6; minute counter at 9.
Strap: black alligator; folding buckle with safety pushbuttons.

MONACO WATCH LADY GRANDE DATE   REF. WAW1313.FC6247

Movement: quartz.
Functions: hours, minutes, small seconds; grande date
Case: polished steel case set with 26 Top Wesselton diamonds on horizontal facets (Ø 2mm, total 0.78 ct); 37x36mm, 11.85mm thickness; antireflective double-sided treatment on the curved sapphire crystal glass; water resistant to 100 meters.
Dial: white mother-of-pearl with vertical snail in the middle, 13 Top Wesselton diamonds (Ø 1.1mm, total 0.081 carats); hand-applied faceted indexes; luminescent markers on diamond shaped hands; monochrome TAG Heuer logo.
Indications: small seconds at 6, grande date at 12.
Strap: white alligator, folding buckle with safety pushbuttons.

MONACO WATCH LADY GRANDE DATE   REF. WAW1316.EB0025

Movement: quartz.
Functions: hours, minutes, small seconds; grande date.
Case: polished steel case set with 26 Top Wesselton diamonds on horizontal facets (Ø 2mm, total 0.78 ct); 37x36mm, 11.85mm thickness; antireflective double-sided treatment on the curved sapphire crystal glass; water resistant to 100 meters.
Dial: brown with sunray effect and vertical snail in the middle, 13 Top Wesselton diamonds (Ø 1.1mm, total 0.081 carats); hand-applied faceted indexes; luminescent markers on diamond shaped hands; monochrome TAG Heuer logo.
Indications: small seconds at 6, grande date at 12.
Strap: provided with brown python strap and Galuchat strap in the same box.

TAG HEUER'S PROFESSIONAL SPORTS WATCH   REF. WAE1113.FT6004

Movement: quartz.
Functions: hours, minutes, seconds; date.
Case: 37.5x36.7mm; fine brushed titanium grade 2 case and stainless steel 316L caseback; stainless steel 316L crown at 9; sapphire glass; massive stainless steel 316L folding buckle incorporated in the case with safety pushbuttons at 10 and 2; water resistant to 50 meters.
Dial: black dial with luminous on hands and beside indexes; monochrome TAG Heuer logo.
Indications: date at 3.
Strap: black silicon extensible strap.
Also available: pink dial with pink silicon extensible strap.

ULYSSE NARDIN
Technological Genius

A brilliant pioneer in the watchmaking industry, Ulysse Nardin has become expert at using silicon elements in its manufacturing processes, as demonstrated with the Sonata Silicium model. The brand also has revamped its signature Freak model with a new color and added the limited edition Blue Seal chronograph to its Maxi Marine collection.

Since Rolf Schnyder acquired the company in 1983, Ulysse Nardin's use of cutting-edge technology has catapulted the brand to the upper echelon of luxury watchmaking—and to leadership status within the industry's evolution.

Recently unveiled in a new version draped in blue, the Freak Blue Phantom's movement turns on itself and displays several major innovations, such as the Dual Ulysse escapement. This exclusive new system was perfected by the manufacturer and is based on several different mechanisms of toothed wheels made of silicon. This new technology limits all defects due to oscillation, ensuring maximum precision of the carrousel-tourbillon movement. To obtain the color of this watch, the brand dyed the components via ionic bombardment of a blue titanium alloy.

The Freak Blue Phantom's components are colored with a blue titanium alloy, applied by ionic bombardment.

This process was also used to construct the movement of the Blue Seal chronograph, produced in two limited editions: 999 rose-gold pieces and 1,846 stainless steel pieces.

For women, Ulysse Nardin designed the Lady Diver. A perfect blend of sport and elegance, the Lady Diver is a fusion of styles that can be worn for any occasion.

> Ulysse Nardin used silicon inside and out to create the high-tech, modern Sonata Silicium.

THE SOUND OF SILICON

With an alarm, second time zone, and large date, the Sonata Silicium features many silicon components. Introduced in 2008, this watch's new movement integrates three special inventions that were first tested in the brand's InnoVision concept watch of 2007: front side/back side etched anchor with integrated silicon safety pin; front side/back side etched roller with integrated silicon impulse finger; silicon (1.1.1) cut hairspring (patent pending). The Sonata Silicium is also Ulysse Nardin's first available timepiece to run without any lubrication and the anchor, oscillator, balance spring, and escapement wheel are made of silicon.

For aesthetic reasons, Ulysse Nardin used silicon to beautify the dial as well. With its gray dial—the raw color of silicon—and its Côtes de Genève decoration, the Sonata Silicium is a high-tech, modern timepiece with classic lines. Limited to two series of 500 pieces each in rose gold and white gold, this watch displays the hours, minutes, seconds, cathedral chime alarm with countdown, second time zone, and date.

TOP   Also available in steel and/or on a bracelet, this rose-gold version of the Blue Seal chronograph is limited to 999 pieces.

CENTER   A dial made partially of silicon gives the Sonata Silicium a totally unique look.

BOTTOM   The Lady Diver is the perfect combination of sport and elegance.

QUADRATO PERPETUAL   REF. 320-90/91

Movement: UN-32.
Functions: perpetual calendar adjustable backwards and forwards from a single crown; second time zone on main dial with patented quickset; permanent home time indicated by third hand.
Case: 18K white gold; 42x42mm.
Suggested price: $53,800

Also available: available in 18K rose gold; various dial combinations; available on bracelet with ceramic elements; available with diamond bezel.

QUADRATO DUAL TIME   REF. 243-92-7/601

Movement: UN-24.
Functions: second time zone on main dial with patented quickset; permanent home time in window at 9; big date in double window.
Case: stainless steel; 42x42mm; exhibition caseback.
Suggested price: $9,300
Also available: available in 18K rose gold; various dial combinations; available with diamond bezel; available on strap.

CAPRICE   REF. 133-91AC/06-02

Movement: UN-13.
Case: stainless steel; 34x35mm; cabochon crown; exhibition caseback.
Suggested price: $18,500
Also available: available in 18K rose and white gold; various dial combinations; on bracelet; with or without diamond bezel.

MAXI MARINE CHRONOMETER   REF. 266-67-8/42

Movement: UN-26; COSC-certified movement.
Functions: power-reserve indicator; oversized small seconds hand.
Case: 18K rose gold; 43mm.
Suggested price: $39,600
Also available: available in stainless steel; various dial combinations; available on leather or rubber strap.

BLUE SEAL
REF. 356-68LE-3

Movement: UN-35.
Functions: chronograph with exclusive 45 minutes register; small seconds at 3; date window at 6.
Case: 18K rose gold; 41mm; exhibition caseback.
Note: limited edition of 999 pieces.
Suggested price: $26,600
Also available: available in stainless steel (limited to 1,846 pieces); available on strap or steel or rose-gold bracelet.

MAXI MARINE CHRONOGRAPH
REF. 356-66-3/355

Movement: UN-35.
Functions: chronograph with exclusive 45 minutes register; date window at 4.
Case: 18K rose gold; 41mm.
Suggested price: $23,400
Also available: available in stainless steel; various dial combinations; bracelet or strap.

MAXI DIVER CHRONOGRAPH
REF. 8003-102-7/91

Movement: UN-800.
Functions: chronograph with central seconds hand and small seconds register at 9.
Case: stainless steel; 42.7mm; unidirectional rotating bezel; exhibition caseback.
Suggested price: $10,000
Also available: available in various dial combinations; available on rubber/titanium strap.

MAXI DIVER CHRONOGRAPH
REF. 8006-102-3A/92

Movement: UN-800.
Functions: chronograph with central seconds hand and small seconds register at 9.
Case: 18K rose gold; 42.7mm; unidirectional rotating bezel; exhibition caseback.
Suggested price: $32,000
Also available: available in various dial combinations; available on bracelet.

MAXI DIVER   REF. 265-90-3/91

Movement: UN-26.
Functions: power-reserve indicator; oversized seconds hand.
Case: titanium/18K rose gold; 45mm; unidirectional turning bezel; screw-down security crown; exhibition caseback.
Suggested price: $19,900
Also available: available in stainless steel/titanium; various dial combinations.

LADY DIVER   REF. 8106-101EC-3C/10

Movement: UN-810.
Functions: date at 6; diamond markers on dial.
Case: 18K rose gold; 40mm; exhibition caseback.
Suggested price: $26,700
Also available: available in stainless steel; various dial combinations; available without diamonds.

DUAL TIME   REF. 246-55/31

Movement: UN-24.
Functions: second time zone on main dial with patented quickset; permanent home time in window at 9; big date in double window.
Case: 18K rose gold; 42mm; exhibition caseback.
Suggested price: $19,900
Also available: available in stainless steel; available on steel or rose-gold bracelet.

DUAL TIME   REF. 243-55-7/92

Movement: UN-24.
Functions: second time zone on main dial with patented quickset; permanent home time in window at 9; big date in double window.
Case: stainless steel; 42mm; exhibition caseback.
Suggested price: $7,300
Also available: available in 18K rose gold; available on steel or rose-gold bracelet.

GMT +- PERPETUAL
REF. 320-60/69

Movement: UN-32.
Functions: perpetual calendar adjustable backwards and forwards from a single crown; second time zone on main dial with patented quickset; permanent home time indicated by third hand.
Case: 18K white gold; 42mm.
Suggested price: $49,800
Also available: available in 18K red gold; various dial combinations; available on bracelet.

SONATA SILICIUM
REF. 676-85

Movement: UN-67.
Functions: chiming 24-hour alarm with countdown indicator; dual time system with instant time zone adjustor.
Case: 18K rose gold; 42mm
Note: limited edition of 500 pieces.
Suggested price: $71,000
Also available: available in 18K white gold.

FREAK BLUE PHANTOM
REF. 020-81

Movement: UN-202; patented "Dual Ulysse" escapement in silicium.
Functions: Carrousel-Tourbillon; 7-day power reserve.
Case: 18K white gold; 44.5mm; exhibition caseback.
Suggested price: $84,800

HOURSTRIKER-EROTICA
REF. 6119-103/P0-P2

Movement: UN-611.
Functions: automatic chime activation; animated Jaquemart.
Case: platinum; 42mm; exhibition caseback.
Suggested price: $130,000
Also available: available in 18K rose gold.

UNIVERSAL GENÈVE
Daring Spirit

More than a century after Universal Genève's founding, the Swiss watchmaker began updating its legendary collection with new timepieces that remain true to the company's historic sense of style and fondness for technological exploration. The latest models embody the range of its collection, with connections to achievements from the past alongside technology that represent the watchmaker's future.

L ast year, Universal Genève introduced the stainless steel Microtor Cabriolet, a descendant of the Cabriolet of 1928, the brand's first reversible watch. Its patented design was born out of necessity: in the 1920s, shattered crystals were common amid the wristwatch's growing popularity. As a clever solution, Universal Genève (then known as Universal Watch) invented a mechanism that allows the case to be flipped over to protect the crystal.

The watchmaker revisits that groundbreaking design with the new Microtor Cabriolet. A button triggers a latch that releases the rectangular case from its mooring at 6:00 while it remains anchored at 12:00 by a pivoting system. Its well-engineered mechanics ensure smooth operation while the case is articulated and help protect the watch and case from scratches.

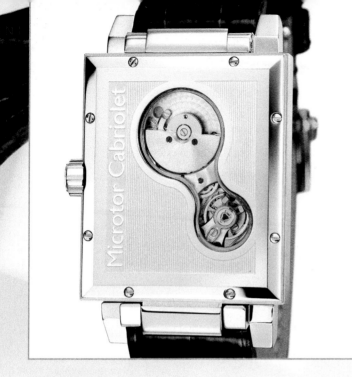

> In the 1940s, the brand earned a reputation innovating pieces still sought by collectors today.

When the case is secured dial-side down, the Microtor UG 101 movement is visible through a crystal aperture. Shaped like an elongated 8, the opening offers a view of the automatic movement's escapement and Microtor, the brand's signature micro-oscillating weight first introduced in 1955. Along with an engraving of the watch's name, the caseback is also decorated with a vertical guilloché.

The Microtor Cabriolet case (32.5mm wide, 52mm long and 11.35mm thick) has beveled edges that frame the dial's dynamic arrangement. Universal Genève offers six dial variations, including different options for both colors (silver, black, anthracite) and numerals (Arabic, Roman). On each, a colored triangle points to the date in an opening at 6:00.

In the 1940s, Universal Genève earned a reputation as an innovator thanks to the Uni-Compax, Aero-Compax, Tri-Compax, and Polerouter—legendary timepieces still sought by collectors today.

When Vincent Lapaire became the company's CEO in 2004, he set out to build on that heritage, starting with new men and women's models. Over the next two years, the

brand unveiled several models powered by the newest proprietary Microtor movements.

In 2008, Universal Genève gave the Microtor UG 101 a different look, offering a new white dial and stainless steel bracelet. A smooth dial replaces the previous year's guilloché wave decoration, while a redesigned minute scale has been relocated to the dial's outer rim. Blue hour markers complement the white dial, as does the blued-steel central seconds hand, a signature detail on a number of Universal Genève watches.

The Microtor UG 101 case features a round shape that measures 41.6mm in diameter. Inside, it houses a movement refined with rhodium-plated bridges decorated with a circular Côtes de Genève pattern.

With its latest generation of timekeeping creations, Universal Genève continues to give voice to the company's daring spirit.

FACING PAGE
The stainless steel case of the Microtor Cabriolet is reversible thanks to an innovative axis at 12:00 that allows the case to rotate 360 degrees in both directions.

THIS PAGE
TOP LEFT A crystal in the Microtor Cabriolet caseback reveals the micro-rotor and escapement of Universal Genève's proprietary Microtor UG 101 movement.

BOTTOM Featuring a new dial design, the Microtor UG 101 houses a proprietary movement that provides 42 hours of power reserve.

MICROTOR CABRIOLET   REF. 8101.129/1A97.CD

Movement: self-winding proprietary Microtor UG 101; 42-hour power reserve; rhodium-plated bridges decorated with circular Côtes de Genève.
Functions: hour, minute, second; date.
Case: stainless steel; 52x32.5mm, thickness: 11.35mm; shaped sapphire crystal with antireflective treatment; reversible rectangular case fitted to the case carrier with a 12:00 axis allowing 360° rotation in both directions; caseback engraving is vertical guilloché with "Microtor Cabriolet" inscription; 8-shaped apertures revealing the micro-rotor and the escapement.
Dial: silver-colored galvanic with black transferred Arabic numerals and lines in the center.
Strap: brown hand-sewn genuine crocodile leather; edge-to-edge cut strap; folding clasp with triple safety blade.
Suggested price: $9,850
Also available: brown Barenia calfskin leather strap; diamond-set version with 80 diamonds.

MICROTOR CABRIOLET   REF. 8101.129/046A.CA

Movement: self-winding proprietary Microtor UG 101; 42-hour power reserve; rhodium-plated bridges decorated with circular Côtes de Genève.
Functions: hour, minute, second; date.
Case: stainless steel; bezel set with 80 diamonds (0.725 ct); 52x32.5mm, thickness: 11.35mm; shaped sapphire crystal with antireflective treatment; reversible rectangular case fitted to the case carrier with a 12:00 axis allowing 360° rotation in both directions; caseback engraving is vertical guilloché with "Microtor Cabriolet" inscription; 8-shaped apertures revealing the micro-rotor and the escapement.
Dial: anthracite galvanic; aubergine-colored transferred Roman numerals.
Strap: black hand-sewn genuine crocodile leather; edge-to-edge cut strap; folding clasp with triple safety blade.
Suggested price: $15,150
Also available: black Barenia calfskin leather strap; with or without diamonds.

MICROTOR CABRIOLET   REF. 8101.129/167.CB

Movement: self-winding proprietary Microtor UG 101; 42-hour power reserve; rhodium-plated bridges decorated with circular Côtes de Genève.
Functions: hour, minute, second; date.
Case: stainless steel; 52x32.5mm, thickness: 11.35mm; shaped sapphire crystal with antireflective treatment; reversible rectangular case fitted to the case carrier with a 12:00 axis allowing 360° rotation in both directions; caseback engraving is vertical guilloché with "Microtor Cabriolet" inscription; 8-shaped apertures enable to admire the micro-rotor and the escapement.
Dial: silver-colored galvanic; midnight-blue transferred Arabic numerals.
Strap: blue hand-sewn genuine crocodile leather; edge-to-edge cut strap; folding clasp with triple safety blade.
Suggested price: $9,850
Also available: black Barenia calfskin leather strap; diamond-set version with 80 diamonds.

MICROTOR CABRIOLET   REF. 8101.129/937.BA

Movement: self-winding proprietary Microtor UG 101; 42-hour power reserve; rhodium-plated bridges decorated with circular Côtes de Genève.
Functions: hour, minute, second; date.
Case: stainless steel; 52x32.5mm, thickness: 11.35mm; shaped sapphire crystal with antireflective treatment; reversible rectangular case fitted to the case carrier with a 12:00 axis allowing 360° rotation in both directions; caseback engraving is vertical guilloché with "Microtor Cabriolet" inscription; 8-shaped apertures revealing the micro-rotor and the escapement.
Dial: black galvanic; white transferred Arabic numerals.
Strap: black hand-sewn genuine Barenia calfskin leather; edge-to-edge cut strap; folding clasp with triple safety blade.
Suggested price: $9,500
Also available: black Barenia calfskin leather strap; diamond-set version with 80 diamonds.

MICROTOR UG 100   REF. 4100.121.125/125A.CD

Movement: self-winding proprietary Microtor UG 100; COSC-certified chronometer; 42-hour power reserve; rhodium-plated bridges and main-plate; diamond-polished snailed bridges.
Functions: hour, minute, second; date.
Case: 18K 5N 750 pink gold; bezel set with 50 Top Wesselton diamonds VVS-VS (1.56 ct); Ø 42.4mm, thickness 10.3mm; cambered sapphire crystal, glareproofed; mineral glass caseback revealing movement; exclusive crown in 18K 5N 750 pink gold; water resistant to 5atm.
Dial: AG920 solid silver.
Strap: brown hand-sewn genuine crocodile leather; pin buckle in 5N 18K750 pink gold.
Suggested price: $27,900
Also available: 18K 3N 750 yellow-gold case; with or without setting.
Note: limited edition.

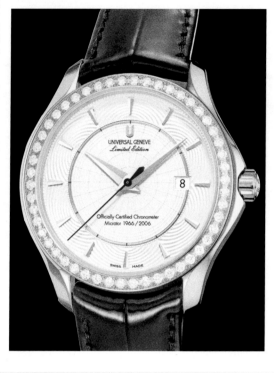

MICROTOR UG 101   REF. 8101.126/368.CA

Movement: self-winding proprietary Microtor UG 101; 42-hour power reserve; rhodium-plated bridges decorated with circular Côtes de Genève motif.
Functions: hour, minute, second; date.
Case: stainless steel; Ø 41.6mm, thickness: 10.32mm; cambered sapphire crystal, glareproofed; mineral glass caseback revealing movement; exclusive crown; water resistant to 5atm.
Dial: white lacquered.
Strap: black hand-sewn crocodile leather; folding clasp with triple safety blade.
Suggested price: $6,050
Also available: black calfskin leather strap or on steel bracelet.

TIMER CHRONOGRAPH   REF. 871.128/1120.CD

Movement: self-winding chronograph caliber UG 71.6; 42-hour power reserve; sun-brushed rhodium-plated oscillating weight, hallowed with a gilded engraved logo.
Functions: 3 counters: 12 hour, 30 minute and 60 second; central chronograph seconds; date.
Case: stainless steel; Ø 41.6mm, thickness: 13.65mm; cambered sapphire crystal, glareproofed; mineral glass caseback revealing movement; exclusive crown; water resistant to 5atm.
Dial: two-tone silver-colored/anthracite.
Strap: brown hand-sewn genuine crocodile leather; folding clasp with triple safety blade.
Suggested price: $6,800
Also available: natural genuine Bulgaro calfskin leather strap or on steel bracelet.

UNI-TIMER   REF. 871.127/0301.AL

Movement: self-winding chronograph caliber UG 71.5; 42-hour power reserve; sun-brushed rhodium-plated oscillating weight, hallowed with a gilded engraved logo.
Functions: 2 counters: 30 minute and 60 second; central chronograph seconds; date.
Case: stainless steel; Ø41.6mm, thickness: 13.65mm; cambered sapphire crystal, glareproofed; mineral glass caseback revealing movement; exclusive crown; water resistant to 5atm.
Dial: two-tone ruthenium/silvered guilloché.
Bracelet: stainless steel with safety folding clasp.
Suggested price: $7,300
Also available: dark brown genuine crocodile leather strap or natural genuine Bulgaro calfskin leather strap.

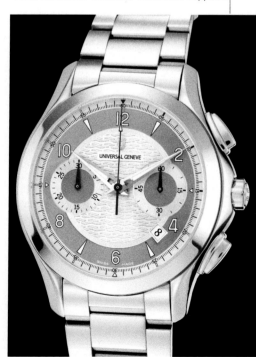

URWERK
Rarified Air

Artistic vision and mechanical expertise go hand-in-hand at Urwerk, an innovative watch-maker passionate about uniting the best ideas from the past with the very latest style in order to achieve an original vision. Watchmaker Felix Baumgartner and designer Martin Frei began working together in 1995, dedicating the next 14 years to blazing trails with timepieces made with cutting-edge science and the experienced hands of artisans.

THIS PAGE Artist and designer Martin Frei and master watchmaker Felix Baumgartner founded Urwerk in 1997.

FACING PAGE Urwerk will produce 10 pieces of the special black edition UR-103 Hexagon. The platinum case (50x36x13.5mm) takes its dark tone from the PE-CVD treatment.

At first glance, Urwerk's watches may appear to be of interstellar origins. But closer inspection reveals that these fantastical machines are indeed designed to articulate time elegantly on the wrists of the earthbound.

Both the company's name and unique watchmaking point-of-view represent an amalgamation of ideas explored by two different cultures.

The first syllable, "Ur" refers to the ancient ciry of Ur in Sumeria (Mesopotamia), where the lunisolar calendar was developed in 6,000 B.C. by dividing a year into 12 lunar months. Much of what we know about horology today is based on the Sumerians' achievements in measuring time during the fifth century B.C.

The final syllable, "werk" is a German term that describes the undertaking of an enterprise with far-reaching implications. In this case, the word is used to represent the evolution of watchmaking through the ages.

Urwerk lives up to its name by developing the technology used for the UR-202 Turbine Automatic, the first watch in the world to regulate winding with compressed air. A three-way selector on the back of the watch tailors the winding resistance to the wearer's level of activity by adjusting the compression generated by the twin turbines.

Seen through the caseback, the winding system operates on the principles of fluid dynamics. The wearer's movements force the turbines to spin, driving air through holes into a small chamber. When the airflow is restricted, it increases pressure, thereby slowing the winding rotor's oscillations and preventing over-winding.

Both turbine blades can be seen spinning freely when the normal setting is engaged during day-to-day activities. The blades can also be locked into place in anticipation of extreme activity. The normal setting provides another benefit, acting as a shock absorber that prolongs the movement's viability.

The connection to black is an emotional one for Baumgartner. "Black evokes mechanical memories of the parts of old clocks that my father restored in his workshop."

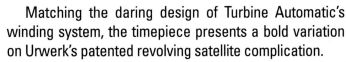

Matching the daring design of Turbine Automatic's winding system, the timepiece presents a bold variation on Urwerk's patented revolving satellite complication.

To create this model, watchmakers replaced the trio of rotating hour discs used for previous models with a complex system of telescoping minute hands. They extend and contract to mirror the arc of the minute scale located on the bottom edge of the dial.

A trio of arms radiates from the carousel at the center of the UR-202 movement to articulate the time. Attached to each arm is a four-sided hour marker with a different number embossed and treated with SuperLumiNova on each side.

The telescopic minute hands extend from the center of the hour markers, providing a reading of the minute. The minute hand achieves its maximum extension (16.6mm) at the 30-minute position, retracting to 1.8mm when it's not passing over the minute scale. Located at both ends of the scale are two additional complications, a moonphase on the left and day/night on the right.

The complex system's smooth operation is ensured by the uncompromising quality standards used to manufacture the rotating hub. The company machines the elements that make up the system at its workshop, where high-tech cutting machines are able to achieve a level of accuracy measured by the 1/1,000 of a millimeter.

The watch's sculptural case (45.6x43.5x15mm) is rendered in white gold, red gold, black PE-CVD platinum and AlTiN coating.

For the past decade, when Urwerk introduced a new model, it also produced a limited edition version of that model in black. The company continues its tradition with the UR-103 Hexagon in black platinum; a limited edition of 10 pieces.

Both of the company's founders say they have a natural affinity for the dark shade. For Frei, who sketches out his ideas in ink on paper, black is part of the creative process. "It is at this moment, when the drawing is without color or artifice, that the true nature of an idea is revealed, and I can really judge the value of a project."

The connection to black is an emotional one for Baumgartner, a talented horologist who was born into a family of watchmakers. "Black evokes mechanical memories of the parts of old clocks that my father restored in his workshop. When I was seven years old I was already rubbing the black patina of time off old wheels to restore their mobility by using a rag soaked in grease remover. Those parts appeared to be ageless, but it was perhaps simply that they were much, much older than me. Since then, black has been synonymous in my mind with timelessness."

URWERK®
BAUMGARTNER & FREI / GENEVE

FACING PAGE
The UR-103 Hexagon's hours and minutes have been treated with SuperLumiNova, making them easy to read during the day and (pictured here) at night.

THIS PAGE
LEFT Turbine Automatic uses a patented carousel system to display the hours with rotating squares and the minutes with telescopic arms. Moonphase and day/night indicators are located at opposite ends of the minute scale.

BELOW Visible from the back, a three-way switch controls the level of air compression inside the case. Restricting airflow increases the air pressure and slows down the turbines and the winding rotor. Creating more resistance against the rotor is recommended when the watch is being worn during strenuous activities.

VACHERON CONSTANTIN
Freedom of Choice

Whether it's a bespoke suit or a custom car, having a status symbol tailored to satisfy a unique taste is truly one of life's most luxurious experiences. Leave it to Vacheron Constantin to extend that rarified pleasure to watch connoisseurs. With its new Quai de l'Ile line, the venerable watchmaker puts collectors at the center of the creation process.

The special collection takes its name from Vacheron Constantin's Geneva address since the late 1800s. The Quai de l'Ile, commissioned by Jean-François Constantin in the late 1800s, is where aristocrats came to order custom timepieces, which were then produced by watchmaking artisans known as *cabinotiers*. Jean-Marc Vacheron, one of the era's most famous *cabinotiers*, is the company's founder. More than 250 years after he established the brand, the world's oldest manufacture continues its tradition of giving people what they want with the Quai de l'Ile.

The new line launched with two automatic models: the Quai de l'Ile Date and the Quai de l'Ile Day-Date and Power-Reserve. Both are available in three standard versions with 41mm cases made of palladium, pink gold or titanium.

Quai de l'Ile Day-Date and Power-Reserve case can be personalized using a combination of those three metals for the lugs, bezel and lateral flanks. Vacheron Constantin also offers different finishes for the dial and movement: gray dial with rhodium-plated movement; white dial with rhodium-plated movement; and black dial with ruthenium movement. In fact, nearly 400 variations are offered.

A world's first in haute horlogerie, this groundbreaking approach epitomizes the company's history of creating exceptional timepieces and provides incomparable personalized service, which reflects Vacheron Constantin's motto: Do better if possible, which is always possible.

Vacheron Constantin ensures authenticity by using the latest anti-counterfeiting technology, such as laser engraving and ultraviolet ink symbols located on the dials of the Quai de l'Ile models.

The Quai de l'Ile provides a chic balance of tradition and technology, combining the fluid lines of a classic cushion-shaped case with an innovative modular construction. It's this union of form and function that makes this model's high level of personalization possible, giving clients the ability to choose different metals for the case middle, back, bezel and crown.

As impressive as the case is, perhaps the most eye-catching aspect of the Quai de l'Ile is its semi-transparent dial: each integrates sophisticated security printing techniques traditionally used to thwart counterfeiting of paper currency and passports.

A combination of secret techniques is used to create these Quai de l'Ile dials. Affixed to the sapphire crystal is the same security polymer used to make bank notes: on the movement side, the film is printed with a pattern of Maltese crosses and concentric circles; concentric rays decorate the dial side. Not only do these graphics protect consumers against fakes, but they also provide spectacular decoration, the likes of which have never been seen in the world of watchmaking.

Vacheron Constantin uses a fine deposit of white gold—called metallization—to create micro-texts on the dials. Each watch features an extract, translated into English, from letters written between Jaques-Barthélémy Vacheron and his associate François Constantin.

With these pioneering techniques, Vacheron Constantin takes the art of watchmaking to a completely new level.

Recognized for generations as one of the greatest Swiss watchmakers, Vacheron Constantin earned its tremendous reputation for technical leadership by adhering to a philosophy that values both cutting-edge technology and extreme precision.

That impressive heritage defines the two automatic movements the company uses to power the Quai de l'Ile models. Designed, developed and produced in-house, both are stamped with the Geneva Hallmark, a prestigious honor bestowed on only the highest quality movements.

The 2460QH caliber used in the Quai de l'Ile Date includes a rotating disc that highlights the date, which is laser engraved on the sapphire crystal. The 2475SC/1 caliber that powers the Quai de l'Ile Day-Date and Power-Reserve incorporates a trio of subdials that indicate what its name suggests: the day of the week, date, and power reserve.

Aesthetically, each movement is carefully embellished with Côtes de Genève decorations, rhodium-plated bridges and circular-grained plates, making an artistic statement that matches its respective technical creativity.

THIS PAGE

TOP LEFT   The Quai de l'Ile timepiece movement is available with two different finishes to the rotor: rhodium or ruthenium. Above, the darker gray ruthenium-plated rotor of the 2460QH movement is seen through the sapphire crystal caseback of the Automatic with Date in 18-karat rose gold.

TOP RIGHT   Vacheron Constantin designed a new triple-fold deployant clasp for the Quai de l'Ile line. Above, the buckle, with its half-Maltese cross design, is shown in 18-karat rose gold against a dark brown alligator strap.

FACING PAGE
This Quai de l'Ile Day-Date and Power-Reserve is customized in palladium and titanium, with a dark dial and a black alligator strap.

The refined approach to luxury expressed by the Quai de l'Ile line extends beyond the wrist with a newly redesigned presentation box. While compact in size, the box features an unusual display window for admiring the watch when it's stored, plus space to hold the watch's accessories. An individually numbered passport guaranteeing the watch's authenticity accompanies each Quai de l'Ile. Employing the same security printing techniques used for the dial, the passport is counterfeit proof.

In addition to this official document, the box includes a magnifying glass to explore the microscopic printing on the dial, a microfiber cloth for cleaning, a second strap and a travel case. It also houses a USB stick that contains the watch's usage and maintenance instructions, along with technical information and a multimedia presentation about the watch.

With the new Quai de l'Ile, the world's oldest manufacture makes itself at home on watchmaking's cutting edge.

QUAI DE L'ILE DATE SELF-WINDING REF. 86050/000D

Movement: mechanical self-winding Vacheron Constantin Caliber 2460QH with Geneva Hallmark; 43-hour power reserve; 27 jewels; 28,800 vph.
Functions: hours, minutes, central seconds; date disc with optimal legibility (numerals engraved and inked on the sapphire dial) and ruthenium-coated with a white mark. **Case:** palladium; Ø 41mm; screw-down back with sapphire crystal; water resistant to 30 meters (100 feet).

Dial: sapphire crystal (galvanic growth of nickel, metallization, and laser engraving with or without inking) and security transparent film (intaglio printing, security inks and micro-printing); numerals 3, 6, 9 and 12 are in galvanic growth of nickel; other numerals are engraved and inked in black or white.
Strap: black or brown hand-stitched, saddle-finished, square-scaled, high-shine alligator leather; triple-blade palladium folding clasp, polished half Maltese cross.
Note: delivered with a second strap in black or brown vulcarbonized rubber.
Suggested price: $35,300
Also available: in 18K pink gold or titanium.

QUAI DE L'ILE DATE SELF-WINDING REF. 86050/000R

Movement: mechanical self-winding Vacheron Constantin Caliber 2460QH with Geneva Hallmark; 43-hour power reserve; 27 jewels; 28,800 vph.
Functions: hours, minutes, central seconds; date disc with optimal legibility (numerals engraved and inked on the sapphire dial) and ruthenium-coated with a black mark. **Case:** 18K pink gold; Ø 41mm; screw-down back with sapphire crystal; water resistant to 30 meters (100 feet).

Dial: sapphire crystal (galvanic growth of nickel, metallization, and laser engraving with or without inking) and security transparent film (intaglio printing, security inks and micro-printing); numerals 3, 6, 9 and 12 are in galvanic growth of nickel; other numerals are engraved and inked in black or white.
Strap: black or brown hand-stitched, saddle-finished, square-scaled, high-shine alligator leather; triple-blade palladium folding clasp, polished half Maltese cross.
Note: delivered with a second strap in black or brown vulcarbonized rubber.
Suggested price: $31,500
Also available: in palladium or titanium.

QUAI DE L'ILE DAY-DATE AND POWER RESERVE SELF-WINDING REF. 85050/000D

Movement: mechanical self-winding Vacheron Constantin Caliber 2475SC with Geneva Hallmark; 43-hour power reserve; 27 jewels; 28,800 vph.
Functions: hours, minutes, seconds; date and day indicated by hands; power reserve.
Case: palladium; Ø 41mm; screw-down back with sapphire crystal; water resistant to 30 meters (100 feet).

Dial: sapphire crystal (galvanic growth of nickel, metallization, and laser engraving with or without inking) and security transparent film (intaglio printing, security inks and micro-printing); numerals 3, 6, 9 and 12 are in galvanic growth of nickel; other numerals are engraved and inked in black or white.
Strap: black or brown hand-stitched, saddle-finished, square-scaled, high-shine alligator leather; triple-blade palladium folding clasp, polished half Maltese cross.
Note: delivered with a second strap in black or brown vulcarbonized rubber.
Suggested price: $49,900
Also available: in 18K pink gold or titanium.

QUAI DE L'ILE DAY-DATE AND POWER RESERVE SELF-WINDING REF. 85050/000R

Movement: mechanical self-winding Vacheron Constantin Caliber 2475SC with Geneva Hallmark; 43-hour power reserve; 27 jewels; 28,800 vph.
Functions: hours, minutes, seconds; date and day indicated by hands; power reserve.
Case: 18K pink gold; Ø 41mm; screw-down back with sapphire crystal; water resistant to 30 meters (100 feet).

Dial: sapphire crystal (galvanic growth of nickel, metallization, and laser engraving with or without inking) and security transparent film (intaglio printing, security inks and micro-printing); numerals 3, 6, 9 and 12 are in galvanic growth of nickel; other numerals are engraved and inked in black or white.
Strap: black or brown hand-stitched, saddle-finished, square-scaled, high-shine alligator leather; triple-blade palladium folding clasp, polished half Maltese cross.
Note: delivered with a second strap in black or brown vulcarbonized rubber.
Suggested price: $44,600
Also available: in palladium or titanium.

QUAI DE L'ILE DATE SELF-WINDING   REF. 86050/000T

Movement: mechanical self-winding Vacheron Constantin Caliber 2460QH with Geneva Hallmark; 43-hour power reserve; 27 jewels; 28,800 vph.
Functions: hours, minutes, central seconds; date disc with optimal legibility (numerals engraved and inked on the sapphire dial) and rhodium-coated with a black mark.
Case: titanium; Ø 41mm; screw-down back with sapphire crystal; water resistant to 30 meters (100 feet).
Dial: sapphire crystal (galvanic growth of nickel, metallization, and laser engraving with or without inking) and security transparent film (intaglio printing, security inks and micro-printing); numerals 3, 6, 9 and 12 are in galvanic growth of nickel; other numerals are engraved and inked in black or white.
Strap: black vulcarbon-ized rubber; triple-blade titanium folding clasp, polished half Maltese cross.
Note: delivered with a second strap in black hand-stitched, saddle-finished, square-scaled, high-shine alligator leather.
Suggested price: $29,900
Also available: in palladium or 18K pink gold.

OVERSEAS CHRONOGRAPH   REF. 49150/000R

Movement: mechanical self-winding Vacheron Constantin Caliber 1137; 37 jewels; 21,600 vph; 40-hour power reserve; anti-magnetic protection.
Functions: hours, minutes, running seconds at 6; 30-minute and 12-hour totalizers at 3 and at 9, respectively; center chronograph seconds; chronograph mechanism to 1/6 of a second; date calendar shown in twin oversized dial apertures at 12.
Case: 18K pink gold; Ø 42mm; solid back stamped with "Overseas" medallion, secured with screws; water resistant to 150 meters (500 feet).
Dial: anthracite; 12 applied 18K pink-gold hour-makers with white luminescent strip.
Strap: hand-stitched alligator leather; pink-gold buckle.
Note: delivered with a second strap in dark brown vulcarbonized rubber.
Suggested price: $33,800
Also available: on 18K pink-gold bracelet.

QUAI DE L'ILE DAY-DATE AND POWER RESERVE SELF-WINDING   REF. 85050/000T

Movement: mechanical self-winding Vacheron Constantin Caliber 2475SC with Geneva Hallmark; 43-hour power reserve; 27 jewels; 28,800 vph.
Functions: hours, minutes, seconds; date and day indicated by hands; power reserve. **Case:** titanium; Ø 41mm; screw-down back with sapphire crystal; water resistant to 30 meters (100 feet). **Dial:** sapphire crystal (galvanic growth of nickel, metallization, and laser engraving with or without inking) and security transparent film (intaglio printing, security inks and micro-printing); numerals 3, 6, 9 and 12 are in galvanic growth of nickel; other numerals are engraved and inked in black or white.
Strap: black vulcarbon-ized rubber; triple-blade titanium folding clasp, polished half Maltese cross.
Note: delivered with a second strap in black hand-stitched, saddle-finished, square-scaled, high-shine alligator leather.
Suggested price: $42,400
Also available: in palla-dium or 18K pink gold.

OVERSEAS DUAL TIME   REF. 47751/000R

Movement: mechanical self-winding Vacheron Constantin Caliber 1222SC; 40-hour power reserve; 28,800 vph; 34 jewels.
Functions: hours, minutes, seconds; power-reserve indicator at 9; second time-zone with day/night indicator at 6; date with hand at 3.
Case: 18K pink gold; Ø 42mm; solid back stamped with "Overseas" medal-lion, secured with screws; set with 88 brilliant-cut diamonds (approx. 0.90 ct); water resistant to 150 meters (500 feet).
Dial: matte white varnish; 10 applied hour-markers in 18K pink-gold with white luminescent strip.
Strap: white hand-stitched, square-scaled alligator leather.
Note: delivered with a second strap in white vulcarbonized rubber; pink-gold buckle.
Suggested price: $36,900
Also available: in white gold.

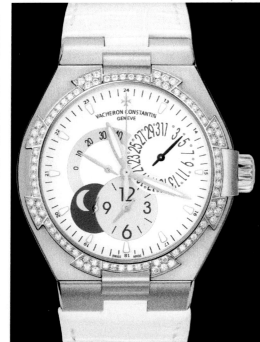

PATRIMONY TRADITIONNELLE AUTOMATIC   REF. 87172

Movement: mechanical automatic-winding Vacheron Constantin Caliber 2455; jewels; 11'''1/5; Ø 25.6mm, thickness: 3.6mm; 40-hour power reserve; 27 jewels; balance with 28,800 vph; decorated with circular-graining and Côtes de Genève patterns, beveled; hallmarked with the Geneva Seal.
Functions: hour, minute, small seconds at 9; date at 3.
Case: 18K white-gold two-piece case; Ø 38mm, thickness: 8.1mm; polished

finish; antireflective curved sapphire crystal; white-gold crown; screw-on back with knurled profile, displaying the movement through a sapphire crystal; water resistant to 3atm.
Dial: very light opaline silvered, finely grained; subdial decorated with circular beads; second and minute rings as black railway track on a dark silvered background; white-gold logo and bâton markers; white-gold Dauphine hands.
Strap: black hand-stitched alligator leather; white-gold clasp.
Suggested price: $20,500
Also available: in pink gold.

PATRIMONY CONTEMPORAINE AUTOMATIC   REF. 85180

Movement: mechanical automatic-winding Vacheron Constantin Caliber 2450; 49-hour power reserve; 27 jewels; 28,800 vph; guilloché 22K pink-gold rotor; hallmarked with the Geneva Seal.
Functions: hours, minutes, seconds; date at 6.
Case: 18K pink-gold, flared three-piece case; Ø 40mm, thickness: 8.5mm; flared, polished finish; curved sapphire crystal; pink-gold crown; snap-on

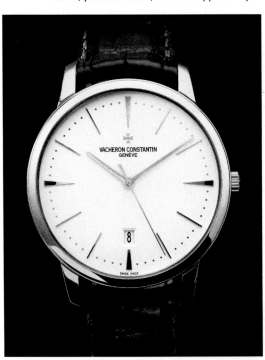

back displaying the movement through a sapphire crystal; water resistant to 3atm.
Dial: silvered, grained; applied pink-gold pointed and bâton markers; hollowed minute track with a gilded cabochon; pink-gold curved index hands.
Strap: alligator leather; pink-gold clasp.
Suggested price: $19,100
Also available: in white or yellow gold.

PATRIMONY CONTEMPORAINE   REF. 81180

Movement: mechanical manual-winding Vacheron Constantin Caliber 1400; 40-hour power reserve; 20 jewels; 28,800 vph; hallmarked with the Geneva Seal.
Functions: hour, minute.
Case: 950 platinum; Ø 40mm; water resistant to 30 meters (100 feet).
Dial: light opaline silvered; grained; with a slightly curved perimeter; applied

white-gold pointed and bâton markers; minute track with a white-gold cabochon; white-gold index hands.
Strap: black hand-stitched alligator leather; 950 platinum clasp.
Suggested price: $33,800
Also available: in pink, white or yellow gold.

PATRIMONY CONTEMPORAINE BI-RETROGRADE   REF. 86020

Movement: mechanical automatic-winding Vacheron Constantin Caliber 2460 R31 R7; 43-hour power reserve; 27 jewels; 28,800 vph; pink-gold rotor guilloché; hallmarked with the Geneva Seal.
Functions: hours, minutes; retrograde day and date.
Case: 18K pink-gold three-piece case; Ø 42.5mm, thickness: 10.3mm; flared, polished finish; curved sapphire crystal; 2 correctors on the middle, for the

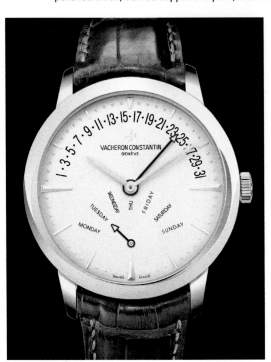

date between 12 and 1; for the day between 9 and 10; pink-gold crown; snap-on back displaying the movement through a sapphire crystal; water resistant to 3atm.
Dial: silvered; grained; curved; applied pink-gold pointed and bâton markers and logo; minute track with hollowed pink cabochons; pink-gold bâton hands.
Indications: minute at 2; hour at 10; sliding disc, day of the week and fan-shaped date with retrograde hands in burnished gold at 6 and 12.
Strap: alligator leather; pink-gold double fold-over clasp.
Suggested price: $34,500

MALTE TONNEAU CHRONOGRAPH   REF. 49180/000G

Movement: mechanical self-winding Vacheron Constantin Caliber 1137; 37 jewels; 21,600 vph; 40-hour power reserve.
Functions: hours, minutes, running seconds at 6; center chronograph seconds; chronograph mechanism to 1/6 of a second; 30-minute and 12-hour totalizers at 3 and at 9, respectively; date calendar shown in twin oversized dial apertures at 12.
Case: 18K white gold; 40x50mm; water resistant to 30 meters (100 feet).
Dial: guilloché "Clou de Paris" center; vertical satin-finished exterior zone.
Strap: hand-stitched alligator leather; white-gold buckle.
Suggested price: $38,300
Also available: in 18K pink gold.

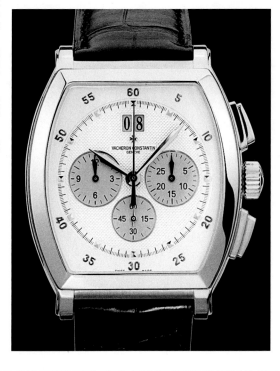

HISTORIQUES AMERICAN 1921   REF. 82035/000R-9359

Movement: mechanical manual-winding Vacheron Constantin Caliber 4400 with Geneva Hallmark; Ø 28mm, thickness: 2.8mm; 21 rubies; 28,800 vph; approx. 65-hour power reserve.
Functions: hours, minutes, off-center small seconds.
Case: 18K 5N pink gold; Ø 40mm; off-center crown; convex sapphire crystal with antireflective coating; transparent sapphire crystal caseback with screws; water resistant to 30 meters (100 feet).
Dial: sand-blasted finishing; painted Arabic numerals and minute track; hands in black oxidized 18K gold.
Strap: brown hand-stitched, saddle-finished, square-scaled alligator leather; 18K 5N pink-gold buckle with polished half Maltese cross.
Suggested price: $24,900

PATRIMONY CONTEMPORAINE BI-RETROGRADE   REF. 86020/000P

Movement: mechanical self-winding Vacheron Constantin Caliber 2460 R31 R7; 43-hour power reserve; 27 jewels; 28,800 vph; pink-gold rotor guilloché; hallmarked with the Geneva Seal.
Functions: hours, minutes; retrograde day and date.
Case: 950 platinum; Ø 42.5mm; snap-on back displaying the movement through a sapphire crystal; water resistant to 30 meters (100 feet).
Dial: 950 platinum sand-blasted dial; special marking "PT950" at 4:30.
Indications: minute at 2; hour at 10; sliding disc; day of the week and fan-shaped date with retrograde hands in burnished gold at 6 and 12.
Strap: dark blue alligator leather strap; 950 platinum buckle.
Suggested price: $87,500

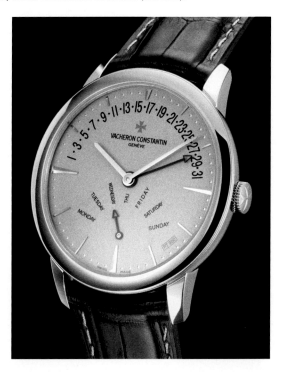

CHRONOMETRE ROYAL 1907   REF. 86122

Movement: mechanical self-winding Vacheron Constantin Caliber 2460 SCC; 40-hour power reserve; 27 jewels; 28,800 vph; 22K pink-gold rotor; COSC-certified chronometer; hallmarked with the Geneva Seal.
Functions: hour, minute, second.
Case: 18K pink gold; Ø 39mm; snap-on back displaying the movement through a sapphire crystal; water resistant to 30 meters (100 feet).
Dial: solid white gold, white Grand Feu enameled; entirely made by hand; black enameled Arabic numerals; black enameled railway minute track; pink-gold Poire hands; burnished second hand.
Strap: brown hand-stitched alligator leather; pink-gold clasp.
Suggested price: $34,000

MALTE POWER RESERVE AND DATE — REF. 83060

Movement: mechanical manual-winding Caliber 1420; Ø 22.35mm, 9''; thickness: 4.2mm; 40-hour power reserve; 20 jewels; 28,800 vph; hall-marked with the Geneva Seal.
Functions: hour, minute, small second; date; power reserve.
Case: 18K pink-gold three-piece case; Ø 38mm, thickness: 9.9mm; bow-shaped lugs; polished finish; antireflective curved sapphire crystal; date corrector on the middle at 4; dual-time pusher corrector at 10 and pink-gold crown; back fastened by 6 screws, displaying the movement through a sapphire crystal; water resistant to 3atm.
Dial: silvered, guilloché; date ring and second subdial decorated with circular beads, grained minute ring; applied bâton markers and logo in pink gold; pink-gold sword-style hands.
Indications: date at 3; small second at 6; power reserve between 10 and 11.
Strap: matte brown hand-stitched alligator leather; pink-gold clasp.
Suggested pice: $22,000
Also available: in white gold.

1972 CAMBERED MODEL — REF. 25510

Movement: quartz Caliber 1202.
Functions: hours, minutes.
Case: 18K white gold; Ø 22.8mm; set with 308 diamonds (2.17 carats); water resistant to a depth of 3atm.
Dial: satin-finished gray; mirror-finished hour markers and Roman numerals.
Strap: hand-stitched alligator leather; buckle set with 25 diamonds (0.1 carat).
Suggested price: $30,600
Also available: in white gold with case and dial set with diamonds; in pink gold with case set with diamonds; in pink gold with case and dial set with diamonds.

MALTE TOURBILLON REGULATOR — REF. 30080/000R

Movement: mechanical manual-winding Vacheron Constantin Caliber 1790 R; tourbillon regulator movement; 27 jewels; 18,000 vph; 40-hour power reserve.
Functions: hours at 12; minutes on regulator display; power-reserve indicator at 9; small second on tourbillon cage at 6.
Case: 18K pink gold; Ø 39.9mm; water resistant to 100 feet.
Dial: pink gold; 5 different kinds of finishing for optimal reading: snailed, guilloched, opaline, vertical satin-finishing and circular satin-finishing.
Strap: hand-stitched alligator leather; pink-gold buckle.
Suggested price: $144,000
Also available: in platinum.

ÉGÉRIE — REF. 25541

Movement: quartz.
Functions: hour, minute.
Case: 18K pink-gold two-piece case in anatomically curved tonneau shape; entirely brilliant pave; 37x38mm, thickness: 9.7mm; curved sapphire crystal; slightly recessed pink-gold crown with a set briolette-cut diamond; back fastened by 8 screws; water resistant to 3atm.
Dial: white mother-of-pearl; black painted bâton markers; applied pink-gold logo and two Arabic numerals with brilliants; pink-gold leaf-style hands.
Strap: hand-stitched alligator leather; recessed attachment; pink-gold clasp with brilliants.
Suggested price: $25,400
Also available: in white gold with brilliant pave on alligator-leather strap or white-gold bracelet with brilliants.

GRAND EXPLORERS CHRISTOPHER COLOMBUS   REF. 47070

Movement: mechanical self-winding Vacheron Constantin Caliber 1126 AT; 38-hour power reserve; 36 jewels; 28,800 vph.
Functions: hours and minutes displayed via three blackened-steel satellite-wheels.
Case: 18K yellow gold; Ø 40mm; solid caseback with inscription of a compass rose in relief; water resistant to 30 meters (100 feet).
Dial: Grand Feu enamel.
Strap: brown alligator leather strap with 18K yellow-gold buckle.
Suggested price: $79,000 for the set.
Note: limited edition of 60 watches.

GRAND EXPLORERS MARCO POLO   REF. 47070

Movement: mechanical self-winding Vacheron Constantin Caliber 1126 AT; 38-hour power reserve; 36 jewels; 28,800 vph.
Functions: hours and minutes displayed via three blackened-steel satellite-wheels.
Case: 18K yellow gold; Ø 40mm; solid caseback with inscription of a compass rose in relief; water resistant to 30 meters (100 feet).
Dial: Grand Feu enamel.
Strap: brown alligator leather strap with 18K yellow-gold buckle.
Suggested price: $79,000 for the set.
Note: limited edition of 60 watches.

CABINOTIERS SKELETON MINUTE REPEATER   REF. 30030/000P

Movement: mechanical manual-winding extra-flat Vacheron Constantin Caliber 1755 SQ; 13'''3/4; Ø 30.8mm, thickness: 3.3mm; 34-hour power reserve; 30 jewels; 18,000 vph; skeletonized, decorated and chased by hand; realized together with the 1755 QP caliber as a limited series of 200 pieces.
Functions: hours, minutes; minute repeater.
Case: platinum 950 three-piece case; Ø 37mm, thickness: 8.35mm; with drop-shaped lugs; polished finish; curved sapphire crystal; repeater slide on the middle; white-gold crown; snap-on back displaying the movement through a sapphire crystal.
Dial: sapphire-crystal disc; applied rosé bâton markers; bâton hands in black oxidized gold.
Strap: blue hand-stitched alligator leather; platinum clasp.
Suggested price: $631,000
Note: limited edition of 15 numbered pieces.

KALLA DUCHESSE   REF. 81750

Movement: mechanical manual-winding Vacheron Constantin Caliber 1400; 40-hour power reserve; 20 jewels; 28,800 vph; hallmarked with the Geneva Seal.
Functions: hour, minute.
Case: 18K white gold; paved entirely with 841 diamonds totaling over 58 carats; 45x36.5mm; water resistant to 30 meters (100 feet).
Bracelet: In 18K white gold set entirely with 380 baguette-cut diamonds totaling 30 carats.
Suggested price: $1,100,000 for the set.

VALENTINO
Worn with Distinction

Valentino brings the glamorous worlds of haute couture and haute horlogerie together with its Timeless collection. This chic group of timepieces includes seven feminine styles designed to dazzle, whether they're parading the fashion runways of Milan or simply out on the town for a romantic rendezvous.

With its Princesse model, Valentino evokes the ruffled flounce seen adorning many of the fashion house's flirtatious evening dresses. Since Valentino Garavani presented his first collection in 1962, well-heeled ladies of every generation—from Princess Margaret and Jacqueline Kennedy-Onassis to Gwyneth Paltrow and Oprah Winfrey—have chosen his designs.

The watch's oval case is trimmed on both sides with a billowing gold ruffle inspired by the flowing lines and precious materials emblematic of Valentino's celebrated elegance. The Princesse's black dial delivers another nod to the Maison's signature élan, using gold hour-markers and Roman numerals to create a bold contrast.

The distinctive look projected by the Princesse is the work of Giorgio Galli, who envisioned the design in cooperation with Valentino's creative department. Galli is the creative director of Timex Group, the company licensed to produce timepieces for Valentino since 2007. With more than 150 years of experience, Timex Group is one of the world's most trusted designers, manufacturers and distributors of luxury watches.

THIS PAGE
Master goldsmiths from Italy's Valenza Gold District craft the golden folds of Valentino Princesse's case.

FACING PAGE
The solid rose-gold ruffle trimming the Princesse's case represents the flowing lines that define Valentino's haute couture collection; it is available polished or enameled.

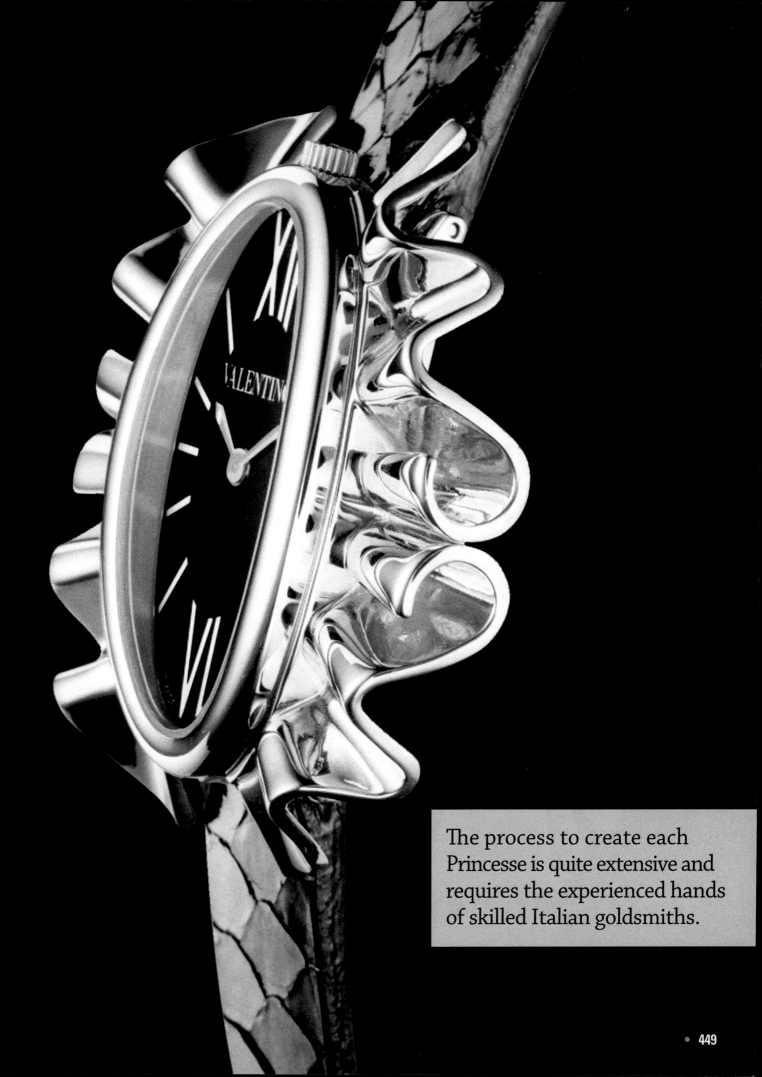

The process to create each Princesse is quite extensive and requires the experienced hands of skilled Italian goldsmiths.

Valentino dresses the Princesse in black enamel, which adds visual depth to the rose-gold folds and gives them the appearance of black silk ribbons.

Valentino offers two solid rose-gold versions of the Princesse: one with a polished case, the other decorated with black enamel. The process to create each is extensive, requiring the experienced hands of skilled Italian artisans to complete.

In fact, master goldsmiths from Italy's famous Valenza Gold District craft the golden folds that frame the Princesse's oval case. Not only is Valenza the most important center in Italy for the production of handcrafted jewelry, it's also a global leader. To put that into perspective, consider that 40 percent of the working population in the province of Alessandria (where Valenza is located) is employed in the gold and jewelry business.

The black enamel Princesse takes the longest amount of time to produce because of the extra time needed to allow the enamel to cure. The polished version, however, requires a higher level of attention in order to accurately polish all of the case's signature undulating lines.

The Princesse's solid gold case, which measures 22x33.4mm, houses a Swiss-made quartz ETA movement. Its sturdy construction ensures the watch is water resistant to 3atm.

In addition to the polished and black enamel models, Valentino has created a unique scintillating jewelry version of the Princesse fit for royalty. Expert gem setters will pave the watch's trademark gold folds with 600 brilliant-cut diamonds. The polished rose-gold oval case will frame a black enameled dial with gold hour-markers. This special edition Princesse has been presented at BaselWorld 2009 and is created exclusively upon request.

The 2008 collection encompasses seven models for ladies—Vanity, Etoile, Gemme, V-Valentino, Seduction, Rose, and Princesse—and two for men—Homme and Prestige.

In February 2009, the Valentino Timeless collection was enriched by a new ladies timepiece, Histoire, inspired by Roman architecture.

Joining Histoire are the 2009 Basel-World releases, even more iconic and linked to Valentino's culture of couture.

Valentino has created a special version of the Princesse that features 600 brilliant-cut diamonds and a black enameled dial. A rare beauty, the watch is available only by request.

VERSACE
The Ultimate in Luxury

Founded by one of the 20th century's most brilliant and prolific fashion designers, Gianni Versace SpA is one of the leading international fashion design houses and a symbol of Italian luxury worldwide.

It designs, manufactures, distributes and retails fashion and lifestyle products including Atelier (Haute Couture), prêt-a-porter, accessories, fine jewelry, watches, eyewear, fragrances, and home furnishings all bearing the distinctive Medusa logo. Upon the death of her brother, Donatella Versace became creative director for the Versace Group. Having previously collaborated with Gianni on the brand's famous advertising campaigns, and herself a talented designer, Donatella was the perfect successor to keep the Versace spirit alive.

Vertime SA, with its headquarters in Switzerland, is the company responsible for the manufacture and worldwide distribution of Versace watches and jewelry on a global scale, and is part of the Timex Group, a market leader in the watch-making sector with over 150 years of experience. Today, Versace and Vertime collaborate to create glamorous timepieces that epitomize Versace's luxury, radical style and passion, positioned in the highest luxury sector and are created to satisfy the demand for exclusive products in increasingly challenging markets.

New materials and the remarkable introduction of movement complications make their appearance in the latest collections, which represent a special alliance between the innovative design of Versace, and the horological expertise of Swiss craftsmanship.

The collections for women are an exclusive expression of how classic style can be re-imagined in a truly contemporary way. These watches have been created by skilfully blending glamour and function, tradition and modernity. They have a precious, exquisitely feminine allure. These are women's timepieces conceived as true items of jewelry, and

TOP LEFT Acron Power Reserve.

ABOVE Era.

LEFT Destiny.

The first flagship store dedicated to Versace's jewelry and watch collections in Rome.

they are remarkable for their perfectly balanced execution. A mosaic in dazzling shades of white and gold, a harmonious combination of different aspects of design: from the pure lines of the product, to the hypnotic geometrics of the graphics, from the sumptuousness of the materials, to the wonders of the handcrafted mechanisms.

There are masculine and classic lines for men's watches in an ongoing dialogue between classic elements, high-tech solutionsand ambitious performance. The warm hues of gold and the concrete solidity of steel, the brilliance of diamonds and the smoothness of ceramics, the bright colors of precious stones and the softness of leather—these elements and singular combinations form the elegant vocabulary that creates the unique style and quality of Versace watches.

The Versace's iconic timepiece is still the DV One which embodies at its best all that the brand stands for: unique design and style, innovative and precious material, high-end Swiss-made technology, in one world luxury. Versace has developed this watch in an anti-scratch, hypo-allergenic, jet-black or off-white ceramic second only to diamonds in hardness and resistance to make this masterpiece last forever. The bezel is also made of ceramic with Versace's Greek fret in relief.

The combination of luxury and refinement has found its most exclusive expression in the Destiny and Era watch lines. A true luxury edition which seduces with the clean lines of its design and the perfection of every element. From the case, available plated with yellow gold, or in stainless steel, to the precious shining dial studded with white diamonds and marked with the Versace logo, to the impeccable Swiss-made movement, this are quite simply exquisite timepieces.

The new Diver City line has a watch's sporty allure skillfully balanced by the introduction of softer, more elegant lines, and by the prevalence of black and the use of innovative combinations of materials. Since the last Diver was launched in 2007, the approach to the ceramic details has and the case is now made entirely out of crystal to reveal the movement. There is a distinctive black nautical calfskin strap marked with the historic

Versace Greek fret motif in relief. Waterproof up to 10 atmospheres, the new Diver City watch is available in a version plated with elegant pink gold, or in tough steel.

The Acron collection reveals the brand's strong identity and it is distinguished by extremely clean lines of its design. The recently launched Acron Tourbillon is an example of top-of-the-line Swiss watchmaking that best represents Versace's elegance. It is manually wound, functions at a frequency of 21,600 rotations/hour and possesses a running time of approximately 120 hours. The Tourbillon's mobile cage completes a full rotation every minute and is visible at the sixth position of the dial.

In 2007 Versace and Vertime opened its first boutique entirely dedicated to the Maison's jewelry and watches in Rome's Via Bocca di Leone 23, exemplifying the company strategy of brand reinforcement in the major locations and represents the first in a series of upcoming openings worldwide.

ACRON
REF. 17A99D009S009

Movement: Swiss Automatic ETA 2824.
Functions: hours, minutes, seconds; date.
Case: stainless steel; Ø 43mm; bezel with Versace logo and indexes engraved, stainless steel crown with Greek key motif; antireflective sapphire crystal; exhibition case; water resistant to 5atm.
Dial: black; stainless steel indexes and details.

Strap: black matte alligator; deployment buckle.

ACRON
REF. 18A99D009S099

Movement: Swiss Automatic La Joux-Perret 3513; 42-hour power reserve.
Functions: hours, minutes, seconds; big date at 12.
Case: stainless steel; Ø 43mm; bezel with applied indexes, stainless steel crown with Greek fret motif; antireflective sapphire crystal; exhibition case; water resistant to 5atm.
Dial: black; stainless steel indexes and details.

Bracelet: stainless steel; deployment buckle.

DIVER CITY
REF. 19A99D009S009

Movement: Swiss Automatic ETA 2824.
Functions: hours, minutes, seconds; date.
Case: stainless steel with body in sapphire crystal; Ø 47mm; stainless steel and black ceramic bezel; screwed-in crown in stainless steel with ceramic detail; antireflective sapphire crystal; exhibition case and site case; water resistant to 10atm.

Dial: black with stainless steel indexes and Arabic numerals; stainless steel details.
Strap: black PU; deployment buckle.

DIVER CITY
REF. 19A99D009S099

Movement: Swiss Automatic ETA 2824.
Functions: hours, minutes, seconds; date.
Case: stainless steel with body in sapphire crystal; Ø 47mm; stainless steel and black ceramic bezel; screwed-in crown in stainless steel with ceramic detail; antireflective sapphire crystal; exhibition case and site case; water resistant to 10atm.

Dial: black; stainless steel indexes and Arabic numerals; stainless steel details.
Bracelet: stainless steel with black ceramic inserts; deployment buckle.

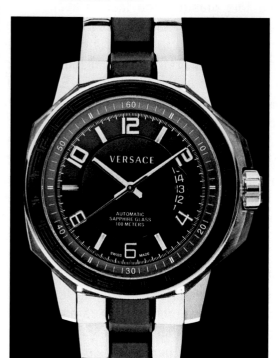

DV ONE   REF. 02ACP1D001SC01

Movement: Swiss Automatic ETA 2824.
Functions: hours, minutes, seconds; date.
Case: white ceramic; Ø 41mm; yellow-gold-plated bezel with white ceramic; yellow-gold-plated crown with ceramic detail; antireflective sapphire crystal; exhibition case ; water resistant to 5atm.
Dial: white enamel with guilloché finishing; yellow-gold-plated indexes and details.
Bracelet: white ceramic; deployment buckle.

DV ONE   REF. 02ACP91D009SC09

Movement: Swiss Automatic ETA 2824.
Functions: hours, minutes, seconds; date.
Case: black ceramic; Ø 41mm; yellow-gold-plated bezel set with white diamonds; yellow-gold-plated crown with ceramic detail; antireflective sapphire crystal; exhibition case; water resistant to 5atm.
Dial: black enamel with guilloché finishing; yellow-gold-plated indexes and details.
Bracelet: black ceramic; deployment buckle.

DV ONE CHRONO   REF. 16CCP11D001SC01

Movement: Swiss Automatic Chrono ETA 2894/2.
Functions: hours, minutes, seconds; date; chronograph.
Case: white ceramic; Ø 43.5mm; yellow-gold-plated bezel set with white diamonds; yellow-gold-plated crown with ceramic detail; antireflective sapphire crystal; exhibition case; water resistant to 10atm.
Dial: white enamel with guilloché finishing; yellow-gold-plated indexes with SuperLumiNova; yellow-gold-plated details.
Bracelet: white ceramic with yellow-gold-plated details; deployment buckle.

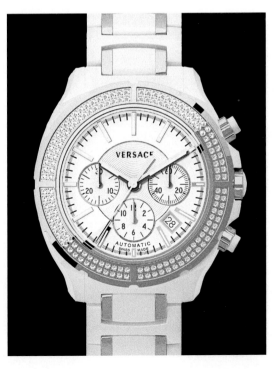

DV ONE CHRONO   REF. 16CCP9D009SC09

Movement: Swiss Automatic Chrono ETA 2894/2.
Functions: hours, minutes, seconds; date; chronograph.
Case: black ceramic; Ø 43.5mm; rose-gold-plated bezel with ceramic detail; rose-gold-plated crown with ceramic detail; antireflective sapphire crystal; exhibition case; water resistant to 10atm.
Dial: black enamel with guilloché finishing; rose-gold-plated indexes with SuperLumiNova; rose-gold-plated details.
Bracelet: black ceramic with rose-gold-plated details; deployment buckle.

ERA
REF. 70Q70D001S001

Movement: Swiss quartz Ronda 1032.
Functions: hours, minutes.
Case: stainless steel and black ceramic; 32x24.8mm; yellow-gold-plated bezel; yellow-gold-plated crown with ceramic insert; antireflective sapphire crystal; water resistant to 5atm.
Dial: white enamel.

Strap: white cocco pattern leather; deployment buckle.

ERA
REF. 70Q91D009SC09

Movement: Swiss quartz Ronda 1032.
Functions: hours, minutes.
Case: stainless steel and black ceramic; 32x24.8mm; bezel set with 34 white diamonds; stainless steel crown with ceramic insert; antireflective sapphire crystal; water resistant to 5atm.
Dial: black enamel.

Bracelet: stainless steel with black ceramic inserts; deployment buckle.

DESTINY
REF. 76Q81SD498S001

Movement: Swiss quartz Techno Time 5180 D.
Functions: hours, minutes.
Case: rose-gold-plated; Ø 36mm; Versace Greca motif, Clous de Paris decoration and 68 white diamonds on bezel; antireflective sapphire crystal; caseback attached with 4 screws; water resistant to 3atm.
Dial: white enamel.

Strap: white python; deployment buckle.

DESTINY
REF. 76Q99D009S009

Movement: Swiss quartz Techno Time 5180 D.
Functions: hours, minutes.
Case: stainless steel; Ø 36mm; Versace Greca motif, bezel with Clous de Paris decoration; antireflective sapphire crystal; caseback attached with 4 screws; water resistant to 3atm.
Dial: black enamel.

Strap: black leather; deployment buckle.

REVE
REF. 68Q99SD009S009

Movement: Swiss quartz Ronda 785.
Functions: hours, minutes, seconds; date.
Case: stainless steel; Ø 35mm; stainless steel bezel engraved with Versace logo; Medusa head embossed on crown; antireflective sapphire crystal; caseback attached with 4 screws; water resistant to 5atm.
Dial: black matte; 8 diamond hour markers; stainless steel details; Arabic 3 and 9.
Strap: black cocco pattern leather; deployment buckle.

REVE CHRONO
REF. 68C80SD009S080

Movement: Swiss quartz chrono ETA 251.471.
Functions: hours, minutes, seconds; date; chronograph.
Case: rose-gold-plated; Ø 40mm; rose-gold-plated bezel with engraved Versace logo; Medusa head embossed on crown; antireflective sapphire crystal; pushers with blue crystal cabochon; caseback attached with 4 screws; water resistant to 5 atm.
Dial: black matte; 6 diamond hour markers; rose-gold-plated details; Arabic 4 and 8.
Bracelet: rose-gold-plated; deployment buckle.

ECLISSI
REF. 84Q80SD009S009

Movement: Swiss quartz Techno Time K62/132.
Functions: hours, minutes.
Case: stainless steel treated in rose PVD; 39x30.5mm; Versace Greca engraved; two half-moon crystals; antireflective sapphire crystal; caseback attached with 4 screws; water resistant to 3atm.
Dial: black guilloché; two diamonds; rose-gold-plated details.
Strap: black leather with Versace Greca and Medusa logos; deployment buckle.

ECLISSI
REF. 83Q80SD009S080

Movement: Swiss quartz Techno Time K62/132.
Functions: hours, minutes.
Case: stainless steel treated in rose PVD; 39x30.5mm; Versace Greca engraved; two half-moon crystals with 8 diamonds; antireflective sapphire crystal; caseback attached with 4 screws; water resistant to 3atm.
Dial: black guilloché; two diamonds; rose-gold-plated details.
Bracelet: stainless steel treated in rose PVD with Versace Greca and Medusa Logos; deployment buckle.

VINCENT BÉRARD
Beauty of the Bulge

Independent watchmaker Vincent Bérard is well trained in the art of making, repairing and restoring timekeepers. He spent years learning at the workbench before opening his watchmaking atelier in 1992 in a former farmhouse overlooking La Chaux-de-Fonds. Today, his skills are in-demand by other watchmakers as collectors clamor for his first collection.

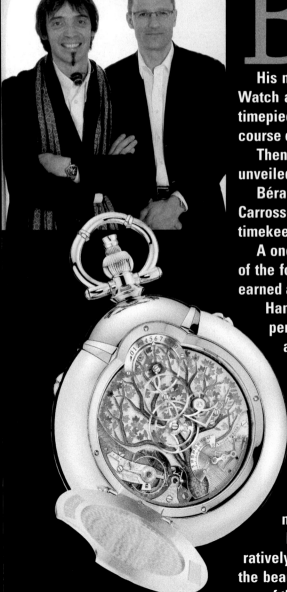

But to understand the watches, it is essential to first understand the watchmaker. Born in France, Bérard studied at the Vallée de Joux watch school where he unraveled the intricacies of the repeater, a mechanism considered by many as high horology's most complex.

His natural aptitude for these kinds of complications led him to the International Watch and Clock Museum, where, at the age of 21, Bérard began restoring antique timepieces. He left after two years, working for various large manufactures over the course of a decade.

Then, in 1992, he founded his own workshop. More than a decade later, Bérard unveiled his first collection at Basel in 2005.

Bérard marked his debut as an independent watchmaker with Quatre Saisons Carrosse, his modern reinterpretation of the clocks once used in carriages as mobile timekeepers.

A one-of-a-kind, the collection includes four pieces; each designed to mirror one of the four seasons. The bold style and skilled craftsmanship of Bérard's brainchild earned a chorus of raves from peers and collectors.

Handcrafted in his workshop, Bérard outfits these grand complications with a perpetual calendar and leap-year display, along with a quarter repeater that animates the season-themed automatons on the dial.

Each generously portioned case (91mm diameter, 32mm thick) is crafted in a different shade of gold: green (spring), yellow (summer), red (autumn), and white (winter).

The natural world again inspires the watch design, this time the portion visible through the caseback. To great effect, the shaped bridge is transformed into a tree by the centuries-old technique of grand feu enamel. Like the dial, the tree reflects the changing seasons, using the budding and falling of leaves. The sublime image provides a gorgeous canvas for the hand-wound movement's kinetic art of meshing gears and mechanical displays.

But it's the subtle bulge atop each case that stands out, both literally and figuratively. Inspiration for the signature bump came to him, Bérard says, while admiring the beautiful pillars at Strasbourg Cathedral. Coincidently, the cathedral is home to one of the largest astronomical clocks in the world.

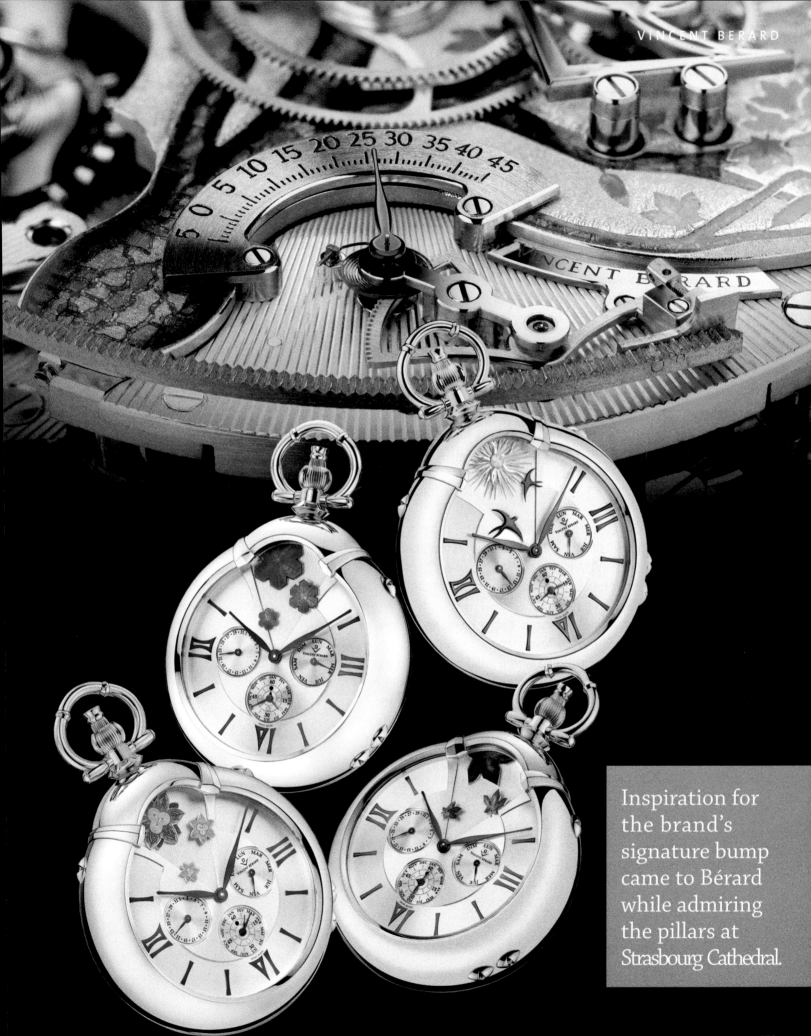

Inspiration for the brand's signature bump came to Bérard while admiring the pillars at Strasbourg Cathedral.

The bulge is back for Luvorene 1, the company's first wristwatch and the inaugural model in Vincent Bérard's Fuseau de l'Infini collection. With Quatre Saisons Carrosse, the space below the bulge served to spotlight the automatons. But with Luvorene 1, the protuberance slides down to 3:00, drawing the eye to an aperture on the dial where an unusual balance oscillates. This unique mechanism (balance with screws and Breguet overcoil balance spring) appears to be missing the escapement and lever wheel.

Covered by a shaped and domed crystal, the elegant dial is decorated with Celtic triskelion at its center, while subdials (seconds, moonphase and day of the week) occupy the rest of the dial.

French for "spindle of infinity," the significance of the Fuseau de l'Infini collection's name is expressed by the spindle motif that connects the openworked hands and applied hour-markers.

The recurring spindle theme continues to Luvorene 1's hand-wound movement, where six bridges rise from the mainplate like spiral stairs. Each "step" is sunray-brushed guilloché-worked, smoothed down to a matte finish and beveled by hand.

A solid-gold caseback flips open to reveal the magnificent construction of Luvorene 1's caliber, which was made completely in-house. When the cover is closed, a pair of sapphire crystals features an additional small seconds opposite a power-reserve gauge.

The Luvorene 1 case measures 42mm in diameter and 13mm thick. Vincent Bérard offers a white- or red-gold version, each available with a choice of four solid-gold, in-house crafted dials colored black, chocolate, ivory or natural gold.

With the company's first wristwatch, Vincent Bérard establishes a distinctive style that resonates with the echoes of watchmaking's past while remaining unambiguously contemporary. Vincent Bérard and the Timex Group are now working together to assure the long-term development and plans for Vincent Bérard S.A.

PREVIOUS SPREAD
Artist and creator Vincent Bérard (left) and veteran CEO Herbert Gautschi are the drive behind the brand's highly skilled team.

The Quatre Saisons Carrosse.

THIS SPREAD
The bump at 3:00 accommodates an extraordinary balance mechanism that appears to be missing the escapement and lever wheel. The remainder of the dial features a trio of subdials for the small seconds, moonphase, and days of the week. Because the crown is located at 9:00 instead of in its traditional position at 3:00, right-handed owners are compelled to flip the watch over when winding, putting the focus on the solid-gold caseback.

ZANNETTI
One of a Kind

Riccardo Zannetti, an authentic designer and artist of our times and a master watchmaker, has decided to explore, through his art, the measuring of time in its many facets. As he is an extremely demanding craftsman he designs and plans only exclusive mechanisms, belonging to the highest historical traditions of his craft. Each single model, in the wake of the long and glorious European tradition, is to be considered unique and, as each piece is numbered and registered.

In Riccardo Zannetti's case, the personalization of each piece is not restricted simply to the aesthetic aspects, as is often the case with this type of watch, that is to say, the case, the dial or the hands or is it limited merely to the mechanism and the movement. Riccardo Zannetti deals with the watch in its totality, creating a timepiece undoubtedly beautiful to behold, while, at the same time, representing a perfect technical creation. To produce a unique piece like this means creating a truly exclusive watch, destined to increase in value in the future while being perfectly wearable in the present.

Designing a watch is a difficult but fascinating challenge. The first aspect to be respected is its functionality, i.e. telling the time, and this must not differ in any way from the accepted manner. It would serve no purpose to produce a fantastic creation, which, on a practical level, does not fulfill its function. On the contrary, it is preferable to favor simplicity and efficacy—guarantees of maximum appreciation on the part of the wearer/owner.

Another obstacle that must always be taken into consideration is the mechanics of the watch and these require specific technical prerequisites which determine the positioning of windows and additional hands in extremely specific places.

> Zannetti favors simplicity and efficacy to guarantee maximum appreciation on the part of the wearer.

The design, therefore, must find a balance between all these specific constructional demands and integrate creativity and good taste in such a way as to stir passion and contentment in the person wearing the watch.

Every watch created by Zannetti is designed and drawn exclusively by hand. It may be the combination of the pencil, the pastels and the carbon lead that transforms a white sheet of paper into an idea, preparing the eye, even before the hand, to imagine and conceive a new and original form.

What makes a person a genius?

Nothing, everything, perhaps simply that little spark in the imagination which some—very few—people have and which moves them continually to be doing things that are absolutely unique. The genius constantly needs to be concentrating on new ideas, to put them into action, to assess their potential, to use them to challenge the certainties and fixed points that are an integral part of our day-to-day life.

FACING PAGE
TOP RIGHT Repeater.
CENTER AND LEFT Rosa Ventorum.
BOTTOM Regent Full Sky.

THIS PAGE
TOP Gioielli Rana.
TOP RIGHT Lady Regent Frog Steel.
TOP LEFT Lady Regent Frog Diamond.
ABOVE Lady Regent Frog Ruby.
LEFT Ovum Mother of Pearl.

REPEATER
REF. REPRA189331

Movement: 5-minute repeater; mechanical automatic-winding; Swiss made; Zannetti re-elaborated; totally skeletonized and hand engraved.
Functions: complicated 5-minute repetition ringing mechanism activated at any moment via a pushpiece and marking hours and its divisions by ringing.
Case: 18K pink-gold three-piece case; new case with redesigned handles; engraved totally by hand; Ø 44mm, thickness: 15mm; pressured closed crown, hand personalized; gold octagonal, engraved pusher at 8 for repeater; antireflective sapphire crystal; pink-gold caseback fixed by 4 pink-gold screws and with central sapphire crystal opening; water resistant to 2atm.
Dial: skeletonized; completely hand-made pink-gold dart-style hands.
Strap: hand-sewn Louisiana alligator leather; hand-engraved 18K pink-gold ardillon buckle.
Note: the Repeater is created exclusively in compliance with the demands and requests of the client, personalized in every single detail.

IMPERO GLADIATORE CHRONOGRAPH
REF. GLRV115.01

Movement: mechanical automatic-winding Valjoux 7750 caliber; rotor hand-engraved with a Greek-column pattern.
Functions: hours, minutes, small seconds; date at 3; 3-counter chronograph: hours at 6, small seconds at 9, minutes at 12.
Case: white-gold three-piece case; Ø 44mm, thickness: 14mm; entirely hand-engraved; antireflective flat sapphire crystal; secret logo; white-gold hexagonal crown and pushers; sapphire crystal exhibition caseback fastened by 8 screws, with hand-engraved laurel crown and individual number; water resistant to 3atm.
Dial: white mother-of-pearl dial with blue enameled, geometrical decorations; brushed white-gold flange with engraved quotation "Veni, vidi, vici"; applied pink-gold frames and markers; luminescent, black enameled leaf-style hands.
Strap: crocodile leather; hand-engraved white-gold fold-over clasp.
Also available: with engraved bezel; in palladium-plated 9K white gold with smooth or engraved bezel.

SQUELETTE XL STEEL
REF. SQFA.116.237

Movement: mechanical automatic-winding 2892A2 ETA caliber; Swiss made; personalized for Zannetti; movement and rotor totally skeletonized and hand engraved.
Functions: hours, minutes, seconds.
Case: steel three-piece case; Ø 41mm, thickness: 9.5mm; jointed central attachment; bezel with hand-engraved Arabic numerals; antireflective flat sapphire crystal with engraved logo; hand-personalized screw-down crown; back fastened by five screws, numbered, displaying the movement through a sapphire crystal; water resistant to 3atm.
Dial: hand-engraved white-gold flange; four round applied markers; blue PVD treatment; leaf-style luminescent SuperLumiNova® hands in blue steel.
Strap: hand-sewn Louisiana alligator leather; steel folding clasp; Zannetti personalized.
Also available: 18K pink-gold three-piece case (below photo), with rodiumed movement.

PALATINO CHRONO
REF. PQYA.011.0434

Movement: mechanical automatic-winding Valjoux 7750 caliber; hand-engraved rotor.
Functions: hour, minute, second; date at 3; chronograph with 3 counters: small seconds at 6, hours at 9, minutes at 12.
Case: stainless steel three-piece case; 36x36mm, thickness: 12.3mm; engraved by hand; sapphire crystal, antireflective with secret logo; bezel with engraved tachometer scale; stainless steel rectangular pushers and crown; back fastened by 4 screws, displaying the movement through a sapphire crystal; numbered; water resistant to 3atm.
Dial: natural mother-of-pearl; enameled Arabic numerals; luminescent black enameled leaf-style hands.
Strap: alligator leather; fold-over clasp with logo.
Also available: black mother-of-pearl dial.
Also available: 18K white-gold case set with white diamonds (below photo).

TIME OF DRIVERS–LIMITED EDITION "LUZZAGO - GIULIETTA SPIDER" REF. TODAV20337AG

Movement: automatic-winding chronograph; 7750 Valjoux caliber; Swiss made; Zannetti re-elaborated. **Functions:** hours, minutes, seconds; Pilotís edition steel chronograph with 2 counters: hours at 6, minutes at 12; date at 3.
Case: stainless steel three-piece case; Ø 42.5mm, thickness: 15.3mm; bezel with hand-engraved index numbers; hand-personalized pressured closed crown; curved antireflective sapphire crystal engraved with logo; stainless steel caseback fixed by 4 screws, central sapphire crystal opening; water resistant to 3atm.
Dial: totally hand engraved; XL leaf-style hands with SuperLumiNova® inside.
Strap: hand-stitched Louisiana alligator leather; polished steel folding clasp with safety pushbuttons and engraved Zannetti logo.
Available dials: Porsche (below photo), Jaguar, Fangio, or traditional double-layer full black, blue or argenté.

TIME OF DRIVERS – CHRONOGRAPH REF. TODAV511.337

Movement: automatic-winding chronograph; 7750 Valjoux caliber; Swiss made; Zannetti re-elaborated.
Functions: hours, minutes, seconds; date at 3; chronograph with 3 counters: hours at 6, small seconds at 9, minutes at 12.
Case: stainless steel three-piece case; Ø 42.5mm, thickness 15.3mm; bezel with hand-engraved and enameled index numbers; hand-personalized pressured closed crown; curved antireflective sapphire crystal with engraved logo; stainless steel caseback fixed by 4 screws, with central sapphire crystal opening; water resistant to 3atm.
Dial: double-layer natural mother-of-pearl; numerals in bombe applied enamel; leaf-style hands with SuperLumiNova®.
Strap: hand-stitched Louisiana alligator leather; and polished steel folding clasp with safety pushbuttons and engraved Zannetti logo.

ZSPORT TITANIUM REF. ZTV11710037

Movement: automatic-winding chronograph 7750 Valjoux caliber; Swiss made; Zannetti re-elaborated; rhodium and perlage plate; Côtes de Genève.
Functions: hours at 6, minutes at 12, center seconds; date at 3.
Case: titanium three-piece case; sand-blasted finish; 45x44mm, thickness: 145mm; 8 pink-gold screws, 4 on the top of the lugs and 4 on the sides; titanium and pink-gold screw-down crown, hand personalized; antireflective sapphire crystal; titanium caseback fixed with 4 screws; water resistant to 10atm.
Dial: multi-layered structure; 4 screws; printed Arabic numerals; 3 chronograph counters.
Strap: hand-sewn Louisiana alligator leather; stainless steel deployant buckle with Zannetti personalization.
Available dials: black or argenté.

REGENT DRAGON REF. RDAA32337

Movement: automatic-winding ETA caliber; Swiss made; Zannetti re-elaborated. **Functions:** off-center hours and minutes. **Case:** stainless steel three-piece case; Ø 42mm, thickness 10mm; bezel with hand-engraved and enameled index numbers; hand-personalized pressured closed crown; antireflective sapphire crystal with engraved logo; stainless steel caseback fixed by 5 screws, with decentralized sapphire crystal opening; water resistant to 5atm. **Dial:** hand-engraved solid gold; translucent colored enamel; dragon figure in bas-relief totally handmade in 18K gold (yellow or white); yellow-gold-plated indexes. **Strap:** hand-sewn Louisiana alligator leather, stainless steel deployant buckle; Zannetti personalized. **Note:** Refined hand-engraved dials are the distinguishing features of the Regent collection models. Imagination, dreams and adventures are represented by designs that have been carefully engraved by hand on a silver base, upon which the translucent red, blue and black colors take on pink, gray and light blue nuances. They are produced exclusively in 500-piece editions for each subject and embody the sheer unadulterated delight of owning a unique piece.

ZENITH
The Legend of Zenith

ZENITH is not a brand that is easily described, but its story is often told, full as it is with watchmaking history. Born in 1865 in Locle, ZENITH created the legendary movement El Primero, the first ever automatic chronograph with a central rotor. It was an historic birth, which gives it the legitimacy even today of a great manufacture on the cutting edge.

ZENITH is one of the rare Swiss manufactures that can claim uninterrupted production of the brand's movements since its creation in 1865. It is a priceless foundation that makes the brand one of today's best-known brands in haute horology. But ZENITH owes this notoriety to its legend, as well, a legend among those told by old watchmakers to their grandchildren: the story of the misadventure of the El Primero movement, which has become the brand's founding myth.

Developed in 1969, and having rapidly become a standard of reference among timepieces, El Primero—whose name in Esperanto means "the first"—illustrates the creative genius and refinement of ZENITH. Conceived according to an almost academic drawing, with no concession made to the unessential, El Primero is a chef d'oeuvre of innovation. This movement is perfectly integrated and, taking little space, it combines accuracy and precision—the position of each plate, each part and every element is optimized. In addition, its column wheel—veritable orchestral leader—centralizes and coordinates instructions transmitted by the pushbuttons.

Unmatched to this day, El Primero is the only chronograph movement capable of measuring short time intervals to one-tenth of a second—a performance made possible by the use of a balance-wheel oscillating at the frequency of 36,000 alternations per hour. This absolute precision enables it to succeed in passing the tests of the COSC (Swiss Official Control of Chronometers). A chronograph with two pushbuttons and autonomous for more than 50 hours, this movement embellished with an instantaneous date-change mechanism can be fitted with other complications—date-day-month indicator, moonphase, and flyback. Precise, accurate, and sophisticated, El Primero, with its exquisite finish and striking profile, is a symbol of excellence—it bears witness to several centuries of the art of watchmaking and represents what is the most accomplished in the field. This year, the El Primero celebrates its 40th anniversary.

ZENITH, the Swiss manufacture founded in 1865, proudly celebrates the 40th anniversary of the legendary El Primero movement.

ZENITH
SWISS WATCH MANUFACTURE
SINCE 1865

From the time he took the reins of ZENITH in 2001, Thierry Nataf saw the potential of this fabled movement. With a power reserve of 50 hours and a dry lubrification from its extremely high frequency, the El Primero was already a very high-tech movement at its birth in 1969. ZENITH's renaissance would become part of the year's challenges. The brand would be generous with everything it had: the 2008 release of the Tourbillon Zero-Gravity would mesmerize watch connoisseurs. Due to its gyroscopic cage, which includes 166 components and a patented transmission system, the escapement is maintained in a horizontal position, no matter what the position of the watch. Incorporated into the Defy Classic and Defy Xtreme collections, which unite the brand's most technical models, it proves ZENITH's capacity for innovation.

The Defy series claims the mantle of an icon of horological research. For the series, ZENITH's engineers specially invented ZENITHIUM©. An alloy of titanium, niobium and aluminum, this exclusive material was designed to be shock-resistant—three times more resistant than steel—and to retain form memory.

THIS PAGE
TOP LEFT Thierry Nataf, President and CEO of ZENITH International since 2001.

TOP RIGHT Defy Classic Zero-Gravity.

LEFT Caliber El Primero 4021 SC with its ZENITHIUM© bridge.

FACING PAGE
LEFT Defy Classic Open.

RIGHT Defy Xtreme Open.

Nataf also hit the bull's eye with the "Open" concept. Through an opening in the dial, the movement was revealed as never before. All the collections would benefit from this innovation, which so artistically expressed the alliance of horological tradition and modernity. The newest member in a successful collection, the elegant ChronoMaster Open Grande Date immediately drew the attention of watch lovers. In the multi-complications department, the Academy Open Minute Repeater attracts attention with its exclusive movement that brings together a chronograph and a minute repeater in the same movement for the first time. Another openworked model, the Mega Port-Royal Open stands out from the crowd with its distinctive angles that embody force and virility.

In the Class collection, ZENITH has also devoted itself to unveiling the mysteries of the movement by openworking the dial, following the example of the Class Traveller Open Multicity, another attention-getting model. Drawing on its history, ZENITH launched the Class New Vintage 1955, an historic model of exceptional purity. It follows in the same spirit and serves as an ambassador to the Class collection, which is full of new sober and aesthetically appealing models.

FACING PAGE

BOTTOM LEFT **ChronoMaster Open Grande Date** immediately drew the attention of watch connoisseurs.

BOTTOM CENTER **The Academy Open Minute Repeater** joins a chronograph and a minute repeater in the same movement for the first time.

THIS PAGE

BELOW LEFT **Mega Port-Royal Open Concept** stands out, thanks to its right angles that evoke power and virility.

BOTTOM CENTER **Class Open,** an icon of the collection.

BELOW RIGHT **Class Traveller Open Multicity,** a hymn to discreet luxury.

To celebrate women, ZENITH has perfected the Starissime Minute Repeater. A complicated watch housing a sonnerie mechanism, it evokes the Starissime Tourbillon, another technical accomplishment. Any roster of feminine versions of ZENITH Classic would have to include the word "Lady." Class Lady, Chrono-Master Lady, with, for example, the remarkable ChronoMaster Lady Moonphase, or even Defy Lady, all embody reworked versions of best-sellers that were originally made for men.

LEFT Starissime Open Minute Repeater.

TOP CENTER Star Love Open.

TOP RIGHT Starissime Open Minute Repeater.

LEFT Class Lady.

RIGHT ChronoMaster Moonphase Lady is available in a feminine version, white and set with diamonds.

CHRONOMASTER TOURBILLON DAY & NIGHT   REF. 18.1260.4034/02.C505

Movement: El Primero 4034 automatic chronograph movement with Tourbillon.
Functions: hours, minutes in the center; date indication around the carriage; moonphase and day/night indicators at 8; tourbillon: carriage positioned at 11, making 1 turn per minute; chronograph: central seconds hand, 30-minute counter at 3; 12-hour counter at 6.
Case: 18K rose-gold case; Ø 45mm; water resistant to 30 meters.

Dial: 18K gold dial with handmade "Grain d'Orge" guilloché; wavy guilloché pattern on the counters.
Strap: handmade black crocodile leather strap lined with silky Alzavel calfskin; 18K gold triple-folding buckle.
Also available: white gold with back dial.

CHRONOMASTER OPEN GRANDE DATE   REF. 03.1260.4039/01.C611

Movement: El Primero 4039 automatic chronograph movement.
Functions: hours, minutes in the center, small seconds hand at 9; 3-disc grand date at 2; power-reserve indicator from hour axis; chronograph: central seconds hand; 30-minute counter at 3.
Case: stainless steel case; Ø 45mm, water resistant to 30 meters.
Dial: silver "soleillé" guilloché; integrated TR90 segments over the calendar disc and power-reserve indicator; opening at 10 revealing heart of 4039 Caliber.
Strap: handmade black crocodile leather strap lined with silky Alzavel calfskin; stainless steel triple-folding buckle.
Also available: stainless steel with black dial; rose gold with silver dial; T-version case: 40mm.

CHRONOMASTER OPEN   REF. 03.1260.4021/21.C505

Movement: El Primero 4021 automatic chronograph movement.
Functions: hours, minutes in the center, small seconds hand at 9; power-reserve indicator from hour axis; chronograph: central seconds hand; 30-minute counter at 3; tachometric scale on guilloché dials.
Case: stainless steel case; Ø 45mm; water resistant to 30 meters.
Dial: silver guilloché; opening at 10 revealing heart of 4021 Caliber.

Strap: handmade black crocodile leather strap lined with silky Alzavel calfskin; stainless steel triple-folding buckle.
Also available: stainless steel with silver dial; rose gold with silver dial; T-version case: 40mm.

CHRONOMASTER LADY MOONPHASE   REF. 16.1230.410/80.C664

Movement: El Primero 410 automatic chronograph movement.
Functions: hours, minutes in the center, small seconds hand at 9; triple calendar (day, date, month) with windows; chronograph: central seconds hand; 30-minute counter at 3, 12-hour counter at 6.
Case: stainless steel case set with diamonds; Ø 37.5mm; water resistant to 30 meters.

Dial: white mother-of-pearl with "Grain d'Orge" pattern beveled and decorated calendar windows.
Strap: handmade white crocodile leather strap lined with silky Alzavel calfskin; stainless steel triple-folding buckle.
Also available: stainless steel with black dial; rose gold with silver dial, with or without diamond.

GRANDE CLASS TRAVELLER MULTICITY REF. 03.0520.4037/22.C660

Movement: El Primero 4037 automatic chronograph movement.
Functions: hours, minutes in the center, small seconds hand at 9; power reserve indicator from hour axis, 3-disc grand date at 2; 24 time-zone system with day/night indicator; chronograph: central seconds hand; 30-minute counter at 3.
Case: stainless steel case; Ø 46mm; water resistant to 50 meters.
Dial: black "Grain d'Orge" guilloché; opening at 10 revealing the heart of the 1037 El Primero caliber beating at 36,000 vph.
Strap: handmade integrated black alligator leather strap lined with silky Alzavel calfskin; stainless steel triple-folding buckle.
Also available: stainless steel with silver dial; rose gold with silver dial.

CLASS OPEN REF. 03.0520.4021/02.C492

Movement: El Primero 4021 automatic chronograph movement.
Functions: hours, minutes in the center, small seconds hand at 9; power-reserve indicator from hour axis; chronograph: central seconds hand; 30-minute counter at 3.
Case: stainless steel case; Ø 44mm; water resistant to 50 meters.
Dial: silver "Grain d'Orge" guilloché; opening at 10 revealing the heart of the 4021 El Primero caliber beating at 36,000 vph.
Strap: handmade black alligator leather strap lined with silky Alzavel calfskin; stainless steel triple-folding buckle.
Also available: stainless steel with black dial; rose gold with silver or brown dial; T version case: 40mm.

CLASS MOONPHASE REF. 18.0510.4100/02.C492

Movement: El Primero 4100 automatic chronograph movement.
Functions: hours, minutes in the center, small seconds hand at 9; complete calendar (day, date, month) with windows; moonphase at 6, chronograph: central seconds hand; 30-minute counter at 3, 12-hour counter at 6.
Case: 18K rose-gold case; Ø 40mm; water resistant to 50 meters.
Dial: silver "Clou de Paris" guilloché; beveled applied calendar windows in gold.
Strap: handmade black crocodile leather strap lined with silky Alzavel calfskin; 18K rose gold triple-folding buckle.
Also available: stainless steel with silver dial, XT version case: 44 mm.

CLASS ELITE AUTOMATIQUE REF. 03.1125.679/02.C492

Movement: Elite 679 automatic movement.
Functions: hours, minutes in the center, central second on hour axis.
Case: stainless steel case; Ø 37mm; water resistance up to 30 meters.
Dial: silver "Clou de Paris" guilloché.
Strap: handmade black crocodile leather strap lined with silky Alzavel calfskin; stainless steel triple-folding buckle.
Also available: stainless steel with black dial, rose gold with silver dial; XT version case: 44mm.

CLAS AUTOMATIQUE   REF: 18.1125.685/01.C490

Movement: Elite 685 automatic movement.
Functions: hours, minutes in the center, small seconds hand at 9.
Case: 18K rose gold; Ø 37mm; water resistance up to 30 meters.
Dial: Grain d'Orge guilloché.
Strap: handmade black crocodile leather strap lined with silky Alzavel calfskin; 18K rose-gold triple-folding buckle.

Also available: stainless steel with black or silver dial; XT version case: 44mm.

CLASS ELITE LADY AUTOMATIQUE   REF: 22.1025.680/80.C665

Movement: Elite 680 automatic movement.
Functions: hours, minutes in the center, small seconds hand at 9; date indicator at 3.
Case: 18K rose-gold case set with diamonds; Ø 34mm; water resistant to 30 meters.
Dial: white mother-of-pearl; "Grain d'Orge" pattern.

Strap: handmade brown skin alligator leather strap lined with silky Alzavel calfskin; 18K rose-gold simple buckle.
Also available: stainless steel with white or black dial; with or without diamonds.

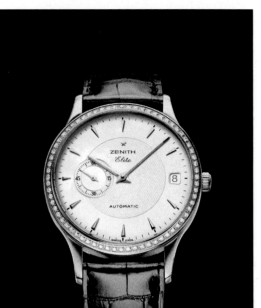

MEGA PORT ROYAL OPEN GRANDE DATE CONCEPT   REF: 96.0560.4039/77.R512

Movement: El Primero 4039 automatic chronograph movement.
Functions: hours, minutes in the center, small seconds hand at 9; horizontal power reserve at 6, 3-disc grand date at 2; chronograph: central seconds hand; 30-minute counter at 3.
Case: black titanium case; 40mm x 57mm, water resistant to 50 meters.
Dial: composite material (PMMA).

Strap: black rubber strap lined; black titanium triple-folding buckle.

PORT ROYAL OPEN   REF. 03.0550.4021/21.R512

Movement: El Primero 4021 B automatic chronograph movement.
Functions: hours, minutes in the center, small seconds hand at 9, power-reserve indicator from hour axis; chronograph: central seconds hand; 30-minute counter at 3.
Case: 36mm x 51mm, stainless steel case, water-resistance up to 50 meters.
Dial: black "Damier" guilloché.

Strap: black rubber strap; stainless steel triple-folding buckle.
Also available: stainless steel with silver or grey dial, on alligator leather or rubber strap; T-version case: 34mm x 48mm.

DEFY CLASSIC OPEN GRANDE DATE   REF. 18.0526.4039/01.C649

Movement: El Primero 4039 SC automatic chronograph movement.
Functions: hours, minutes in the center, small seconds hand at 9; power-reserve indicator from hour axis; 3-disc grand date at 2; chronograph: central seconds hand; 30-minute counter at 3.
Case: brushed 18K rose-gold graduated unidirectional rotating bezel; Ø 46.5mm; water resistant to 100 meters.
Dial: silver guilloché; opening at 10 revealing heart of 4039 SC Caliber.
Strap: handmade brown stamped integrated alligator leather; brushed 18K rose-gold triple-folding buckle.
Also available: brown rubber strap or gold bracelet.

DEFY CLASSIC OPEN SEA   REF. 03.0529.4021/51.R674

Movement: El Primero 4021 SC automatic chronograph movement.
Functions: hours, minutes in the center, small seconds hand at 9; power-reserve indicator from hour axis; chronograph: central seconds hand; 30-minute counter at 3.
Case: brushed stainless steel; graduated unidirectional rotating bezel in blue-tinted stainless steel; Ø 46.5mm; water resistant to 300 meters.
Dial: blue wavy guilloché; opening at 10 revealing heart of 4021 SC Caliber.
Strap: blue vulcanized rubber strap with wavy pattern on central links; stainless steel tongue buckle.

DEFY CLASSIC OPEN   REF. 03.0516.4021/21.R642

Movement: El Primero 4021 SC automatic chronograph movement.
Functions: hours, minutes in the center, small seconds hand at 9; power-reserve indicator from hour axis; chronograph: central seconds hand; 30-minute counter at 3.
Case: brushed stainless steel; Ø 43mm; graduated unidirectional rotating bezel; water resistant to 300 meters.
Dial: black guilloché; opening at 10 revealing heart of 4021 SC Caliber.
Strap: black vulcanized rubber strap; stainless steel tongue buckle.
Also available: stainless steel with silver dial on black alligator leather or rubber strap; XT-version: 46.5mm.

DEFY CLASSIC LADY CHRONOGRAPH   REF. 16.0506.4000/01.R666

Movement: El Primero 4000 SC automatic chronograph movement.
Functions: hours, minutes in the center, small seconds hand at 9; date at 4½; chronograph: central seconds hand; 30-minute counter at 3; 12-hour counter at 6.
Case: brushed stainless steel set with diamonds; Ø 38mm; graduated unidirectional rotating bezel; water resistant to 300 meters.
Dial: white guilloché.
Strap: white vulcanized rubber strap; stainless steel tongue buckle.
Also available: stainless steel with black dial; rose gold with white dial, with or without diamonds; alligator leather or rubber strap.

DEFY XTREME TOURBILLON ZERO G REF. 96.0525.8800/21.M525

Movement: El Primero 8800 automatic chronograph movement; gyroscopic tourbillon.
Functions: hours, minute excentered at 11; self-regulating module "Zero-G Tourbillon" at 5; second indicator at 5.
Case: black titanium; Ø 46.5mm; water resistance up to 100 meters.
Dial: multi-layered dial made of Hesalite glass, carbon fiber and aluminum.

Bracelet: black titanium bracelet; black titanium triple-folding clasp.

DEFY XTREME OPEN SEA REF. 96.0529.4021/51.M533

Movement: El Primero 4021 SX automatic chronograph movement.
Functions: hours, minutes in the center, small seconds hand at 9; power-reserve indicator from hour axis; chronograph: central seconds hand; 30-minute counter at 3.
Case: black titanium case; Ø 46.5mm; graduated unidirectional rotating bezel in black titanium; fitted with carbon fiber inserts; helium valve at 10; water resistant to 1,000 meters.
Dial: multi-layered see-through structure composed of shock-resistant transparent hesalite® glass; carbon fiber layer and varnished dial plate.
Bracelet: black titanium bracelet with blue-tinted central links; reinforced by composite lateral inserts; black titanium triple-folding buckle.

DEFY XTREME OPEN GOLD & TITANIUM REF. 96.0528.4021/21.R642

Movement: El Primero 4021 SX automatic chronograph movement.
Functions: hours, minutes in the center, small seconds hand at 9; power-reserve indicator from hour axis; chronograph: central seconds hand; 30-minute counter at 3.
Case: black titanium case; Ø 46.5mm; graduated unidirectional rotating bezel in rose gold and black titanium; helium valve at 10; water resistant to 1,000 meters.
Dial: multi-layered crystal structure composed of shock-resistant transparent hesalite® glass; carbon fiber layer and varnished dial plate.
Strap: black vulcanized rubber strap; black titanium triple-folding buckle.
Also available: rose gold and black titanium bracelet.

DEFY XTREME STEALTH OPEN GRANDE DATE REF. 96.0527.4039/21.M529

Movement: El Primero 4039 SX automatic chronograph movement.
Functions: hours, minutes in the center, small seconds hand at 9; power-reserve indicator from hour axis; patented 3-disc grand date over 2; chronograph: central seconds hand; 30-minute counter at 3.
Case: black titanium case; Ø 46.5mm; graduated unidirectional rotating bezel; helium valve at 10; water resistant to 1,000 meters.
Dial: multi-layered crystal structure composed of black or silver carbon fiber layer and varnished dial plate; 9-branched open bridge in red eloxed aluminium.
Strap: titanium bracelet with lateral inserts in Kevlar; black titanium triple-folding buckle.
Also available: Silver Titanium.

ACADEMY OPEN REPETITION MINUTES   REF. 18.1260.4043/01.C611

Movement: El Primero 4043 automatic chronograph movement.
Functions: hours, minutes in the center, small seconds hand at 9; minute repeater; chronograph: central seconds hand; 30-minute counter at 3.
Case: 18K rose-gold case; Ø 45mm; water resistant to 30 meters.
Dial: 18K gold dial, handmade "Grain d'Orge" guilloché; opening at 10 revealing heart of 4043 Caliber.
Strap: handmade black crocodile leather strap lined with silky Alzavel calfskin; 18K gold triple-folding buckle.
Also available: concept version in white gold with sapphire transparent dial.

ACADEMY TOURBILLON CHRONOGRAPH   REF. 65.1260.4005/23.C505

Movement: El Primero 4005 automatic chronograph movement.
Functions: hours, minutes in the center; date indication positioned around the carriage; tourbillon: carriage positioned at 11 making 1 turn per minute; chronograph: central seconds hand; 30-minute counter at 3; 12-hour counter at 6.
Case: 18K white-gold case; Ø 45mm; water resistant to 30 meters.
Dial: 18K gold handmade "Grain d'Orge" guilloché.
Strap: handmade black crocodile leather strap lined with silky Alzavel calfskin; 18K gold triple-folding buckle.
Also available: rose gold or platinum with silver dial.

STAR LOVE   REF: 03.1230.4021/35.C677

Movement: El Primero 4021 automatic chronograph movement.
Functions: hours, minutes in the center, small seconds hand at 9; 30-minute counter at 3; power reserve indicator from the hour axis.
Case: stainless steel; Ø 37.5mm; water resistance up to 30 meters.
Dial: silver guilloché dial.
Strap: hand made leather strap; stainless steel triple-folding buckle.
Also available: stainless steel with black or Bordeaux guilloché dial.

STAR ROCK EL PRIMERO   REF. 16.1230.4002/02.C664

Movement: El Primero 4002 automatic chronograph movement.
Functions: hours, minutes in the center, small seconds hand at 9; date indicator at 4½; chronograph: central seconds hand; 30-minute counter at 3.
Case: stainless steel case set with diamonds; Ø 37.5mm; water resistance up to 30 meters.
Dial: silvered dial with "Onde" guilloché pattern.
Strap: white alligator leather strap; stainless steel triple-folding buckle.
Also available: stainless steel with black dial.

Brand Directory

AUDEMARS PIGUET
1348 Le Brassus
Switzerland
Tel: 41 21 845 14 00
USA: 646 375 0811

B.R.M
2 Impasse de l'Aubette
ZAC des Aulnaies
95420 Magny-en-Vexin
France
Tel: 33 1 61 02 00 25
USA: 214 235 9127

BAUME & MERCIER
50, Chemin de la Chênaie
1293 Bellevue
Switzerland
Tel: 41 22 999 51 51
USA: 212 593 0444

BELL & ROSS
350 Rue Saint Honoré
75001 Paris, France
Tel: 33 1 42 86 61 27
USA: 203 604 6840

BERTOLUCCI
Route des Acacias 43
1211 Genève 26
Tel: 41 22 756 95 00
USA: 212 204 0580

BOUCHERON
20 Rue de la Paix
75002 Paris, France
Tel: 33 1 42 44 09 43
USA: 866 983 3747

BOVET FLEURIER SA
9 Rue Ami-Lévrier
1211 Geneva 1
Switzerland
Tel: 41 22 731 46 38
USA: 305 965 3277

BVLGARI
34 rue de Monruz
2000 Neuchâtel
Switzerland
Tel: 41 32 722 78 78
USA: 646 397 7800

CARL F. BUCHERER
Carl F. Bucherer N.A.
1805 South Metro Parkway
Dayton, OH 45459 USA
USA: 800 395 4306

CARTIER SA
Boulevard James-Fazy 8
1201 Genève, Switzerland
Tel: 41 22 721 24 00
USA: 212 753 0111

CHANEL
25 Place du Marché
St Honoré
75001 Paris, France
Tel: 33 1 55 35 50 00
USA: 212 688 5055

CHOPARD
Rue de Veyrot 8
1217 Meyrin-Geneva 2
Switzerland
Tel: 41 22 719 31 91
USA: 212 821 0300

CHRONOSWISS
Dr.-Johann-Heitze-Strasse 4
85757 Karlsfeld bei
München, Germany
Tel: 49 8131 292 77 0
USA: 609 524 2567

CLERC
Rue de Lausanne 37A
1201 Geneva, Swizerland
Tel: 41 22 716 25 50
USA: 212 397 1662

CONCORD
MGI Luxury Group SA
Rue de Nidau 35
2501 Bienne, Switzerland
Tel: 41 32 329 34 00
USA: 800 547 4073

CORUM SA
Rue du petit Château
2301 La Chaux-de-Fonds
Switzerland
Tel: 41 32 967 06 70
USA: 949 788 6200

CUERVO Y SOBRINOS
220 Congress Park Dr
Suite 100
Delray Beach, FL 33445 USA
USA: 561 330 0088

DANIEL ROTH
Haute Horlogerie S.A.
Chemin du Grand Puits, 42
1217 Meyrin Switzerland
Tel: 41 21 719 17 17
USA: 212 315 9700

DAVID YURMAN USA
24 Vestry Street, 12th Fl
New York, NY 10013 USA
USA: 646 264 7346

de GRISOGONO
176 bis Route de St. Julien
1228 Plan-les-Ouates
Switzerland
Tel: 41 22 817 81 00
USA: 212 439 4240

DEWITT
2, Rue du Pré-de-la-Fontaine
Satigny - 1217 Meyrin 2
Switzerland
Tel: 41 22 750 97 97
USA: 305 531 6004

DIMIER
9595 Wilshire Blvd.
Suite 511
Beverly Hills, CA 90212 USA
USA: 310 205 5555

DIOR WATCHES
8, Rue Fourcroy
75017 Paris, France
Tel: 33 1 44 29 36 61
USA: 973 467 1890

EBEL
MGI Luxury Group
113 Rue de la Paix
2301 La Chaux-de-Fonds
Switzerland
Tel: 41 32 912 31 23
USA: 800 920 3153

F. P. JOURNE
13 Place Longemalle
1204 Geneva, Switzerland
Tel: 41 22 322 09 03
USA: 305 572 9802

FRANC VILA
Rue du petit Château
2301 La Chaux-de-Fonds
Switzerland
Tel: 41 32 967 06 70
USA: 949 788 6200

GÉRALD GENTA
Haute Horlogerie S.A.
42 Chemin du Grand Puits
1217 Meyrin, Switzerland
Tel: 41 21 719 17 17
USA: 800 969 1989

GREUBEL FORSEY
19-21 Rue du Manège
2300 La Chaux-de-Fonds
Switzerland
Tel: 41 32 751 71 76
USA: 310 205 5555

GUY ELLIA
21, Rue de la Paix
75002 Paris, France
Tel: 33 1 53 30 25 25
USA: 800 235 5464

H. MOSER & CIE.
Rundbuckstrasse, 10
8212 Neuhausen AM
Rheinfall, Switzerland
Tel: 41 52 674 00 50
USA: 561 330 0088

HUBLOT
44 Route de Divonne
1260 Nyon 2, Switzerland
Tel: 41 22 990 90 00
USA: 800 536 0636

INVICTA
1 Invicta Way
3069 Taft Street
Hollywood, FL 33021
Tel: 954 921 2444

IWC
Baumgarten Strasse 15
8201 Schaffhausen
Switzerland
Tel: 41 52 635 62 37
USA: 212 891 2460

JACOB & CO.
Richelien 39
1290 Versoix
Switzerland
Tel: 41 22 775 33 33
USA: 212 888 2330

KRIEGER
1000 5th Street, Suite 300
Miami Beach, FL 33139
USA: 305 534 8433

LEVIEV
31 Old Bond Street
London W1S4QH
Tel: 44 20 7493 3333
USA: 212 763 5333

LONGINES
2610 Saint-Imier
Switzerland
Tel: 41 32 942 54 25
USA: 201 271 1400

LOUIS MOINET
Rue de Temple 1
PO Box 28
2072 Saint-Blaise
Switzerland
Tel: 41 32 753 68 14
USA: 919 521 5610

MCT
Rue du Coq d'Inde 24
2000 Neuchatel
Switzerland
Tel: 41 22 301 49 67
USA: 310 205 5555

MONTBLANC MONTRE
Hellgrundweg 100
22525 Hamburg
Germany
Tel: 49 40 84 001 0
USA: 908 508 2334

MOVADO
MGI Luxury Group SA
Rue de Nidau 35
2501 Bienne, Switzerland
Tel: 41 32 329 34 00
USA: 800 810 2311

PANERAI
Via Ludovico di Breme, 44/45
20156 Milan, Italy
Tel: 39 02 30261
USA: 212 888 8788

PARMIGIANI FLEURIER
Rue du Temple 11
2114 Fleurier, Switzerland
Tel: 41 32 862 66 30
USA: 949 489 2885

PATEK PHILIPPE
Chemin du Pont du
Centenaire 141
1228 Plan-les-Ouates,
Switzerland
Tel: 41 22 884 20 20
USA: 212 218 1272

PIAGET
37 Chemin du Champ-
des-Filles
1228 Plan-les-Ouates
Switzerland
Tel: 41 22 884 48 44
USA: 212 355 6444

RAYMOND WEIL S.A.
Avenue Eugène-Lance 36-38
1211 Geneva 26
Switzerland
Tel: 41 22 884 00 55
USA: 212 355 3350

RICHARD MILLE
11 rue du Jura
2345 Les Breuleux Jura
Switzerland
Tel: 41 32 959 43 53
USA: 310 205 5555

ROLEX
Rue François Dussaud 3-7
1211 Geneva 24
Switzerland
Tel: 41 22 302 22 00
USA: 212 758 7700

ROMAIN JEROME
Rue Robert Céard 8
1204 Geneva
Switzerland
Tel: 41 22 319 29 39
USA: 813 792 0402

SALVATORE FERRAGAMO
Vertime SA
Via Cantonale-Galleria 1
6928 Manno, Switzerland
Tel: 41 91 610 87 00
USA: 203 523 7249

STÜHRLING ORIGINAL
449 20th Street
Brooklyn, NY 11215 USA
USA: 718 840 5760

TAG HEUER
Louis-Joseph Chevrolet 6A
2300 La Chaux-de-Fonds
Switzerland
Tel: 41 32 919 80 00
USA: 973 467 1890

ULYSSE NARDIN
3, Rue du Jardin
2400 Le Locle
Switzerland
Tel: 41 32 930 74 00
USA: 561 988 8600

UNIVERSAL GENEVE
Route de Acacias, 6
1211 Geneva 4
Switzerland
Tel: 41 22 307 78 80

URWERK
34 rue des Noirettes
1227 Carouge-Geneva
Switzerland
Tel: 41 21 900 20 25
USA: 310 205 5555

VACHERON CONSTANTIN
Rue des Moulins 1
1204 Geneva, Switzerland
Tel: 41 22 316 17 40
USA: 212 713 0707

VALENTINO
Vertime SA
Via Cantonale-Galleria 1
6928 Manno, Switzerland
Tel: 41 91 610 87 00
USA: 203 523 7263

VERSACE
Vertime SA
Via Cantonale-Galleria 1
6928 Manno, Switzerland
Tel: 41 91 610 87 00
USA: 203 523 7263

VINCENT BERARD
Boulevard des Endroits 24
2300 La Chaux-de-Fonds
Tel: 41 32 926 16 46
USA: 310 205 5555

ZANNETTI
Via Monte d'Oro 19
00186 Rome, Italy
Tel: 39 06 68 192 566

ZENITH
2400 Le Locle
Switzerland
Tel: 41 32 930 62 62
USA: 973 467 1890